COLLECTED ESSAYS IN LAW

Islam and Human Rights

Collected Essays in Law Series

General Editor: Tom D. Campbell

Crime, Compliance and Control

Doreen McBarnet

ISBN: 978 0 7546 2349 6

Democracy Through Law

Johan Steyn

ISBN: 978 0 7546 2404 2

Legal Reasoning, Legal Theory and Rights

Martin P. Golding

ISBN: 978 0 7546 2669 5

Meaning, Mind and Law

Dennis Patterson

ISBN: 978 0 7546 2749 4

Living Law

Roger Cotterrell

ISBN: 978 0 7546 2710 4

Law as Resistance:
Modernism, Imperialism, Legalism

Peter Fitzpatrick

ISBN: 978 0 7546 2685 5

Legal Scholarship and Education

Mark Tushnet

ISBN: 978 0 7546 2673 2

Beyond Law in Context

David Nelken

ISBN: 978 0 7546 2802 6

Abdullahi An-Na'im,
edited by Mashood A. Baderin

Islam and Human Rights

Selected Essays of Abdullahi An-Na'im

Routledge
Taylor & Francis Group
LONDON AND NEW YORK

First published 2010 by Ashgate Publishing

Published 2016 by Routledge
2 Park Square, Milton Park, Abingdon, Oxon OX14 4RN
605 Third Avenue, New York, NY 10017

First issued in paperback 2021

Routledge is an imprint of the Taylor & Francis Group, an informa business

Publisher's Note
The publisher has gone to great lengths to ensure the quality of this reprint but points out that some imperfections in the original copies may be apparent.

British Library Cataloguing in Publication Data
An-Na'im, Abdullahi Ahmad, 1946-
Islam and human rights : selected essays of Abdullahi An-Na'im.
1. Human rights–Religious aspects–Islam. 2. Human rights–Islamic countries.
I. Title II. Baderin, Mashood A.
341.4'8'091767-dc22

Library of Congress Control Number: 2009924481

ISBN 13: 978-1-03-209944-6 (pbk)
ISBN 13: 978-0-7546-2823-1 (hbk)

Contents

Acknowledgements vii

Series Editor's Preface ix

Biography xi

Introduction xiii

PART ONE: ISLAM BETWEEN UNIVERSALISM AND SECULARISM

1 What Do We Mean by Universal?
Index on Censorship, 1994, pp. 120–8. 3

2 Islamic Law, International Relations and Human Rights: Challenge and Response
20 *Cornell International Law Journal*, **2**, 1987, pp. 317–35. 13

3 A Kinder, Gentler Islam?
52 *Transition*, 1991, pp. 4–16. 33

4 Re-affirming Secularism for Islamic Societies
New Perspectives Quarterly, **3**, 2003, pp. 36-45. 47

5 Islam and Human Rights: Beyond the Universality Debate
94 *Proceedings of the American Society of International Law*, 2000, pp. 95–101. 57

PART TWO: ISLAM AND HUMAN RIGHTS IN THE MUSLIM WORLD

6 Human Rights in the Muslim World: Socio-Political Conditions and Scriptural Imperatives
3 *Harvard Human Rights Journal*, 1990, pp. 13–52. 67

7 Civil Rights in the Islamic Constitutional Traditions: Shared Ideals and Divergent Regimes
25 *The John Marshall Law Review*, **2**, 1992, pp. 267–93. 107

8 Human Rights in the Arab World: A Regional Perspective
23 *Human Rights Quarterly*, **3**, 2001, pp. 701–32. 135

9 Human Rights and Islamic Identity in France and Uzbekistan: Mediation of the Local and Global
22 *Human Rights Quarterly*, **4**, 2000, pp. 906–41. 167

10 'The Best of Times' and 'the Worst of Times': Human Agency and Human Rights in Islamic Societies
1 *Muslim World Journal of Human Rights*, 2004 **1**, Article 5. 203

PART THREE: SOME TOPICAL ISSUES IN ISLAM AND HUMAN RIGHTS DISCOURSE

11 The Islamic Law of Apostasy and its Modern Applicability: A Case from The Sudan
16 *Religion*, 1986, pp. 197–223. 219

12 Religious Minorities under Islamic Law and the Limits of Cultural Relativism
9 *Human Rights Quarterly*, 1987, **1**, pp. 1–18. 247

13 The Rights of Women and International Law in the Muslim Context
9 *Whittier Law Review*, **3**, 1987, pp. 491–516. 265

14 The Contingent Universality of Human Rights: The Case of Freedom of Expression in African and Islamic Contexts
10 *Emory International Law Review*, **3**, 1997, pp. 29–66. 291

15 Why Should Muslims Abandon *Jihad*? Human Rights and the Future of International Law
27 *Third World Quarterly*, **5**, 2006, pp. 785–97. 329

PART FOUR: CONCLUSION: A THEORY OF INTERDEPENDENCE

16 The Interdependence of Religion, Secularism, and Human Rights: Prospects for Islamic Societies
11 *Common Knowledge*, **1**, 2005, pp. 65–80. 345

Name Index 371

Acknowledgements

The chapters in this volume are taken from the sources listed below, for which the editor and publishers wish to thank their authors, original publishers or other copyright holders for permission to use their materials as follows:

Chapter 1: What Do We Mean by Universal? *Index on Censorship*, 1994, pp. 120–8.

Chapter 2: Islamic Law, International Relations and Human Rights: Challenge and Response 20 *Cornell International Law Journal*, **2**, 1987, pp. 317–35.

Chapter 3: A Kinder, Gentler Islam? 52 *Transition*, 1991, pp. 4–16.

Chapter 4: Re-affirming Secularism for Islamic Societies *New Perspectives Quarterly*, 3, 2003, pp. 36-45.

Chapter 5: Islam and Human Rights: Beyond the Universality Debate 94 *Proceedings of the American Society of International Law*, 2000, pp. 95–101

Chapter 6: Human Rights in the Muslim World: Socio-Political Conditions and Scriptural Imperatives 3 *Harvard Human Rights Journal*, 1990, pp. 13–52.

Chapter 7: Civil Rights in the Islamic Constitutional Traditions: Shared Ideals and Divergent Regimes 25 *The John Marshall Law Review*, **2**, 1992, pp. 267–93.

Chapter 8: Human Rights in the Arab World: A Regional Perspective 23 *Human Rights Quarterly*, **3**, 2001, pp. 701–32. Copyright © 2001 by The Johns Hopkins University Press.

Chapter 9: Human Rights and Islamic Identity in France and Uzbekistan: Mediation of the Local and Global 22 *Human Rights Quarterly*, **4**, 2000, pp. 906–41. Copyright © 2000 by The Johns Hopkins University Press.

Chapter 10: 'The Best of Times' and 'the Worst of Times': Human Agency and Human Rights in Islamic Societies 1 *Muslim World Journal of Human Rights*, (2004) **1**, Article 5. Copyright © 2004 by the author.

Chapter 11: The Islamic Law of Apostasy and its Modern Applicability: A Case from The Sudan 16 *Religion*, 1986, pp. 197–223. Copyright © Academic Press Inc. (London) Ltd.

Chapter 12: Religious Minorities under Islamic Law and the Limits of Cultural Relativism 9 *Human Rights Quarterly*, 1987, **1**, pp. 1–18. Copyright © 1987 by The Johns Hopkins University Press.

Chapter 13: The Rights of Women and International Law in the Muslim Context 9 *Whittier Law Review*, **3**, 1987, pp. 491–516.

Chapter 14: The Contingent Universality of Human Rights: The Case of Freedom of Expression in African and Islamic Contexts 10 *Emory International Law Review*, **3**, 1997, pp. 29–66.

Chapter 15: Why Should Muslims Abandon *Jihad*? Human Rights and the Future of International Law 27 *Third World Quarterly*, **5**, 2006, pp. 785–97. Copyright © 2006 Third World Quarterly.

Chapter 16: The Interdependence of Religion, Secularism, and Human Rights: Prospects for Islamic Societies 11 *Common Knowledge*, **1**, 2005, pp. 65–80. Copyright © 2005 Duke University Press.

Series Editor's Preface

Collected Essays in Law makes available some of the most important work of scholars who have made a major contribution to the study of law. Each volume brings together a selection of writings by a leading authority on a particular subject. The series gives authors an opportunity to present and comment on what they regard as their most important work in a specific area. Within their chosen subject area, the collections aim to give a comprehensive coverage of the authors' research. Care is taken to include essays and articles which are less readily accessible and to give the reader a picture of the development of the authors' work and an indication of research in progress.

Abdullahi An-Na'im

Abdullahi Ahmed An-Na'im is Charles Howard Candler Professor of Law at Emory University in Atlanta, Georgia, USA.

He holds an LLB (Hons) University of Khartoum, Sudan, 1970; LLB (Hons) and Diploma in Criminology, University of Cambridge, England, 1973; and PhD in Law, University of Edinburgh, Scotland, 1976. His previous positions include Associate Professor at the University of Khartoum, Sudan until 1985; Visiting Professor of Law at the University of California at Los Angeles, 1985-87; Ariel F. Sallows Professor of Human Rights at the University of Saskatchewan, Canada, 1988-91; Olof Palme Visiting Professor at Uppsala University, Sweden, 1991-92. He served as Executive Director of Human Rights Watch/Africa from 1993 to 1995 before joining the Faculty of Emory Law School in 1995.

In February 2009, An-Na`im received an Honorary Doctorate from the Universite Catholique de Louvain (UCL, Louvain-la-Neuve) and Katholieke

Universiteit Leuven (K.U. Leuven, Leuven), Belgium. He also serves as Global Legal Scholar at the Law School, University of Warwick, UK (Sept. 2007 to Aug. 2010); and Extraordinary Professor at the Centre for Human Rights, Faculty of Law, University of Pretoria (Jan 2009 to December 2010).

He is the author of *Islam and the Secular State: Negotiating the Future of Shari`a* (Indonesian 2007, English 2008); *African Constitutionalism and the Role of Islam* (2006); and *Toward an Islamic Reformation: Civil Liberties, Human Rights and International Law* (1990) (translated into Arabic, Indonesian, Russian and Farsi). His edited publications include *Human Rights under African Constitutions* (2003); *Islamic Family Law in a Changing World: A Global Resource Book* (2002); *Cultural Transformation and Human Rights in Africa* (2002); *The Cultural Dimensions of Human Rights in the Arab World* (in Arabic, 1994); *Human Rights in Cross-Cultural Perspectives: Quest for Consensus* (1992); *Human Rights in Africa: Cross-Cultural perspectives,* with Francis M. Deng (1990). He has also published more than sixty articles and book chapters on human rights, constitutionalism, Islamic law and politics.

Introduction

Abdullahi An-Na'im's Philosophy on Islam and Human Rights[1]

> "I am proposing the principles of constitutionalism, human rights and citizenship, which can work only when they enjoy sufficient cultural and religious legitimacy to inspire and motivate people to participate in organized and sustained political and legal action. An Islamic discourse is essential for legitimizing the necessary strategies for regulating the public role of Islam. At the same time, that discourse cannot emerge or be effective without the security and stability provided by the secular state."
> - Abdullahi An-Na'im.[2]

The relationship between Islam and human rights forms an important aspect of contemporary international human rights discourse. Current international events and the increasing public role of Islam in modern Muslim states have made the subject more relevant than ever. Many international human rights courses around the world now cover issues relating to Islam and human rights. Some universities and academic centres have specific postgraduate courses or modules on the subject. The importance of the subject as a specific theme in general human rights discourse is portrayed by the volume of literature currently available on its different aspects. Professor Abdullahi Ahmed An-Na'im is one of the leading scholars and contributors on the subject. In fact, he remains one of the most cited authorities in the subject area. His contributions on the subject span more than three decades during which he has engaged with almost every topical issue on the subject. He has been described as one of the non-Western jurists from "the South" "who have made substantial contributions to the theory and practice of human rights" generally.[3] It is therefore a great honour to be commissioned to compile and write an introduction to a selection of his

1 This introductory chapter and revision of manuscript for this volume was completed during my professorial visit to the Faculty of *Syariah* and Law, Islamic Sciences University of Malaysia, Malaysia in December 2008. I thank the University for the opportunity and for the facilities provided, which enabled me to complete this work during the period. I particularly express my gratitude to the Dean of the Faculty, Professor Dr. Abdul Samat Musa, and to Mohammad Nizam bn Awang and Ahmad Anis bn Muhammad Fauzi for their kind hospitality during the period.

2 A.A. An-Na'im, *Islam and the Secular State: Negotiating the Future of Shari'a* (Cambridge: Harvard University Press, 2008) p. 44.

3 W. Twining, "Human Rights: Southern Voices; Frances Deng, Abdullahi An-Na'im, Yash Ghai and Upendra Baxi" (2007) 1 *Law, Social Justice & Global Development Journal* (*LGD*) http://www2.warwick.ac.uk/fac/soc/law/elj/lgd/2007_1/twining at p. 3. (Last accessed 16 December 2008)

scholarly essays on the subject. This single volume brings together, coherently, his thoughts as developed on the subject over the years. It will provide easy access and convenience to students, academics, researchers, practitioners, policy-makers and all those interested in this important subject area.

The quotation at the top of this introductory chapter is taken from An-Na'im's latest book, *Islam and the Secular State: Negotiating The Future of Shari'a*, which he describes as "the culmination of my life's work, the final statement I wish to make on issues I have been struggling with since I was a student at the University of Khartoum, Sudan, in the late 1960s".[4] While the quotation summarises, succinctly, his ultimate standpoint on Islam and human rights in modern Muslim states, the evolution of that standpoint can only be better appreciated and understood through the reading of his scholarly writings over the years. Thus, for a comprehensive insight into his general philosophy on the subject, this volume presents sixteen of his scholarly journal essays published between 1986 and 2006 illustrating the progression and consistency of his arguments over a period of twenty years. The essays are presented herein, not chronologically, but coherently, in a way that takes the reader on a scholarly journey through An-Nai'm's general philosophy on Islam and human rights in a consistent way. In essence, this volume cuts across twenty years of An-Nai'm's expressed thoughts on a complex subject before his ultimate arrival at the standpoint portrayed in his quotation cited at the beginning of this introductory chapter.

It is important to state that this prologue is not intended to be a critical analysis or a critique of An-Na'im's work contained herein. Rather, it presents the work "as it is", providing a brief summary of each of the essays contained in the volume and identifying in the process, what I consider to be the main elements of his general philosophy on the subject. Based on their content, the essays are grouped into four parts as follows.

I. Islam between Universalism and Secularism

Universalism is considered to be at the heart of human rights today, while the modern nation-state is considered more often in secular terms. This literally puts Islam between universality of human rights and secularity of the modern nation-state particularly in modern Muslim states. Read together, the five essays in this part reflect An-Na'im's perception of the position of Islam in relation to the considered universality of human rights and secularity of the modern nation-state.

4 A.A. An-Na'im, *supra*, note 2 above, at vii.

The usual starting point of human rights discourse is the question of its universality. The first United Nations (UN) human rights instrument adopted in 1948 is called Universal Declaration of Human Rights (UDHR), which clearly indicates that the international human rights agenda was meant to be a universal one from the beginning. Yet, there have been two persistent questions in that regard since the concept of universal human rights was mooted under the UN system. The first question is, what do we mean by universality of human rights?, and the second is, how can that universality be achieved? It is on record that one of the earliest questions posed to the UN Commission on Human Rights, then drafting the UDHR, was the statement submitted to the Commission by the American Anthropological Association (AAA) on 24 June 1947 about the proposed universality of human rights and how that would be achieved. The AAA had observed then that:

> Because of the great numbers of societies that are in intimate contact in the modern world, and because of the diversity of their ways of life, the primary task confronting those who would draw up a Declaration on the Rights of Man is thus, in essence, to resolve the following problem: How can the proposed Declaration be applicable to all human beings, and not be a statement of rights conceived only in terms of the values prevalent in the countries of Western Europe and America? …Today[5] the problem is complicated by the fact that the Declaration must be of world-wide applicability. It must embrace and recognize the validity of many different ways of life. It will not be convincing to the Indonesian, the African, the Indian, the Chinese, if it lies on the same plane as like documents of an earlier period. The rights of Man in the Twentieth Century cannot be circumscribed by the standards of any single culture, or be dictated by the aspirations of any single people. Such a document will lead to frustration, not realization of the personalities of vast numbers of human beings.[6]

Although the UDHR has, today, established itself as an instrument of great influence globally, those questions have not been fully subdued in international human rights discourse and, in relation to the socio-cultural and politico-legal influence of Islam in Muslim societies, they remain part of the fundamental questions in the Islam and human rights discourse.

---

5 That was in 1947 when the statement was issued, but this question has not fully disappeared from international human rights discourse even today.

6 *See* American Anthropological Association, 'Statement on Human Rights' (1947) 49 *American Anthropologist,* pp. 539–43, at pp. 539 and 542–3. Cf. the 1999 AAA Declaration on Anthropology and Human Rights available at: http://www.aaanet.org/stmts/humanrts.htm [29/12/08] and K. Engle, "From Scepticism to Embrace: Human Rights and the American Anthropological Association from 1947–1999" (2001) 23 *Human Rights Quarterly,* No.3, pp. 536–59, for an analysis of the two Statements.

This volume thus opens with an essay first published in 1994 by An-Na'im entitled "What do we mean by universal?" in which he articulates his views on the universality of human rights in relation to Islam. The essay was written in the context of the 1990 Salman Rushdie affair and the consequent *fatwa* of Iran's Ayatollah Khomeini against Salman Rushdie. An-Na'im is certainly a universalist and a staunch believer in the universal nature of human rights as is reflected in the first paragraph of this essay where he states that "[h]uman rights ought, by definition, to be universal in concept, scope and content as well as in application: a globally accepted set of rights or claims to which all human beings are entitled by virtue of their humanity and without distinction on grounds such as race, gender or religion" (p. 120). He also notes, however, that "[y]et there can be no prospect of the universal application of such rights unless there is, at least, substantial agreement on their concept, scope and content" (p. 121). Thus, his philosophy on the universality of human rights, as he manifests in this essay and consistently restates at appropriate points in all his other writings, is what may be described as a philosophy of cross-cultural universality. I identify this as the first element of his general philosophy on Islam and human rights. In relation to Islam, he reflects this philosophy of cross-cultural universality in the last paragraph of the essay wherein he concludes that "There are potentially powerful and vigorous constituencies for universal human rights worldwide – including the Islamic world. But those constituencies can never be mobilised in a global project on purely Western liberal notions of individual civil and political rights. Along with other rights and new formulations of familiar rights, all human rights will only command genuine universal respect and validity through discourse and dialogue" (p. 128). Between the first paragraph earlier quoted and this last paragraph of the essay, An-Na'im clearly articulates his views on the different paradoxes raised by the question of universality in theory and practice. He emphasises throughout the essay that the dialogue for cross-cultural universality must be "undertaken in good faith, with mutual respect for, and sensitivity to, the integrity and fundamental concerns of respective cultures, with an open mind and with the recognition that existing formulations may be changed – or even abolished – in the process" (p. 122).

But what kind of contribution can Islam bring to this dialogue towards the realisation of a cross-cultural universality of human rights? An-Na'im identifies that in "[r]eading the Qur'an and *Sunna*, one will find authority for liberalism as well as conservatism, and Muslim history gives clear examples of both tendencies". This matter, he argues "is determined by the choices Muslims make, and the struggle they wage in favour of their choices, in their own historical context" (p. 125). Thus, for Islam to be able to make a meaningful contribution to the dialogue for cross-cultural universality of human rights,

Muslims must, in the view of An-Na'im, choose liberal interpretations of Islamic sources to make Islamic law amenable to modern international relations and human rights. He develops this point further in the next essay, which serves as the basis for the second element of his general philosophy on Islam and human rights.

The second essay, "Islamic Law, International Relations, and Human Rights: Challenge and Response", was first published in 1987. In it An-Na'im proposes "solutions to the drawbacks of historical *Shari'a* from a religious rather than secular perspective, because Muslims do not separate the religion of Islam from the law of Islam" (p. 318). He argues here that a reformation of Islamic law through a modern interpretation of the *Shari'a* would work better for the advancement of human rights in Muslim states than a secular approach. He observes, *inter alia*, in that regard that "because *Shari'a* signifies the positive law of historical Islam, its general principles continue to bind and motivate Muslims" (p. 319) and that the appeal of the *Shari'a* amongst the majority of Muslims makes it imperative for it to be "authoritatively reformed from within the Islamic traditions and in ways acceptable to Muslims themselves, [o]therwise, such reform would lack legitimacy and practical viability" (p. 319). He also notes, however, that "although Muslims will not accept secular reforms to their religious law and practice, they have made some concessions to the demands of constitutionalism and the rule of law in national and international relations" (p. 319). He summarizes his arguments in this essay to the effect that "for Islamic states, smooth and successful transition to complete secularism is neither likely nor desirable because Muslims are obligated to live in accordance with Islamic law" (p. 320). However, in his view, "[f]ulfilling that obligation by re-introducing historical *Shari'a* would be disastrous for international relations and human rights" (p. 320). He therefore proposes that "the Muslims' religious duty may be satisfied by applying a modern version of Islamic law that is consistent with peaceful international relations and respect for human rights" and that "[t]his modern version will [still] be Islamic *Shari'a* because it will be derived from the fundamental sources of Islam, without being identical in every respect to historical *Shari'a*" (p. 320).

An-Na'im then goes on, in this essay, to analyse the historical *Shari'ah* and the Medina model of the Islamic state, arguing at the end of that analysis that "[m]odern jurists must not confine Islam to [historical] *Shari'a*", noting that if they do so it would unjustifiably condemn Islam "to *Shari'a*'s contextual limitations and deem it incapable of responding to changes in the physical and social environment that are, according to Muslim belief, willed and manifested by God Himself" (p. 323). He also critically examines the theory of international relations under the *Shari'a*, discussing the traditional concept of *jihad* and its implications to modern theory of international relations and human rights. He emphasises in the end that while "*Shari'a*'s [historical] view of civil liberties compared favourably with civil rights under Roman and Persian law prevailing at the time…criticism and strong objection must be raised to any attempt to reintroduce historical public *Shari'a* today because it is inconsistent with prevailing human rights standards" (p. 331). But he also argues conversely that "[w]hile this Article criticizes historical public *Shari'a* as being inconsistent with prevailing human rights standards, it does not unqualifiedly endorse those standards that originated with the western liberal tradition" (p. 332). Rather he proposes solutions from within Islam, stating that a "legitimate and lasting constitutional and legal order that can address modern international relations and domestic human rights must develop from within Islam" (p. 333), for which he argues that the best solution must be based on the methodology of his late mentor *Ustadh* Mahmoud Mohamed Taha, who was executed in Sudan in 1985 for the alleged offence of apostasy under Sudanese law then.[7] An-Na'im consistently proposes *Ustadh* Mahmoud Taha's methodology as the best means of transforming Islamic law to meet the standards of modern human rights and international relations in all the essays contained herein as well as in his other major works on the subject. This may be described as the philosophy of internal reformation of Islamic law based on the methodology of his mentor *Ustadh* Mahmoud Mohamed Taha, which I identify as the second element of his general philosophy on Islam and human rights.

An-Na'im's proposition for the internal reformation of Islamic law is taken further in the third essay, "A Kinder, Gentler Islam?" first published in 1991. In this essay, he argues essentially for a kinder, gentler interpretation of the Islamic sources. The essay is framed in the context of right to self-determination and principle of reciprocity. Here, An-Na'im focuses on "the need to transform the historical traditions of Muslim peoples in ways that would enable them to exercise their legitimate rights to self-determination without violating the rights of others" (p. 4). He identifies with the fact that Muslim peoples have the right to choose an Islamic definition of their self but argues that this should not be by reference to what he calls "historical *Shari'a*"; a point he made in the previous essay and consistently reiterates in other essays contained in this volume and throughout his writings. He proposes here that self definition by Muslims must be properly clarified and updated, for which he asserts again that "the Islamic tradition must undergo its own reformation and develop a modern conception of *Shari'a* that can be implemented today" (p. 8). He again acknowledges that the norms of "historical *Shari'a*" were far more enlightened and humane than corresponding principles and conceptions of its time, but argues that most of those norms cannot stand up to the minimum standards of

7 *See* Chapter 11 "The Islamic Law of Apostasy and its Modern Applicability: A Case from The Sudan" in this volume.

modern human rights, which are universal and must be enjoyed by everyone including Muslims. He therefore makes it clear that his "criticisms are not … addressed to *Shari'a* in its own proper historical context but rather against those who wish to resurrect dated concepts and principles and implement them under radically transformed domestic and international conditions" (p. 11).

In An-Na'im's view it is possible, indeed imperative, "to develop a new version of *Shari'a* based on a modern interpretation of the sources of Islam" (p. 11) in ways that would promote a kinder, gentler Islam. He states: "Far from advocating the abandonment of the Islamic tradition, I am calling on Muslims to achieve their own 'reformation' in order to transform their tradition into a viable and just ideology for their modern exercise of their right to self-determination" (p. 11). He then goes on to elaborate on his proposed methodology of transforming this tradition, which is again the methodology of his late mentor *Ustadh* Mahmoud Mohamed Taha. He argues "In the Muslim belief that I share, Islam is perfect and eternal from God's point of view, but in the affairs of the world, it is open to competing interpretations and practical policies reflecting the moral and intellectual capabilities of its adherents and their need to adapt to changing material and political conditions" (p. 11). He continues, "In the formula I propose, the constant part of the Islamic tradition is the texts of its divine sources while the interpretation and implementation of those sources must now be transformed" (p. 11). To illustrate his arguments against the application of "historical *Shari'a*" he cites Sudan as an example of where "efforts on behalf of a misconceived Islamic identity seeking to implement historical *Shari'a* … led to a total deadlock politically and contributed to the militarization of the entire country" (p. 15). He asserts that the ideal would be to ensure the right of Muslims "to self-determination in terms of an Islamic identity without violating the right of self-determination of others" (p. 16). Failing that, he states in conclusion that he "as an Arabized Muslim whose loyalty is to the cause of justice and peace for all Sudanese, would rather live in a secularised Sudan than in one ruled by totalitarian Islamic *Shari'a*" (p. 16), thereby introducing a refined argument for secularism which appears to be a departure from his previous position that secularism may lack legitimacy and practical viability for his proposed reforms in Muslim societies.[8] This refined position of secularism is pursued further by him in the next essay.

The fourth essay, "Re-affirming Secularism for Islamic Societies" was first published in 2003. His argument in this essay is against the background of the debate "about whether a new system of government that is both Islamic and democratic can be built as some kind of model for the [Middle East] region" (p. 36) after the overthrow of Saddam Hussein's Ba'athist regime in Iraq. He first identifies that "the central issue that must be debated among Iraqis

8 *See* Chapter 2 in this volume.

– as among modernizing Muslims everywhere – is the relationship between Islam and secularism in any new political system" (p. 36). He then proceeds to provide his reflections on that point from an Islamic perspective.

In addressing the issue of Islam versus secularism, An-Na'im first argues that "[t]he commonly presumed incompatibility between Islam and secularism needs to be re-evaluated" (p. 36). He observes that there is both a definitional and terminological as well as substantive confusion about the presumed incompatibility between Islam and secularism, which needs to be deconstructed. In trying to deconstruct the traditional understanding of secularism he argues that the traditional equation of secularism with complete disregard for religion, or a diminishing role for religion in public life is problematic. He criticises "the tendency to limit secularism to the experiences of west European and North American countries with Christianity since the 18th century", pointing out that in its west European and North American sense the term secularism "has come to Africa and Asia in the suspect company of colonialism". In his view "secularism should be understood in terms of the type of relationship between religion and the state, rather than a specific way in which that relationship has evolved in one society or another". After that terminological deconstruction of the concept of secularism, he then proceeds to argue for the re-affirmation of secularism in Muslim states and proposes that "the most compelling argument for an Islamic rationale for secularism is its necessity for pluralistic nation states that are able to safeguard the freedom of religion and belief of believers and non-believers alike" (p. 37), meaning that "the freedom of religion and belief of Muslims as well as non-Muslims is more likely to be violated by a state that seeks to promote a particular religious doctrine than one that is neutral on the matter". He illustrates his points by citing examples of Muslim intellectuals and political dissidents who have sought refuge in Western countries "because they enjoy more freedom of belief and political action in "secular" states that are more or less neutral on issues of religion" (p. 38). He further argues that the notion of an Islamic State is a contradiction in terms and that the diversity of opinion among Islamic schools of thought and scholars makes it impossible for the state to enact the *Shari'a* into positive law as that would lead to the selection of some opinions over others by the state and consequently deny Muslims the freedom to follow other equally legitimate Islamic opinions of their choice. In his view, Muslims actually "need the protection of human rights, and political and social space secured by secularism to live up to the ideals of their own religion" and asserts that such "protection and space cannot be sustained among Muslims without an internal transformation of their own understandings and practice of Islam" (p. 39). This may be described as his philosophy of re-affirming secularism for Muslim states, which I identify as the third element of his general philosophy on Islam and human rights.

It is important to bear in mind An-Na'im's redefinition of secularism in this context.

To drive his arguments home, he gives some examples of the issue of women's rights in Egypt and of Islamic identity in the Sudan and Iran to illustrate that a "secular space" is necessary for the realisation and enjoyment of human rights in Muslim states. Based on those three identified elements of his general philosophy of Islam and human rights, An-Na'im then introduces in this essay, a theory of "synergy and interdependence" of religion, human rights and secularism by arguing that: "The synergy and interdependence of religion and human rights enable Muslims to observe their own understanding and practice of Islam through an assertion of human rights, while using their Islamic identity to promote their human rights within their own Muslim communities. By ensuring that minority and dissident voices within a religious tradition are able to challenge dated and regressive understandings and practices of Islam, human rights and secularism help Muslims avoid the difficult choice of either rejecting their religion entirely or abandoning their own human rights" (p. 41). His conclusion in this essay is to the effect that "[m]aintaining a dynamic synergy and interdependence among human rights, religion and secularism will enable all citizens to live by their religious convictions while respecting the right of others to do the same, instead of expecting people to choose between competing religions or religious interpretations" (p. 45). He elaborates further on this theory of synergy in the concluding essay in this volume.[9]

The essay, "Islam and Human Rights: Beyond the Universality Debate", first published in 2000, rounds up the part on Islam between universality and secularism and takes us back to the issue of universality. Certainly, universality of human rights is only a means to an end and not an end in itself. An-Na'im begins the essay by acknowledging that the "implementation of international human rights norms in any society requires thoughtful and well-informed engagement of religion (broadly defined) because of its strong influence on human belief systems and behaviour, regardless of the formal characterization of the relationship between religion and the state in any society" (p. 95) and that "religious considerations are too important for the majority of people for human rights scholars and advocates to continue to dismiss them simply as irrelevant, insignificant, or problematic" (p. 95). In relation to the universality debate, he then raises the question of "whether the secular Western origin of human rights, as defined by the UDHR, necessarily mean that these rights are not (or cannot be) truly universal" (p. 96). He then proceeds to try and answer that "key question" in relation to Islam and Islamic societies. He restates his theory of synergy by indicating the need to understand the synergy between internal discourse and cross-cultural dialogue in the universality debate and

---

9 See Chapter16 in this volume.

concludes, *inter alia*, that "universality of human rights must be realized through the implementation of deliberate strategies that are likely to attract popular support, instead of on the basis of assumptions that such universality already exists, or can be achieved by proclamation in international documents" (pp. 100–101) alone.

II. Islam and Human Rights in the Muslim World

Today, the Muslim world may be perceived narrowly in the geographical sense of modern Muslim states or broadly in a diasporic sense to include Muslim peoples living as minorities in different non-Muslim states worldwide. In either case, the relationship between Islam and human rights is often an issue. In the five essays in this part An-Na'im addresses, respectively, some of the problems regarding Islam and human rights in the Muslim world both in relation to Muslim states and in relation to Muslim minorities living in non-Muslim states.

This part starts with the essay, "Human Rights in the Muslim World: Socio-Political Conditions and Scriptural Imperatives", which was first published in 1990. In this essay An-Na'im presents a preliminary enquiry on the practice of human rights in the Muslim world in the geographic sense. The essay starts by defining the *Shari'a* as a historical formulation of Islamic religious law and acknowledges its legitimising role in Muslim states. An-Na'im reiterates his argument on the need for the cultural legitimacy for human rights stating that human rights violations in a particular society is often a reflection of "the lack or weakness of cultural legitimacy of international standards in [that] society" and that as long as "these standards are perceived to be alien to or at variance with the values and institutions of a people, they are unlikely to elicit commitment of compliance". He therefore asserts that the "underlying causes of any lack or weakness of legitimacy of human rights standards must be addressed in order to enhance the promotion and protection of human rights in that society" (p. 15).

With regard to Islam and human rights in Muslim states, he observes that Muslims have recently been challenging "the gradual weakening of *Shari'a* as the basis for their formal legal systems", which has led to "mounting demands for the immediate application of *Shari'a* as the sole, or at least primary, legal system of the land" in many Muslim countries (p. 20). He however identifies that there are obvious conflicts between historical *Shari'a* and certain human rights, especially women's rights and the rights of non-Muslims, and indicates the need to focus on how those areas of conflict could be resolved. He emphasises that "a modern version of Islamic law can and should be developed", which would be the modern *Shari'a*, arguing that such "a modern "*Shari'a*" could be ... entirely consistent with current standards of human rights" (p. 21). However, part of the problem, in An-Na'im's view, is that only a tiny minority of Muslims appreciate this, and that the overwhelming majority of Muslims today, still view "historical *Shari'a*" as the sole valid interpretation of Islam that ought to prevail over all other laws and policies. He also points out the fact that the relationship between Islam and human rights in Muslim states is not only influenced by the historical scriptural imperatives of the *Shari'a* but also by political and sociological considerations in most Muslim states. He illustrates the political factors with examples of Muslim countries such as Pakistan, Indonesia, Iran, Saudi Arabia, Egypt and Morocco. With regard to the sociological factors, he provides examples on the different classes of Islamic activists in different Muslim states and how they influence social attitudes and behaviour and also states the relevant counter-arguments and counter-methods against the approaches of the different activists. Against that background, he again presents case studies on the *Shari'a* and women's rights in its different contexts citing practical examples from some of the Muslim states earlier discussed in the essay.

Finally, An-Na'im addresses the issue of Islamic reform and highlights again his preference for the reform methodology of his late mentor *Ustadh* Mahmoud Mohamed Taha in that regard. He argues that "the proposal is not as radical as it may seem because the proposed new rule would also be based on the Qur'an and *Suuna*, albeit on a new interpretation of the text" (p. 49). He however notes that "the proposed reform will probably be resisted because it challenges the vested interests of powerful forces in the Muslim world and may upset male-dominated traditional political and social institutions". He therefore states that "the acceptance and implementation of this reform methodology will involve a political struggle within Muslim nations as part of a larger general struggle for human rights". Based on his conviction of "the extreme importance of Islamic legitimacy in Muslim societies" he not only urges "[Muslim] human rights advocates to claim the Islamic platform and not concede it to the traditionalists and fundamentalist forces in their societies" but "also invite[s] outside supporters of Muslim human rights advocates to express their support with due sensitivity and genuine concern for Islamic legitimacy in the Muslim world" (p. 50).

The seventh essay, "Civil Rights in the Islamic Constitutional Traditions: Shared Ideals and Divergent Regimes" was first published in 1992. In it An-Na'im presents "an internal critique of civil rights in the Islamic constitutional tradition in the modern context" (pp. 267–8). He restates his previous conviction from the beginning that "Muslim people have the right to conduct their constitutional and legal affairs in conformity with the principles of Islam" but also emphasises that this must be "subject to the obligation of respecting the legitimate rights of all individuals and groups within Islamic countries". He then asserts that his task "as a Muslim" is "to seek ways of fulfilling this obligation from an Islamic point of view" (p. 268). While he argues that "various normative traditions may legitimately pursue different approaches to realizing the shared ideals of human dignity, liberty and well-being" he notes that "these approaches must remain open to criticism and reform in order to ensure and improve their practical ability to realize these ideals" (p. 269). In relation to the Muslim world, he suggests that the "key to conducting constructive discourse about civil rights in the Islamic constitutional tradition ...is the candid admission of the historical contradictions and ambivalence inherent to the subject itself, and an appreciation of the underlying causes thereof" (p. 270). He then proceeds to address the challenge of realizing the shared ideals, commencing with the observation that "the pursuit of the ideals of dignity, liberty and well-being is universal to all human societies" but that the matter is, however, complicated "by the fact that perceptions of dignity, permissible limitations on liberty and the conditions believed to be conducive to well-being vary from one society to another" (p. 271). Thus, in his view this challenge can be addressed "only if the proposed approach is appreciative of, and sensitive to, global cultural diversity in relation to the precepts, institutions and mechanisms of civil rights". He therefore reiterates that "the need for a civil rights regime in a given state society must be legitimized and rooted in the local culture(s) of that society" (p. 272).

An-Na'im then examines the origins and development of Islamic constitutional theory through a critical analysis of the constitutional theory of the Medina state, the evolution and present status of Islamic constitutional theory, and Islamic constitutionalism in the modern context. He also discusses the issue of civil rights in modern Islamic constitutional theory under which he addresses the issue of *Shari'a* and civil rights, highlighting the issue of women's rights, the rights of non-Muslims, and civil rights in the present Muslim world. He illustrates his arguments in that regard with examples from different Muslim states to ultimately show that the relationship between [historical] *Shari'a* and civil rights is negative, especially in relation to the civil rights of women and non-Muslims. He however notes that despite the "apparently poor status of civil rights in Islamic countries" he does "not believe that the situation is hopeless" (p. 292). He maintains "that Islam can and should still be used as a valuable cultural resource to legitimize and enhance civil rights in Islamic societies" (p. 291) reiterating that "the struggle for civil rights in Islamic countries should utilize the processes of internal discourse and cross-cultural dialogue to realize the shared ideals of dignity, liberty and well-being for all" (p. 292). His conclusion in this essay is that: "While it is true that modern formulations of civil rights emerged from the Western liberal tradition, their underlying values of dignity, liberty and well-being are shared by Islamic societies" and that "[i]n adopting modern civil rights regimes, and adapting them to their own cultures and circumstances, Islamic societies are merely responding to the challenge of realizing ideals they already share in the modern context" (p. 293).

The eighth essay, "Human Rights in the Arab World: A Regional Perspective" was first published in 2001. Here, An-Na'im argues that "the wide variety of strategies for the effective and sustainable protection of [human] rights should always be determined and implemented in specific local, regional and global context" (p. 701). He notes that his particular concern in this essay is "with identifying and promoting ways of diminishing, and eventfully breaking" what he calls "human rights dependency" (p. 702) of developing countries on international pressure for the protection of human rights of their own people. He identifies the different problems associated with "human rights dependency" of developing countries and proceeds to engage with those problems. He restates his consistent position that "moral or philosophical justifications for the universality of human rights can be found in all major religious and cultural traditions of the world, which should be emphasized through an internal discourse within each tradition that also addresses those features of the religion or culture which are negative or hostile to human rights norms" (p. 703).

In relation to the Arab world, he observes that "[w]hile Islam is often assumed to be a major factor in the presumed unity of 'Arab culture', there are some strong differences in the way it is understood and practiced in various parts of the region, especially in terms of its relationship to the state and public life, from Tunisia to Saudi Arabia, and from Somalia to Syria and Iraq" (p. 707). He therefore observes the need for a "clear appreciation of the complexity of interests, as well as the diversity of factors and contexts, that condition the policy and practice of each Arab state, especially regarding the protection of human rights" and more particularly in respect of "the impact of the Arab-Israeli conflict, Arab nationalism(s), and political Islam on the current status and future prospects of the protection of human rights in this region". He notes that "since these factors have been cited as justification or explanation of human rights violations at various times in different Arab countries, they should be taken into account in any analysis of the current status, and assessment of future prospects" (p. 708). The essay then proceeds to address relevant issues such as governmental action, the Arab League, and non-governmental organizations (NGOs). In respect of the latter, he observes that "Arab human rights NGOs are consistently denied official registration and face systematic harassment by the majority of the governments of the region" and that this is true both of "traditionalist purportedly Islamic governments like those of the Gulf states and Saudi Arabia or so-called secular governments like those of Iraq, Syria and Libya" (p. 723). In analysing the conceptual difficulties, he notes that a particular troubling difficulty to the Arab human rights movement is "the strong emergence of Islamic activism during the last two decades" (p. 729) and the consequent problem of "how to deal with Islamist and other militant ideological groups which seek to manipulate the processes of democratization and protection of human rights in order to seize political power without genuine commitment to these values" (p. 724). He notes also that "the personal background of the secular Arab intellectuals who became leaders of human rights organizations is not conducive to open dialogue with the leaders of the Islamic groups" and that "these leaders of human rights organizations find it difficult to openly challenge calls by Islamic groups for the application of Islamic Law (*Shari'a*) for fear of being branded as 'anti-Islamic' despite the obvious fundamental contradictions between [historical] *Shari'a* principles and international human rights norms on such issues as the rights of women, non-Muslims and freedom of belief among Muslims" (p. 729). An-Na'im concludes this essay philosophically with the observation that the challenge that ultimately confronts human rights in the Arab world "is how to be 'visionary yet realistic', because there are no 'magic solutions' that can materialize immediately for any of the obstacles and problems facing the protection of human rights in the Arab world. Because one has to take the world as it is, not as one would like it to be, strategies for promoting the protection of human rights must take into account the deep-rooted nature of the problems in devising incremental solutions that address immediate short term needs, while seeking to achieve long term ends" (p. 732).

The ninth essay, "Human Rights and Islamic Identity in France and Uzbekistan: Mediation of the Local and Global" was first published in 2000. It relates to the Muslim world in the diasporic sense, in relation to the human rights problems raised by Muslim minorities living in non-Muslim states and trying to maintain their identity as Muslims in those states. Here, An-Na'im discusses "current expressions of Islamic identity in Western Europe and Central Asia" as part of his "wider and continuing concern with issues of cultural transformation in Islamic societies and communities" (p. 906). The importance of the Muslim world in the diasporic sense, is reflected in An-Na'im's reference to the fact that some "Muslim scholars, like late Fazlur Rahman and Zaki Badawi, have suggested that Islamic renewal may come from Muslims in the West", with Zaki Badawi adding that "the most profound formulations will come from France, where Muslims will be challenged by the hardness of life, the deeply held convictions of Republican secularism, and the depth of racism" (p. 917). The essay focuses specifically on "the role of the human rights paradigm in the dynamics of the formation and transformation of Islamic identity in France and Uzbekistan today". An-Na'im notes, in that regard, that "despite differences in their historical experiences and specific present context, both types of complex Muslim communities face the question of the relationship between Islam and the state" (p. 908).

In relation to France, he identifies that local "Muslim communities are currently negotiating with the wider national French identity and culture about the meaning and relevance of their Islamic identity in the context of a highly developed and effective national and regional European human rights framework" (p. 908). He observes in that regard that major issues of contestation include education, religion, language, political participation, and immigration policies. On the other hand he notes that "Uzbekistan is struggling with the meaning and relevance of an Islamic identity in the context of a post-Soviet-state society that is only beginning to discover the possibilities and benefits of a human rights framework" (p. 909). Thus, An-Na'im asserts the need for Muslims to "adopt a human rights paradigm (including its norms and institutions and its popular advocacy) in order more effectively to assert their Islamic identity" (p. 940) but in doing so he argues that "Muslims in France and Uzbekistan *may have to modify aspects of their understanding of what an Islamic identity means in the process of claiming that identity in the modern context*" (emphasis not mine). He reiterates again in this essay that "for the universalist human rights project of the second half of the twentieth century to succeed ... it needs to engage possibilities of internal discourse and cross-cultural dialogue in promoting its own normative legitimacy as well as its political and legal efficacy" (p. 910). He also discourses the complexities of identity formation and transformation, Islamic identity and nationality and citizenship in France, and the politics of transformation in Uzbekistan, respectively. With regard to France he argues that "the human rights paradigm precludes the coerced assimilation of migrant populations into French culture and nationality in the traditional sense", which he notes "forces an adjustment of dominant understandings of what it means to be French". He also notes, however, that "immigrant Muslims will also have to adjust their understandings of what it means to be a Muslim precisely in order to be able to claim an Islamic identity in France" (p. 917). With regard to Uzbekistan he analyses the "role of Islam in the social and political transformation of the country in the post Soviet era, while highlighting some features that may be relevant to an assessment of the possibilities and limitations of using the human rights paradigm in mediating Islamic identity in that country" (p. 922). The essay then examines the relationship between Islam and culture and considers the "possible role of the human rights paradigm in the transformation of Islamic identity in these two countries" (p. 933).

In conclusion An-Na'im appreciates that "it may appear paradoxical to say that Muslims, or any other religious or ethnic group for that matter, will have to accept the incorporation of an external normative system, namely, universal human rights standards and institutions, into their own identity in order to claim that identity. However, the paradox is resolved or mediated to the extent that Muslims are active actors in (not merely subjects of) the articulation, interpretation, and implementation of human rights" and that the "human rights paradigm is necessary for the formation and transformation of Islamic identity". He closes his arguments by stating that "Muslims have a choice in either rejecting this imperative paradigm as 'alien' to their cultures or accepting it as integral to those cultures in today's interdependent world" (p. 941).

Often, when discussing the relationship between Islam and human rights in Muslim societies, the important role of human agency is often not well highlighted or is forgotten completely. This is what An-Na'im addresses in the tenth essay, "The Best of Times and the Worst of Times: Human Agency and Human Rights in the Islamic Societies". This was first published in 2004 during very difficult times for Islam and Muslims generally, principally as a consequence of reactions to the September 11 terrorist attacks in the United States of America in 2001. An-Na'im begins this essay with the premise that "there are good reasons for 'pragmatic optimism' about human rights in all Islamic societies, precisely because they are experiencing multiple and profound crises of unprecedented scale and magnitude" (p. 1). He argues that the crises confronting Islam and Muslims "are opening new opportunities for creative human agency, which is the ability of people to take control of their own lives and realize their own objectives, thereby becoming the source and cause of transformation", meaning that the best of times can "materialize out of the worst of times through human agency of persons, acting individually, collectively or institutionally". He states however that "outcomes are contingent upon what Muslims and others make of these opportunities, hence the qualification of my optimism as pragmatic, drawing on realistic prospects in the real world to inspire appropriate action, rather than simply assuming that respect for human rights will necessarily improve as a matter of course" (p. 1). An-Na'im emphasises that we "should be concerned about human rights in Islamic societies generally in view of the fact that Muslims are estimated at 19.6% of the total world population, living in every continent and region, and constituting the clear majority of the population in 44 states, a quarter of the total membership of the United Nations" which "represent[s] too large a proportion of the field to be overlooked by any systematic study or monitoring of the status of human rights around the world" (p. 2).

With regard to the role of human agency, he notes that the question of the relationship between Islam and human rights "can be meaningful only when it is about Muslims not Islam... because "the question is always about people's understanding and practice of their religion, not the religion itself as an abstract notion, and about human rights as a living and evolving body of principles and rule, not as a theoretical concept". He argues further that "[w]hether regarding religion or human rights, reference to states, countries or international organizations like the United Nations is really to people who control the state apparatus, inhabit a country or work through international institutions", and that "[w]hether institutions and organizations are religious, political or diplomatic, the question about their relationship to human rights is always about how people negotiate power, justice, and pragmatic self-interest, at home and abroad" (p. 2). Thus, in relation to Islam, he argues on the one hand that through a proper use of human agency, "the attitudes and practice of Muslims … can change in favour of the equal human rights of women and non-Muslims through internal debate within present Islamic societies", but on the other hand he also notes importantly that "the manner in which Muslims are likely to interact with human rights will be conditioned by such factors as what other societies are doing about the same issues". In his view, "Muslim responses are likely to be affected by whether they perceive that they are required to 'prove' their allegiance to the human rights paradigm while others are not expected or required to do so" and that "Muslims are more likely to resist commitment to these rights when they are presented as being alone in struggling with the principle, while the commitment of other cultural or religious traditions is taken for granted" (p. 4). He then strongly condemns both the terrorists attacks of September 11 2001 as well as the unilateral military retaliation by the United States describing the United States' occupation of Iraq in 2003 as a "colonial venture" which by definition is "the usurpation of the sovereignty of a people by military conquest without legal justification" as well as a "reckless and unaccountable invasion and occupation was neither justified by self-defense principles nor authorized by the Security Council of the United Nations" (p. 5). He however raises a challenge to Muslim societies arguing as a Muslim himself that a "critical part of that process in the present global context is to confront terrorism within our own societies, as it is ultimately a challenge to our human decency and responsibility for what we do, or is done on our behalf or in our name, with our approval or acquiescence". He adds that "Terrorism could not exist or thrive as it does at present if we have not somehow supported or encouraged it, at least by our indifference to the broader phenomenon of political violence and its underlying causes" (p. 7). He argues further that "[n]either the terrorist attacks nor the American retaliation could have happened without the support of a wider constituency on each side, a much wider circle of complicity for having justified, condoned or facilitated those acts of violence" (p. 9).

In relation to human rights, he asserts that "Muslims must exercise their human agency in choosing peaceful co-existence and mediation of conflict over the arbitrary and indiscriminate use of violence to achieve political objectives" (p. 8). Thus he notes that despite the "worst of times" scenario confronting Muslim societies, "this is also the 'best of times' for a positive engagement of international legality and peaceful co-existence" and that among the many lessons and insights that can be drawn by all societies from the atrocities of September 11 is what he describes as "our shared human vulnerability – the recognition that all human beings everywhere are vulnerable to arbitrary violence" (p. 8). Against this background, An-Na'im then notes that the relationship between Islam and human rights "is open to engagement and transformation precisely because it is contingent on an interactive web of internal and external factors and forces" and that "[l]ike other major religious and cultural traditions, Islam provides a basis for upholding human rights and dignity through its own account of what it means to be human". He however contends that "these dimensions of the Islamic traditions (in the plural) should be seen as open to critical reflection and reformulation among the believers themselves, because of the inherent and permanent diversity of the tradition itself. There are not only similarities as well as variations in perceptions and practices of human rights and dignity among Muslims and Islamic societies, but also possibilities of change in relevant attitudes and practices" (pp. 9–10). He concludes *inter alia* that the point "is simply to say that the practical relevance and utility of the social order of Islam are contingent upon human understanding and practice, which testifies to its ability to provide for the practical needs of its adherents. This point is critical for the theological basis of the relationship between Islam and human rights today" and that "these are the best of times and the worst of times for Muslims, with infinite possibilities in either direction, dependent on the way we all use or abuse our human agency" (p. 12).

III. Some Topical Issues in Islam and Human Rights Discourse

Within the general theme of Islam and human rights, there are specific substantive topical issues that usually feature prominently in the discourse. In the five essays contained in this part of the book, An-Na'im addresses some of those topical substantive issues, namely, the questions of apostasy, religious minorities, women's rights, freedom of expression and *jihad,* respectively.

The part opens with the eleventh essay, "The Islamic Law of Apostasy and its Modern Applicability: A Case from The Sudan", first published in 1986. The traditional Islamic law on apostasy is a very controversial issue in relation to the right to freedom of thought, conscience and religion under international human rights law. Article 18 of the UDHR provides that the right to freedom of thought, conscience and religion "includes freedom to change [one's] religion or belief", which was one of the reasons for Saudi Arabia's abstention from the adoption of the UDHR in 1948 on the ground that this contradicts the prohibition and punishment of apostasy under traditional Islamic law.[10] An-Na'im notes that the tension between faith and legalism is most obvious in the classical *Shari'a* ruling on apostasy. He addresses this tension against the background of the execution of his mentor *Ustadh* Mahmoud Muhammad Taha by the Sudanese military regime under President Ja'far Numeri on 18 January 1985 for the alleged offence of apostasy among other charges under Sudanese state law. He argues that the "real importance of *Ustadh* Mahmoud's trial and execution is in the questions it raises about the place of [historical] *Shari'a* in the modern world" especially "the relation between sincere Muslim belief and compliance with laws purporting to be derived from that belief". In his view, a candid admission by Muslims of this element of religious intolerance under [historical] *Shari'a* is "an essential prerequisite for the success of any attempt to secure complete respect for freedom of religion under Islamic law and in Muslim states". Through this essay, he hoped to contribute "to the building of a theological, philosophical and legal case for religious freedom in Islam" (p. 197).

The essay starts with a detailed legal, political and religious background to the Mahmoud Taha case in the Sudan before analysing the traditional Islamic law of apostasy. An-Na'im then argues that it is a "fact that the traditional Islamic law of apostasy is not only liable to be abused, but that it is a also inherently in contradiction with more universally accepted standards of constitutional civil liberties and international human rights". He asserts strongly that the "case of *Ustadh* Mahmoud in the Sudan cannot, unfortunately, be dismissed as an isolated and curious example of despotic and oppressive brutality" but a genuine question of Islamic law that "confronts Muslims all over the world with very real and fundamental questions" (p. 211). He then analyses the traditional legal basis of the offence under Islamic law and its civil and human rights implications in modern times. He examines and critiques the different approaches advanced by different modernist Muslim scholars and identifies what, in his view are the shortcomings of each of those approaches. In the end he again proposes *Ustadh* Mahmoud Taha's approach as a new approach and best method for dealing with the issue of apostasy under traditional Islamic law in relation to the right to freedom of religion under modern international human rights law.

---

10 The prohibition and punishment of apostasy under traditional Islamic law is currently a hotly debated issue amongst contemporary Muslim scholars. *See e.g.* M. Baderin, *International Human Rights and Islamic Law* (Oxford: OUP, 2003) pp. 123–125; S. El-Awa, *Punishment in Islamic Law* (Indianapolis: IIIT, 1982) pp. 50–56; M. H. Kamali, *Freedom of Expression in Islam* (Cambridge: ITS, 1997) pp. 87–107.

The twelfth essay, "Religious Minorities under Islamic Law and the Limits of Cultural Relativism" was first published in 1987. In it An-Na'im addresses the issue of religious minorities under Islamic law within the context of cultural relativistivism in human rights discourse. He begins with the argument that, "Non-Muslim minorities within an Islamic state do not enjoy rights equal to those of the Muslim majority". He also notes that "although most of the constitutions of modern Muslim states guarantee against religious discrimination, most of these constitutions also authorize the application of *Shari'ah*" which, he argues is contradictory and raises important questions for urgent and candid discussion. He first anticipates and counteracts what he identifies as "possible arguments which may be used to justify or rationalize the inferior status of religious minorities under *Shari'ah*" (p. 1). The article then provides an extensive analysis of cultural relativism and human rights, whereby he discusses the importance of cultural considerations to the development of human rights, thereby restating his erstwhile philosophy that "the implementation of the international human rights standards will improve if they can be shown to be the natural and legitimate evolution of the cultural tradition of the particular community", on grounds that the genesis of human rights norms "can be found in almost all major cultural traditions" (p. 3). He however notes, importantly, that emphasizing "the need for cultural contribution and legitimacy… does not mean that we should concede the claim to extreme cultural relativism that there are no universal standards of human rights", arguing that to do so "would defeat the purpose of cultural relativism itself" (p. 4). He then goes on to discuss the universal nature of the rights of religious minorities by analysing relevant human rights instruments and constitutional provisions, including those of Muslim states, that guarantee this right.

Against that background, An-Na'im then discusses the issue of religious minorities under *Shari'ah*, observing that traditional *Shari'ah* must be understood in the context of the prevailing period of its development and that "now that the problems have changed, and the historical answers ceased to be valid … new answers must be developed out of the Qur'an and *Sunnah*", which are the main sources of Islamic law, and that those new answers "would be the Islamic *Shari'ah* of today" rather than the historical *Shari'ah*. To find new answers to the issue of religious minorities in Muslim states, he first outlines the historical *Shari'ah* positions on the issue and argues that were we to apply those historical *Shari'ah* principles "to a modern nation-state, such as Sudan, we [will] find that the human rights implications are very serious indeed" (p. 12). He also cites the constitutional provisions of Iran and points out that the "constitutional manifestations of *Shari'ah* [therein] are obviously radically inconsistent with the universal human rights of religious minorities outlined" earlier in the essay (p. 13). He also mentions other Muslim states that constitutionally declare Islam as the religion of the state and *Shari'ah* as a main source of legislation. He states that the argument of cultural relativism can never be allowed to go so far as allowing for the discrimination against religious minorities sanctioned under historical *Shari'ah*.

He however states clearly in this article that he believes "Islamic *Shari'ah* can be reformed from the fundamental sources of Islam to fully accommodate and even contribute to the further development of the current universal standards" and then proceeds to outline "one way in which *Shari'ah* can be brought into full accord with universal human rights" particularly the rights of religious minorities (p. 14). He argues in the end that "it is my firm conviction that *Shari'ah* has developed in the only way it should, and could possibly, have developed in that historical context" and that the "early jurists...did an excellent job and succeeded in serving the needs and aspirations of their community for centuries" but that "by the same token ... it should be open to modern Muslim jurists to state and interpret the law for their contemporaries even if such statement and interpretation were to be, in some respects, different from the inherited wisdom" (pp. 16–17). He then makes propositions for such new interpretations based, again, on the work of his mentor *Ustdah* Mahmoud Taha. He asserts in his conclusion that "[s]ince the Muslims cannot, and should not, be allowed to justify discrimination against and persecution of non-Muslims on the basis of Islamic cultural norms, the Muslims themselves must seek ways of reconciling *Shari'ah* with fundamental human rights" (p. 18).

The thirteenth essay, "The Rights of Women and International Law in the Muslim Context" was first published in 1987. In it, An-Na'im discusses "some aspects of the relationship between [historical] *Shari'a* and current international standards on the rights of women" (p. 492). The essay first analyses the main principles of *Shari'ah* on the rights of women both in the historical context and in view of the "likely re-establishment of *Shari'a* in the public domain" of modern Muslim states (p. 492). He starts with an analysis of the theory of the rights of women under the *Shari'ah,* identifying that "[f]rom its very beginning in the seventh century, *Shari'a* guaranteed all Muslim women an independent legal personality, including the capacity to hold and dispose of property in their own right, a specific share in inheritance, access to education... and some participation in public life" (p. 495). He notes that while "[t]his level of achievement may not appear impressive by some modern standards, ... it has made very significant improvements in women's rights when viewed in historical perspectives", thereby reaching the conclusion that "*Shari'a* on the rights of women, ... compares very favourably with any other legal system until the nineteenth century" (p. 495).

He however argues that "A historical perspective is a poor excuse for the current inferior status of women under *Shari'a* when compared to other contemporary legal systems or when judged by the emerging international standards" (p. 495). He thus points out that this needs to change, arguing that "the provisions of the Qur'an and *Sunna* on women's rights can be interpreted differently" and that we should in fact, "now rely on this alternative interpretation of the Qur'an and *Sunna* in the reformation of *Shari'a* on the rights of women". He warns however that "[t]he possibility of an alternative interpretation … should not be confused with the current authoritative view of *Shari'a* as accepted by the vast majority of Muslims" (p. 497). In relation to the question of equality, An-Na'im states notably that "I do not believe, however, that complete legal equality between men and women is achievable and must be our objective in the Muslim world today" but rather it is the ideal of substantive equality between men and women that must be realistically pursued. He further argues in that regard that complete emancipation of women in the Muslim world cannot be fully achieved through secular movements and that the best way to achieve women's rights "is through what may be described as alternative Islamization through the reformation of *Shari'a*" (p. 500), by which he means "the assumption of an Islamic platform in advocating fundamental reform of *Shari'a* on the rights of women and the provision of Islamic foundations for these rights". He notes that "Islam is too powerful a political and cultural force to abandon to fundamentalists" and that "Islamic movements can easily mobilize mass support for their agenda by appealing to the religious sentiments and allegiances of the vast majority of Muslims", and that the "best way … is to show that the rights of women are Islamic and not alien western notions, albeit they may find expressions in other cultural and religious traditions, both western and non-western". He says this must be done internally through the adoption of imaginative reform techniques for the evolution and reformation of *Shari'a* rules relative to women's rights" (p. 501).

The essay then provides an analysis of women's rights under international law and Muslim reactions to those international standards. He illustrates his arguments with examples of the practices of some Muslim states and concludes with a discussion of his proposed approach to solving the problem of the rights of women in Islam in modern times.

The fourteenth essay, "The Contingent Universality of Human Rights: The Case of Freedom of Expression in African and Islamic Contexts" was first published in 1997. An-Na'im starts by citing example of incidents on freedom of expression in relation to Islamic law and Muslim states to establish the effect of the interplay of the domestic and the international on the realisation of universal human rights generally. He states that the main premise of the essay "is that freedom of expression (and other human rights) possess a contingent universality" (p. 30) which he then goes on to elaborate. He "explores the nature and dynamics of internal and external variables in relation to the normative and empirical standing of freedom of expression at both the domestic and international levels", the understanding of which he argues is "necessary for the development of appropriate strategies for promoting the universality of freedom of expression" (p. 31). He then proposes that "African and Islamic societies... should seek to promote universality of human rights as a necessary response to the realities of hegemonic neo-colonial designs of the developed world" and that "the needs of Islamic and African societies to attain and sustain national unity, political stability, and economic development, even as they safeguard their cultural and religious integrity, are all better served by a greater protection and promotion of freedom of expression than by its violation" (p. 32). He also addresses the issue of universality of freedom of expression before discussing freedom of expression in African and Islamic contexts. With regard to the African and Islamic contexts, he observes that "[t]he post-independence experiences of almost all African and Islamic countries ... clearly show that decades of bad planning and poor implementation of economic policies, corruption and incompetence were sustained in part through systematic denial of freedom of expression" (p. 46). He, among others, discusses the Egyptian case of Nasr Hamd Abu Zaid, which, he observes, "brought additional concerns about Islamic *Shari'a* law as personal law for Muslims in Egypt" (p. 52). The essay further examines freedom of expression in Kenya and Sudan, using the latter to illustrate how a Muslim state could, through its implementation of Islamic law, acutely limit the right to freedom of expression in ways that had contributed to the continuation of the civil war in the Sudan. In conclusion, An-Na'im proposes specific strategies for integrating the protection of freedom of expression in the political and legal systems of African and Islamic countries based on the earlier analysis of its contingent universality.

The fifteenth essay, "Why should Muslims abandon *jihad*?: Human Rights and the Future of International Law" was first published in 2006. An-Nai'm's intention here is to, realistically and rhetorically, question "the basis of prohibitions of *jihad* and upholding the universality of human rights in ways that can reaffirm the commitment of Muslims to international legality". The essay starts by first addressing the different meanings of *jihad* and indicates that it is used here "to refer to the unilateral use of force by Muslims in pursuit of political objectives and outside the institutional framework of international legality and the rule of law in general". He argues that "[s]ince the framework of legality and rule of law is lacking in 'the real world', there would be no basis for expecting Muslims to abandon *jihad*, as defined" in the essay. He notes that "human beings everywhere are responsible for protecting each other against the risks of our shared vulnerability to arbitrary violence, poverty and injustice generally" and argues that the important question, in his view, is "how can we all fulfil this mutual responsibility, instead of seeing the issues in terms of an 'Islamic threat' to human rights or to the security of some Western countries?" (p. 785). However this objective of protecting our shared vulnerability, he notes, "would neither be coherent nor politically viable in the absence of consistent observance of these norms and mechanisms of the rule of law in international relations". To achieve such observance and mechanisms of the rule of law in international relations, he states that Muslims should be called upon to abandon *jihad* in the sense of unilateral use of force in pursuit of political objectives, in conformity with the provisions of international law. However he notes the need to "realise that such calls will not be heeded in practice if those principles are not also honoured by other societies [and that] these principles cannot be true to their underlying rationale if they are not inclusive of all of humanity, including Muslims" (p. 786).

The essay also addresses the issue of how international and lawful is international law, wherein he tries to "affirm and promote the legitimacy and efficacy of international law as the indispensable means for realising universal ideals of peace, development and the protection of human rights everywhere". He notes that "For international law to play its role in realising shared ideals of justice and equality under the rule of law for all human beings it must be both truly international and legitimately lawful. It has to be equally accepted and implemented by all human societies, not something that some may choose to ignore while others are required to observe it". He asserts that under international law "the use of military force is not allowed except in accordance with the Charter of the United Nations, namely, in strict self-defence under Article 51 of the Charter, or when sanctioned by the Security Council under Chapter VII. There cannot by any possibility of lawful use of force beyond these two grounds, whether claimed as 'pre-emptive self-defence', 'just war' or Islamic *jihad*" (p. 787). He then states that "It is incoherent and futile to prohibit aggressive Islamic *jihad* without doing the same for any use of force outside the ambit of the UN Charter in the name of national self-interest. From this perspective, there is no moral, political or practical difference between international terrorism in the name of Islamic *jihad*, on the one hand, and so-called pre-emptive self-defence or humanitarian intervention claimed by the USA in Iraq, on the other. Both are instances of 'self-regulated' use of force outside the institutional framework of the UN, and are so inherently arbitrary and unaccountable that they undermine the very possibility of international law". He further emphasises the fact that "it is futile for state actors to demand observance of international law principles by non-state actors when they are unwilling to abide by those principles themselves" (p. 788). The essay then discusses the terrorist act of 9/11 and the American response to it in relation to the universality of human rights. He states that "[t]he Islamic tradition at large is basically consistent with most human rights norms, except for some specific, albeit very serious, aspects of the rights of women and freedom of religion and belief" (p. 791).

Finally, the essay addresses the issue of the mutual responsibilities for shared vulnerabilities, which, An-Na'im argues depends largely on "how to develop the necessary institutions and global culture of the rule of law in international relations and the protection of human rights throughout the world". He states that "[o]n the Islamic side of the issue, the persistent failure of Muslims to respond effectively enough to the responsibilities of sovereignty at home and peaceful international relations abroad is as damaging for the prospects of international legality and universality of human rights as the unilateral invasion of Iraq by the USA" (p. 795). He concludes that "[c]onfronting terrorism would therefore include combating this underlying culture of political violence, as well as the immediate causes and consequences of the use of arbitrary and indiscriminate violence in the furtherance of political ends, whoever the perpetrators and however we may feel about their alleged justification" (p. 796).

IV. Conclusion: A Theory of Interdependence

The sixteenth and last essay in this volume harnesses all three elements of Abdullah An-Na'im's general philosophy on Islam and human rights. The essay, "The Interdependence of Religion, Secularism, and Human Rights", was first published in 2005. In it, An-Na'im argues that the apparent tensions between or among religion, secularism and human rights "can be overcome by their conceptual synergy" (p. 56). He notes that he is "not suggesting the collapse of all related ideas, institutions, and policies into [this] framework" but that his purpose "is to highlight the dynamics of one complex process that might contribute to individual freedom and social justice" for all (p. 56). While he believes that his proposition of synergy was applicable to various religious and political contexts, his "primary concern as a Muslim is the prospect for this approach in Islamic societies" and "would like to encourage the determined promotion – the strengthening – of this synergy in the interest of legitimizing human rights, regulating the role of religion in public life, and affirming the positive place of secularism in Islamic societies" (p. 57). He then analyses the moral and philosophical foundation of human rights as well as its universality, the exclusivity of religion and specificity of secularism. As earlier noted in Chapter 4, this is a slight departure from, or modification of, his earlier position adduced in Chapter 2, where he had initially asserted, *inter alia*, that: "Muslim belief precludes a purely secular approach to law and the state" and argued therefore that "the benefits of western secularism in the Muslim world are temporary" (p. 333). The current position should however be understood in the context of his deconstruction and redefinition of the concept of secularism in Chapter 4 as well as in the present essay, where he states, *inter alia*, that "[w]idespread confusion and suspicion are attendant on the term *secularism* especially in Islamic societies, which regard it as a European, Christian concept imposed by colonial and neo-colonial forces" and then tries to redefine it in a way that "is deeply contextual and dynamic" to be consistent with an Islamic and human rights perspective (p. 61).

In this essay, he re-emphasises the important role of human agency in every society as well as in his proposed synergic process by arguing that each of the three paradigms, i.e. religion, secularism, and human rights, is an enabling factor of human agency and equally susceptible to be influenced by it". The question therefore is "how to secure the best conditions for human agency to achieve the transformations required" (p. 64). While he notes the fact that "[h]uman agency is always integral to the interpretation and implementation of every doctrine" he also acknowledges that "the guardians of orthodoxy everywhere claim eternal validity for their own interpretation and practice" (p. 65) so he argues that it is the principles of human rights that can guarantee the conditions that will facilitate the atmosphere to challenge such orthodox claims from within. He then analyses how human rights depend on both secularism and religion on the one hand, and how religion depends on both secularism and human rights on the other, and finally how secularism also depends on both religion and human rights. He proceeds to analyse this interdependence in Islamic contexts with examples again from the issue of women's rights in Egypt, and the negotiation of identity and politics in the Sudan and in Iran. He ends this essay with a strong assertion that "peoples and individuals need make no choice among religion, secularism, and human rights". In his view, "[t]he three can work in synergy" (p. 80). He therefore urges "both scholars and policymakers to take responsibility for that mediation rather than permit further damage to be done by belief in the incompatibility of religion with secular government and human rights", a human choice, he argues, that will be made by individuals.

From these selected essays, I have endeavoured to identify Abdullahi Ahmed An-Na'im's general philosophy on Islam and human rights as a three-angled philosophy, namely: (i) the philosophy for cross-cultural universality of human rights, (ii) the philosophy for internal reformation of Islamic law based on the methodology of his mentor *Ustadh* Mahmoud Mohamed Taha, and (iii) the philosophy for re-affirming secularism for Muslim states. Based on this three-angled philosophy, An-Na'im advocates a theory of interdependence between Islam, human rights and secularism through which he believes that Muslims should be able to practice their religion faithfully and at the same time enjoy the guarantees of human rights without hindrance.

Whether one agrees, or not, with every aspect of An-Na'im's three-angled philosophy on Islam and human rights and his theory of interdependence, there is no doubt that he is a great scholar whose views make significant contributions to human rights discourse generally and to the topic of Islam and human rights particularly. The factual point is that the questions he raises and engages with regarding the relationship between Islam and human rights in the modern world generally and in modern Muslim states particularly, are very valid and complex questions, which he himself acknowledges could be addressed from many different perspectives. He states, for example, in Chaper 4 that "I am not suggesting the collapse of all related ideas, institutions, and policies into the framework I am describing. My purpose here is to highlight the dynamics of one complex process that might contribute to individual freedom and social justice". As the discourse continues and as Muslims and human rights advocates continue to seek answers to these complex but valid questions, there is no doubt that Abdullahi Ahmed An-Na'im's thoughts as expressed in these essays will continue to be relevant to the debates on the subject for a very long time, which indicates the importance of this volume. Happy reading!

Mashood A. Baderin,
Professor of Law,
SOAS, University of London
October 2009

Part One

Islam between Universalism and Secularism

[1]
What Do We Mean by Universal?

RAY ROBERTS: CAMERA PRESS

The Mosque in Córdoba, Spain: the glory of Islam in Europe

Any concept of human rights that is to be universally accepted and globally enforced demands equal respect and mutual comprehension between rival cultures

Human rights ought, by definition, to be universal in concept, scope and content as well as in application: a globally accepted set of rights or claims to which all human beings are entitled by virtue of their humanity and without distinction on grounds such as race, gender or religion. Yet there can be no prospect of the universal application of such rights unless there is, at least, substantial agreement on their concept, scope and content.

What is at issue — between those who support a universal concept and those who argue for a relativist approach — is how and by whom these rights are to be defined and articulated. Universality requires global agreement, a consensus between different societies and cultures, not the application of one set of standards derived from the culture and context of a particular society to all other societies. The normative system in one society may not necessarily be appropriate for other societies who need to elaborate their own systems based on their particular cultural context.

Hence the paradox in which the international human rights movement is presently caught: the concept and essential characteristics of currently accepted international standards on 'universal' human rights have been primarily conceived, developed and established by the West; they cannot be accepted and implemented globally by the peoples of other parts of the world unless they are seen to be valid and legitimate from their perspectives. If they are to be more widely accepted and implemented, they must be premised on a genuinely universal model rather than the universalisation of a certain culturally specific, 'Western', model. To attempt to deny or disguise the dilemma only plays into the hands of those who may wish to manipulate it and undermines the credibility of those who attempt to uphold the contested human rights norms by making them appear to reject what their own constituency sees as obvious and important.

The paradox can only be resolved by first acknowledging the historical facts and then by arguing that although the universal validity of these standards cannot be assumed or taken for granted, they are not necessarily or inherently invalid from the perspective of other cultures. The question of whether and to what extent there is fundamental and irreconcilable difference between a particular international human rights standard and the norms, values and institutions of any other culture, can then be debated internally and across cultures.

All cultures have an element of ambivalence and contestability in the sense that prevailing practices and institutions are open to constant challenge and change. Not only is this essential for the survival of the culture as a whole, it provides a range of debatable options, any one of which may prevail at a particular time. While a particular interpretation or perception of certain cultural norms and institutions may appear to be

ABDULLAHI AN-NA'IM

in fundamental conflict with existing international human rights standards, this does not make it impossible to articulate an alternative interpretation which may begin to resolve the conflict.

If dialogue is to broaden and deepen global consensus it must be undertaken in good faith, with mutual respect for, and sensitivity to, the integrity and fundamental concerns of respective cultures, with an open mind and with the recognition that existing formulations may be changed — or even abolished — in the process. Ideally, participants should feel on an equal footing but, given existing power relations, those in a position to do so might seek ways of redressing the imbalance.

Where the Islamic world is concerned it is important to appreciate the profoundly defensive and reactive mode of internal discourse and cross-cultural exchange. Following the failure of secular liberalism or national socialism in the post-independence era, Muslims are now channelling their frustration and powerlessness into radical and militant Islamic revivalism as an assertion of their right to self-determination. The insistence on one universally valid set of human rights, therefore, risks the sort of confrontation we have seen in the Rushdie affair and forces debate under the worst possible circumstances.

The value and validity of a given concept of human rights is neither necessarily diminished nor validated by the fact that it is historically or geographically specific. It may well be that the 'democratic way of life' which presupposes the existence and acceptance of a certain concept of individual human rights is superior to other forms of political life. However, there are many parts of the world in which Western conceptions of democracy and human rights have not taken root. Instead of simply asserting the inherent superiority of those conceptions in the abstract, it would be more constructive to examine the reasons for this failure in regions that might be more receptive to their own equivalent or corresponding concepts.

Individual civil and political rights are integral to fundamental human rights, as are economic and social rights and collective rights to development and self-determination. Support for this holistic and interdependent concept of human rights includes efforts to promote their legitimacy in all cultures of the world as well as the need to protest their violation by exerting pressure on offending governments to respect them.

The present dynamics of the international protection of human rights operates primarily through the monitoring by Northern organisations of violations in the South in order to lobby Northern governments to pressure Southern governments to respect the human rights of their own populations. A truly universalist dynamic of protection would rely on monitoring and advocacy by local constituencies within the South, such as those that exist in the North, as well as in both directions across the North-South divide. I am not suggesting the abandonment of international monitoring and advocacy as we know it today, but rather seeking to enhance its genuinely global nature by multiplying and diversifying its centres and axes through rooting and legitimating it in the cultures and experiences of all peoples.

Given general agreement that freedom of expression can be limited, by law, to protect the rights of others, we must then ask, which rights, when and how? Who is to articulate and enforce such limits, to what end and on what basis? Since I purport to present an 'Islamic' perspective, the basis and nature of claims of Islamicity is the key to the present discussion. Not only do such claims determine the conceptual framework which informs and conditions responses to the sort of questions raised here, they are the criteria by which others, whether insiders or outsiders, can understand and evaluate the substance, content and implications of the claim.

Religion is not excluded from the ambivalence and contestability that characterise all cultures. Even when a religion is, like Islam, believed to be founded on divine scripture and the traditions of the Prophet and other significant communities or personalities, the human interpretation of those sources remains significant. Given unavoidable differences in interpretation of textual sources in historical context, what the religion is believed to be at any given point in time, or to say on any specific matter, is the product of competing human perceptions and prevailing socio-economic factors and forces that have become the prevailing view.

To believers, Islam is primarily and essentially defined by the Quran and Sunna of the Prophet, but, historically, the interpretation and application of these has always been conditioned by the understanding of the Muslim community at any given time or place. While the traditions of early Muslim communities are believed to be authoritative, those who subsequently seek to invoke this authority are themselves similarly conditioned. What Islam means or says on any given matter is therefore what the Muslims of the time and place believe it to be. There is no

ABDULLAHI AN-NA'IM

ALBERTO TESSORE: CAMERA PRESS

Senegal: the community will decide

other way for any religion, to have relevance to the lives of believers.

The dominance of a particular theological interpretation at any time is determined by a variety of factors. Historians may debate the relevance or relative significance of one factor or another, or speculate about the possibility of alternative results given a different set of factors, but the existence and nature of the process itself is beyond dispute.

During the second and third centuries of Islamic history, for example, there was a major debate between the so-called textualists and rationalists *(Ash'ariya* and *Mu'tazila)* on some fundamental issues of theology and politics which ended with the dominance of the former and suppression of the latter. One may debate why one view prevailed, or what might have happened under different circumstances, but the facts of the debate and its outcome are accepted by all historians of Islam. It is also clear that, although the *Mu'tazila* may not subsequently have won the day, elements of their approach and thought have survived and continue to be reflected in internal Muslim debates to the present day.

Whichever group or position a modern Muslim may support in that debate, the need to protect the freedom of expression which allows this sort of debate to take place cannot be denied. The same is true for any set of competing views in the past, present or future of Islamic experience. It is equally true that the winning side would want to curtail the freedom of expression of its opponents in the name of protecting and preserving the integrity of tradition and the stability of religious doctrine.

But since it is the totality of the community of Muslims of the time and place who have the legitimate right to decide which conception of the tradition is to be protected and preserved, and which religious doctrine should be maintained, freedom of expression remains of paramount importance. This conclusion does not yield definitive answers to the questions above — who is to articulate and enforce its limits, to what end and on what basis — but it does provide a clear presumption and orientation in favour of wider freedom of expression, and generally indicates by whom and how limitations may be set in practice.

This may sound exactly like a liberal justification of freedom of expression, but that does not make it necessarily non-Islamic. It is fully and coherently Islamic by virtue of its frame of reference, theological rationale and historical substantiation. This is perhaps the sort of overlapping consensus suggested by Jacques Maritain in a 1949 UNESCO study on the bases of an International Bill of Human Rights whereby different cultures come to a common understanding of the concept and its content, despite their disagreement on its justification.

The issue is not whether Islamic cultures, or any other cultures, are either inherently restrictive or tolerant of relatively greater freedom of expression. Such orientations tend to change over time. Neither is it a matter of citing textual sources or historical experiences as 'evidence' of greater or lesser 'Islamic' restriction or tolerance since texts are open to competing interpretations and historical experiences are susceptible to shifting characterisations. Reading the Quran and Sunna, one will find authority for liberalism as well as conservatism, and Muslim history gives clear examples of both tendencies. The matter is determined by the choices Muslims make, and the struggle they wage in favour of their choices, in their own historical context.

Secularism came to the Islamic world in the suspect company of colonialism, and is often confused with a particular experience of Western Christianity. Most Muslims believe there is a strong, organic link between Islam and politics since several verses of the Quran clearly instruct them to implement its dictates in their public as well as private affairs. The Quran and Sunna of the Prophet are also explicit in requiring

ABDULLAHI AN-NA'IM

Muslim communities to enforce certain principles regarding taxation, commercial and financial dealings, penal sanctions and so forth.

Although Muslims have in fact lived under varying degrees of secularism for most of their history, the ideal of an Islamic state in full accordance with the *sharia* (Islamic law) has always been kept, even invoked, by secular rulers to legitimise their power. Nevertheless, if confronted today with a categorical and immediate choice between an Islamic *sharia* state and an openly and unequivocally secular state that relegates *sharia* to the purely personal and private domain, most Muslims would probably opt for the former since most find it extremely difficult openly to oppose the application of *sharia* in public affairs.

Without ruling out the possibility altogether, it seems highly improbable, given the present predilection for majority rule and self determination, that a strictly secular state could be sustained in the Islamic world today, at least in countries with an overwhelming Muslim majority. Whatever degree of secularism earlier authoritarian rulers like Ataturk of Turkey or Bourguiba of Tunisia were able to construct, the prospects of open secularism appear to be diminishing: the failure of post-independence secularism and nationalism gave Islamic fundamentalism its impetus. Using the tools of 'modern' political organisation, international finance and the technology of mass communication, Islamic fundamentalism is now confronting an increasing number of Muslims with a stark choice between the 'divine' law of God and the 'anti-religious' law of man.

In the present context, I see more hope in trying to expose the fallacy of that formulation and in constructing an alternative modern version of *sharia* based on a radical reinterpretation of Islamic sources — something I have tried to do in my book *Toward an Islamic Reformation* — than in openly arguing for Western secularism. *Sharia* is neither as divine as its advocates claim nor secularism as anti-religious as its opponents allege. Should that exercise fail, even on its own terms, it might still make a useful contribution to the development of a modernist Islamic moral philosophy fully consistent with the concepts and principles of constitutionalism and universal human rights. A modern Islamic moral philosophy is unlikely to achieve its desired objectives, however, unless it succeeds in fulfilling the dual function of presenting Muslims with a justification for setting *sharia* aside and providing them with sound foundations for a political and legal order they can accept as Islamic.

The Rushdie affair in perspective

While I would maintain that the West has not overreacted to the *fatwa* on Salman Rushdie as a result of its own prejudices, I cannnot agree that the Muslim response is the act of a small minority of Shia fundamentalists. The Western reaction to a serious challenge to what most people around the world, Muslims and non-Muslims alike, hold to be fundamental and universal human rights is perfectly normal. And even though few non-Shia Muslims have spoken out in condemnation of the *fatwa,* the Shia response is shared by many Sunni Muslims.

The model can also operate through an alternative scenario whereby Islamic fundamentalism seizes power in a number of Islamic countries, is seen to have failed, and is replaced by a renewed drive for open secularism legitimised by a reconstruction of Islamic moral philosophy. I am convinced, however, that moral rights cannot be 'constitutionalised' in Islamic countries without some form of religious legitimacy.

Muslim responsibility goes much wider. Formalistic objections to the *fatwa* should not be allowed to hide the fact that its underlying justification in the *sharia* has not been challenged even by Muslims who would oppose this use of apostasy for procedural reasons. At the same time, simplistic condemnations of the Muslim failure to uphold universal norms of freedom of expression are equally inadequate and unlikely to succeed in mediating and resolving the issues.

The ultimate importance of the Rushdie affair is that it confronts the proponents of both sides with a serious challenge to their convictions. It casts individual freedom of belief and expression in global terms because of totally novel circumstances in human history. Whereas such issues have always been debated, mediated and resolved in relative privacy within relatively homogenous settings, they are now cast, and demand resolution, at a global, public and publicised level. This is happening at a time when global power relations are shifting away from gunboat diplomacy and the more recent superpower rivalries towards attempts to resolve conflict by mediation.

In this global and public confrontation, Muslims are required openly either to defend their belief in the validity of the *sharia* law of apostasy and its wider implications for freedom of belief and expression, or uphold the latter and thereby concede the invalidity of a law they believe to be divine. The 'Rushdie Defence Committees' and their constituencies, in turn, face the challenge of how to achieve their objective without frustrating the universality of human rights to which they claim allegiance.

I began with a discussion of relativity and universality, emphasising the need for discourse and dialogue to promote a global culture of human rights and break the current dependency of the South on Northern initiatives, priorities and resources. The course of the international advocacy of human rights will never be secure and consistent with its own rationale as long as 'Rushdie Defence Committees' are only set up in the North to pressure governments in the South.

There are potentially powerful and vigorous constituencies for universal human rights worldwide — including the Islamic world. But those constituencies can never be mobilised in a global project on purely Western liberal notions of individual civil and political rights. Along with other rights and new formulations of familiar rights, all human rights will only command genuine universal respect and validity through discourse and dialogue.

RACHAD EL KOUSSY: CAMERA PRESS

Al-Azhar, Egypt: the inviolate word

[2]

Islamic Law, International Relations and Human Rights: Challenge and Response*

I. INTRODUCTION 317
II. HISTORICAL *SHARI'A*: THE MEDINA MODEL OF THE ISLAMIC STATE 320
III. THE THEORY OF INTERNATIONAL RELATIONS IN *SHARI'A* 323
A. *Jihad* and Its Implications 323
B. The Modern Theory of International Relations 326
IV. RESTRICTED HUMAN RIGHTS UNDER *SHARI'A* . 328
A. Muslim Men 329
B. Muslim Women and Non-Muslims 330
C. *Shari'a* in Light of Minimum Human Rights Standards 332
V. SOLUTIONS FROM WITHIN ISLAM 333
VI. CONCLUSION 335

I. INTRODUCTION

When recently asked whether Chinese Muslims aspire to conduct all aspects of their public and private affairs in accordance with Islam, a distinguished Chinese Muslim scholar responded by saying that the Chinese Muslims live in *dar al-harb*,[1] the territory of war, and must therefore accept the status of a religious minority unable to assert its

* This Article was presented at a symposium on Human Rights and International Relations in Islamic Law co-sponsored by the School of Law and the Center for Near Eastern Studies, UCLA, March 21-22, 1986.

1. The theory of Islamic law did not accept permanent peace with the non-Muslim states. In accordance with this principle, the world is divided in terms of *dar al-Islam*, territory under Muslim rule, and *dar al-harb*, territory at war with the Muslims. *See infra* notes 37-40 and accompanying text.

full religious identity.[2] Conversely, a spokesperson for a non-Muslim minority living within *dar al-Islam*—an Islamic state ruled by *Shari'a*, Islamic religious law—would no doubt mention the restrictions and various civil limitations imposed on his or her community.[3] Further, Muslim women would also be aware of gender-based limitations that the Islamic state imposes on them.[4]

Shari'a's strict classifications of territories in terms of *jihad*,[5] and people in terms of religion and gender, are very much alive in the hearts and minds of Muslims and those non-Muslims with whom they interact. This Article argues that these principles of public *Shari'a*, as distinguished from private *Shari'a* of family law and devotional rites,[6] are both morally indefensible and practically impossible to maintain today.

This Article discusses solutions to the drawbacks of historical *Shari'a* from a religious rather than secular perspective, because Muslims do not separate the religion of Islam from the law of Islam. The author submits, as a Muslim, that God communicates through the social and physical environment as well as through the *Qur'an*, His literal and final word, and through the *Sunna*, traditions of His final Prophet, Mohammed Ibn Abdillah.[7] This Article contends that God's instructions must be understood and applied in light of all social and material phenomena He has manifested in the world. This religious perspective is important for several reasons.

First, Muslims are fully entitled to assert their Islamic identity and comply with their religious duty to apply Islamic law to every aspect of their public and private lives. This is a legitimate exercise of their substantive right to self-determination enshrined in the United

2. I do not have the permission of this Chinese scholar to identify him by name, or by reference to the occasion.

3. *See* D. MARTIN, THE PERSECUTION OF THE BAHA'IS OF IRAN, 1844-1984 (1984); E. WATKIN, A LONELY MINORITY, THE MODERN HISTORY OF EGYPT'S COPTS (1963); Masriya, *A Christian Minority: The Copts in Egypt*, in 4 CASE STUDIES ON HUMAN RIGHTS AND FUNDAMENTAL FREEDOMS, A WORLD SURVEY 90 (W. Veenhoven ed. 1976) [hereinafter WORLD SURVEY]; Rondat, *Minorities in the Arab Orient Today*, in MAN, STATE AND SOCIETY IN THE CONTEMPORARY MIDDLE EAST 276 (J. Landau ed. 1972); *see also* B. YE'OR, THE DHIMMI, JEWS AND CHRISTIANS UNDER ISLAM (1985).

4. *See, e.g.*, C. LUCA, *Discrimination in the Arab Middle East* in 1 WORLD SURVEY, *supra* note 3, at 213, 219-25.

5. The principle and implications of *jihad* are discussed *infra* notes 35-51 and accompanying text.

6. *Shari'a is* the Muslim comprehensive religious law derived from the basic sources, namely the *Qur'an*, the Muslim holy book, and *Sunna*, the traditions of the Prophet Mohammed. This Article is concerned only with certain public law aspects of *Shari'a*, such as questions of public international law, civil liberties, and human rights.

7. Belief in the *Qur'an* and Prophet Mohammed is the essence of the Muslim creed, but it has no validity for non-Muslims. Discussion of Islamic law must proceed along religious lines because the Muslims have no equivalent of the Western doctrine of separation of church and state.

Nations Charter[8] and other relevant international documents and supported by modern national and international practice.[9]

Second, because *Shari'a* signifies the positive law of historical Islam, its general principles continue to bind and motivate Muslims.[10] Therefore, passive non-assertion of *Shari'a*'s norms is unworkable because a significant number of Muslims advocate the immediate application of historical *Shari'a*.[11] The appeal of this movement makes it imperative that *Shari'a* be authoritatively reformed from within the Islamic traditions and in ways acceptable to Muslims themselves. Otherwise, such reform would lack legitimacy and practical viability.[12]

Third, although Muslims will not accept secular reforms to their religious law and practice, they have made some concessions to the demands of constitutionalism and the rule of law in national and international relations.[13] Clearly, they are sensitive to tensions between inherited wisdom and the realities of the modern world. However,

8. Under the United Nations Charter, one of the purposes of the United Nations is "[t]o develop friendly relations among nations based on respect for the principle of equal rights and self-determination of peoples, and to take other appropriate measures to strengthen universal peace." U.N. CHARTER art. 1, para. 2.

9. African Charter of Human and Peoples' Rights (Banjul Charter), Jan. 7-19, 1980, art. 20, OAU Doc. CAB/LEG/67/3/Rev. 1; International Covenant on Civil and Political Rights, Dec. 16, 1966, art. 1, G.A. Res. 2200 (XXI), 21 U.N. GAOR Supp. (No. 16) 52, U.N. Doc. A/6316; International Covenant on Economic Social and Cultural Rights, Dec. 16, 1966, art. 1, G.A. Res. 2200 (XXI), 21 U.N. GAOR Supp. (No. 16) 49, U.N. Doc. A/6316. *See generally* A. COBBAN, THE NATION STATE AND NATION SELF-DETERMINATION (1970); D. GORDON, SELF-DETERMINATION AND HISTORY IN THE THIRD WORLD (1971); R. SUREDA, THE EVOLUTION OF THE RIGHT OF SELF DETERMINATION: A STUDY OF UNITED NATIONS PRACTICE (1973); U. UMOZURIKE, SELF-DETERMINATION IN INTERNATIONAL LAW (1972).

10. *See generally* J. ESPOSITO, VOICES OF RESURGENT ISLAM (1983); G. JANSEN, MILITANT ISLAM (1979).

11. The Muslims have known periodic movements demanding the purification of the faith and the rigorous application of *Shari'a*. In the 19th century, these so-called Islamic "fundamentalist" movements included the *Maydiya* of the Sudan and the Fulani *jihad* of West Africa. *See, e.g.*, M. HISKETT, THE SWORD OF TRUTH: THE LIFE AND TIMES OF SHEHU USMAN DAN FADIO (1973); P. HOLT, THE MAHDIST STATE IN THE SUDAN, 1881-1898 (1958); Waldman, *The Fulani Jihad: A Reassessment*, 6 J. AFR. HIST. 333 (1956).

More recently, the movement of the Muslim Brothers, originating in Egypt in the 1920s, has vigorously advocated the immediate and total application of *Shari'a* for many years. On the ideology and organization of this movement, see R. MITCHELL, THE SOCIETY OF THE MUSLIM BROTHERS (1969).

The same demand is also voiced by a number of other groups and prominent individuals throughout the Muslim world. *See generally* ISLAMIC RESURGENCE IN THE ARAB WORLD (A. Dessouki ed. 1982); J. ESPOSITO, *supra* note 10; D. PIPES, IN THE PATH OF GOD, ISLAM AND POLITICAL POWER 124-42 (1983).

12. The Muslims feel a strong sense of religious duty to conduct all their public and private affairs in accordance with their divinely ordained law. The *Qur'an* describes those who fail to apply the law ordained by God as "unbelievers" and "wrong-doers." *Qur'an* 5:44-49 (R. Bell trans. 1937) [hereinafter *Qur'an*].

13. Khadduri, *Islam and the Modern Law of Nations*, 50 AM. J. INT'L L. 358 (1956); G. JANSEN, *supra* note 10, ch. 7; D. PIPES, *supra* note 11, at 52.

such concessions are limited and temporary because the division of loyalty between tradition, on the one hand, and a pressing sense of fairness and practicability, on the other hand, creates a dangerous ambivalence in Muslim attitudes and policies.[14]

To resolve this paradox and secure modern advances, modern Muslims must settle these tensions with reference to resources available within their own traditions. Otherwise, they will continue an unstable situation of subscribing to an unrealistic ideal of *Shari'a* while attempting to conduct their affairs in accordance with secular norms and institutions.

To summarize, this Article argues that, for Islamic states, smooth and successful transition to complete secularism is neither likely nor desirable because Muslims are obligated to live in accordance with Islamic law.[15] Fulfilling that obligation by re-introducing historical *Shari'a* would be disastrous for international relations and human rights. This Article proposes that the Muslims' religious duty may be satisfied by applying a *modern* version of Islamic law that is consistent with peaceful international relations and respect for human rights. This modern version will be Islamic *Shari'a* because it will be derived from the fundamental sources of Islam, without being identical in every respect to historical *Shari'a*.

II. HISTORICAL *SHARI'A*: THE MEDINA MODEL OF THE ISLAMIC STATE

Shari'a is often mistakenly equated with Islam. In fact, it only represents the early Muslims' understanding of the two fundamental sources of Islam: the *Qur'an*, and the life-examples of the Prophet, the *Sunna*. A brief survey of *Shari'a*'s historical development demonstrates this preliminary proposition.[16]

The Prophet was born in Mecca, a commercial town in western Arabia, around 570 C.E.[17] He started to receive the *Qur'an*, which Muslims believe to be the literal and final word of God, around 610.[18] Continuous persecution, culminating in a plot to kill the Prophet, prompted him and his followers to migrate to Medina, another town in western Arabia, in 622.[19] The growing Muslim community, in alli-

14. *See* D. Pipes, *supra* note 11, chs. 5-8. For a more sensitive and sympathetic analysis of the Muslim dilemma, see W. Smith, Islam in Modern History, ch. 8 (1957).

15. *Qur'an, supra* note 12, at 4:65, 5:44-49, 24:51.

16. For surveys of the nature, sources, and development of *Shari'a* see, e.g., N. Coulson, A History of Islamic Law (1964); J. Schact, The Origins of Muhammadana Jurisprudence (1950).

17. *See generally* A. Ali, The Spirit of Islam chs. 1-10 (1922); T. Arnold, The Preaching of Islam ch. 2 (1913).

18. *See* sources cited *supra* note 17.

19. *See* sources cited *supra* note 17.

ance with the sizable Jewish population of Medina, established the first Islamic state.[20]

A written treaty between the two communities determined the relationships between the dominant Muslims and subordinate Jews of Medina.[21] A similar treaty regulated the relationship between the Muslims and the Christians of Najran.[22] These and other treaties concluded by the Prophet and his immediate successors, the *Khulaffa*,[23] became the basis of the *dhimma* system governing the status and rights of non-Muslim communities "tolerated" within the borders of the Muslim state.[24] Similar treaties concluded with alien powers became the basis of Muslim inter-communal relations, the equivalent of modern international law.[25]

As the religious and political head of the Muslim state of Medina, the Prophet had the dual roles of prophet, continuing to receive revelation, and ruler, interpreting and applying revelation to all the public and private affairs of the community. His companions, and succeeding generations of Muslims, made no distinction between the two roles. Under the Medina model of the Muslim state, the religious head of the community combines all executive and judicial functions.

Early Muslim jurists purported to severely restrict the Islamic state's legislative function on the assumption that the law was divinely revealed. In fact, the *Qur'an* and *Sunna* did not provide a comprehensive system of law. The early *Khulaffa* and their provincial governors exercised legislative functions through *ijtihad*, creative independent juristic reasoning.[26] The theo-political *Khulaffa* consulted with the

---

20. *See* sources cited *supra* note 17.

21. The subordinate status of the Jewish community was signified by their submission to the Prophet's rule, or in modern terms, Muslim sovereignty. The Jews, however, were guaranteed equality before the law, security of person and property, and freedom of religion. For a translation of the text of that first treaty, see M. KHADDURI, WAR AND PEACE IN THE LAW OF ISLAM 206-09 (1979).

22. *Id.* at 179-80. The terms of the treaty signified the submission of this Christian community to the Muslim sovereignty.

23. *Id.* at 180.

24. The word *dhimma* literally means "honor" or "pledge." As a technical term of *Shari'a*, it means the pledge given by the Muslim ruler to certain non-Muslim communities. It secures their persons and property, and guarantees their right to worship and to conduct their personal affairs in accordance with their own religion and customs, in exchange for submission to Muslim sovereignty and payment of a poll tax (*jizyah*). *See* M. KHADDURI, *supra* note 21, at 175-220.

25. *Id.* at 42-48, 175-201.

26. The Prophet sanctioned *ijtihad*, or independent juristic reasoning, in the absence of clear and definite ruling in the *Qur'an* or *Sunna*. However, Muslim jurists came to agree that no fresh *ijtihad* was allowed after the tenth century. *See* Anderson, *Law as a Social Force in Islamic Culture and History*, 20 BULL. SCH. ORIENTAL & AFR. STUD. 13 (1957). For the view that *ijtihad* is still permissible, see Halla, *Was the Gate of Ijtihad Closed?*, 16 INT'L J. MIDDLE EAST STUD. 3 (1984).

leading companions, but were not bound by their opinion.[27] To that extent, under the Medina model, the Muslim ruler combined all legislative, executive, and judicial functions. Although the Muslim ruler was theoretically bound by the *Qur'an* and *Sunna*, he was the ultimate judge of what those sources meant in any given situation. The actions of the *Khaliffa* (singular of *Khulaffa*) were limited by his conscience and piety, rather than by objective constitutional safeguards.[28]

This concentration of religious and legal authority is the most telling criticism of public *Shari'a* in a modern context. The Medina model was the appropriate structure in its historical context. However, it was never intended to be the final model of an Islamic state.[29] After fourteen-hundred years, the need for safeguards such as separation of powers and an independent judiciary is evident.

The need for an effective limitation on the powers of modern government is beyond dispute. The Medina model of public *Shari'a*, however, fails to provide these vital safeguards. This Article will propose that adequate safeguards are possible within alternative models of the Islamic state. Although the alternative models are not entirely consistent with the Medina model, they are equally Islamic.

Muslim history itself clearly illustrates that the Medina model was workable only within its immediate historical context, the reign of the first four *Khulaffa*. With the assassination of the fourth *Khaliffa*, Ali, and the establishment of the Amawy and Abbasy dynasties, political pragmatism and expedience rather than public *Shari'a* governed Muslim public life.[30] The jurists continued to theorize, but it had little

---

27. The *Qur'an* requires consultation among the Muslims, but as the word *Shwra* itself means consultation (*Qur'an*, *supra* note 12, at 3:159, 42:38), these verses only support the right to give non-binding advice. *Id.* The Prophet and his successors did consult the Muslims and often accepted their advice, but they also retained the right to reject such advice and did in fact sometimes act against the advice of the vast majority of the Muslims. *See, e.g.*, A. MUTWALY, MABADI' NIZAM AL-HUKM FI AL-ISLAM [PRINCIPLES OF THE SYSTEM OF GOVERNMENT IN ISLAM] 667-69 (1966).

28. Coulson, *The State and the Individual in Islamic Law*, 6 INT'L COMP. L.Q. 49 (1957). One commentator described this aspect of *Shari'a* as follows:

> The Islamic state did not rest on any assumption that the public should act as a check restraining the ruler, even if he transgressed the sacred law .... In matters such as the interpretation of law and religion, the caliph [*Khaliffa*] was expected to consult the *'ulama* [*scholars*]. But if the caliph ignored the *'ulama*'s advice or chose to act without it, they might warn him of evil consequences or pray that God might change his heart. Rarely did the *'ulama* even seek to influence the Caliph via public opinion.

M. KHADDURI, POLITICAL TRENDS IN THE ARAB WORLD 47 (1970).

29. *See generally* U. TAHA, THE SECOND MESSAGE OF ISLAM (1987).

30. For historical surveys of early Muslim public and political life and institutions, see generally A. ALI, THE SPIRIT OF ISLAM (1974); 1 T. HUSSEIN, AL-FITNA AL KUBRA [THE GREAT UPHEAVAL] (1959); 2 T. HUSSEIN, AL-FITNA AL KUBRA [THE GREAT UPHEAVAL] (1961); W. MUIR, THE CALIPHATE, ITS RISE, DECLINE AND FALL (1975) (providing extensive and authoritative treatment of the subject).

relationship to the actual state of affairs.[31] State authorities tolerated the jurists because they did not pose a serious threat to political power and continued to expound public *Shari'a* as a theoretical ideal. In mutual appreciation of each other's limitations, the jurists and statesmen stayed apart.[32]

This historical perspective provides valuable insights into the origins and nature of *Shari'a* and its applicability to a modern state. Although *Shari'a* is often represented as the only valid and necessary implication of the *Qur'an* and *Sunna*, the early jurists interpreted the meaning of those sources in the context of the prevailing socio-economic and political conditions.[33]

Because of their exceptional intellectual and moral caliber, the early jurists were able to develop a sophisticated and flexible legal system that sustained the Muslim civilization for many centuries. For a long time, public *Shari'a* could adapt to changing conditions through its internal flexibility and variety of juristic opinions. This process, however, has now been exhausted, and public *Shari'a* is no longer capable of adequate response. The magnitude of change from the time of the formative era of public *Shari'a*, in the Middle East of the eighth to the tenth centuries, to twentieth century global, social, and political relations, is too much for *Shari'a* to handle.

Modern jurists must not confine Islam to *Shari'a*. This would unjustifiably condemn it to *Shari'a*'s contextual limitations and deem it incapable of responding to changes in the physical and social environment that are, according to Muslim belief, willed and manifested by God Himself.

III. THE THEORY OF INTERNATIONAL RELATIONS IN *SHARI'A*

A. *Jihad* and Its Implications

The early *Shari'a* model was consistent with its historical context and was a substantial improvement upon contemporary legal systems. However, certain assumptions and principles of *Shari'a* are diametrically opposed to those of modern international law and practice.[34]

One such principle is the theory of *jihad*. *Jihad* emphasizes the Muslims' duty to propagate their faith through aggressive war if necessary, until the whole world embraces Islam or submits to Muslim

31. T. Arnold, The Caliphate ch. 5 (1965).
32. *See generally* Coulson, *supra* note 28.
33. *See* sources cited *supra* note 11. *But see* U. Taha, *supra* note 29.
34. Khadduri, *Islam and the Modern Law of Nations*, 50 Am. J. Int'l L. 358, 358 (1956).

sovereignty.[35] Under this theory, Muslims ought not recognize the territorial sovereignty of non-Muslim states with whom they deem themselves to be in a constant state of war. Muslim rulers may temporarily suspend active *jihad* to prepare better for the next confrontation, but such suspension should never be for too long. Some jurists specifically mention ten years as the maximum duration of suspension of active *jihad*.[36]

In accordance with this theory the world is divided into *dar al-Islam*, territory subject to Muslim sovereignty, *dar al-sulh*, territory enjoying a peace treaty, and *dar al-harb*, territory at war with the Muslims.[37] Muslims determine the rights of individuals according to the territorial classification of their residence.[38] To avoid some of the negative consequences of classifying a territory as *dar al-harb*, Muslim jurists set very strict qualifications and insisted that they should be

---

35. Khadduri described the position of *Shari'a* accurately when he said:

> But the *jihad* did not always mean war, since Islam's objective might be achieved by peaceful as well as violent means. Thus the *jihad* may be regarded as an intensive religious propaganda which took the form of a continuous process of warfare, psychological and political, no less than strictly military. From a legal viewpoint it meant a permanent state of war between Islam and enemy territory. But this state of war should not be construed as actual hostilities; it was rather equivalent, in Western legal terminology, to non-recognition. This, however, did not imply, as in the modern law of nations, the impossibility of initiating negotiations and concluding treaties, for such actions were considered neither to imply equality between the two contracting parties nor necessarily to possess a permanent character. The nearest equivalent, perhaps, to this situation is the recognition of insurgency which neither precludes an intention of later *de facto* or *de jure* recognition nor approval of the regime under insurgency; it merely means that an authority to enforce the law in a certain territory is needed under certain circumstances [citation omitted]. The Islamic state, in like manner, in entering into diplomatic negotiations with a non-Muslim state, did not intend to recognize that state, but merely to admit that a certain authority or authorities were needed in the *dar al-harb* so long as it remained beyond Muslim sovereignty.

Id. 359-60; *see also* Shihata, *Islamic Law and the World Community*, 4 HARV. INT'L L.J. 101, 107 (1962). For a documented summary of the doctrine of *jihad*, see M. KHADDURI, *supra* note 21, at 55-73.

36. LAW IN THE MIDDLE EAST 345 (M. Khadduri & H. Liebesny ed. 1955) [hereinafter LAW IN THE MIDDLE EAST]. The Shafi' School of Islamic jurisprudence set the ten-year maximum limit on suspension of *jihad* by analogy to the Hudaybiya treaty in which the Prophet agreed to postpone war with the polytheists of Mecca for ten years. For a translation of the text of this treaty, see M. KHADDURI, *supra* note 21, at 212. The Hanafi and Maliki Schools of Islamic jurisprudence argue that because that treaty was violated by the non-Muslim side within two years, and the Prophet retaliated by marching on Mecca and capturing it, the Hudaybiya treaty cannot be taken as precedent for suspension of *jihad* for ten years. According to this view, *jihad* should not be suspended except for the absolute necessity of settling Muslim internal differences or in the face of overwhelming enemy power. *See* Khadduri, *supra* note 21, at 134.

37. As Shihata explained, the original classification was in terms of territories of war and peace, *dar al-hard* and *dar al-Islam*. The intermediate category of *dar al-sulh* was devised by the jurists around the ninth century in recognition of the extended, if not indefinite, state of peace established by treaty. Shihata, *supra* note 35, at 107.

38. *See, e.g.*, M. KHADDURI, *supra* note 21, at 147-201.

applied rigorously.[39] For example, Abu Hanifa set three conditions for designating a territory as *dar al-harb*: 1) that the law applied there be apparently non-Islamic; 2) that the territory border the Muslim world, creating an expectation of aggression; and 3) that no Muslim or *dhimmi* (a person protected by the Islamic state) is safe in such territory except by a special contract.[40]

Some modern Muslim scholars dispute that *jihad* was aggressive, and argue that it was exclusively defensive war.[41] They cite those verses of the *Qur'an* that authorize Muslims to repel aggression in defense of themselves and property.[42] These scholars fail, however, to take account of verses of the *Qur'an* that suggest aggressive *jihad*.[43] *Sunna* and the actual practice of the early Muslims also support the idea of *jihad* as aggressive war.[44] These sources instruct the Muslims to initiate *jihad* by seeking out the unbelievers and offering them the choice to either embrace Islam, submit to Muslim rule in accordance with *Shari'a*, or fight.[45] If they should fight and are defeated, the victors may seize their property as spoils of war, and surviving men, women, and children may be taken as slaves.[46] These were the imperative consequences of *jihad* under *Shari'a* even when *jihad* was defensive war. Religious and historical evidence clearly shows *jihad* and its

39. Shihata, *supra* note 35, at 108.

40. Abu Zahrah, *Nazaria't Al-Harb Fi Al-Islam*, 14 REVUE EGYPTIENNE DU DROIT INT'L 1, 17 (1958). Khadduri states the Hanafi position in slightly different terms: "[F]irst, the law of the unbelievers is enforced; second, it becomes separated for *dar al-Islam* by non-Muslims territory; and third, no believer or dhimmi could safely reside in the territory." M. KHADDURI, *supra* note 21, at 156.

41. *See, e.g.*, Abu Zahrah, *supra* note 40; M. SHALTUT, AL-ISLAM WA AL-'ALAGAT AL DAWLIA [ISLAM AND INTERNATIONAL RELATIONS] 38 (1951).

42. The *Qur'an* states "[I]f any make an attack upon you, make a like attack upon them; show piety towards Allah, and know that Allah is with those who show pity." *Qur'an*, *supra* note 12, at 2:190. The defensive dimension of *jihad* is not disputed here.

43. The *Qur'an* states: "When the sacred months have slipped away, slay the polytheists wherever ye find them, seize them, beset them, lie in ambush for them everywhere; if they repent, and establish the prayer and pay the Zakt, then set them free; For Allah is forgiving, compassionate." *Qur'an*, *supra* note 12, at 9:5.

> Fight against those who do not believe in Allah nor in the Last Day, and do not make forbidden what Allah and his messengers have made forbidden, and do not practice the religion of truth, who have been given the Book [Christians and Jews], until they pay the *Jizya* off-hand, being subdued.

Id. at 9:29.

"Oh ye who have believed, fight the unbelievers who are near to you, and let them feel a rough temper in you, and know that Allah is with those who show piety." *Id.* at 9:124.

44. *See* M. KHADDURI, *supra* note 21, at 55-82.

45. These options were based on the explicit instructions given by the Prophet to army and detachment commanders. Because the object of *jihad* was to spread the faith and not material gain, Islam had to be offered first, and if accepted, the Muslims were not entitled to fight. If Islam was not accepted, then the second and third options would follow in accordance with *Shari'a*. *See* Shihata, *supra* note 35, at III.

46. M. KHADDURI, *supra* note 21, at 118-32.

consequences cannot be rationalized as exclusively defensive war.[47]

Jihad is best seen as employing the prevailing method of conducting international relations for the superior purpose of propagating Islam and achieving what Muslims believed to be the just and enlightened rule of *Shari'a* over the conquered territory. Historically, *jihad* was a positive phenomenon because it humanized the practice of warfare in the Middle Ages. First, *Shari'a* prohibited the prevalent practice of using war for material gain or revenge.[48] Second, the Prophet and his companions, acting in accordance with the *Qur'an* and *Sunna*, laid down very specific and strict rules for honorable combat.[49]

According to these rules, Muslims must first offer their foes the option of accepting Islam or submitting to Muslim sovereignty. In other words, there can be no *jihad* under *Shari'a* without a formal declaration of war following the enemy's rejection of Islam and of a status equal to that of Muslims or at least the status of a protected *dhimmi* community. Once they declare war, Muslims must never kill non-combatants, destroy property, or conduct war-like activities outside the battlefield. The *Qur'an* encourages peace and emphasizes the strict duty to observe treaties and covenants with the enemy.[50] *Shari'a* also protects aliens such as diplomats and international travellers who are allowed into Muslim territory under safe conduct.[51]

Subject to these limitations, *jihad* remains a fundamental obligation under *Shari'a*. There should be no permanent peace until the whole world submits to Muslim sovereignty. This aim clearly repudiates the most fundamental premise of the theory of modern international relations: peaceful coexistence of equal sovereign states.[52]

B. The Modern Theory of International Relations

After the *bellum jestum*, the European equivalent of *jihad*,[53] the

47. For an account of the Muslim expansion, see J. Glubb, The Great Arab Conquests (1980).

48. Law in the Middle East, *supra* note 36, at 110.

49. M. Hamidullah, Muslim Conduct of State 204-08 (1953); M. Khadduri, *supra* note 21, at 102-05.

50. *Qur'an*, *supra* note 12, at 4:90, 8:61. As the terms of these verses and the verses which sanction *jihad* to spread the faith clearly show, peace treaties are to be concluded on the Muslims' terms. *See supra* note 43. Ideally this would be when non-Muslims embrace Islam, or at least submit to Muslim rule. The Muslims may also conclude a peace treaty to gain time to strengthen themselves or settle internal differences. But once they do conclude a treaty, the Muslims are strictly bound by it until the other party repudiates it by clear violation. Shihata, *supra* note 35, at 112-13.

51. M. Khadduri, *supra* note 21, at 162-69. It is interesting to note that the seizure of American diplomats in Iran in 1979 and recent abductions and assassinations in Lebanon of non-combatant aliens who enjoy safe-conduct (*aman*), violate *Shari'a* itself. Shihata, *supra* note 35, at 108-09.

52. U.N. Charter art. 2, paras. 1, 4.

53. I. Walker, A History of the Law of Nations 300, 306-07 (1899).

European powers came to appreciate the need for peaceful coexistence among themselves and with non-European powers.[54] During the nineteenth century, the community of "civilized" nations was gradually extended to include the Muslims as represented by the Ottoman Empire.[55] Western European legal norms became the basis of international relations.[56]

Although the Muslims and other peoples of the world initially joined the community of nations on Europe's own terms, they now challenge some of these norms as repugnant to international justice, the principles of equality of states, and national self-determination.[57] Some of these criticisms of traditional international law norms are valid. Certain aspects of international law must be renegotiated and improved to ensure world peace and the survival of world civilization.[58] This does not, however, justify *jihad*, which would repudiate the basic premise of sovereign equality and peaceful coexistence. The Islamic world must address the limitations of historic public *Shari'a* if it wishes to maintain world peace and stability. First, the Islamic nations must reassess the validity of *jihad* and whether the aggressive propagation of Islam by violence is viable in the modern world. Second, Muslims must question whether non-recognition of sovereign non-Muslim states and classification of them as *dar al-harb*, territories of war, can continue when peaceful coexistence is imperative. Given these aspects of public *Shari'a*, it is arguable that this system is both morally indefensible and practically untenable today.

Some contend that the Muslims have already abandoned these aspects of public *Shari'a* and accepted membership in the modern community of nations on the basis of the principles of peaceful coexistence and sovereign equality of all nations.[59] However, because these principles of *Shari'a* continue to influence Muslim attitudes and

---

54. *Id.*

55. For a brief survey of the process of assimilation, see Khadduri, *supra* note 34, at 360-72.

56. *See generally* I. WALKER, *supra* note 53.

57. *See, e.g.*, H. KELSEN, THE COMMUNIST THEORY OF LAW 188 (1955); L. OPPENHEIM, 1 INTERNATIONAL LAW 52 (8th ed. 1963); R. SCHLESINGER, THE SOVIET LEGAL THEORY 286 (2d ed. 1951).

58. C. JENKS, THE COMMON LAW OF MANKIND ch. 1 (1958). *See generally* P. CORBETT, LAW AND SOCIETY IN THE RELATIONS OF STATES (1951); Q. WRIGHT, THE STRENGTHENING OF INTERNATIONAL LAW (1959).

59. All Muslim countries are members of the United Nations and are bound by the U.N. Charter. R. LILLICH & F. NEWMAN, INTERNATIONAL HUMAN RIGHTS 66 (1976); Lauterpacht, *The International Protection of Human Rights*, 70 RECUEIL DES COURS 5, 24 (1947). The Charter states:

> The Purposes of the United Nations are:
>
> 1. To maintain international peace and security, and to that end: to take effective collective measures for the prevention and removal of threats to the peace . . . .

U.N. CHARTER art. 1, para. 1; *see also id.* art. 1, para. 2.

practice today, the danger of Muslim repudiation of the basic premise of international law and peaceful coexistence remains.

IV. RESTRICTED HUMAN RIGHTS UNDER *SHARI'A*

Under *Shari'a* rule, some basic human rights are at serious risk.[60] Had Muslims not temporarily abandoned public *Shari'a* during secular rule, there would have been massive violations of the most basic human rights.[61] Recent attempts to re-introduce public *Shari'a* in Iran and Pakistan provide horrific examples of persecution of religious minorities and violation of individual civil liberties.[62] Islamic governments sometimes commit these atrocities in violation of *Shari'a* itself.[63] This transgression is due to a lack of institutionalized safeguards to ensure compliance with *Shari'a* limitations on the powers of rulers.[64] But even if *Shari'a* is observed, gross violations of human rights would still occur.

As explained below, *Shari'a* classifies all the subjects of an Islamic state in terms of gender and religion. At the top of the hierarchy are Muslim men, who enjoy the highest level of civil and political rights, followed by Muslim women and "tolerated" non-Muslim minorities.

60. The important question of the validity of moral and philosophical foundations of human rights is beyond the scope of this Article.

61. For example, it should be noted that slavery has been abolished in the Muslim world as a matter of secular law and not through the reform of the relevant rules of *Shari'a*. Despite the call to formally abolish slavery as a matter of *Shari'a* law, see A. ALI, *supra* note 17, at 267, abolition was achieved only through secular law.

In theory, there is nothing to prevent the re-establishment of slavery if *Shari'a* is the exclusive legal system. For *Shari'a*'s effort to improve the lot of the slaves, see M. KHADDURI, *supra* note 21, at 130-32. Nevertheless, slavery as such is not unlawful under *Shari'a*.

62. Documenting current human rights violations is problematic because of the scarcity of objective and verifiable information. Moreover, it is often difficult to distinguish between the various sociological and political causes in relation to a given country. The available information nevertheless provides support for the statement that certain human rights violations are at least closely associated with the application of *Shari'a* law in Iran and Pakistan. This is particularly true when the frequent incidence and gravity of such violations coincide with the move to apply *Shari'a* in these countries. *See, e.g.*, AMNESTY INTERNATIONAL, LAW AND HUMAN RIGHTS IN THE ISLAMIC REPUBLIC OF IRAN: A REPORT COVERING THE EVENTS WITHIN THE SEVEN MONTHS PERIOD FOLLOWING THE REVOLUTION OF FEBRUARY 1979 (1980); AMNESTY INTERNATIONAL, DOCUMENTATION ON IRAN (1982); AMNESTY INTERNATIONAL, EVIDENCE OF TORTURE IN IRAN, (1984).

In relation to Pakistan, see AMNESTY INTERNATIONAL, THE ISLAMIC REPUBLIC OF PAKISTAN: AN AMNESTY INTERNATIONAL REPORT INCLUDING THE FINDINGS OF A MISSION TO PAKISTAN, 23 April-12 May 1976 (1977); AMNESTY INTERNATIONAL, SHORT REPORT OF AN AMNESTY INTERNATIONAL MISSION TO THE ISLAMIC REPUBLIC OF PAKISTAN, 20-25 January 1978 (1978).

63. The scope of the present Article does not permit a detailed discussion of the various sociological, political, and economic reasons why the Muslims are plagued by oppressive authoritarian regimes that exploit and manipulate *Shari'a* in this way. It is significant for the purposes of this Article to note that historical public *Shari'a* lends itself to such exploitation and manipulation.

64. *See supra* notes 23-31 and accompanying text.

Shari'a treats aliens who are admitted under temporary safe conduct (*aman*) under the terms of their license, unless their stay in the Muslim state is an extended one, whereupon they are treated as members of a tolerated non-Muslim community (*dhimmis*).[65] None of the subjects of a *Shari'a* state, including Muslim men, enjoy the full rights of a citizen in the modern sense of the term.[66]

This Article now analyzes the human rights of various groups under the Muslim's historical development of *Shari'a* as positive law. As will be made clear, historical *Shari'a* did not provide for constitutional civil rights and safeguards limiting the power and discretion of its rulers. The *Qur'an* and *Sunna* do provide sources that support the development of constitutional safeguards today,[67] but these sources have yet to be developed into positive law.

A. Muslim Men

Under traditional *Shari'a*, the Muslim male enjoyed full civil capacity, but his political rights fell short of modern standards. He had no effective voice in government because *Shari'a* did not provide for the popular election of rulers.[68] As evidenced by the history of the *Khulaffa*, the executive heads of state, *Shari'a* made no provision for

65. Shihata, *supra* note 35, at 108 (citing AL-MAWARDI, AL-AHKHAM AL SULTANIYYA [THE PRINCIPLES OF GOVERNMENT] 252 (1853)).

66. Khadduri states:

> Human Rights in Islam, as prescribed by the Divine Law [*Shari'a*], are privileges only of persons of full legal capacity. A person with full legal capacity is a living human of mature age, free, and of Moslem faith. It follows accordingly, that non-Moslems and slaves who lived in the Islamic states were only partially protected by law or had no legal capacity at all.

Khadduri, *Human Rights in Islam*, 243 ANNUALS 77, 79 (1946). This substantially true statement should be qualified in two ways. First, the rights of a Muslim male who enjoyed full capacity as prescribed by *Shari'a* do not exactly correspond to the full rights of a citizen in the modern sense of the term. Second, Muslim women did not enjoy civil and political rights equal to those of Muslim men. There is also a distinction between Islam and the "Divine law," by which I take Khadduri to be referring to *Shari'a*. An appreciation of the fact that *Shari'a* did not enact into positive law the whole of Islam is crucial to the reform methodology proposed at the end of this Article.

67. *See generally* Ishaque, *Al-Ahkam Al-Sultanivah: Law of Government in Islam*, 4 ISLAMIC STUD. 275 (1965); M. ASAD, PRINCIPLES OF STATE AND GOVERNMENT IN ISLAM (1966).

68. Popular elections were utterly unthinkable in the seventh century A.D., which is precisely the point. So long as the manner of succession of the first four *Khulaffa*, a mixture of selection by leading Muslims and direct appointment by the preceding *Khaliffa*, is taken as definitive and the most authoritative Islamic model, we cannot say that *Shari'a* provides for general elections on universal suffrage.

For the *Shi'a* sect of Islam, the office of *Khaliffa* (*Imam* in their terminology) is determined by direct descent from the Prophet and appointment by the preceding *Imam*. For the majority of *Shi'a*, known as Twelvers, now living mainly in Iran, there is no question of any election of the *Imam*. Note that these *Shi'a* believe that the current incumbent *Imam* is absent and expected to reappear soon.

On the majority *Sunni* and minority *Shi'a* views on the selection of the executive head of the state, see LAW IN THE MIDDLE EAST, *supra* note 36, chs. 1 and 5.

peaceful and orderly change of government.[69] Similarly, *Shari'a* provided no effective limitations on the powers of the ruler.[70]

Islamic law, as developed by the early jurists, does allow Muslim male community leaders to advise the ruler, although they cannot compel him to comply.[71] The ruler may impose criminal sanctions for dissent at his complete discretion.[72] These sanctions dampen freedom of speech and create a sense of intellectual and political impotence.[73] Furthermore, if Muslim men express views that the ruler deems heretical, they may be put to death as apostates.[74]

B. Muslim Women and Non-Muslims

Women and tolerated communities of non-Muslims suffer more restrictions than Muslim men. *Shari'a* does not allow either group to advise the ruler or participate on equal terms with Muslim men in the public life of the Muslim state.

Shari'a treats women as the wards of men. As such, women lack the capacity to hold high-ranking general executive or judicial office.[75] While *Shari'a* achieved significant advances over contemporary practice in improving the status of women,[76] it generally inhibits women's

69. *See* sources cited *supra* note 30.

70. *See* sources cited *supra* note 28.

71. *See* sources cited *supra* note 28.

72. Islamic criminal law provides for a few specific offenses and punishments, *hudud* and *qasas*, and leaves the rest to the discretion of the ruler. *See generally* M. El-Awa, Punishment in Islamic Law (1982).

73. Khadduri states this aspect of the Muslim historical experience as follows:

> While, in early Islam, Muslim public opinion was not inclined to support an *imam* [*Khaliffa*] who himself seemed to have departed from the law, the jurist-theologians seem to have gradually tended to support the authority of the *imam* against any element revolting against him. They upheld the theory that the *imam*, even if he committed an error, must be obeyed. The *Ash'aris* and almost all the latter *Sunni* jurists supported authority against dissension and argued that rebellion is worse than tyranny. To them once the *bay'a* (homage or fealty) was given to the new *imam* there was no legal way of taking it back. . . . Thus in practice the *imam* has the ultimate authority in the state, and he can invoke the *jihad* to enforce his commands. It follows that *baghi*, in the sense of dissension, would constitute the negation of the *imam*'s authority; hence both the *imam* and his subject must oppose the dissenters in order to re-establish the unity of the *imamate* [leadership of the Muslim community].

M. Khadduri, *supra* note 21, at 78-79.

74. *See, e.g.*, Peters & DeVries, *Apostasy in Islam*, 17 Die Welt de Islams 1 (1976). For a modern application of this law in the Sudan in 1985, see An-Na'im, *The Islamic Law of Apostasy and its Modern Applicability: A Case from the Sudan*, 16 Religion 197 (1986).

75. *See Qur'an*, *supra* note 12, at 2:282; 4:34, 33:33, 33:53. For a general explanation of *wilaya*, the male guardianship over women, see Shorter Encyclopedia of Islam 633 (H. Gibb & J. Kramers, eds. 1953) [hereinafter Encyclopedia] (stating that the sovereign's power he holds or delegates is *willaya*. Holders of high or judicial office have a special *willaya*. Women are excluded from possessing either general or special *willaya*).

76. *See* A. Ali, *supra* note 17, at 255-57; P. Hitti, History of the Arab 28 (1956); R. Levy, The Social Structure of Islam 91-134 (1957); R. Smith, Kinship and Marriage in Early Arabia 92-94 (1903).

participation in public life.[77]

Non-Muslims suffer limitations on their access to public offices that exercise authority over Muslims because their allegiance to the Muslim state is in doubt. *Shari'a* allows them a degree of communal autonomy and power to conduct the private affairs of their religious community,[78] but they may not hold responsible office or join the military service of the Islamic state.[79] In exchange for being *dhimmis*, a tolerated community governed and defended by the Muslims, non-Muslims pay *jizia*, a personal poll-tax that signifies submission to Muslim rule and sovereignty.[80]

Some modern Muslim scholars justify the payment of *jizia* because non-Muslims are exempt from military service and should therefore share in the cost of defending the realm.[81] The truth of the matter, however, is that they are disqualified, and not merely exempt, from military service. Exemption implies request or at least the choice of the person excused. Non-Muslims have no choice in accepting the status of being defended by the Muslims in exchange for payment of *jizia*.[82]

It must be emphasized that the object of critically noting all these limitations on the basic civil rights of Muslim men, women, and non-Muslims is not to doubt the validity of such limitations in their proper historical context. *Shari'a*'s view of civil liberties compared favorably with civil rights under Roman and Persian law prevailing at the time. Rather, criticism and strong objection must be raised to any attempt to reintroduce historical public *Shari'a* today because it is inconsistent with prevailing human rights standards.

---

77. *See* Higgins, *Women in the Islamic Republic of Iran: Legal, Social, and Ideological Changes*, 10 SIGNS: J. WOMEN IN CULTURE & SOC'Y 477 (1985).

78. On the degree of internal autonomy allowed to *dhimmis*, see Goiten, *Minority Self-Rule and Government Control in Islam*, 31 STUD. ISLAMICA 101 (1970).

79. This restriction was done under charters granted by the Muslim state to its non-Muslim subjects called "compacts of dhimma." For samples of the terms of these charters, see M. KHADDURI, *supra* note 21, at 177-78; *see also* ENCYCLOPEDIA, *supra* note 75, at 16-17, 75-76.

80. The concept of *dhimma* is not, of course, a purely legal concept, but rather a social and political institution based on religio-legal principles. *See* A. TRITTON, THE CALIPHS AND THEIR NON-MUSLIM SUBJECTS (1970) (providing an extensive review of the institution and its implications throughout Muslim history).

81. M. HAMIDULLAH, MUSLIM CONDUCT OF STATE 244-45 (1968).

82. T. ARNOLD, THE PREACHING OF ISLAM (1913). Arnold gives several examples of Christian groups who were exempt from payment of *jizia* in exchange for serving in Muslim armies. *Id.* at 62-63. This occurence was rather exceptional and contrary to the predominant practice. Such positive features of the historical Muslim experience should be emphasized and developed further into complete equality between the citizens of an Islamic state, regardless of sex or religion.

C. *Shari'a* In Light of Minimum Human Rights Standards

While this Article criticizes historical public *Shari'a* as being inconsistent with prevailing human rights standards, it does not unqualifiedly endorse those standards that originated within the western liberal tradition.[83] As in the case of international law,[84] the emergence of the socialist and third world blocs has already had a significant impact in reformulating human rights standards.[85] Economic, social, cultural, and collective peoples' rights such as a right to development are increasingly finding expression in United Nations documents and in regional human rights instruments.[86] Claims of cultural relativism are gradually modifying the definition and implementation of human rights.

This line of development does not negate the validity of the objections raised against public *Shari'a*. Claims of cultural relativism, including allegiance to a religious legal system such as *Shari'a*, are limited by minimum standards of universal human rights.[87] For example, slavery and torture cannot be justified with reference to any set of prevailing social norms or traditional cultural standards. To concede the unlimited claims of an ideological or cultural tradition can lead to absurd and manifestly unjust results.

Discrimination on grounds of gender or religion is as objectionable as discrimination on grounds of race.[88] The Muslims condemn the racist policies of the Republic of South Africa, for example, while condoning discrimination on grounds of gender and religion under their own law. Furthermore, the modern nation state is based on the fundamental premise of equal rights and duties for all its citizens, which are

83. *See* F. Dowrick, Human Rights, Problems, Perspectives and Texts (1979); A. Robertson, Human Rights in the World (1982); Minogue, *The History of the Idea of Human Rights*, in The Human Rights Reader 3 (W. Laqueur & B. Rubin eds. 1978); Van Dervyver, *The Concept of Human Rights: Its History, Contents and Meaning*, in Acta Juridica 10 (1979).

84. *See supra* notes 53-57 and accompanying text.

85. For a general survey of this process, see Henkin, *Rights: Here and There*, 81 Colum. L. Rev. 1582 (1981). For the Marxist perspective, see, e.g., Przetacznik, *The Socialist Concept of Human Rights: Its Philosophical Background and Political Justification*, 13 Revue belge de droit Int'l 238 (1977).

86. *See generally* International Covenant on Civil and Political Rights, *supra* note 9; International Covenant on Economic, Social and Cultural Rights, *supra* note 9; African Charter on Human and Peoples' Rights, *supra* note 9; American Convention on Human Rights, Nov. 22, 1969, O.A.S.T.S. No. 36, at 1, O.A.S. Off. Rec. OEA/Ser.L/V/II.23, doc. 21, rev. 6.

87. *See* An-Na'im, *Religious Minorities under Islamic Law and the Limits of Cultural Relativism*, 9 Hum. Rts. Q. 1 (1987).

88. It is not being claimed here that current state practice is fully consistent with these standards. However, the effective prohibition of discrimination on grounds of race, gender, or religion is one of the objectives of the international human rights movement. A discussion of the moral and philosophical base of these standards is beyond the scope of this Article.

often enshrined in formal constitutional documents.[89] Thus a modern Islamic state cannot justify discrimination among its own citizens on grounds of gender or religion.

Muslim scholars do not justify such discrimination as a matter of principle.[90] Rather, Muslim writings are apologetic and uncritical.[91] If the Muslims are seriously contemplating the application of an Islamic public law to replace or at least supplement the secular Western model they inherited from colonial rule, they must meet the challenge of modern international law and basic universal human rights.

V. SOLUTIONS FROM WITHIN ISLAM

A legitimate and lasting constitutional and legal order that can address modern international relations and domestic human rights must develop from within Islam. Although Muslims presently live with superficial patterns of western-style government, Muslim belief precludes a purely secular approach to law and state.[92]

Therefore, the benefits of western secularism in the Muslim world are temporary. Islamic states lack native support for western governmental institutions because these institutions are perceived as purely secular and un-Islamic.[93] Furthermore, despite western-style constitutional safeguards and international obligations regarding human rights, massive violations continue to occur in the region.[94]

The movement among some Muslim jurists to re-institute the Medina model of historical public *Shari'a* may be seen, in at least one sense, as a positive step. Islamic fundamentalism confronts Muslims with the implications of *Shari'a* in a modern context, and forces them to conceive of alternative Islamic responses.

It is impossible to reconcile every aspect of historical public *Shari'a* with the full range of domestic civil liberties and peaceful co-

89. Most modern Muslim countries have written constitutions that expressly guarantee equality before the law for all citizens. This is true not only of the secular Muslim states, but also of the states that purport to apply *Shari'a*. *See* CONST. OF THE ISLAMIC REPUBLIC OF IRAN art. 20; CONST. OF THE ISLAMIC REPUBLIC OF PAKISTAN arts. 25-27; CONST. OF THE REPUBLIC OF SUDAN art. 14. The Iranian constitution nevertheless makes provision for discrimination on grounds of religion. CONST. OF THE ISLAMIC REPUBLIC OF IRAN arts. 11-14. *See generally* CONSTITUTIONS OF THE COUNTRIES OF THE WORLD (A. Beaustein & G. Flanz ed. 1985).

90. Works such as S. Tabandeh, A MUSLIM COMMENTARY ON THE UNIVERSAL DECLARATION OF HUMAN RIGHTS (1970) are exceptional in this regard.

91. For a critical review of modern Muslim reformist movements see, for example, M. KERR, ISLAMIC REFORM (1966); FAZLUR RAHMAN, ISLAM, ch. 13 (1966); W. SMITH, ISLAM IN MODERN HISTORY (1957).

92. *See* sources cited *supra* note 11.

93. *See* sources cited *supra* note 11.

94. *See generally* sources cited *supra* note 3.

existence in the international sphere.[95]

The best solution to the current Muslim dilemma of legitimizing peaceful coexistence and basic human rights from within Islam is based on the work of the late Sudanese Muslim reformer *Ustadh* Mahmoud Mohamed Taha.[96] According to Taha, public *Shari'a* did not enact the whole of Islam.[97] The jurists were working primarily on the model of the Medina state and speculating on the basis of their knowledge and understanding of the *Qur'an* and *Sunna*.[98] Both the Medina model and the jurists' understanding of the sources were bound to their historical context. One may find the modern model of an Islamic state in the broad principles of justice and equality contained in the *Qur'an* and *Sunna* of the earlier stage of Mecca before migration to Medina.[99]

Taha's approach provides a framework for the discovery of solutions from within Islam. Such a model would emphasize that Islam suits *all* ages and places, not just its early historical context. Muslims must recall that the Prophet was a man of his time and for all times. In delivering the whole of the *Qur'an* and living up to its values, the Prophet faithfully executed his role as the Prophet of the universal and eternal message of Islam. Working out of the totality of Islam, the Prophet then constructed the best workable model and left the rest for the Muslims to develop and implement in light of their own needs and experience. Thus, Islam suits all ages and places by providing a flexible framework from which the right answers may be developed according to the demands of the times.

There are some major obstacles to instituting the framework this Article proposes. First, such changes require Muslims to encourage free discussion and tolerate political dissent. However, the prevailing attitudes inherited from *Shari'a* do not tolerate unorthodoxy or dissent.[100] Most Muslim scholars are either silent, in exile, or in prison.[101] For example, Sheikh Ali Abdel Razig of Cairo's Al Azhar Islamic University suffered severe persecution after publication of his

---

95. *See supra* notes 16-82 and accompanying text.

96. All Taha's books are in Arabic. For a new English translation, see M. TAHA, THE SECOND MESSAGE OF ISLAM (A. An-Naim trans. 1987). For an explanation of some aspects of Taha's approach, see An-Na'im, *supra* note 74; An-Na'im, *The Elusive Islamic Constitution: The Sudanese Experience*, 26 ORIENT 329 (1985); El Naiem, *A Modern Approach to Human Rights in Islam: Foundations and Implications for Africa*, in HUMAN RIGHTS AND DEVELOPMENT IN AFRICA 75 (C. Welch & R. Meltzer eds. 1984).

97. *See generally* M. TAHA, *supra* note 29.

98. *See* sources cited *supra* notes 96-97.

99. *See* sources cited *supra* notes 96-97.

100. *See supra* notes 72-74 and accompanying text.

101. Miller, *The Embattled Arab Intellectuals*, N.Y. Times, June 9, 1985, § 6 (Magazine), at 6.

thesis on Islamic government.[102] Islamic authorities banned his book, burned available copies, revoked the author's degree, and threatened him with execution as a heretic.[103]

Similarly, *Ustadh* Mahmoud Mohammed Taha, whose work is central to the proposals in this Article, was executed in Khartoum on January 18, 1985.[104] The authorities burned his books and outlawed his movement.[105]

VI. CONCLUSION

It is impossible to reconcile every aspect of public *Shari'a* as developed by the early Muslim jurists with civil liberties and peaceful international coexistence. Fortunately, to opt out of that version of public *Shari'a* is not to opt out of Islam itself. On the contrary, to insist on all aspects of historical public *Shari'a* today is tantamount to saying that Islam stands for repression and discrimination at home and aggression abroad.

In advocating international peaceful coexistence and respect for human rights at home and abroad, one is fully aware of the many problems Muslims have with these principles today. From the Muslim third world perspective, there are problems with international law and relations as defined and developed by western colonial powers. From the Muslim cultural perspective, there are problems with human rights as defined and developed by the western liberal tradition. Nevertheless, in these same standards we already have a very good beginning. Western dominance in both spheres has already been challenged and eroded by contributions from socialist and third world countries.[106] The Muslims must overcome their historical biases in order to participate and make their own original contributions to this process. What they should not do is sit back and watch passively, as they have been doing so far, or make the negative contribution of resurrecting historical public *Shari'a*. International peace, justice, and human rights have already been partially achieved through the Grace of God, and are to be enhanced and promoted through His Grace too. It is the paramount religious duty of all Muslims to participate in this ultimate act of worship.

102. A. Razig, Al-Islam Wa'usul Alhukm [Islam and the Basis of Government] (1966).

103. Al-Islam Wa 'Usul Al Hukm 5 (M. Haqi ed. 1966); A. Hourani, Arabic Thought in the Liberal Age 183-92 (1962); D. Pipes, *supra* note 11, at 122.

104. An-Na'im, *Detention Without Trial in the Sudan: The Use and Abuse of Legal Power*, 17 Colum. Hum. Rts. L. Rev. 159 (1986); Lesch, *The Fall of Numieri*, 1985 U. Field Staff Int'l Rep. 22.

105. *See* sources cited *supra* note 104.

106. *See* sources cited *supra* notes 83 and 85.

[3]
A Kinder, Gentler Islam?

Throughout history, conquerors have deprived conquered people of much of their material resources, human dignity, and moral integrity; they have distorted the self-identity of the conquered and robbed them of their history as a people. But modern colonialism did more than that by transforming the world almost beyond recognition, thereby affecting the ability of colonized peoples to retrieve their lost resources, dignity, and integrity even long after the colonial period. By imposing the nation-state model and integrating local economies into a global capitalist economic system, the modern colonizers made precolonial forms of social and political organization and economic relations largely obsolete. Given this state of affairs, how can the colonized peoples recover from the colonial intrusion by resolving their present predicament and exercising their right to self-determination in a meaningful and constructive manner?

As a Muslim, the reflections I am offering here address this question in relation to the experience of Muslim peoples, but my comments may also be relevant to other parts of the world, including the situation of aboriginal peoples living within the developed North as victims of internal colonization. My focus is the need to transform the historical traditions of Muslim peoples in ways that would enable them to exercise their legitimate right to self-determination without violating the rights of others. This process requires expanding the terms of discourse over the essential nature and foundations of the Islamic traditions in order to reevaluate their content and relevance to the lives of their modern adherents now living under radically transformed circumstances. (My thesis and arguments can only be presented in a brief form here. Greater detail and technical support for these ideas can be found in my recent book, *Toward an Islamic Reformation: Civil Liberties, Human Rights and International Law*).

Self-Determination

While it is perfectly legitimate, indeed imperative, for all peoples to assert and ex-

Abdullahi Ahmed An-Na'im.

ercise their right to self-determination, we must clarify any ambiguities in the subjective sense in which the collective "self" is identified and recognize the complexities of the objective conditions under which it seeks to assert and exercise this fundamental right today. During the struggle to end colonialism, and even after achieving formal political independence, little attention has been given by colonized peoples to clearly identifying the "self" or recognizing the complexities of its present situation, especially in the Islamic context. Whatever the reasons may have been for this failure, it must be rectified immediately if the right to self-determination is to be exercised in a meaningful and constructive manner.

Discourse over self-determination and its implications now takes place in a world of nation-states. This fundamental fact has far-reaching consequences for such discourse whether it is taking place internally within a particular state or, more usually, in relation to other states. It is therefore remarkable that participants in this discourse in the Islamic context fail to take due account of this fact. They speak, whether explicitly or implicitly, of a coherent historical self which has somehow survived the colonial intrusion or can now be resurrected to continue its precolonial existence regardless of the new radically transformed reality of national and international relations. In my view, this romantic myth, which some Muslims actually believe and others manipulate as a political ploy, must be categorically repudiated in order to have meaningful discourse and effective action on the principle of self-determination.

Whatever the historical self of Islamic peoples may have been, it is neither possible nor desirable to redeem it in the modern intensely interdependent and interacting world of nation-states and sharp international boundaries. The colonial intrusion has not only diminished our collective memory of how things used to be, or are alleged to have been, but also changed the conditions under which that memory may be retrieved. Throughout their history, Muslim peoples have been governed by imperial states which claimed, at least in theory, to have universal sovereignty and totalitarian jurisdiction. Within the framework of those universal totalitarian states, the collective self of various Islamic peoples was effectively determined by religious and ethnic criteria. In contrast, their modern self must now be defined within the framework of a limited "national" state in a way which requires transcending some of the basic exclusive assumptions of religious or ethnic identity. Instead of being determined by cultural unity emanating from common religion and ethnicity, the modern national self is now largely defined in territorial terms.

This is not to say that cultural unity and modern national territorial identity are mutually exclusive. On the one hand, the territorial integrity of the nation itself presupposes a minimum degree of cultural unity. The lack of this minimum degree is one of the underlying causes of secessionist movements, especially in Africa. A mature and stable nation, on the other hand, may achieve a high degree of broad cultural unity, but this would be a consequence rather than a cause of subscribing to a common national identity. Such a broad national cultural unity would subsume and accommodate a variety of subcultures, including those determined by religious and ethnic criteria. Moreover, the creative tension between cultural diversity and national unity is both a permanent and desirable feature of human relations. I am emphasizing the overlap of cultural and national identity and not their mutual exclusiveness. Whereas the historical self was primarily defined in terms of cultural unity, the modern self must include both national and cultural components.

Assuming a satisfactory identification of the self, which is entitled to exercise the right to self-determination, we must also be clear on the moral and political conditions which determine the content of the right and manner of its exercise. Briefly stated, both types of conditions emanate from the fundamental moral principle of reciprocity, also known as the golden rule, that one must treat others as s/he wishes to be treated by them. This moral principle is also sanctioned and supported by the political consideration that the "others" will revolt or react against the violation of the golden rule of reciprocity. Whether in international relations, intercommunal relations within a nation-state, or in relations of individuals among themselves or with the state/community at large, the lack of reciprocity will inevitably produce severe negative political consequences. The ultimate safeguard for every nation, community, or individual person is that whoever fails to observe due reciprocity in dealing with others will be forced to comply with its dictates. While this is easily substantiated from historical and contemporary experience, it needs further clarification in concept and regulation of methods.

Since every state, community, or person needs the protection of the principle of reciprocity and is a likely target of its assertion, it is in everybody's interest to perfect mechanisms that will ensure its orderly and practical efficacy. This requires the prevalence of the rule of law in regulating relations among nations and between communities and individuals within a nation-state. If existing state, community, or individual power relations should frustrate the orderly and peaceful practical efficacy of that ultimate safeguard for the time being, the victim will probably resort to whatever available means in order to redress the situation. Although violent force and self-help have historically been regarded as legitimate avenues for realizing claims of reciprocity and justice in human relations, the rule of law is increasingly gaining greater supremacy in this regard. In any case, humanity can no longer afford to do without the rule of law, and must therefore strive to uphold it in every aspect of national and international relations.

The term *rule of law* is used here in the substantive sense of the regular application of rules and procedures which are consistent with the principle of reciprocity itself. Unfair power relations in the past have affected the content and mechanisms of the relevant legal systems, namely, international law and domestic constitutional law. The rule of law does not simply mean the consistent and orderly application of these sets of laws regardless of their content. While maintaining the basic notion that human relations should be regulated through principles of general application applied in a peaceful and orderly manner, the rule of law also means that the applicable principles must be fair and reasonable. Complaints against the fairness of traditional international law and domestic constitutional and legal arrangements do not justify repudiating the principle of the rule of law. Such complaints, however, must be redressed. Otherwise, people will resort to self-help and violent force in asserting the demands of reciprocity.

The Islamic tradition must undergo its own reformation

It must also be emphasized that self-determination is not an end in itself but a means to communal interests in political stability, economic prosperity, and social harmony which are, in turn, means to personal integrity and well-being of individual human beings. All of this relates equally to every community and individual person in accordance with the principle of reciprocity. By definition, the communal and individual interests to be derived from exercising the right to self-determination include the equal right of others to the same. Any conception of self-determination which does not serve these

Mahmoud Mohemed Tal about 1982.

ends in a balanced and rational fashion will be counterproductive and must therefore be revised. In light of these considerations, I now turn to the present Muslim predicament.

The Elusive Past

Following national liberation, whether from direct or indirect colonial intrusion, Muslim peoples throughout the world have rightly sought to assert and exercise their right to self-determination. In this ongoing process of trial and error, many Muslims have tended to define their "self" in Islamic terms and sought to exercise their right through the implementation of historical principles of Islamic law and ethics, commonly known as *Shari'a*. I personally support the right of Muslim peoples to choose an Islamic definition of their self, but find that this involves very dangerous ambiguities, especially as it is generally perceived to lead to the conclusion that it requires the implementation of historical Shari'a today. Muslims are entitled to define their self in Islamic terms provided that this definition is properly clarified and updated. I also maintain that they are entitled to pursue the implications of that self-identity through the implementation of Islamic principles in their public and private lives, but those principles cannot be historical Shari'a. As I will argue below, the Islamic tradition must undergo its own reformation and develop a modern conception of Shari'a that can be implemented today.

Powerful images of cordial and pious tribal and religious patriarchs managing the affairs of their domestic and general subjects with loving care and scrupulous justice dominate the imagination of modern Muslims seeking to redeem an alleged historical Islamic self. As any knowledge of Islamic history will reveal, however, this has been the ethical ideal more than concrete reality. In any case, that model presupposes traditional highly personalized social and political relations and simple localized economic systems. None of this can be found anywhere in the Muslim world today. In this world of large impersonal urban centers, complex political relations, and globalized economies, the patriarch model is neither appropriate nor possible to operate. The modern world requires well-defined channels and structures for political relations, forms of social interaction and control, and types of economic relations which are simply nonexistent in the historical Islamic model.

That historical model is impossible and undesirable to achieve today because it contemplates the implementation of Shariʿa which involves massive discrimination against women and non-Muslims at the domestic level and hostile aggressive relations with non-Muslim states abroad. According to Shariʿa's scheme of things, the subjects (not citizens in the modern sense of the term) of an Islamic state are strictly classified by gender and religion, with each group having its categorically assigned role, rights, and obligations. Some proponents of the historical Islamic model today argue that the rights of women and non-Muslims are better protected under Shariʿa because they are strictly secured by divine law. The actual history of Muslim peoples does not support this claim because Shariʿa itself was consistently violated more than honored. Even if true in practice, this argument avoids the issue of the equality of women and non-Muslims demanded by the principle of reciprocity which is the fundamental moral and political foundation of modern standards of human rights. As indicated earlier, it is not enough to have scrupulous observance of the rule of *any* law. The substance of the law must also conform with the principle of reciprocity.

Another claim of the modern proponents of Shariʿa which must also be categorically repudiated is that Shariʿa recognized and protected human rights fourteen centuries ago. This claim is based on a fundamental misconception of human rights as rights to which each and every person is entitled by virtue of being a human being. Shariʿa sought to protect the rights it ascribed to Muslim men, women, and non-Muslims as such but not as human beings. Furthermore, the modern conception of human rights followed specific recent intellectual developments, and their realization presupposes certain political, economic, and social prerequisites which did not exist anywhere in the world until recently as well.

In order to achieve the religiously sanctioned ultimate objective of Islamizing the whole world, the Islamic state under Shariʿa, known as *Dar al-Islam* or the abode of Islam, should never be at permanent peace with non-Muslim territories, significantly called *Dar al-harb* or the abode of war. Shariʿa permits the Islamic state to conclude treaties of temporary peace (*sulh* or *ahd*) with non-Muslim states in order to prepare for the next round of hostilities, demanding the strict observance of the terms of such treaties while they last but never allowing permanent peace with them and recognition of their equal sovereignty. While not necessarily a true measure of Muslim behavior throughout history, it is the basis of Shariʿa's view of international law and intercommunal relations (*siyar*) and continues to color Muslims' relations with non-Muslims, whether internationally or among communities within the same modern nation-state.

Take, for example, the Salman Rushdie affair, in which the head of an Islamic state, the late Ayatollah Khomeini of Iran, ordered the murder of the citizen of another country because, from the former's point of view, the British author committed blasphemy or heresy. Even if Rushdie were subject to the jurisdiction of Iran, Khomeini's act can only be characterized as incitement to murder because Rushdie was not afforded the protection of the due process of law even by Shariʿa standards. The case is further aggravated by the fact that, in so doing, Khomeini violated the sovereignty of another nation and flouted established standards of responsible behavior in the modern world. Yet very few voices were raised in the Muslim world in condemnation of this criminal act. I think that part of the reason for this inexcusable failure by all Muslims who remained silent is the belief that their right to protect their faith is paramount to all other considerations, including the right of others to protect and act in accordance with their convictions. This Muslim belief and failure to accord reciprocity to others can be traced to historical conceptions of Shariʿa that sanction hostile aggressive relations with non-Muslims and refuse to recognize their equal sovereignty.

Unless we set our own house in order, we will never have the moral credibility to challenge and redress Western dominance, exploitation, and bias

Muslim apologists and some of their sympathizers tried to confuse the issues by talking of Britain's colonial and postcolonial aggression and the bias of the Western media, and so on. These issues are real and deserve to be addressed, but only by those who are willing to speak the truth and fairly apportion blame and responsibility. The Prophet of Islam said that whoever remains silent in the face of the truth is a mute demon. Historical grievances against colonial and postcolonial exploitation and abuse can never be redressed by incitement to murder. Khomeini's reckless and lawless behavior only succeeded in giving credence and greater influence to biased elements in the Western media. Unless we set our own house in order and hold ourselves to the standards of decent human behavior, we will never have the moral and political credibility to challenge and redress Western dominance, exploitation, and bias.

In my view, the above-mentioned aspects of Shariʿa were fair and reasonable in the historical context in which Muslim jurists elaborated the relevant principles, that is to say, between the seventh and ninth centuries. In fact, Shariʿa principles concerning the status and rights of women and non-Muslims and its conception of international and intercommunal relations were far more enlightened and humane than corresponding principles and conceptions of other systems until modern times. For example, Shariʿa recognized the independent legal personality of women and their right to hold and dispose of property centuries before women were accepted as persons by any other legal system in the world. It also accorded them certain minimum rights in personal law and inheritance which for a very long time exceeded those secured by other legal systems. Similar points can be made regarding the status of religious minorities and international law under Shariʿa. My criticisms are not therefore addressed to Shariʿa in its own proper historical context but rather against those who wish to resurrect dated concepts and principles and implement them under radically transformed domestic and international conditions.

I also maintain that Shariʿa is not the whole of Islam, but rather a historically conditioned interpretation of the fundamental sources of Islam, namely the Qur'an, which Muslims believe to be the final and conclusive revelation, and Sunna, or traditions attributed to the Prophet Muhammad. It is possible, indeed imperative in my view, to develop a new version of Shariʿa based on a modern interpretation of the sources of Islam. Far from advocating the abandonment of the Islamic tradition, I am calling on Muslims to achieve their own "reformation" in order to transform their tradition into a viable and just ideology for their modern exercise of their right to self-determination.

It is imperative to develop a new version of Shariʿa based on a modern interpretation of Islamic sources

Transformation of Tradition

Since the term "tradition" signifies the authority of inherited wisdom and the continuity of norms and institutions based on past experience, it is necessary to clarify the sense in which I propose the transformation of the Islamic tradition. Islam is perhaps the ideal model of a scriptural religion because it is based on explicit textual sources, the Qur'an and Sunna. As with all other texts, however, there is no access to these sources except through the agency of human interpretation. Whereas, as a Muslim, I believe in the divine authority and finality of the Islamic message as contained in the Qur'an and Sunna, I also know that that message can never be implemented except through the understanding of human beings and through their actions on the basis of that understanding. In the Muslim belief that I share, Islam is perfect and eternal from God's point of view, but in the affairs of this world, it is open to competing theoretical interpretations and practical policies reflecting the moral and intellectual capabilities of its adherents and their need to adapt to changing material and political conditions. From the human point of view, therefore, Islam is perfect and eternal precisely because its interpretation and implementation evolve and adapt to changing circumstances. In the formula I propose, the constant part of the Islamic tradition is the texts of its divine sources while the interpretation and implementation of those sources must now be transformed.

The notion of reformation evokes images of Lutheran revolt against the dogma and hierarchy of the Catholic church and the evolution of the European "Enlightenment." This should not deter us from applying the term to other situations because, in essence, it signifies the challenge of any dogma and the exposure of any tradition to a different or novel interpretation. Each tradition should be subject to reformation on its own terms and, in fact, contains the seeds of such reformation. To the extent that traditions and their environments are different, the nature, timing, and consequences of their reformation will also differ. In this way, an Islamic reformation does not mean secularization because Islam is not Christianity and the Muslim world is not Europe. The link between the divine and temporal is much more organic in Islam than it has been in Christianity as historically practiced, though not necessarily as originally conceived by its founder; and the relationship between the public and private domains in Muslim societies is significantly different from that prevailing in Europe at the time of its reformation. An Islamic reformation cannot be a belated and poor copy of the European Christian model. It will have to be an indigenous and authentically Islamic process if it is to be a reformation at all.

The fundamental mistake of Islamic modernists is that they sought reform within the framework of Shariʿa

Many Muslim intellectuals have advocated reform and sought the elusive goal of Islamic modernism since at least the second half of the nineteenth century. While adding my voice to theirs, I am not satisfied with their methods and achievements. In my view, the fundamental mistake of Islamic modernists is that they sought to achieve their goal through reform within the framework of Shariʿa. Some of them may have been intimidated by the prospects of challenging what they perceived to be a divine system, while others may have been persuaded to adopt this course of action out of tactical or political reasons, thinking that their views would have greater popular appeal if they remained within the confines of Shariʿa. To the first group I would say that Shariʿa is not divine, though it is based on the human interpretation of divine sources; this is clearly established by the actual historical evolution of Shariʿa and techniques used by its founding jurists. The second group of Islamic modernists should realize that reforms within the framework of Shariʿa, albeit more readily acceptable to the majority of Muslims, are simply inadequate and hardly worth the effort. This last point can be briefly explained without too much technical detail before proceeding to outline a proposed way out of the present predicament of Islamic modernism.

Any movement should be clear on its objectives and the best means for achieving them. In my view, Islamic modernism should seek to enable Muslim peoples to effectively exercise their right to self-determination in accordance with the principle of reciprocity. This would require, for example, the elimination of institutionalized discrimination against women and non-Muslims and the authoritative repudiation of hostile and aggressive conceptions of international and intercommunal relations. Some Islamic modernists believe these reforms can be accomplished by means of independent juristic reasoning (*ijtihad*) as recognized by Shariʿa. According to the branch of Shariʿa that regulates the derivation of principles and rules of Islamic law and ethics, *ijtihad* can only be exercised in matters not covered by clear and categorical texts of the Qurʾan and Sunna. While the detailed elaboration of these features of Shariʿa is the product of juristic commentary or Islamic jurisprudence (*fiqh*) and thus is open to challenge through modern *ijtihad*, some of the relevant general principles and specific rules are based on clear and categorical texts of the Qurʾan and Sunna.

This means that *ijtihad*, as defined by Shariʿa itself, cannot be used to rectify, for example, the inferior status of non-Muslim citizens within an Islamic state. Equality before the law is unattainable—inequality is based on some clear and categorical texts of the Qurʾan and Sunna. In this way, the advocates of reform within the framework of Shariʿa quickly reach a dead end. Faced with an aspect of Shariʿa that is totally incompatible with modernity, they are unable to change it through the techniques they propose to adopt. The only way to resolve this deadlock, in my view, is to revise the concept of *ijtihad* itself so that it can deal even with matters governed by clear and categorical texts of the Qurʾan and Sunna. This novel reform methodology, proposed by the late Sudanese Muslim reformer *Ustadh* Mahmoud Mohamed Taha, can be explained as follows.

The totality of Islam should be seen in light of an important fact: it had to fill the needs of a specific community of Muslims of seventh-century Arabia at the same time that eternal and universal principles of justice and human dignity were being formulated. Owing to this duality of purpose, the sources of Islam inevitably contained a rather contradictory set of principles, one designed to be applied immediately in order to satisfy the real needs of early Muslim communities and the other intended for future implementation under the appropriate conditions. In effect, argued *Ustadh* Mahmoud Mohamed Taha, Islam consists of two messages, one transitional in nature and localized in application and the other eternal in nature and universal in application. (For a full explanation of his thesis, see my English translation of his major work, *The Second Message of Islam.*)

However, Islam also had to communicate these two messages in a way that did not confuse the early Muslims and prevent them from developing a comprehensive and coherent set of legal and ethical principles to govern their social and political lives. This was achieved by stating the eternal set of principles in general and broad terms while expressing the transitory set of principles in clear and categorical terms for immediate application. To reconcile the two sets of principles, early Muslim jurists employed a technique called *naskh* whereby they deemed certain texts of the Qurʾan and Sunna to have been abrogated or repealed for the purposes of Shariʿa. According to *Ustadh* Mahmoud, this process should now be seen as one of postponement rather than final and conclusive abrogation. Otherwise, there would have been no sense in having revealed those texts in the first place.

Once *naskh* is seen in this light, it would be possible for the purposes of modern Shari^ca to revive and implement previously "abrogated" texts and to abrogate or repeal previously enacted texts. In other words, Muslims should now reverse the process of *naskh* by enacting what has been repealed and abrogating what has been enacted in the past as historical formulations of Shari^ca. This effort would be legitimate from the Islamic point of view because it merely replaces one set of texts that has exhausted its purposes with another set of texts that is more appropriate for application today. After all, it was past Muslim jurists who selected the verses which they deemed to apply to Shari^ca—modern Muslims would be simply substituting their own judgment as to how to interpret and implement Islamic principles. The divine nature of the revelation is not an issue at all. Rather, it is the human understanding of the dictates and implications of that revelation which is being challenged and replaced.

I find this approach an intellectually honest and perfectly legitimate means of achieving the *necessary degree* of reform and thereby effecting an Islamic reformation. Nevertheless, I am open to considering any reform methodology capable of achieving the same objectives of Islamic modernism. My purpose is to initiate, not conclude, the search for ways to transform the Islamic tradition. The process of reformation I am advocating must be, by definition, open and undogmatic in its pursuit of its goals or else it will be an exercise in futility.

The Sudan and the Politics of "Lebanonization"

My own country, the Sudan, represents a tragic illustration of the dangers of a misconceived and bungled effort at self-determination. Without minimizing the complexities of the historical background, ethnic and cultural diversity, and the impact of local, regional, and international geopolitical factors, I maintain that the Sudanese disaster is largely due to narrow-minded and shortsighted, if not deliberately manipulative, efforts to exercise an alleged right to self-determination in violation of the principle of reciprocity. It is reminiscent of Lebanon, where religious and ethnic factions are so consumed by prejudice and intolerance of the "other," so dominated by a narrow and dated conception of the self entitled to exercise the right to self-determination, that they are incapable of finding a formula for peaceful coexistence. It is just a matter of time before such a situation accelerates into an irreversible cycle of violence and uncontrollable militarization and foreign intervention. Several of the features of the politics of Lebanonization can be seen in the Sudan today.

The Sudan is a prime example of ethnic and cultural diversity and competition over scarce resources. Its total population of about 22 million people identify with over five hundred tribes and subtribes and speak more than twenty-five distinct languages in over a hundred dialects. While the majority are Arabized Muslims, a large minority profess Christianity and a variety of traditional African beliefs. This widely diverse population has to share scarce material resources while maintaining a fragile environment. In addition to all this, we now have an oppressive military regime, in power since the end of June 1989, which professes a totalitarian Islamic ideology seeking to implement Shariʿa at all costs. The country's unique geographical location and demographic and cultural composition make it a political and sociological as well as a physical bridge between the rest of the continent and the Arabized Islamic North Africa, the Middle East, and beyond. As such, the Sudan represents a real test case for nation building in many parts of the postcolonial world.

The analysis of this article applies to the Sudan in that efforts on behalf of a misconceived Islamic identity seeking to implement historical Shariʿa have led to a total deadlock politically and contributed to the militarization of the entire country. There are other obviously legitimate causes of grievance among the non-Muslim southern Sudanese against the north. Although the country as a whole is poor and underdeveloped, southern and other marginalized regions are particularly so and their population has had less than its fair share of political power. These regions lack educational, health, and other essential facilities in comparison with the north. But the northern drive to impose an Arabized Islamic identity and implement Shariʿa throughout the country is certainly one of the primary causes of the current phase of the civil war.

Both sides in the present conflict, and some other thinking Sudanese, often try to underplay the role of religious and racial factors in the war. While I respect the good motives of some Sudanese who take this position and see the devious motives of others, I think that this argument has been overstated. The real and apparently irreconcilable protagonists in this conflict, in my view, are, first, those who insist on asserting a historical Islamic identity and implementing Shariʿa and, second, those who oppose those same developments precisely because, by denying citizens their right to a non-Islamic identity and imposing on them a religious legal system against their will, they would constitute a violation of the principle of reciprocity. Furthermore, if not strictly racial, the difference between these two positions certainly has racial connotations because the proponents of Shariʿa are largely Arabized northerners and those who oppose it are African southerners. While not all northern Sudanese Muslims support the establishment of a Shariʿa state, their leadership has been sufficiently ambivalent to justify

I would rather live in a secularized Sudan than one ruled by totalitarian Islamic Shariʿa. This is my choice as a Muslim and human being . . .

southern accusations of regional and cultural loyalty overriding the claims of national identity and unity.

Despite the fact that the Islamic factor is complicating Sudanese politics, I can see no way to exclude it completely. Islam means too much to too many Sudanese to be irrelevant to the political and social life of the country as a whole. Furthermore, the organic link between the divine and temporal is too strong in Islam to admit of a stable and lasting secularization. The ideal answer would therefore appear to be an Islamic reformation that will enable Sudanese Muslims to realize their aspirations to exercise their right to self-determination in terms of an Islamic identity without violating the right of self-determination of others. I believe that this is perfectly feasible. Failing that or until it is realized, however, I, as an Arabized Muslim whose loyalty is to the cause of justice and peace for all Sudanese, would rather live in a secularized Sudan than in one ruled by totalitarian Islamic Shariʿa. This is my choice as a Muslim and human being who aspires to live in accordance with the principle of reciprocity in the interest of my own personal human dignity and well-being.

As clearly shown by the Sudanese situation, the transformation of tradition is an essential and urgent condition for the immediate alleviation of untold human suffering, never mind achieving the goals of political stability, economic development, and social justice in many parts of the world. Such a transformation must be legitimate in internal cultural, in this case Islamic, terms without conceding too much to claims of ethical or cultural relativism. Muslims and all other peoples have a right to their own identity and right to self-determination, provided they fully respect the rights of others to the same. This is the most essential and indispensable condition for a just and stable human existence.

[4]
Re-affirming Secularism for Islamic Societies

ATLANTA — In the wake of the overthrow of Saddam Hussein's Baathist regime in Iraq, a new debate has emerged, primarily among the Shiite majority, about whether a new system of government that is both Islamic and democratic can be built as some kind of model for the region.

I am totally opposed to the American occupation of Iraq, which I see as nothing short of a regression to 19th-century colonialism. As repeatedly confirmed throughout human history, colonialism is by definition incapable of establishing democracy or protecting the human rights of its subjects. Nevertheless, the constructive question now is how to make the best of a disastrous situation, to think of the way forward despite the American invasion.

As I see it, the best scenario in the aftermath of the invasion is to establish an effective "caretaker" government to provide security and essential services, and to create and protect a "public space" for Iraqis to debate the political future of their country. Realistically, this transitional period should last at least five years, before a constitutional convention is convened to establish a long-term system.

In my view, this whole process can only be legitimately achieved under United Nations sponsorship, perhaps under the UN Trusteeship Council, which is still legally possible under the UN Charter though the council has been disbanded in the years since the end of colonialism.

Certainly the central issue that must be debated among Iraqis — as among modernizing Muslims everywhere — is the relationship between Islam and secularism in any new political system. Here are some reflections on this question from an Islamic perspective.

The central issue that must be debated among Iraqis — as among modernizing Muslims everywhere — is the relationship between Islam and secularism in any new political system.

ISLAM VS. SECULARISM | The commonly presumed incompatibility between Islam and secularism needs to be reevaluated. It should first be emphasized that the confusion is definitional and terminological as well as substantive. This does not mean that the issue is not real and serious, especially in view of the drastic practical consequences of common confusion on the matter. Rather, the point is that one needs to begin with clarifying questions of definition and terminology in order to frame the substantive side of the debate in more precise terms.

The main problem on the definition side, in my view, is the tendency to limit secularism to the experiences of west European and North American countries with Christianity since the 18th century. Whether viewed as "separation of church and state" or "disestablishment of religion," such definitions are obviously specific to certain situations and do not address the continuing social and political role of religion in public life, even in those settings. For instance, efforts to sever institutional links between religion and the state cannot apply to the role of religion in politics, since there is no way of knowing the motives of people's political action, let alone attempting to control that.

It is also problematic to equate secularism with disregard for religion, or a diminishing role for it in public life, as some scholars have argued in relation to Western societies. Since that could not possibly mean that religion has no influence whatsoever in the public life of any society, as that is obviously false, the question becomes what sort of influence, and how is it diminishing? From this perspective, I suggest that secularism should be understood in terms of the type of relationship between religion and the state, rather than a specific way in which that relationship has evolved in one society or another.

I would also emphasize that the form that relationship should take in pluralistic societies has to be the product of organic development over time, and be accepted as legitimate by the population at large, instead of expecting it to drastically change immediately by constitutional enactment or political rhetoric.

As a matter of terminology that is relevant to this deeply contextual approach, it should be noted that the term "secularism" in its west European and North American sense has come to Africa and Asia in the suspect company of colonialism. For the Islamic societies in particular, this term is commonly associated with militantly anti-religious attitudes of the French Revolution, in relation to Christianity. Nevertheless, this term can be used in relation to experiences of African and Asian societies, provided it is understood and applied in the specific context of each society, rather than as a feature of liberal political or constitutional transplant. This view of secularism, I believe, will redress much of the apprehension about the concept as a tool of Western imperialism.

The term "secularism" in its west European and North American sense has come to Africa and Asia in the suspect company of colonialism.

On the substantive side of the issue, the most compelling argument for an Islamic rationale for secularism is its necessity for pluralistic nation states that are able to safeguard the freedom of religion and belief of believers and non-believers alike.

That is, the freedom of religion and belief of Muslims as well as non-Muslims is more likely to be violated by a state that seeks to promote a particular religious doctrine than one that is neutral on the matter.

Whether it is the Shi'a of eastern Saudi Arabia, Sunni of Iran or Shi'a of Pakistan, Muslims can suffer serious violations of their right to uphold and live by their belief in Islam, as they know and understand it. Indeed, many Muslim intellectuals and political dissidents are seeking refuge in Western countries, including leaders of Islamist movements like Rashid Qanushi of Tunisia who lives in the United Kingdom at the time of writing, rather than in other predominantly Muslim countries, because they enjoy more freedom of belief and political action in "secular" states that are more or less neutral on issues of religion.

It is commonly claimed that Islam mandates the establishment of an "Islamic state" which will implement and enforce Shari'a (the normative system of Islam) as the law of the land. But in my view, the notion of an Islamic state is a contradiction in terms because whatever principles of Shari'a are enacted by the state as positive law cease to be the normative system of Islam by the very act of enacting it as the law to be enforced by the state. Since there is so much diversity of opinion among Islamic schools of thought and scholars, any enactment of Shari'a principles as law would have to select some opinions over others, thereby denying believers their freedom of choice among equally legitimate competing opinions.

There is neither a historical precedent of an Islamic state to be followed, nor is such a state practically viable today.

Moreover, there is neither a historical precedent of an Islamic state to be followed, nor is such a state practically viable today. As the most avowed advocate of an Islamic state today would concede, there has never been such a state throughout Muslim history, since that of the Prophet in Medina, which was so exceptional as to be useful as a model to be applied today. Recent experience has also shown that the implementation of Shari'a as the official law of the state is untenable in economic and political terms in the modern nation state in its present global economic and political context because it conflicts with international law.

In short, Muslims need the protection of human rights, and political and social space secured by secularism to live up to the ideals of their own religion. But that protection and space cannot be sustained among Muslims without an internal transformation of their own understandings and practice of Islam. Here are some illustrations of the basic points I am trying to make.

1. Women's Rights in Egypt

The women's movement in Egypt is multi-faceted and fractured. Although the chasm is often explained as a rift between Islamist (conservatives) and secular liberals, one survey of the so-called secular women's movement in Egypt reveals that it is united not by an anti-religious or anti-Islamic position, but by the view that Shari'a should not be the main or sole source of legislation within Egypt.

It is also clear that the majority of women consider themselves to be very religious. Many of these women do not see religion as antithetical to feminism, and perceive religious affiliation as integral to their struggle for human rights on many different levels. According to this survey, "most secular women activists [recognize] that religion does not constitute the only source of values and axis of orientation in peoples' lives."

The best way to conceive of religious and secular attitudes in Egypt is on a continuum rather than a strict dichotomy because dichotomous conceptions serve to sustain Islamist notions of secular as "being against religion."

On the other hand, however, some women activists do view their religious traditions as inherently mired by the patriarchal system in which they were created, and therefore reject the religious framework altogether.

In this light, the best way to conceive of religious and secular attitudes in Egypt is on a continuum rather than a strict dichotomy because dichotomous conceptions serve to sustain Islamist notions of secular as "being against religion."

The case of the Egyptian women's movement supports the idea that religion needs human rights and secularism for several reasons. For instance, this case reflects the belief of Muslim women in the ability of human agency to promote the understanding and practice of both religion and secularism. Egyptian women are reinterpreting and renewing their religious traditions from within. Moreover, the alleged Western origin of human rights doctrine does not prevent these women from claiming these rights for themselves, and seeking to reevaluate and adapt these norms to suit their own cultural, religious and political situations.

The idea of human agency in this context is illustrated by the ability of women to initiate their struggle from within their particular religious tradition by working among a variety of understandings of Islam. The human rights norm of freedom of religion gives these women the power to choose among competing views of their religious tradition, and their choices are informed by their belief in human rights in general. Their broader religious tradition is enhanced by this internal synergy that allows them to maintain their own religious convictions, while striving to attain a higher level of human dignity through international human rights standards.

The synergy and interdependence of religion and human rights enable Muslims to observe their own understanding and practice of Islam through an assertion of human rights, while using their Islamic identity to promote their human rights within their own Muslim communities. By ensuring that minority and dissident voices within a religious tradition are able to challenge dated and regressive understandings and practices of Islam, human rights and secularism help Muslims avoid the difficult choice of either rejecting their religion entirely or abandoning their own human rights.

At the same time, the combination of the protection of human rights and observance of secularism enables people to challenge dated understandings of their own tradition without fearing drastic consequences for charges of heresy or apostasy. They can choose to either leave the tradition in safety and dignity, or stay within its parameters while contesting its dominant dogma also in safety and dignity, as some of the members of the secular women's movement in Egypt are doing. It is critical for the moral integrity of the religious tradition itself that people are free to stay or leave the community at will, instead of being forced or intimidated into the hypocritical pretense of conformity with dominant beliefs and practices.

Unfortunately, in attempting to respond to the threat of militant Islamic fundamentalism, the present Egyptian government tends to limit freedom of religion and other human rights for all segments of its population.

It is also instructive for our purposes here to note that the relative "neutrality" of the Egyptian state is critically important for maintaining the peace and stability of the country as a whole, which has a significant Christian minority, in addition to diversity of beliefs among the Muslim majority.

Unfortunately, in attempting to respond to the threat of militant Islamic fundamentalism, the present Egyptian government tends to limit freedom of religion and other human rights for all segments of its population.

One example of this is the 1992 decision to "nationalize" private mosques in order to dictate sermons to all Muslim Egyptians in the name of preventing their use to promote violent extremist activities. Ironically, such state control of Islamic discourse tends to inhibit the human rights of the majority of Muslims, without necessarily succeeding in suppressing Islamic militancy. The fact that the mosque has become a contested political arena, instead of a place for religious workshop and reflection, in a narrow or strict sense, undermines the role of the state as the guardian of human rights and secularism.

2. Negotiating Islamic Identity and Politics: The Case of Sunni Sudan

In Sudan, profound ambiguities about the relationship between Islam and the state, and Islam and politics more broadly, have been a primary factor in political instability and retarded economic and social development of the country since independence from Anglo-Egyptian colonial rule in 1956. These ambiguities are also part of the underlying causes of civil war that has raged in the southern part of the country, first from 1955 to 1972, and then again since 1983.

The basic dilemma can be summarized as follows. On the one hand, the main political parties in the predominantly Muslim northern part of the country are unable to challenge the claims of the National Islamic Front that the country must be governed by an Islamic state in order to enforce Shari'a as the positive law of the land. This situation gave the National Islamic Front a grossly exaggerated influence in the country, and promoted the general belief that the regulation of the role of Islam in public life in Sudan is not an option.

On the other hand, that notion of an Islamic state is obviously untenable in view of the profound religious and cultural diversity of the country as a whole. The imposition of a particular understanding of Islam as the positive law of the whole country violates the human rights of Muslim as well as non-Muslim citizens. Since that view of Shari'a is commonly believed to be divine, any political opposition to the government of the day becomes tantamount to apostasy which is a capital crime punishable by death under section 126 of the Sudan Penal Code of 1991.

Minority religious traditions will also suffer serious violations of their fundamental human rights. In this light, the benefits of secularism and human rights are obvious, but neither is achievable in a sustainable manner without clarifying the role of Islam in the politics of the country. That is, given the wide belief in the necessity of a role for Islam in public life, human rights cannot be founded on purely secular grounds, and secularism cannot be justified in human rights terms, without relating both to an Islamic justification. Yet, this process itself depends on the protection of freedom of belief and dissent. That is how and why the case of Sudan is a clear illustration of the need for the proposed synergy and interdependence of religion and secularism.

The benefits of secularism and human rights are obvious, but neither is achievable in a sustainable manner without clarifying the role of Islam in the politics of the country.

3. Negotiating Islamic Identity and Politics: The Case of Shi'a Iran.

Another case that makes the same point is that of Iran since April, 1979, when the revolution declared an Islamic Republic that fused the state and a particular interpretation of Islam (that was exceptional even within the particular Shi'a tradition of Iran itself) under the novel notion of "guardianship by the clergy" (vilayat-i faqih).

The 1979 constitution of Iran, on which that so-called Islamic state was based, is a complex system of paradoxes and contradictions. For example, Article 2 states, "[t]he Islamic Republic is a system based on belief in . . . One God . . . His exclusive sovereignty and right to legislate, and the necessity of submission to His commands. . . ." Article 4 states, "[a]ll civil, penal, economic, administrative, cultural, military, political and other laws and regulations must be based on Islamic criteria. . . ." Paradoxically, Article 6 states that "[i]n the Islamic Republic of Iran, the affairs of the country must be administered on the basis of public opinion, expressed by means of elections...." Yet, the clergy retain the ultimate power to ensure that "public opinion" is consistent with "the sovereignty of God" as determined, of course, by those self-appointed guardians.

The Constitution announces Islam as the "eternally immutable" religion of Iran, but recognizes Zoroastrianism, Judaism and Christianity as the only accepted religious minorities, giving their adherents freedom to practice their religion "within the limits of the law." Moreover, an "absolute religious Leader and the Leadership of the Ummah" have ultimate authority over the executive: the Islamic Assembly is made up of 270 members, of which "[t]he Zoroastrians and Jews will elect one representative; Assyrian and Chaldean Christians will jointly elect one representative; and Armenian Christians in the north and in the south of the country will each elect one representative."

The clergy retain the ultimate power to ensure that "public opinion" is consistent with "the sovereignty of God" as determined, of course, by those self-appointed guardians.

Further, the constitution ensures the equality of males and females and the equal rights of women, but only "in conformance with Islamic criteria." These contradictory clauses of the constitution, mixing notions of divine authority, as exercised by an "absolute religious Leader and the Leadership of the Ummah," who are fallible human beings, with modern ideas of popular sovereignty and democratic elections, have resulted in untold suffering for all segments of the population, including Shi'a Muslims themselves.

Political struggles among competing religious and civic authorities have locked the state in unworkable policies, and forced the country into a devastating international isolation. Reports of the United Nations' Special Representative on Iran in 1991 as well as 1998 documented horrendous human rights violations throughout the country. Yet, the fact that the second UN report also reported some improvement in the human rights situation indicates the real possibility of recovery from the total disaster of the 1980s and early 1990s.

What is clear from the sad, yet hopeful, experience of Iran's notion of an Islamic state is that a secular space between religion and state is critically important for political stability, social and economic development as well as general well being of Islamic societies. As clearly shown by Iran's relations with a range of other countries, from conservative Sunni Islamic Saudi Arabia to the liberal, secular United States, carefully regulating the relationship between religion and the state is necessary for maintaining positive cooperative relations with other nations, whether so-called Islamic or not. In view of the well-documented daily human rights violations in Iran, the notion of an Islamic government undermines the validity of Islam as a religion, even among its own adherents. When the government is identified with the religion, both are blamed for the social and political problems of the state.

What is clear from the sad, yet hopeful, experience of Iran's notion of an Islamic state is that a secular space between religion and state is critically important for political stability, social and economic development as well as general well being of Islamic societies.

I do not assume or imply that religion, secularism and human rights are totally autonomous or independent concepts or paradigms, because they all exist in constant interaction with political, economic, constitutional and governmental processes and institutions, both locally and globally. Therefore, the human rights of women, or of citizens in general, whether in Egypt, Iran or any other Islamic society, cannot be protected simply by ratifying international treaties or adopting national legislation. Secularism cannot be sustained in Sudan by "proclaiming" the idea at a national constitutional conference, or even enacting it in the constitution of the country.

State policy and legislation in Islamic countries must be founded on the institutionalized practice of secularism, as an indigenous concept, rather than an externally imposed Western notion. Such practice needs to be legitimized in Islamic terms for the population to take it seriously. It also requires the development of the necessary constitutional, judicial, economic and political institutions, all from an internal perspective of each society, but with due regard to its regional and global context. In each case, the success or failure of initiatives will depend on a complex web of historical developments and context, institutionalization and consistent practice in accordance with clear principles and politics, a well-informed and an active civil society that will hold its government officials accountable for their actions.

In conclusion, the positive working of Islam, secularism and human rights, and of the relationship among all three of them, will remain dependent upon sound economic policy, stable state constitutionalism and genuine democracy, all interacting within an and active civil society. A constitution that reflects particular religious beliefs is static precisely because it is grounded in a claim of divinity. A democracy that allots political positions according to religious affiliation not only violates the fundamental rights of citizens, but is also too rigid and simplistic because believers do not necessarily act politically in accordance with their religious beliefs.

As civil wars throughout Muslim history clearly show, believers can be deeply divided in their political beliefs and practice.

In any case, how is one to judge the relative level of piety and fidelity to the faith among citizens as the bases of state policy and practice in every day life? As civil wars throughout Muslim history clearly show, believers can be deeply divided in their political beliefs and practice. Maintaining a dynamic synergy and interdependence among human rights, religion and secularism will enable all citizens to live by their religious convictions while respecting the right of others to do the same, instead of expecting people to choose between competing religions or religious interpretations.

▲

[5]
Islam and Human Rights: Beyond the Universality Debate

Religion and the Universality of Human Rights

The implementation of international human rights norms in any society requires thoughtful and well-informed engagement of religion (broadly defined) because of its strong influence on human belief systems and behavior, regardless of the formal characterization of the relationship between religion and the state in any society. While it is true that the behavior of believers is not always motivated by total fidelity to their faith, religious considerations are too important for the majority of people for human rights scholars and advocates to continue to dismiss them simply as irrelevant, insignificant, or problematic.

In emphasizing the need for advocates of human rights to seriously engage religion, I do not assume that there is either immediate compatibility or permanent contradiction between human rights and any religion. On the contrary, my suggestion is premised on the paradox of the reality of tension between the two, on the one hand, and the importance of reconciliation, on the other. This paradox is often depicted in terms of the polar extremes posed by the universality of human rights and the relativity of religion. In my view, to posit such a dichotomy is misleading, because of the interdependence between the two. While the universality of human rights cannot be realized among believers unless they accept it as consistent with their religious beliefs, the integrity of religious faith and its relevance to the lives of its adherents is dependent on the effective protection of human rights. Accordingly, it is more useful to see this relationship in terms of synergy and mutual influence, than to envision it as one of permanent antagonism.

In this essay, I use the case of Islam and Islamic societies for illustration, while emphasizing that similar issues arise in relation to other religions and societies. My argument is that the terms of this debate should be expanded, to include the role of local and global social, economic and political factors, instead of focused on purely theological analyses of the relationship between religion and human rights. In my view, this approach is more conducive to mediating between the polar extremes of universality and relativity by emphasizing common features of human experience over differences in abstract theological terms. This mediation is more likely to be effective when the focus is on the actual perception and practice of Muslims and other believers in their specific context. In other words, I am advocating that religious factors be understood in their proper perspective or context, instead of disregarded altogether or granted exaggerated impact as theological ideals.

For the purpose of this essay, it is necessary to distinguish between the two senses in which the term *human rights* is often used. In one sense, the term *human rights* refers to historical struggles for freedom and social justice in general. While prevalent in popular discourse, this general sense of the term is not useful for an analysis of the compatibility of human rights with any specific religious, political or ideological tradition, as each of these paradigms would claim its own understanding of human rights. As used here, the term *human rights* refers to the particular conception of freedom and social justice that was articulated in the Universal Declaration of Human Rights (UDHR) of 1948, and more specifically defined in subsequent treaties and effectuated through a variety of implementation mechanisms.

The key feature of human rights as defined in the UDHR is that these rights are *due to all human beings by virtue of their humanity, without distinction on such grounds as race, sex (gender), religion, language or national origin*. There is no doubt that the most immediate antecedents and articulation of this concept of human rights have emerged from Western

(European and American) experiences since the late eighteenth century. As commonly acknowledged, however, those experiences were premised on the Enlightenment, rather than Christian or Jewish theologies, though the latter have tended to reconcile themselves with the former over time. In particular, the concept of human rights as defined in the UDHR is essentially a "universalization" of the idea of fundamental constitutional rights as developed by Western countries, although the actual set of rights provided for in the Declaration surpasses what can be found under the constitutional system of any country, Western or non-Western.

It is important to note here that while it is not binding as such under international law, the UDHR is clearly the enabling document for efforts to define human rights and devise mechanisms and strategies for their implementation. Given the realities of national sovereignty and international relations, it was imperative to strike a balance between the need for international supervision and respect for the domestic jurisdiction. Thus, in universalizing certain notions of fundamental rights, international human rights systems seek to make these rights binding under international law, while leaving application on the ground to the agency of the nation-state. The mitigation of this paradox of self-regulation by states of their own human rights performance requires a clear understanding of domestic and international factors and processes, including religion and the role of religious institutions, which influence the actual conduct of states in this regard.

Since there is no reliable international mechanism for "enforcing" human rights standards against the will of national governments,[1] the crucial question is how to encourage governments to ratify human rights treaties, and motivate them to comply with the obligation to protect these rights within their respective territories. An effective and sustainable way of doing this is to generate a local constituency to advocate for the ratification and implementation of human rights within the national context. Even if the elite in control of government want to respect some human rights, it is unlikely to do so against the wishes of its own population. For such a local constituency to emerge and be effective in its advocacy of human rights, these rights must be seen by the general public as consistent with its own religious beliefs. In other words, international human rights norms are unlikely to be accepted by governments as legally binding, and respected in practice, without strong legitimation within national politics. Popular perceptions of human rights as consistent with the religious beliefs of the population are essential for these rights' legitimation in each country. Even in so-called secular states, such as the United States and France, a clear understanding and appreciation of the political and sociological importance of religion is essential to efforts to influence the human rights policies and practices of the state.

As noted earlier, I am not suggesting that consistency between religion and human rights can be assumed, or taken for granted, in any part of the world. On the contrary, one can easily identify some fundamental tensions, if not open conflict, between religious precepts and human rights norms. Therefore, a key question in the universality debate is whether the secular Western origins of human rights, as defined by the UDHR, necessarily mean that these rights are not (or cannot be) truly universal.

The response I am proposing to this question is based on the following interrelated propositions:

1. The moral or philosophical foundation and political justification of the conception of human rights as defined by the UDHR *can be* found in different religious and cultural traditions. However, since the traditional theology of the major religions of the world, including Christianity, is not readily consistent with this specific conception of human rights, reconciliation will require a reinterpretation of some of the precepts of those religions.

[1] While "humanitarian interventions" and actions by the UN Security Council can be cited as examples of coercive measures for the protection of human rights against the will of national governments, these mechanisms apply only in extreme cases and are too dependent on the political calculations of the major powers to qualify as part of a reliable system for the regular international enforcement of human rights norms.

2. Reconciliation is necessary because of the fundamental value of international protection of human rights in checking the abuse of the powers of the state. Since the European model of the nation-state has been universalized through colonialism, there is need for effective protection against excessive or abusive state power. The corresponding universalization of fundamental constitutional rights through the UDHR is the best available means of providing that protection.
3. While there will necessarily be a theological dimension to the reinterpretation of religious precepts, the process itself must be understood in the specific political, social and economic context of the community of believers. The concrete historical context in which believers live is integral to all human understandings of religion, explained below in terms of an anthropological approach to religion. This context is also the framework within which the reinterpretation of religious precepts can emerge and be accepted in practice.

To develop these propositions in relation to Islam and Islamic societies, I will first attempt to briefly explain what I believe to be the key issue in current Islamic discourse, and explain its relevance to the subject of this essay. The framework I propose for addressing this issue in particular societies consists of an internal discourse and a cross-cultural dialogue with other societies.[2] To illustrate the application of this proposal, I will briefly outline how it might work in relation to Islamic societies. Drawing on a recent experience in Mauritius, I will examine some of the factors and conditions that affect the prospects of internal discourse and cross-cultural dialogue.

Islam, Sharia *and Human Rights*

Like other believers, Muslims have always sought to experience their faith in terms of individual and collective conformity with its normative system, commonly known as *sharia*, which is supposed to regulate their daily lives as Muslims. While Muslims tend to ascribe divine authority to historical formulations of *sharia* by jurists of the eighth and ninth centuries, it is clear that the precise content of that normative system has always been, and will continue to be, the product of human understanding in specific historical context.[3] As a scholar of Islamic studies recently explained, "Although the law [*sharia*] is of divine provenance, the actual construction of the law is a human activity, and its results represent the law of God *as humanly understood*. Since the law does not descend from heaven ready-made, it is the human understanding of the law—the human *fiqh* [literally, understanding]—that must be normative for society."[4]

While readily understandable, the common confusion between *sharia* as divinely ordained, on the one hand, and human efforts to discover what it means, on the other, needs to be clarified if Islam itself is to play a positive role in the lives of Muslims today. Given drastic changes in the social, economic, and political circumstances of Islamic societies throughout the world, an understanding of *sharia* that was developed more than a thousand years ago is bound to face some practical difficulties today. Yet, significant reform of any problematic aspect of *sharia* cannot occur as long as preexisting human formulations of it are taken to be divine. As a result of this "man-made" deadlock, Muslims everywhere continue to subscribe to a conception of *sharia* that none of them are willing or able to live by. For example, religious condemnation of *ribba* (usury) is understood to mean that the payment of any interest on loans is totally prohibited. Similarly, religious objections to *gharar* (uncertainty and speculation in commercial dealings) is taken to invalidate contracts of insurance where the

[2] *See, generally*, HUMAN RIGHTS IN AFRICA: CROSS-CULTURAL PERSPECTIVES (Abdullahi Ahmed An-Na'im & Francis Deng, eds.) (1990); HUMAN RIGHTS IN CROSS-CULTURAL PERSPECTIVES: QUEST FOR CONSENSUS (Abdullahi Ahmed An-Na'im, ed.) (1992).

[3] On the origins and development of that historical understanding of *sharia*, see ABDULLAHI AHMED AN-NA'IM, TOWARD AN ISLAMIC REFORMATION: CIVIL LIBERTIES, HUMAN RIGHTS AND INTERNATIONAL LAW ch. 2 (1990).

[4] BERNARD WEISS, THE SPIRIT OF ISLAMIC LAW 116 (1998). Emphasis in original.

obligations of the parties are contingent on whether or not something happens in the future. In practice, however, Muslim individuals and their governments routinely charge and pay interest on loans, and conclude and enforce contracts of insurance because it is impossible to have viable economic systems today without these practices. This discrepancy between theory and practice can be bridged through an appreciation of the fact that all specific definitions of concepts such as *ribba* and *gharar* are necessarily the product of human understanding in specific historical context, not direct divine decree.

Failing to distinguish between the two meanings of human rights noted earlier, some Muslims claim that historical formulations of *sharia* have always secured human rights in theory, though such a situation may not have materialized in practice. In my view, by securing a relatively advanced degree of protection for the rights of women and non-Muslims, historical formulations of *sharia* did provide for better protection of human rights than other normative systems in the past. For example, from the very beginning, *sharia* was understood to require an independent legal personality for women, and the protection of certain minimum rights for them in inheritance and family relations, beyond what was possible under other major normative systems until the nineteenth century. Similarly, *sharia* guarantees specific rights for the so-called People of the Book (mainly Christians and Jews) more than what had been provided for under other major normative systems in the past. However, since the rights of women and non-Muslims under *sharia* are not equal to those of men and Muslims, respectively, the level of protection of rights under *sharia* is not sufficient when judged by the standards set by the UDHR, which require equal rights for all human beings, without distinction on such grounds as sex, religion, or belief.[5]

A possible response to this criticism of *sharia* is the argument that Muslims (and other believers) should strive to live by the dictates of their religion, not according to some fallible, humanly devised set of human rights norms. However, since divine commands are always understood and applied by human beings, the contrast between orthodox perceptions of "the dictates of religion" and new or unorthodox views on the matter is really between two *human understandings* of what the religion requires of its adherents. Accordingly, a reinterpretation of Islamic sources that demonstrates agreement with human rights norms should be considered on its own terms, rather than dismissed as un-Islamic because it is inconsistent with previously established human understandings of *sharia*. For Muslims, a reinterpretation should be accepted or rejected in terms of its own foundation in Islamic sources, instead of being rejected simply because it is new or unorthodox. Space does not permit a detailed discussion of possible Islamic reform methodologies that can achieve consistency between human rights and modern understandings of *sharia*.[6] What I wish to emphasize here is the possibility of establishing the religious legitimacy of such an interpretation through what might be called an anthropological approach to Islam.

As I have explained elsewhere,[7] this approach is premised on an organic and dynamic relationship between the sacred texts of a religion, the Qur'an and Sunna (traditions of the Prophet) in the case of Islam, on the one hand, and the comprehension, imagination, judgment, behavior, and practical experience of human beings, on the other. Such an approach is not only justified, but in fact required by the terms of the Qur'an, which in numerous verses invites individuals, or the community, to reflect and reason independently. Indeed, verse 12 of chapter 2 and verse 43 of chapter 3 proclaim that human reflection and understanding is the whole purpose of revealing the Qur'an. The rich diversity of opinion among Muslim jurists over almost every significant legal principle or issue of public policy clearly indicates a dynamic

[5] For a detailed discussion of discrepancies between historical formulations of *sharia* and modern international standards, *see* AN-NA'IM, *supra* note 3, at 4–7.

[6] AN-NA'IM, *supra* note 3, at ch. 3.

[7] Abdullahi Ahmed An-Na'im, *Toward an Islamic Hermeneutics for Human Rights*, *in* HUMAN RIGHTS AND RELIGIOUS VALUES: AN UNEASY RELATIONSHIP ch. 16 (Abdullahi A. An-Na'im et. al., eds., 1995).

relationship between the Qur'an and Sunna, on the one hand, and human comprehension, imagination and experience, on the other.

Since the historical context of the community and the personal experiences of individual believers substantially influence human perception and behavior, drastic changes in the conditions of individual and communal life should lead to reconsideration of the meaning and implications of the divine message. By the same token, one must appreciate the differential impact of these factors on the perception and orientation of each community of Muslims today. To emphasize the importance of the specific historical context within which Islamic principles are understood and practiced is to call for clear understanding of the nature of these factors and careful consideration of their consequences for each society. In other words, one should address these issues for each Islamic society in its own context, instead of treating all such societies in the same way.

This contextualization is particularly important because of the role of the state as the framework for the articulation and implementation of public policy for Islamic societies today. Whatever role *sharia* may play in the lives of contemporary Muslims, that role will necessarily be mediated through the agency of their respective national states, rather than by the autonomous action of the global Muslim community as such. As an essentially political institution, any state has to balance a variety of competing claims and interests. It is true that some of those claims and interests will probably reflect the religious sentiments of the population. But in view of the religious and political diversity of the population of Islamic countries today, and the complexity of their regional and global economic and security concerns, it is totally unrealistic to expect any state to be solely motivated by the religious sentiments of even the vast majority of its population.

In addition to the above-mentioned elements of internal discourse and its processes, consideration must also be given to factors and processes of cross-cultural dialogue. First, the realities of global interaction and interdependence mean that cross-cultural dialogue is already taking place in different ways among various participants, and around a variety of national and international concerns. The question here is to what extent these processes can be used to promote acceptance of international human rights norms within different religious communities. Second, as is the case with all forms of human communication, the nature and outcomes of such dialogue are conditioned by the perspectives or agendas of different participants, their perceptions of historical and current power relations, levels of trust or misapprehension, and other features of both the immediate and the broader contexts. Moreover, these factors tend to interact over time not only in the context of experience but in that of shifting perceptions of self-interest, mounting or diminishing solidarity, and other variable factors. Third, with regard to the relationship between religion and human rights in particular, it is important to understand the synergy between internal discourse and cross-cultural dialogue, as these two aspects of the process can reinforce or undermine each other, depending on the interaction of the contextual factors indicated above. While the preceding remarks may indicate the sort of factors and considerations that I believe should be taken into account, I can only conclude by calling for further exploration of local and global conditions that are likely either to facilitate or to hinder the legitimation of human rights within different religious traditions in general.

Possibilities of Reconciliation in the Modern Context: The View from Mauritius

During a visit to Mauritius in November 1999, I gave a lecture on Islamic family law (also known as Muslim personal law, or MPL) from a human rights perspective. In that lecture, I made the obvious point that historical formulations of *sharia* discriminate against women, and called for the reinterpretation of Islamic sources to secure equality between men and women in all aspects of MPL. I was speaking in the context of a debate over the enforcement of the MPL by the state, an issue that has been simmering in Mauritius since the constitutional conference of 1965.[8] After the lecture, I was denounced as a "heretic" in the press of some Islamic groups, and by imams and other speakers at local mosques, because I said that those formulations of *sharia* should not be enacted by the state since *sharia* discriminates against women. Some activists who claimed to speak in the name of the Muslim community in the country also called for me to be declared persona non grata in the country, citing financial support by the Ford Foundation for my work on Islamic family law as conclusive evidence that I was an agent of American imperialism seeking to undermine the stability of Islamic societies from within.

The intense and hostile Muslim reaction to my remarks clearly indicated that the issue of MPL has become proxy for broader cultural and political concerns in the historical tensions between the Muslim minority and other segments of the population. As the managing editor of *Impact News*, the weekly newspaper that led the attack, told me on the telephone, "You should understand how important it is for us to have MPL enacted as the law for our community in this country. If we fail in doing that, all of our freedom of religion will be lost, including the right to hold Friday prayers in our mosques." I find that claim unjustified by any independent criteria, but also appreciate the fact that this view is firmly held by many Muslims in the country, who tend to understand their local and regional situations against the background of a long and bitter history of interreligious strife in India, the land of origin of both the Hindu majority and the Muslim minority in Mauritius.

There was also a clear awareness among the Mauritians that the international legitimacy of their island country requires a good human rights record. This was true among Muslims who supported the move to enforce MPL through the official legal system. Otherwise, they would not have been as concerned with my saying that *sharia* violates human rights by discriminating against women. It is probably true that Muslim activists were more concerned about the government's rejection of the idea of a MPL code on human rights grounds than they were about upholding the fundamental human rights principle of nondiscrimination on the grounds of sex. Nevertheless, an awareness of the relevance of human rights norms to domestic policies is precisely the sort of influence the international system is supposed to exert.

This dialectic between the global and the local, which is commonly appreciated now, is part of the cross-cultural dialogue mentioned earlier in this essay. The point I wish to emphasize here is the need for a variety of strategies to enhance the influence of human rights standards in both the domestic and the global context of each society. In relation to the role of religion in particular, it is imperative to engage in an internal discourse within the framework of the religious community in question, in order to overcome objections to human rights norms. Whether such a discourse is conducted through the reform methodology suggested in this essay, or by some other means, an internal discourse about the religious validity of human rights is essential if these rights are indeed to be universal at the global level.

Concluding Remarks

The term *human rights* is popularly used to refer to a variety of systems for negotiating competing claims and interests in regard to how a society should be organized to achieve the best possible degree of freedom and justice. As used in this essay, however, this term means the particular normative and institutional system for realizing those objectives in the context of the state throughout the world today. Despite their clearly secular Western origins, human rights must also be legitimated in the context of different religious traditions because of the importance of those perspectives for the vast majority of people around the world. This process of religious legitimation requires creative approaches to theological questions in the specific socioeconomic and political context of each society. The universality of human rights must be realized through the implementation of deliberate strategies that are likely to attract popular

[8] Bhewa and Alladeen v. Government of Mauritius, 1990 Mauritius Reports, 79–90.

support, instead of on the basis of assumptions that such universality already exists, or can be achieved by proclamation in international documents.

The proposed approach to the relationship between religion and human rights strongly emphasizes commonalities as well as differences in the experience of societies. These commonalities are easier to appreciate in light of a clear understanding of the dynamics of local struggles over power and resources, than by exclusively focusing on abstract theological precepts. This approach will enable human rights scholars and advocates to address the role of Islam (or any other religion) as a source of motivation and mobilization for particular political and social agendas, without appearing to challenge its legitimacy as the faith of a significant segment of the population of any country.

The experience I had in Mauritius clearly demonstrates that a more realistic and contextualized appreciation of the practical difficulties facing the universal acknowledgment of human rights in each society is essential to devising the best strategies for influencing the processes of cultural transformation in favor of better protection of those rights. The way out of the vicious cycle of the "universality-relativity debate" is to go deeper into the local context of each issue in order to find sustainable points of mediation. As with other public policy issues, the legitimacy and efficacy of the protection of human rights must be promoted through deliberate strategies that combine visionary belief in the possibilities of social and political change with a realistic appreciation of the difficulties.

In closing, I wish to express my personal appreciation of the fact that Professor Louis Henkin is the commentator on this presentation. With profound respect, I take the liberty of noting that both of us strive to combine adherence to our respective religious traditions with a strong commitment to the universality of human rights. While gladly accepting the possibility of disagreement between the two of us about how to reconcile religious adherence with a commitment to the universality of human rights, I still believe that our collaboration somehow resonates with the argument I have attempted to make in this lecture.

Part Two

Islam and Human Rights in the Muslim World

[6]
Human Rights in the Muslim World: Socio-Political Conditions and Scriptural Imperatives*

To hundreds of millions of Muslims, the historical formulations of Islamic law known as Shari'a determine the boundaries of legal and ethical conduct. In this Article, Professor An-Na'im explores the implications of Shari'a for Muslim observance of international human rights standards. Part I addresses the legitimacy of these standards in Muslim countries, focusing on the international legal principles of equality and nondiscrimination. Part II traces the development of Shari'a in Islamic history and its influence on Muslims. Professor An-Na'im discusses several conflicts between Shari'a and human rights standards, rejecting the contention that such inconsistencies do not exist. Part III explores the political and social forces associated with Islamization in Muslim countries. Professor An-Na'im argues that such pressures heighten the need to examine critically the effect of Shari'a on human rights violations. Part IV presents a case study on Shari'a and Muslim women's rights. Finally, in Part V, Professor An-Na'im offers a methodology for human rights advocates in the Muslim world: to reexamine the scriptural imperatives in the Qur'an to make the dictates of Shari'a consistent with international human rights norms.

INTRODUCTION

Historical formulations of Islamic religious law, commonly known as Shari'a,[1] include a universal system of law and ethics and purport

* I wrote this Article while holding the Ariel F. Sallows Chair in Human Rights at the College of Law, University of Saskatchewan, Canada. I am grateful for the research assistance of Charmaine Spencer and the editorial help and useful suggestions of Anne McGillivray.

1. In Islamic literature, the term Shari'a is used to refer to Divine Law based on the Qur'an and Sunna (traditions of the Prophet Muhammad), while the term *fiqh* (jurisprudence) refers to the opinions and commentaries of Muslim jurists. Some Muslim authors emphasize this distinction in order to suggest that they are criticizing merely *fiqh* and not Divine Law itself. *See, e.g.*, K. FARUKI, ISLAMIC JURISPRUDENCE 12–19 (1962); A. FYZEE, OUTLINES OF MUHAMMADAN LAW 14–24 (4th ed. 1974).

I use the term Shari'a because the aspects of Islamic law I discuss are directly based on the Qur'an and Sunna and not upon personal opinions and commentaries of jurists. As a Muslim, I am not challenging the divine nature of the Qur'an and Sunna. Rather, I am challenging the failure of contemporary Muslims to appreciate the impact of historical context upon the interpretation and application of those fundamental sources of Islam. I argue that given the historical to regulate every aspect of public and private life. The power of Shari'a to regulate the behavior of Muslims derives from its moral and religious authority as well as the formal enforcement of its legal norms. As such, Shari'a influences individual and collective behavior in Muslim countries through its role in the socialization processes of such nations regardless of its status in their formal legal systems. For example, the status and rights of women in the Muslim world have always been significantly influenced by Shari'a, regardless of the degree of Islamization in public life. Of course, Shari'a is not the sole determinant of human behavior nor the only formative force behind social and political institutions in Muslim countries.

In this Article, I explore the implications of Shari'a for the status of human rights[2] in the Muslim world.[3] After briefly discussing my methodological choice in Part I, in Part II I explain Shari'a and the human rights violations which result from the dominant interpretation of Shari'a. In Part III, I describe some of the political and social forces which translate this scriptural interpretation into action. In Part IV, I analyze in some detail the impact of Shari'a and Islamization on the status and rights of women in Muslim communities. And in Part V, I argue that human rights reform requires reinterpretation of Shari'a and I offer one possible reformulation.

---

contexts of both initial revelation and subsequent interpretations of the texts of the Qur'an and Sunna, some texts are no longer applicable while others need to be interpreted differently. I believe that divine revelation must be understood and applied in historical context because it addresses us in our human condition and circumstances which change over time.

2. This Article is not concerned with the origins and philosophical meaning of the term "human rights" and does not detail contemporary human rights standards. Rather, I take the International Bill of Human Rights as the source of international human rights standards. *See infra* note 7.

3. It is not possible in a work of this nature to offer extensive surveys and analyses of the situation in even a selected group of countries. I therefore focus on a number of broad human rights issues while illustrating my arguments with reference to conditions prevailing in representative Muslim countries. I have chosen Egypt, Indonesia, Iran, Morocco, Pakistan, and Saudi Arabia as reflecting varying degrees of secularization, fundamentalism; and traditionalism. The analysis is applicable to other Muslim countries provided, of course, that factors and conditions peculiar to each country are taken into account.

For the purpose of this Article, a "Muslim country" is one in which the majority of the population perceive themselves to be Muslims. Because I do not believe that it is within the realm of human discourse to agree on an objective conception of Islam, I must accept a people's self-perception. It should be borne in mind during the discussion that variation in the conception of Islam is inevitable.

As to the size of the Muslim majority which qualifies a country as a "Muslim country," 80% appears to be reasonable because such a majority normally would be large enough to significantly influence public policy and action. In other words, I assume that if 80% of the population is Muslim, then Islam is a significant factor in the life of that society regardless of whether the state is constituted as an "Islamic state" or whether Shari'a is the formal legal system of the land. All six countries selected for this discussion satisfy my criteria. *See, e.g.*, MUSLIM PEOPLES: AN ETHNOGRAPHIC SURVEY 887, 891, 893, 900–902 (R. Weeks ed. 1984); D. PIPES, IN THE PATH OF GOD: ISLAM AND POLITICAL POWER 338–39 (1982).

I conclude that human rights advocates in the Muslim world must work within the framework of Islam to be effective. They need not be confined, however, to the particular historical interpretations of Islam known as Shari'a. Muslims are obliged, as a matter of faith, to conduct their private and public affairs in accordance with the dictates of Islam, but there is room for legitimate disagreement over the precise nature of these dictates in the modern context. Religious texts, like all other texts, are open to a variety of interpretations. Human rights advocates in the Muslim world should struggle to have their interpretations of the relevant texts adopted as the new Islamic scriptural imperatives for the contemporary world.

A. *Cultural Legitimacy for Human Rights*

The basic premise of my approach is that human rights violations reflect the lack or weakness of cultural legitimacy of international standards in a society. Insofar as these standards are perceived to be alien to or at variance with the values and institutions of a people, they are unlikely to elicit commitment or compliance. While cultural legitimacy may not be the sole or even primary determinant of compliance with human rights standards, it is, in my view, an extremely significant one. Thus, the underlying causes of any lack or weakness of legitimacy of human rights standards must be addressed in order to enhance the promotion and protection of human rights in that society.

Some commentators have focused on this lack of cultural legitimacy of international standards in the non-Western world to challenge the basic validity of international human rights standards. In fact, conduct which would amount to human rights violations under existing international standards has been justified precisely because these standards were perceived to be culturally illegitimate. This cultural illegitimacy, it is argued, derives from the historical conditions surrounding the creation of the particular human rights instruments. Most African and Asian countries did not participate in the formulation of the Universal Declaration of Human Rights[4] because, as victims of colonization, they were not members of the United Nations. When they did participate in the formulation of subsequent instruments, they did so on the basis of an established framework and philosophical assumptions adopted in their absence. For example, the preexisting framework and assumptions favored individual civil and political rights over collective solidarity rights, such as a right to development, an outcome which

4. *Universal Declaration of Human Rights*, G.A. Res. 217A (III), U.N. GAOR Res. 71, U.N. Doc. A/810 (1948) [hereinafter *Universal Declaration*].

remains problematic today. Some authors have gone so far as to argue that inherent differences exist between the Western notion of human rights as reflected in the international instruments and non-Western notions of human dignity.[5] In the Muslim world, for instance, there are obvious conflicts between Shari'a and certain human rights, especially of women and non-Muslims.[6]

Concern for the lack of universal participation in formulating international human rights instruments does not lead me to invalidate those existing instruments. On the contrary, for the purposes of this study, I take the International Bill of Human Rights as the source of these standards.[7] It is true that not all Muslim countries have endorsed or ratified these instruments, but neither have they publicly repudiated them.[8] The human rights idea is too powerful and popular now for any government to oppose openly. The governments of Muslim countries are no exception to this general rule. In this discussion, I focus on the principles of legal equality and nondiscrimination contained in many human rights instruments.[9] These principles relating to gender and religion are particularly problematic in the Muslim world.

---

5. *See, e.g.*, Donnelly, *Human Rights and Human Dignity: An Analytic Critique of non-Western Conceptions of Human Rights*, 76 AM. POL. SCI. REV. 303 (1982); Panikkar, *Is the Notion of Human Rights a Western Concept?* 120 DIOGENES 75 (1982).

6. *See infra* notes 101–137 and accompanying text.

7. The term "International Bill of Human Rights" refers to a collection of three United Nations instruments: *Universal Declaration, supra* note 4; *The International Covenant on Economic, Social and Cultural Rights*, G.A. Res. 2200 (XXI), 21 U.N. GAOR Supp. (No. 16) at 49, U.N. Doc. A/6316 (1966) (entered into force Jan. 3, 1976); and *International Covenant on Civil and Political Rights*, G.A. Res. 2200 (XXI), 21 U.N. GAOR Supp. (No. 16) at 52, U.N. Doc. A/6316 (1966) (entered into force Mar. 23, 1976).

8. During the first few years after the Iranian revolution, official representatives of the Islamic Republic of Iran expressed reservations toward international human rights standards, favoring what they believed to be Islamic standards. *See* E. MORTIMER, INDEX ON CENSORSHIP 5 (1983). Nevertheless, Iran remains a party to the International Covenant on Economic, Social and Cultural Rights and the International Covenant on Civil and Political Rights, *supra* note 7. *See* INTERNATIONAL HUMAN RIGHTS INSTRUMENTS 170.42, 180.18 (R. Lillich ed. rev. 1988).

9. Article 1 of the Universal Declaration states that "all human beings are born free and equal in dignity and rights." Article 2 specifies that "everyone is entitled to all the rights and freedoms set forth in this Declaration without distinction of any kind, such as race, colour, sex, language, religion, political or other opinion, national or social origin, property, birth or other status." *Universal Declaration, supra* note 4, at arts. 1, 2.

Article 2.2 of the International Covenant on Economic, Social and Cultural Rights obliges state parties to guarantee that the rights enunciated in the Covenant will be exercised without discrimination on grounds such as race, color, sex, language, and religion. Article 3 of the same Covenant creates the obligation to ensure the rights of men and women to the equal enjoyment of all economic, social, and cultural rights set forth in the Covenant. *See International Covenant on Economic, Social and Cultural Rights, supra* note 7, at arts. 2.2, 3.

Articles 2.2 and 3 of the International Covenant on Civil and Political Rights create similar obligations to ensure nondiscrimination and equality in relation to rights set forth in that Covenant. *See International Covenant on Civil and Political Rights, supra* note 7, at arts. 2.2, 3. The same principles underlie numerous specific rights set forth in both Covenants.

I realize that formal equality before the law and the implementation of nondiscrimination policies are necessary but insufficient conditions for the realization of substantive economic,

I adopt a constructive approach[10] to the problem of the cultural legitimacy of human rights norms. This approach posits that such problems can be overcome through a process of reinterpreting the fundamental sources of the Islamic tradition. The proposed new interpretation will have to be undertaken in a sensitive, legitimate manner, and time will be required for its acceptance and implementation by the population at large. The availability of such reinterpretation is a vital prelude to the political struggle which is integral to the whole process. The reformulation I offer in the final part of this Article is but a brief presentation of my arguments for a reinterpretive approach which I have explored in more detail elsewhere.[11] In the final part of this Article, I offer a brief presentation of the thesis and the prospects of its implementation in the Muslim world today.

II. ISLAM, SHARI'A AND HUMAN RIGHTS

In this part, I first discuss the formation of the Shari'a and address the impact which Shari'a has had upon the thinking and conduct of Muslims. I conclude with a discussion of recent mounting pressure in Muslim countries to adopt the Shari'a as their formal legal systems.

A. *The Development and Current Application of Shari'a*

To the over nine hundred million Muslims of the world, the Qur'an is the literal and final word of God and Muhammad is the final Prophet. During his mission, from 610 A.D. to his death in 632 A.D., the Prophet elaborated on the meaning of the Qur'an and supplemented its rulings through his statements and actions. This body of information came to be known as Sunna.[12] He also established the first Islamic state in Medina around 622 A.D. which emerged

political, and social equality. Questions remain of systemic discrimination and issues of affirmative action, as well as debates about equality of opportunity as opposed to equality of result. Nevertheless, these questions and issues must be discussed in the context of particular societies and mediated through the political and social processes of each society. An exploration of these questions and issues, even with respect to the countries selected, is outside the scope of this Article. With respect to India, see generally M. GALANTER, COMPETING EQUALITIES: LAW AND THE BACKWARD CLASSES IN INDIA (1984).

10. For a detailed discussion of this approach, see An-Na'im, *Problems of Universal Cultural Legitimacy for Human Rights*, in HUMAN RIGHTS IN AFRICA: CROSS-CULTURAL PERSPECTIVES (An-Na'im & Deng eds. forthcoming 1990); An-Na'im, *Religious Minorities under Islamic Law and the Limits of Cultural Relativism* 9 HUM. R. Q. 1 (1987).

11. A. AN-NA'IM, TOWARD AN ISLAMIC REFORMATION: CIVIL LIBERTIES, HUMAN RIGHTS AND INTERNATIONAL LAW (1990) [hereinafter TOWARD AN ISLAMIC REFORMATION]; An-Na'im, *The Rights of Women and International Law in the Muslim Context*, 9 WHITTIER L. REV. 491 (1987); An-Na'im, *Islamic Law, International Relations and Human Rights: Challenge and Response*, 20 CORNELL INT'L L. J. 17 (1987).

12. On these formative stages of Islam, see M. HODGSON, I THE VENTURE OF ISLAM, 146–230 (1974); I. LAPIDUS, A HISTORY OF ISLAMIC SOCIETIES, 21–80 (1988).

later as the ideal model of an Islamic state.[13] In addition, the practices of the first four caliphs, successors of the Prophet, are also binding or at least highly authoritative for the ninety percent of Muslims commonly known as Sunnis.[14] In contradistinction, the Shi'a minority insists that the fourth caliph Ali (the Prophet's cousin and son-in-law) and his descendants from Fatima, the Prophet's daughter, were the only rightful *imams*, leaders of the Muslim community.[15]

While the Qur'an was collected and recorded soon after the Prophet Muhammad's death, it took almost two centuries to collect, verify, and record the Sunna. Because it remained an oral tradition for a long time during a period of exceptional turmoil in Muslim history, some Sunna reports are still controversial in terms of both their authenticity and relationship to the Qur'an.[16]

Because Shari'a is derived from Sunna as well as the Qur'an, its development as a comprehensive legal and ethical system had to await the collection and authentication of Sunna. Shari'a was not developed until the second and third centuries of Islam.[17] The concept itself, in the sense of a unified body of law, was a relatively late development.[18] The first generation of Muslim legal scholars worked independently in various centers, discussing their views on the meaning of the Qur'an and Sunna and issuing individual opinions upon request.[19]

Shari'a, therefore, was constructed by Muslim jurists over a long period of time and did not become a comprehensive legal and ethical

13. For a detailed account and analysis of the Mecca and Medina phases of early Islam, see generally W. WATT, MUHAMMAD AT MECCA (1953); W. WATT, MUHAMMAD AT MEDINA (1956).

14. It should be noted, however, that those early caliphs enjoy authority among Muslims by virtue of their religious standing and not their political role. In fact, their political role is seen as a result of their religious learning and piety. Many other early companions of the Prophet share in those qualities and would therefore be accepted as authoritative jurisprudential and theological figures in Muslim history. *See* F. RAHMAN, ISLAM 79 (1979).

15. Upon the Prophet's death, the majority of Muslims accepted Abu Bakr as the first caliph, and they subsequently selected Umar and Uthman as the se ond and third caliphs before Ali became the fourth caliph. To a minority group, known at the time as *Shi'at* Ali, or the partisans of Ali, the first three caliphs were usurpers of the rightful position of the Prophet's cousin and son-in-law. This group eventually developed into a separate sect of Islam, following their line of "rightful" *imams* and developing their own schools of Islamic jurisprudence. At the present time, the main Shi'a groups are the Twelvers of Iran; the Isma'ilis of the Indian sub-continent, central Asia, Syria, and the Persian Gulf region; and the Zaydis of southern Arabia. *See* Fyzee, *Shi'i Legal Theories*, in LAW IN THE MIDDLE EAST 113 (Khadduri & Liebesny eds. 1955). For a theological account of these Shi'a sects see W. WATT, ISLAMIC PHILOSOPHY AND THEOLOGY, 122–28 (1985).

16. *See* Rahman, *supra* note 14, at 53–59; Vesey-Fitzgerald, *Nature and Sources of the Shari'a*, in LAW IN THE MIDDLE EAST 93 (Khadduri & Liebesny eds. 1955).

17. For explanations of this long and complicated process, see generally J. SCHACHT, AN INTRODUCTION TO ISLAMIC LAW 28–68 (1964); N. COULSON, A HISTORY OF ISLAMIC LAW 9–74 (1964).

18. *See* RAHMAN, *supra* note 14, at 101–09.

19. *See* A. HASAN, THE EARLY DEVELOPMENT OF ISLAMIC JURISPRUDENCE 20–21 (1970).

system until well into the third century of Islam. The jurists who founded the main schools of Islamic jurisprudence that are followed by the vast majority of modern Muslims did their founding work between the middle of the eighth century and the middle of the ninth century, one to two hundred years after the Prophet's death.[20] In fact, the techniques and methods for the derivation of general principles and specific rules of Shari'a, such as *ijma* (consensus) and *qiyas* (analogy), were not settled until the time of Shafi'i who died in 819.[21]

Shari'a is not a formally enacted legal code. It consists of a vast body of jurisprudence in which individual jurists express their views on the meaning of the Qur'an and Sunna and the legal implications of those views. Although most Muslims believe Shari'a to be a single logical whole, there is significant diversity of opinion not only among the various schools of thought, but also among the different jurists of a particular school.[22] The original founding jurists themselves were not attempting during the second and third centuries of Islam to establish permanent opinions of general application.

Furthermore, Muslim jurists were primarily concerned with the formulation of principles of Shari'a in terms of moral duties sanctioned by religious consequences rather than with legal obligations and rights and specific temporal remedies.[23] They categorized all fields of human activity as permissible or impermissible and recommended or reprehensible.[24] In other words, Shari'a addresses the conscience of the individual Muslim, whether in a private, or public and official, capacity, and not the institutions and corporate entities of society and the state.[25] Each Muslim is in theory entitled to follow whatever view

---

20. These were, for Sunni Muslims, Abu Hanifa, d. 767; Malik, d. 795; Shafi'i, d. 819; and Ibn Hanbal, d. 855. The majority of Shi'a Muslims follow the school attributed to Ja'far Al-Sadiq, d. 765.

21. For a detailed discussion and substantiation of this conclusion, see TOWARD AN ISLAMIC REFORMATION, *supra* note 11, at 14–27.

22. *See* N. COULSON, *supra* note 17, at 47–51; K. FARUKI, *supra* note 1, at 166–94 (1975).

23. *See* N. COULSON *supra* note 17, at 82–83.

24. *See id.* at 83–84; A. HASAN, *supra* note 19, at 34–39.

25. It is true that Muslims are required to constitute an Islamic society, *Umma*, and enforce the positive law aspects of Shari'a that entail the establishment of what might be called in modern terminology the executive and judicial organs of an Islamic state. But the relevant provisions of Shari'a are inherently matters of individual conscience. For example, the selection of the chief executive, caliph, is supposed to be based on subjective individual evaluation of his piety and religious knowledge as expressed through a religious oath of allegiance, *by'a*. Appointment to judicial office by the caliph or his representatives is also supposed to be based on similar subjective evaluation of piety and religious knowledge. Given its historical context, it is not surprising that Shari'a did not provide for an "institutionalized" executive and an independent judiciary. Such institutions may be developed today on the basis of some historical sources and practices, but they did not exist in Shari'a.

For detailed discussion of these issues and citation of sources, see TOWARD AN ISLAMIC REFORMATION, *supra* note 11, at 75–100.

is acceptable to his or her private conscience.[26] As a general rule, Muslims to the present day tend to identify themselves as observers of one or another of the established schools of thought.[27] One is entitled to choose not only from among the various views available within his or her school of thought, but also from those views available within other schools. In accordance with this principle, modern official legal reforms in the Muslim world have employed a technique known as *talfiq*: constructing a composite general principle or specific rule from a variety of sources regardless of whether they belong to the same school of thought.[28]

Shari'a, as a religious and moral body of principles and directives, has had and continues to have a significant impact on the thinking and behavior of Muslims. It forms an integral part of the socialization of every Muslim child and is one of the primary forces behind the institutions and customs of the vast majority of Muslim societies.

Whatever may have been the historical status of Shari'a as the legal system of Muslim countries, the scope of its application in the public domain has diminished significantly since the middle of the nineteenth century. Due to both internal factors and external influence, Shari'a principles had been replaced by European law governing commercial, criminal, and constitutional matters in almost all Muslim countries. Only family law and inheritance continued to be governed by Shari'a.[29] Even countries such as Saudi Arabia which claim always to have maintained Shari'a as their sole legal system have enacted numerous "regulations" based on European law and practice in the commercial and public administration fields.[30]

Recently, many Muslims have challenged the gradual weakening of Shari'a as the basis for their formal legal systems. Most Muslim countries have experienced mounting demands for the immediate application of Shari'a as the sole, or at least primary, legal system of the land. These movements have either succeeded in gaining complete control, as in Iran, or achieved significant success in having aspects of Shari'a introduced into the legal system, as in Pakistan and the Sudan. Governments of Muslim countries generally find it difficult to resist these demands out of fear of being condemned by their own populations as anti-Islamic. Therefore, it is likely that this so-called Islamic

26. *See* J. SCHACHT, *supra* note 17, at 68 n.1.

27. Most Sunni Muslims identify with the Hanafi, Maliki, Shafi'i, or Hanbali schools while the majority of Shi'a Muslims follow the Ja'fari school of thought.

28. *See* J. SCHACHT, *supra* note 17, at 106; N. COULSON, *supra* note 17, at 197–201.

29. *See generally* H. LIEBESNY, THE LAW OF THE NEAR AND MIDDLE EAST 46–76, 77–117, 118–25 (1975).

30. *See* Seaman, *Islamic Law and Modern Government: Saudi Arabia Supplements the Shari'a to Regulate Development*, 18 COLUM. J. TRANSNAT'L L. 413 (1980).

fundamentalism will achieve further successes in other Muslim countries.[31]

The possibility of further Islamization may convince more people of the urgency of understanding and discussing the relationship between Shari'a and human rights, because Shari'a would have a direct impact on a wider range of human rights issues if it became the formal legal system of any country.[32] To my mind, however, this need is urgent regardless of the official status of Shari'a. As a Muslim, I appreciate the extralegal power that Shari'a has on the minds and hearts of Muslims. Given this power, it is difficult to see how Muslim governments can honor their obligations to promote and protect human rights, even if they wish to do so, where those obligations are perceived to be contrary to Shari'a.

The above survey of the development and nature of Shari'a clearly indicates that Shari'a, as a unified body of moral and legal principles derived from both the Qur'an and Sunna, reflects specific historical interpretations of the scriptural imperatives of Islam. Other interpretations are possible and were in fact anticipated by the founding jurists of Shari'a themselves. Although modern Muslim reformers have expressed some support for this proposition, usually in more moderate terms, very little has been done to develop an adequate reform technique.[33] I believe that a modern version of Islamic law can and should be developed. Such a modern "Shari'a" could be, in my view, entirely consistent with current standards of human rights. These views, however, are appreciated by only a tiny minority of contemporary Muslims. To the overwhelming majority of Muslims today, Shari'a is the sole valid interpretation of Islam, and as such *ought* to prevail over any human law or policy.

---

31. *See generally* 10 THIRD WORLD QUARTERLY (1988) (a special issue on Islam and politics); Haddad, *Muslim Revivalist Thought in the Arab World: An Overview* 76 MUSLIM WORLD 143 - 66 (1986). *See also* sources cited *infra* note 53.

Some authors object to the use of the term "fundamentalism" in relation to the Muslim world. *See, e.g.*, Munson, Jr., *The Social Base of Islamic Militancy in Morocco*, 40 MIDDLE E. J. 267 (1986). Others find the term appropriate. Dessouki, for example, adopts the term "fundamentalism" to refer to "the affirmation, in radically changed environment, of traditional modes of understanding and behavior". Dessouki, *The Resurgence of Islamic Organizations in Egypt: An Interpretation*, in ISLAM AND POWER 107, 108 (Cudsi & Dessouki eds. 1981).

Whether one adopts the term "fundamentalism" or the term "Islamic activism" used in this study, the important thing is to be clear on the nature and context of the phenomenon under discussion. What are the world view and objectives of Islamic fundamentalists/activists? What are the likely consequences for Muslim countries? In particular, what is the probable impact on human rights? To the extent that the activists' objectives reflect a desire to expand and consolidate certain aspects of existing social realities, how do those realities affect human rights today?

32. This relationship has already been noted and discussed. *See, e.g.*, Note, *Human Rights Practices in the Arab States: The Modern Impact of Shari'a Values* 12 GA. J. INT'L & COMP. L. 55 (1982).

33. For a survey and critique of modern Islamic reforms, see TOWARD AN ISLAMIC REFORMATION, *supra* note 11, at 35–51.

B. Shari'a and Human Rights

In this part, I illustrate with specific examples how Shari'a conflicts with international human rights standards. Specifically, I will focus on discrimination against women and non-Muslims. Some contemporary Muslim authors have claimed that Shari'a is fully consistent with and has always protected human rights. Ali A. Wafi, for example, contends that "the most important human rights" can be classified into five principal rights relating to five kinds of liberty: "religious liberty; liberty of opinion and expression; liberty of work; liberty of instruction and culture; and civil liberty."[34] Wafi cites general Islamic sources in support of each liberty and concludes that "Islam" provided for that particular liberty.[35] I find this approach to be both simplistic and misleading. It is simplistic in its classification of human rights and failure to consider conceptual and structural aspects of the modern human rights movement. According to Wafi, civil liberty is the right to conclude contracts, shoulder civil obligations and to dispose freely of property.[36] This is hardly an adequate description of civil liberty as a human right even in the most formal and minimal sense. Wafi's approach is also misleading because it is highly selective and fails to mention other Islamic sources which contradict his contentions in relation to each of the five liberties. He fails to mention the ways in which jurists of Shari'a interpreted these sources and the manner in which Muslim states applied those interpretations through the ages.

The claim that Shari'a is fully consistent with and has always protected human rights is problematic both as a theoretical and a practical matter. As a theoretical matter, the concept of human rights as rights to which every human being is entitled by virtue of being human was unknown to Islamic jurisprudence or social philosophy until the last few decades and does not exist in Shari'a. Many rights are given under Shari'a in accordance with a strict classification based on faith and gender and are not given to human beings as such. As a practical matter, fundamental inconsistencies exist between Shari'a as practiced in Muslim countries and current standards of human rights. For example, many aspects of Shari'a discriminate against women and violate their fundamental human rights. I will discuss this further in Part IV. Three other specific examples of human rights violations can be cited here to illustrate the point.

Although slavery was formally abolished in all Muslim countries through secular law, the institution itself remains lawful under Shari'a

34. Wafi, *Human Rights in Islam*, 11 ISLAMIC Q. 64 (1967).
35. *See id.*
36. *See id.* at 69.

to the present day.[37] It is true that Islam originally discouraged slavery by restricting the "legitimate" sources of slaves and encouraging their emancipation, but it did not directly prohibit slavery and the institution of slavery has never been abolished under Shari'a. In fact, treatises on Shari'a discuss at length contractual and other arrangements relating to slaves.[38] In my view, the original intention of Islam was to eliminate slavery in due course, but that intention has never been realized through Shari'a.[39]

The second example is the Shari'a law of apostasy. According to Shari'a, a Muslim who repudiates his faith in Islam, whether directly or indirectly, is guilty of a capital offense punishable by death.[40] This aspect of Shari'a is in complete conflict with the fundamental human right of freedom of religion and conscience. The apostasy of a Muslim may be inferred by the court from the person's views or actions deemed by the court to contravene the basic tenets of Islam and therefore be tantamount to apostasy, regardless of the accused's personal belief that he or she is a Muslim.

The Shari'a law of apostasy can be used to restrict other human rights such as freedom of expression. A person may be liable to the death penalty for expressing views held by the authorities to contravene the official view of the tenets of Islam. Far from being an historical practice or a purely theoretical danger, this interpretation of the law of apostasy was applied in the Sudan as recently as 1985, when a Sudanese Muslim reformer was executed because the authorities deemed his views to be contrary to Islam.[41]

---

37. *See* S. TABANDEH, MUSLIM COMMENTARY ON THE UNIVERSAL DECLARATION OF HUMAN RIGHTS 27 (1970).

38. *See* N. COULSON, *supra* note 17, at 32–33, 44–46, 50; J. SCHACHT, *supra* note 17, at 127–30, 162, 166, 170, 174, 177–78, 186–87, 193.

39. *See* TOWARD AN ISLAMIC REFORMATION, *supra* note 11, at 172–75.

40. *See* M. EL-AWA, PUNISHMENT IN ISLAMIC LAW: A COMPARATIVE STUDY 43 (1982).

41. *See* An-Na'im, *The Islamic Law of Apostasy and its Modern Applicability: A Case from the Sudan*, 16 RELIGION 197 (1986).

The Salman Rushdie affair illustrates the serious negative implications of the law of apostasy to literary and artistic expression. Mr. Rushdie, a British national of Muslim background, published a novel entitled, *The Satanic Verses*, in which irreverent reference is made to the Prophet of Islam, his wives, and leading companions. Many Muslim governments banned the book because their populations found the author's style and connotations extremely offensive. The late Imam Khomeini of Iran sentenced Rushdie to death *in absentia* without charge or trial.

There are obvious procedural objections to that sentence from a Shari'a point of view, namely, that Mr. Rushdie was not subject to the jurisdiction of Iran and was not formally charged and allowed to defend himself. But beyond this formal objection remains the basic fundamental objection to the law of apostasy itself as a violation of freedoms of belief and expression. If Shari'a procedural requirements can be satisfied, an author can be sentenced to death under Shari'a for his views.

For a fuller discussion of this case and its implications, see TOWARD AN ISLAMIC REFORMATION, *supra* note 11, at 182–84.

A third and final example of conflict between Shari'a and human rights relates to the status and rights of non-Muslims. Shari'a classifies the subjects of an Islamic state in terms of their religious beliefs: Muslims, *ahl al-Kitab* or believers in a divinely revealed scripture (mainly Christian and Jews), and unbelievers.[42] In modern terms, Muslims are the only full citizens of an Islamic state, enjoying all the rights and freedoms granted by Shari'a and subject only to the limitations and restrictions imposed on women. *Ahl al-Kitab* are entitled to the status of *dhimma*, a special compact with the Muslim state which guarantees them security of persons and property and a degree of communal autonomy to practice their own religion and conduct their private affairs in accordance with their customs and laws. In exchange for these limited rights, *dhimmis* undertake to pay *jizya* or poll tax and submit to Muslim sovereignty and authority in all public affairs.[43] Unbelievers may be granted *aman* or safe conduct which secures their persons and property for the duration of the *aman* period.[44] Moreover, unbelievers that are permanent residents of an Islamic state may be recognized as *dhimmis*.

According to this scheme, non-Muslim subjects of an Islamic state can aspire only to the status of *dhimma*, under which they would suffer serious violations of their human rights. *Dhimmis* are not entitled to equality with Muslims. Their lives are evaluated as inferior in monetary terms as well: they are not entitled to the same amount of *diya* or financial compensation for homicide or bodily harm as Muslims.[45] The reputation of a *dhimmi* is not protected by Shari'a on equal terms with that of a Muslim since the *hadd* of *qadhf*, the special criminal penalty for an unproven accusation of fornication, does not apply unless the victim is a Muslim.[46] In the private law of Shari'a, discrimination against non-Muslims includes the rule that a Muslim man may marry a *dhimmi* woman but a *dhimmi* man may not marry a Muslim woman.[47]

Some of these restrictions against non-Muslims have not been enforced in most Muslim countries for some time, but they all remain

42. "Unbelievers," as defined by Shari'a, are those who do not believe in one of the recognized heavenly revelations. Originally, this category was taken to include all non-Muslims except Christians, Sabi'is, and Jews, but some jurists have argued that adherents of other religions such as Zoroastrians and Hindus should be included on the assumption that they have revealed scriptures. *See* SHORTER ENCYCLOPAEDIA OF ISLAM 16–17 (Gibb & Kramers eds. 1974); A. YUSUF, KITAB AL-KHARAJ 128–30 (1302 Hijri) (Arabic). Animists would not qualify as believers regardless of their own view of their belief in God.

43. *See* verse 9:29 of the HOLY QUR'AN. *See also* M. AL-SHAFI'I, 4 KITAB AL-UMM 172 *passim* (1961) (Arabic); M. KHADDURI, WAR AND PEACE IN THE LAW OF ISLAM 177, 195–99 (1955).

44. *See* M. KHADDURI, *supra* note 43, at 166–69.

45. See AL-SHAFI'I, 6 KITAB AL-UMM 105–6 (1961) (Arabic).

46. See I. RUSHD, 2 BIDAYAT AL-MUJTAHID WA NIHAYAT AL-MUQTASID 330 (Arabic); Safwat, *Offences and Penalties in Islamic Law*, 26 ISLAMIC Q. 149, 159 (1982).

47. *See* AL-SHAFI'I, 5 KITAB AL-UMM 6–9, 44, 50. (Arabic).

part of Shari'a, and consequent violations of the human rights of non-Muslims recently have occurred in some modern Muslim countries.[48] Not only are these human rights violations committed against those who identify themselves as non-Muslims, such as the Copts of Egypt,[49] but they are also committed against minority Muslim sects which are deemed by the majority to be apostates from Islam, such as the Ahmadis of Pakistan.[50] Members of these minorities are not only persecuted by governments, but are also frequently attacked and murdered by mobs unfettered by legal restrictions.[51]

The broader implications of the law of apostasy are also relevant to understanding the status and rights of other minority sects, such as the Shi'a of Pakistan and Saudi Arabia, who do not conform to orthodox Sunni beliefs dominant in those countries. Serious human rights violations are committed against these minorities by official and private actors.[52]

III. THE POLITICS AND SOCIOLOGY OF ISLAMIZATION

To appreciate the likely impact of Shari'a on human rights it is important to understand not only its historical formulations, but also the socio-political context of what has often been called the process of Islamization in various Muslim countries. Although there appears to be an obvious development toward greater Islamization in many Muslim countries, it is a process of fits and starts, backward and forward movements, reflecting general trends and the peculiar experience of

48. See, for example, the evaluation of Sudan's application of Shari'a since 1983 in TOWARD AN ISLAMIC REFORMATION, *supra* note 11, at 125–33.

49. *See generally* An-Na'im, *Religious Freedom in Egypt: Under the Shadow of the Dhimma System*, in RELIGIOUS LIBERTY AND HUMAN RIGHTS IN NATIONS AND RELIGIONS 43 (L. Swidler ed. 1986).

50. In Pakistan, the government of Z. Bhutto yielded to pressures to declare the Ahmadis a non-Muslim minority and as such exclude them from important official positions. J. ESPOSITO, ISLAM AND POLITICS 163 (rev. ed. 1987).

The Baha'is claim to be adherents of an independent religion and specifically state that they are not a sect of Islam. Iranian authorities reject this claim, because Islam does not accept the possibility of revelation after the Qur'an. The Baha'i faith cannot therefore qualify as an independent religion according to Shari'a. The Baha'is of Iran have been subjected to severe persecution since the founding of their faith during the nineteenth century. *See generally* G. NASH, IRAN'S SECRET POGROM (1982); D. MARTIN, THE PERSECUTION OF THE BAHA'IS OF IRAN, 1844-1984 (1984).

51. Government officials often instigate violence against members of these groups. Former President Zia ul-Haq of Pakistan, for example, said that "Ahmadis will not be tolerated. There is no place for infidels in Pakistan. If a man's honor is attacked he does not even hesitate from committing murder." Parker, *Pakistani sect's death sentence*, San Francisco Examiner, May 25, 1986, at A14 col. 4.

52. *See, e.g.*, Ziring, *From Islamic Republic to Islamic State in Pakistan*, 24 ASIAN SURV. 931 (1984); Ahmed, *The Shi'is of Pakistan*, in SHI'ISM, RESISTANCE AND REVOLUTION 275 (M. Kramer ed. 1987); Goldberg, *The Shi'i Minority in Saudi Arabia*, in SHI'ISM AND SOCIAL PROTEST 230 (Cole & Keddie eds. 1986).

each society.[53] Consequently, Shari'a-inspired impact on human rights varies significantly from Islamic nation to nation.[54] Governments facing mounting pressure to implement Islamic laws and policies, however, have tended to enunciate policies that have a differential impact upon the weaker segments of society. These governments adopt policies which restrict the rights of women and minorities, who have minimal influence and voice in society, rather than taking measures that challenge the status quo or effect vested interests.[55]

A. *Political Context and Developments*

The complexity of the politics of Islamization is illustrated by the recent history of almost any Muslim country. The dynamics of domestic politics and personalities, together with regional and international geopolitical factors, often render the whole process seemingly unpredictable and paradoxical. For example, the supposedly secular socialist regime of Zulfikar Ali Bhutto was the first to substantially advance the cause of Islamization in Pakistan's history. On the other hand, General Suharto in Indonesia, who came to power to counter a communist coup d'etat in 1965, has proven to be most resistant to Islamization in that country. Yet each situation has its own internal logic.

Bhutto was attempting to respond to a crisis in national identity caused by the secession of Bangladesh, to seek Muslim Arab financial support, and to dispel domestic charges of being un-Islamic.[56] This led him to implement policies that had drastic long-term human rights consequences, such as the persecution of the Ahmadi minority. Ironically his efforts to appease Islamic activists failed and opposition to his regime from Islamic groups eventually contributed to Zia ul-Haq's coup of July 1977. According to one author, Bhutto's introduction of Islamic measures and promise of more Shari'a law, rather than defusing the Islamic revival movement "served to reinforce the Islamic character

---

53. The literature on this subject is extensive. *See generally* D. PIPES, IN THE PATH OF GOD: THE POLITICS OF ISLAMIC REASSERTION (M. Ayoob ed. 1981); RELIGION AND POLITICS IN THE MIDDLE EAST (M. Curtis ed. 1981); ISLAM IN THE POLITICAL PROCESS (J. Piscatori ed. 1983); VOICES OF RESURGENT ISLAM (J. Esposito ed. 1983); J. ESPOSITO, *supra* note 50.

54. This does not mean that a greater role for Islam in public life will necessarily lead to more violations of human rights. In fact, it may well be the case that resistance to such demands leads to more human rights violations where the government is willing and able to oppress Islamic activists.

55. The regime of General Zia ul-Haq in Pakistan, for example, was unwilling to heed demands by Islamic activists to lift martial law or conduct national elections, but was prepared to introduce a range of Islamic measures, including restrictions on women's rights. *See* J. ESPOSITO, *supra* note 50, at 167–70, 175; Faruki, *Pakistan: Islamic Government and Society*, in ISLAM IN ASIA 68–70 (J. Esposito ed. 1987).

56. *See* Richter, *The Political Dynamics of Islamic Resurgence in Pakistan*, 19 ASIA SURV. 547–57 (1979); Faruki, *supra* note 55, at 57–58.

of the conflict. Most importantly, a turning point had been reached. Islam and Pakistan's Islamic identity had re-emerged as the dominant theme in Pakistani politics in a manner and to a degree that had not been seen since Pakistan's establishment."[57]

Islam's dominance of Pakistani political discourse has been reinforced by more than ten years of Zia ul-Haq's rule. This dominance probably will continue unabated despite the return of democratic government and the election of Ali Bhutto's daughter, Benazir Bhutto, as Prime Minister. The paradox, however, continues: despite previously implemented Islamization measures, which included the drive to exclude women from public office in accordance with Shari'a provisions, a woman was elected as Prime Minister of Pakistan.

In contrast to Pakistan, Indonesia presents a different picture of Islamization. One author has suggested that the restriction of Islam under the New Order of General Suharto

> reflects, on the one hand, the proclivities of state leaders influenced by both technocratic and pre-Islamic ideas and fearful of any institutions they do not control. It also, however, continues the experience of Indonesian Islam over a far longer time . . . . The ambiguity of Islam's political strength and role has been mirrored in the ambivalence of Indonesia's rulers towards it; by and large, while trying to use it as a source of legitimacy, they have held it at arm's length.[58]

While Islam currently plays a fairly minimal part in Indonesian politics, the situation is far from static. The present regime's policies on the role of Islam in Indonesian politics may change in the near future. Islamic activists may either achieve some moderate success with the present government by modifying their strategies or perhaps they will contribute to the regime's overthrow.[59]

The impact of the international Islamic dimension affects in different ways the internal politics of Islamization in Indonesia and other parts of south and southeast Asia.[60] While international Islam tends to affect the situation in Pakistan and Bangladesh by influencing government policies, it offers support for the Islamic opposition to

---

57. J. ESPOSITO, *supra* note 50, at 166.

58. McVey, *Faith as the Outsider: Islam in Indonesian Politics*, in ISLAM IN THE POLITICAL PROCESS 199, 201 (J. Piscatori ed. 1983).

59. *See* Liong, *Indonesian Muslims and the State: Accommodation or Revolt*, 10 THIRD WORLD Q. 869 (1988); McVey, *supra* note 58, at 212–21.

60. *See* Gunn, *Radical Islam in Southeast Asia: Rhetoric and Reality in the Middle Eastern Connection*, 16 J. CONTEMP. ASIA 30 (1986).

the government in Indonesia.[61] For example, the Iranian Revolution has had more than a purely inspirational impact on the politics of Islamization in Indonesia.[62]

Currently, the politics of Islamization in Indonesia are apparently producing human rights violations from official as well as private sources. The situation in Indonesia is a paradigmatic example of the demand for greater Islamization leading to gross violations of the human rights of Muslim activists at the hands of official authorities.[63] In the private arena as well, Islamic politics appear to be associated with some of the sectarian violence in Indonesia giving rise to many human rights violations.[64]

Other Muslim countries present their own surprising developments and peculiar politics of Islamization. In Iran, Muslim activists achieved their most spectacular success this century when one of the most secularized countries in the Muslim world was transformed into a totalitarian Islamic state in 1979. The stages and personalities of that "unexpected" development are well known and need not be described here.[65]

The Kingdom of Saudi Arabia may appear to most outsiders as the embodiment of Islam itself. In fact, the Saudi dynasty endeavors to cultivate this image and to manipulate Islam as the primary source of its legitimacy.[66] But, as dramatically evidenced by the seizure of the Great Mosque of Mecca in 1979, and by repeated Shi'a riots in eastern

---

61. *See* von der Mehden, *The Political and Social Challenge of the Islamic Revival in Malaysia and Indonesia*, 76 MUSLIM WORLD 219, 225, 231 (1986).

62. *See* Gunn, *supra* note 60, at 45–46.

63. *See id.* at 43–44. Of course, Islamic activists are not the only ones having to bear the brunt of the Indonesian government policies. The persecution of communists and other political activists of the 1960s is a continuing source of human rights violations in Indonesia. *See* Budiardjo, *The Abuse of Human Rights in Indonesia*, III CASE STUDIES ON HUMAN RIGHTS AND FUNDAMENTAL FREEDOMS: A WORLD SURVEY 211 (1976); AMNESTY INTERNATIONAL, INDONESIA: AN AMNESTY INTERNATIONAL REPORT 1 *passim* (AI PUB 77/00/77 1977) "Tens of thousands of political prisoners in Indonesia are held captive without trial, or used as servants by local military commanders, or exploited as forced labour, or subjected to an archaic policy of transportation to penal colonies." *Id.* at 9; *Indonesia in the 1980's*, 16 ASIAN AFFAIRS 125 (1985). Events in East Timor, which has been occupied by Indonesian troops since 1975, present another gruesome chapter of human rights violations unrelated to the politics of Islamization in that part of the world. *See generally* ASIA WATCH, HUMAN RIGHTS IN INDONESIA AND EAST TIMOR (1989).

64. McVey, *supra* note 58, at 202–3. Neither of the above-mentioned sources of human rights violations, however, are peculiar to Indonesia. Syria presents an example of an official source while recent events in Northern Nigeria illustrate the operation of a private source of human rights violations.

65. Literature on the subject is extensive. *See, e.g.*, R. RAMAZANI, REVOLUTIONARY IRAN: CHALLENGE AND RESPONSE IN THE MIDDLE EAST (1986); THE IRANIAN REVOLUTION AND THE ISLAMIC REPUBLIC (Keddie & Hooglund eds. 1986); A. HUSSAIN, ISLAMIC IRANI REVOLUTION AND COUNTER-REVOLUTION (1985); S. IRFANI, REVOLUTIONARY ISLAM IN IRAN (1983).

66. J. Piscatori, *Ideological Politics in Sa'udi Arabia*, in ISLAM IN THE POLITICAL PROCESS 57–63 (J. Piscatori ed. 1983).

Saudi Arabia, Islam can also provide a significant source of challenge to the Saudi regime.[67]

As a result of rapid modernization in Muslim countries, a new technocratic middle class has emerged, which has, somewhat surprisingly, espoused Islamic fundamentalist positions rather than an enlightened Islamic interpretation or a secular ideology. It may appear paradoxical to speak of "modernized" segments of society adopting a fundamentalist posture; however, as indicated by studies in countries such as Egypt[68] and Morocco,[69] young, educated, urbanized Muslims often opt for Islamic fundamentalism. Moreover, the victimization of significant numbers of the population as a result of rapid modernization likely will cause the Saudi regime to confront challenges from both the left and right—"the secular radicals and the religious conservatives."[70] The dilemma facing the Saudi regime—which would trouble any ruling elite attempting to balance the push and pull of such conflicting forces—is that whatever measures it takes to satisfy one source of dissent will necessarily antagonize the other.

Accomodation may be particularly difficult for the Saudi regime given their Islamic ideology, namely the Hanbali school of Islamic jurisprudence as interpreted by Muhammad ibn Abd al-Wahab in the eighteenth century.[71] Western scholars differ in their evaluation of the central feature of Saudi ideology. Whereas most scholars perceive the Hanbali school as strict and rigid, others argue that it has proven to be particularly flexible, at least in Saudi hands. In espousing the latter view, Piscatori has argued that the former "misinterprets Hanbali conservatism: there must be faithful adherence to the Qur'an and the *hadiths* (the traditions of the Prophet), but when these have nothing to say on a subject, there are no rigid guidelines."[72]

I tend to agree with the first evaluation and disagree with that of Piscatori. The Hanbali school is generally the most strict of all Sunni schools in its interpretations of the Qur'an and Sunna, and the least likely to accept that these sources have nothing to say on a subject. The Hanbali school is therefore more likely to hold that the sources of Islam are explicit on a given subject—and more likely to adopt the stricter interpretation of these sources—than any of the other three

67. *See id.* at 66–67.

68. *See, e.g.*, Ibrahim, *Anatomy of Egypt's Militant Islamic Groups: Methodological Note and Preliminary Findings*, 12 INT'L J. MIDDLE E. STUD. 438, 439–40 (1980); Altman, *Islamic Movements in Egypt*, 10 JERUSALEM Q. 87, 96, 100 (1979).

69. *See* Munson, *The Social Base of Islamic Militancy in Morocco*, 40 MIDDLE E. J. 267, 269, 276, 278 (1986).

70. Piscatori, *supra* note 66, at 68.

71. *See* SHORTER ENCYCLOPEDIA OF ISLAM, *supra* note 42, at 20–21; H. WAHBA, JAZIRAT AL-'ARAB FI AL-QARN AL-'ISHRYN 324–31 (1961) (Arabic).

72. Piscatori, *supra* note 66, at 62.

schools of Sunni jurisprudence. In political terms, the severity of the Hanbali school, especially under Wahabi interpretations, probably will increase the tension between conflicting forces in Saudi Arabia today, making it harder for the Saudi dynasty to maintain the necessary balance between the conservative and modernized segments of its population.

Despite apparent differences from the Saudi case, and between themselves, Egypt and Morocco are open to similar analyses. Both the republican regime of Egypt and the Moroccan monarchy are trying to maintain Islamic legitimacy of their rule while containing the fundamentalist threat posed by Islamic activists.[73] The Moroccan government initially favored the growth of Islamic activism for the same reason Sadat initially supported similar movements in Egypt, namely, to curb Marxist and leftist groups. Both governments eventually realized that Islamic activism could pose a greater threat to their regimes.[74] The difficult balance these regimes are attempting to maintain is having negative consequences for human rights in both countries.[75]

B. Sociological Considerations

In this part, I consider the role of sociological factors in this analysis, which are important not only for their influence on political developments and impact on the accessibility and efficacy of legal remedies, but also because they underlay private or nonofficial human rights violations. This section puts forward some observations about who makes up the class of Islamic activists, how these activists influence social attitudes and behavior, what social forces counter their influence,

---

73. On Egypt see, *e.g.*, Hanafi, *The Relevance of the Islamic Alternative in Egypt*, 4 ARAB STUD. Q. 54 (1982); Ajami, *In the Pharaoh's Shadow: Religion and Authority in Egypt*, in ISLAM IN THE POLITICAL PROCESS, *supra* note 53, at 12. In relation to the situation in Morocco, see Munson, *Islamic Revivalism in Morocco and Tunisia*, 76 MUSLIM WORLD 203 (1986).

74. *See* Munson *id.* at 205.

75. These problems are extensively documented by human rights monitoring organizations, such as Amnesty International, Human Rights Internet, Middle East Watch, and the Arab Human Rights Organization. *See, e.g,* AMNESTY INTERNATIONAL, EGYPTIAN GOVERNMENT MUST ACT URGENTLY TO END TORTURE (Bulletin, MDE 12/03/88, 1988) ("Many reports of torture had followed the arrest of thousands of political suspects after the attempted assassinations in May and August last year of the former Interior Ministers . . . . The alleged victims [of torture] were mostly supporters of Islamic groups."); AMNESTY INTERNATIONAL, ARREST OF CHRISTIANS IN EGYPT (Bulletin, MDE 12/02/86, 1986) ("Amnesty International is concerned by reports it has received of the arrest of four converts from Islam to Christianity in Cairo in January 1986. The organisation believes that the detainees may be prisoners of conscience, detained for practising the Christian religion."); *see also* AMNESTY INTERNATIONAL, URGENT ACTION, UA 313/85 (1985) (Amnesty received reports that 37 people were arrested in Morocco for exercising freedoms of association and expression, held incommunicado, and ill-treated in prison.); MIDDLE EAST RESEARCH AND INFORMATION PROJECT (MERIP), HUMAN RIGHTS IN THE MIDDLE EAST (No. 149, Nov.-Dec. 1987).

and what arguments and methods are available to those who would counter the activists.

In Morocco, the overwhelming majority of Islamic activists are university and high school students. The movement also appeals to other segments of the "new middle class," as well as to some members of the traditional strata of society.[76] Studies of other Muslim societies generally confirm a similar composition of such Islamic fundamentalist movements.[77] Furthermore, the numbers of students and other youths who passively support the goals of Islamic activists are far greater than the numbers who become actively involved.[78] For example, while fewer than fifteen percent of Moroccan university students surveyed in a 1976 study were actively involved in protests and demands for reform, thirty-two percent favored the reestablishment of Islamic law (Shari'a), and thirty-eight percent saw a sincere return to Islamic values as the sole way for Morrocans to free themselves.[79] Despite their numerical insignificance, students in most Muslim countries tend to be much more politically active than the peasantry which constitutes the majority of the population.[80]

Another characteristic of student Islamic activists is that most of them come from the poorest strata,[81] which constitutes the vast majority of the population. They can therefore be presumed to be representative of the majority view or at least expected to receive its support.

The basic message of Islamic activists—a genuine return to Islam and outrage at moral and political decay and economic injustice—is deeply rooted in the Islamic tradition. The current cycle of Islamic activism draws on the long-established belief in the universality and centrality of Islam in the lives of Muslims, as the essential basis and focus of their identity and loyalty.[82] As explained by Smith, throughout the modern period, almost every Islamic movement has been, in some way, a variation on the double theme of protest against internal

---

76. Munson, *supra* note 69, at 267, 269, 276, 278 (1986). By the "new middle class" Munson refers to people who are neither extremely poor nor extremely rich and who have had considerable exposure to Western culture, usually in basically secular public schools. *Id.* at 276.

77. *See, e.g.*, Ibrahim, *Anatomy of Egypt's Militant Islamic Groups: Methodological Note and Preliminary Findings*, 12 INT'L J. MIDDLE E. STUD. 438, at 439–40 (1980); Altman, *Islamic Movements in Egypt*, 10 JERUSALEM Q. 87, 96, 100 (1979).

78. *See* Munson, *supra* note 69, at 272–75.

79. *See* Munson, *supra* note 69, at 275 (reporting on a study for a doctoral thesis by Mohamed Tozy, *Champ et contre champ politico-religieux au Maroc* 248, 250–52. Université de Droit, d'Economie et de Sciences d'Aix-Marseille, 1984).

80. *See* Munson, *supra* note 69, at 271.

81. *See id.* at 275–76; Kupferschmidt, *Reformist and Militant Islam in Urban and Rural Egypt*, 23 MIDDLE E. STUD. 403 (1987).

82. *See* Lewis, *The Return to Islam*, in RELIGION AND POLITICS IN THE MIDDLE EAST, *supra* note 53, at 11.

deterioration and external encroachment.[83] Islamic activism can therefore be seen as a response to a protracted crisis of political, economic, and military dimensions, presenting Islam as "a practical political alternative as well as a secure spiritual niche and psychological anchor in a turbulent world."[84] Muslims are reminded of the Golden Age of the Islamic civilization, an age of political power, economic prosperity, and social justice as well as religious piety and spiritual well-being. Current political, economic, and social problems are attributed to a departure from Islam and the failure to implement Shari'a. The cure, obviously, is a return to Islam and the reestablishment of Shari'a.

In delivering this powerful message, Islamic activists enjoy two main advantages. First, they share with their audience a common belief, language, and history which enables them to draw on easily appreciated and highly effective symbols from the Islamic tradition. Second, they are delivering a message which their audience wants to accept, a single cause for all their problems and an apparently simple solution. Instead of looking for reasons or causes of Islamic activism, one should perhaps ask why it is not as successful as the power of its message and the nature of its methods would indicate.

One author has observed that the message of Islamic activists should be particularly appealing to the more traditional and less privileged strata of Muslim societies.[85] Yet, there is little evidence of widespread support for Islamic activists from these strata in Morocco and elsewhere in the Muslim world, notwithstanding the activism of Islamic students from these same strata.[86] Although many Islamic activists originate from among these less privileged sectors of society, they seem to have had little success in mobilizing the poor masses in support of their cause. The causes of this apparent lack of support can best be appreciated in the context of a particular society, but a few rather speculative general observations may be illustrative.

In the first place, the lack of evidence of support does not necessarily mean the support itself is lacking. The lack of evidence of popular support may be due to political factors, such as the suppression of freedom of expression or the lack of technological and other means of communication. There is usually little inclination and opportunity for conducting opinion polls in the Muslim world. Very few observers

---

83. *See* W. SMITH, ISLAM IN MODERN HISTORY 47 (1957).

84. Dekmejian, *The Anatomy of Islamic Revival: Legitimacy Crisis, Ethnic Conflict, and the Search for Islamic Alternatives*, in RELIGION AND POLITICS IN THE MIDDLE EAST, *supra* note 53, at 39. Many authors in the field offer similar analysis. *See, e.g.*, Dessouki, *supra* note 31, at 110–16; Esposito, *Introduction: Islam and Muslim Politics*, in VOICES OF RESURGENT ISLAM 11–13 (J. Esposito ed. 1983); Munson, *supra* note 69, at 215–18.

85. *See* Munson, *supra* note 69, at 279.

86. *See id.* at 279.

saw evidence of widespread support for Khomeini in 1979, yet Khomeini had enough support to overthrow a regime which was generally believed to be one of the most stable and durable in the Muslim World. As one author concluded in relation to Morocco, "it would be a mistake to assume that militant Islam will remain as politically impotent as it now appears to be."[87] I believe this conclusion is generally true of other Muslim countries as well.

Furthermore, the aspiration of Muslim peoples to establish an Islamic state has been dormant for so many centuries that it is no longer taken seriously as a realistic prospect by the lower, unsophisticated strata of society. Their hopes have been frustrated so many times and manipulated by their leaders for so long that ordinary Muslims have simply resigned themselves to postponing the idea indefinitely.

A related consideration is that the present rulers of the Muslim world are successful in claiming Islamic legitimacy. King Hassan II of Morocco, for example, is venerated by the majority of his subjects as a descendent of the Prophet and accepted as *Amir al-Mu'minin*, Commander of the Believers or the legitimate ruler of an Islamic state. In addition, the Saudi dynasty seems to have succeeded in cultivating the image of an Islamic state. Why should the people demand the establishment of an Islamic state, at considerable risk to their personal safety and well-being, if they are led to believe that they already have one?

My own hypothesis is that, despite their assumed or declared belief in the desirability of an Islamic state based on Shari'a, the majority of Muslims know instinctively that such a state is not really workable and may not be desirable in practice. I believe that it is this almost subconscious knowledge, more than colonialism and external influence, which caused the role of Shari'a in the public domain to diminish so drastically in modern times.

Nevertheless, I realize that Muslims find it extremely difficult to admit this fact even to themselves. So long as they are not forced to make an open decision on the matter, they will continue believing or pretending to believe in the myth of an Islamic state based on Shari'a. Consequently, they will probably remain passive to the demands of Islamic activists until they are forced to decide. Demographic, cultural, and other factors and forces may influence their decision. While these factors exist in all Muslim countries, the Indonesian case may provide better insights into the complexity and specificity of the issues.

The manner of the initial Islamization of Indonesia and the demographic composition of the country seem to be significant factors in the present status of Islamic activists there. It is generally accepted

87. *Id.* at 284.

that Islam was brought to that part of the world by Muslim merchants during the fourteenth and fifteenth centuries, or earlier.[88] Islam was consolidated on the main islands of Java and Sumatra and on other islands between the fifteenth and seventeenth centuries. Other developments followed which need not be detailed here. The point to emphasize is that the

> Muslim community in what is now Indonesia, then, is the heir to a variety of modalities by which Islam achieved a presence at particular points in Southeast Asia. In some, it remained simply a presence, in others, it disappeared and, in still others, it developed as the opportunities of time and place allowed.[89]

The interplay of local factors and external Dutch encroachment produced a complex mixture of Islamic and non-Islamic cultures in the region. For example, in Javanese society,

> [the term *santri*] denote the religiously observant orthodox Muslims as a group in society, in contradiction to the *abangan* (those who followed the old Javanese folk religion, intermingled with Islam) and the *priyayi* (the Javanese aristocrats and their descendants) who followed an Islam which had strong admixture of Hindu-Buddhist elements.[90]

Moreover, there are too many animist, regional, and ideological variations in perceptions of Islam to allow for unified or even vaguely allied action by Islamic activists.[91]

There has never been a real Muslim state in Indonesia in the sense experienced by Muslims in the Middle East, North Africa, and the Indian sub-continent.[92] This "has left a deep impact on Indonesian politics, particularly on the role of Muslim political as well as religious organizations."[93] The representatives of the Muslim community have consistently been assigned an outsider's role throughout Indonesian

88. Soebardi & Woodcroft-Lee, *Islam in Indonesia*, in THE CRESCENT IN THE EAST 180–82 (R. Israel ed. 1982).

89. Johns, *Modes of Islamization in Southeast Asia*, in RELIGIOUS CHANGE AND CULTURAL DOMINATION 61, 62 (1981).

90. Soebardi & Woodcraft-Lee, *supra* note 88, at 186. *See generally* C. GEERTZ, THE RELIGION OF JAVA (1960).

91. Johns, *Indonesia: Islam and Cultural Pluralism*, in ISLAM IN ASIA 202, 226 (J. Esposito ed. 1987).

92. Some states of the past, such as Acheh, could probably come close to full fledged Islamic states. *See* Johns, *supra* note 89, at 69.

93. Utrect, *Religion and Social Protest in Indonesia*, 25 SOC. COMPASS 395, 398 (1978).

history.[94] Therefore, ordinary Indonesian Muslims have difficulty relating to a total political Islamic experience or envisaging the application of Shari'a in the public domain, despite the intellectual efforts of elites to supplement this deficiency.

Another factor relevant to the status of Islamic activism in Indonesia today is the sheer distance between that country and the majority of Muslim countries. This inhibits communication between Indonesian and Middle Eastern Islamic activists and also reinforces the barriers of language and culture in general. Distance may not overly hamper elites in this age of jet travel and electronic communications, but it certainly diminishes the impact of religious and intellectual influences from the Middle East and North Africa on the majority of ordinary Indonesian Muslims.

Despite these factors, Islam does have a political role in Indonesia, although somewhat weak in comparison to its role in other Muslim countries. There is so much spiritual, intellectual, and organizational Islamic activism that some observers were led to suggest that Indonesia might be close to an Islamic revolution.[95] Paradoxically, although Islam was the banner of Indonesian nationalism during the struggle for independence, its political role declined after independence, especially during the last three decades.[96] The influence of Islam in that country is strongest, however, on human relations, especially in family law and inheritance.[97] The human rights implications of this aspect of Shari'a will be discussed later.[98]

The nature and rationale of factors and forces opposing the reestablishment of Shari'a are, in general, secular education and cross-cultural interaction. These forces have raised the consciousness and expectations of some segments of the population. Many women, for instance, have had the benefits of secular higher education and have travelled abroad or otherwise been exposed to external feminist influences. These women have also experienced some degree of equality and have had access to opportunities in public life through the somewhat secularized political regimes and legal systems of most Muslim countries. They have learned how to organize and lobby for their rights and how to establish networks with other women's rights groups. These women's organizations have engaged in some forms of resistance to Islamization

94. *See* Wertheim, *Islam in Indonesia: A House Divided*, in TEN YEARS' MILITARY TERROR IN INDONESIA 75 (M. Caldwell ed. 1975).

95. *See, e.g.*, G. JANSEN, MILITANT ISLAM (1979).

96. *See* Utrecht, *supra* note 93, at 408–11; Soebardi and Woodcroft-Lee, *supra* note 88, at 189–204; Johns, *supra* note 89, at 209–20. *See also* von der Mehden, *supra* note 61, at 222–25.

97. Utrecht, *supra* note 93, at 407.

98. *See infra* notes 102–38 and accompanying text.

in Pakistan and protested against measures which affected their status and rights during Zia ul-Haq's era.[99]

Although I appreciate the apprehensions of these groups about the strict application of Shari'a, I can see that they face a deep dilemma. Because what they are protesting is perceived by the Muslim populations of their countries to be the law of Islam, they can expect little sympathy and political support from those populations. These groups are therefore faced with a difficult choice: on the one hand, if they submit to the strict application of Shari'a they would be accepting the institutionalization of the violation of their human rights. Yet, resistance would lay them open to charges of being anti-Islamic, making it easy for the proponents of Islamization to mobilize public opinion against their cause. Moreover, to the extent that members of these vulnerable groups are Muslims themselves, they also face a strong psychological barrier against criticizing Shari'a, the embodiment and authoritative voice of their faith. Thus, the socio-political forces encouraging greater Islamization will exacerbate the difficulty of this dilemma faced by women in Muslim countries.

IV. A CASE STUDY: THE ISLAMIC DIMENSION OF THE STATUS OF WOMEN

Given the rising tide of Islamization in Muslim countries and its call for wider recognition of Shari'a as the primary legal basis of Muslim nations, concerns about Shari'a's conflict with human rights standards must be addressed. Such conflict and tension between historical formulations of Shari'a and modern standards of human rights is readily illustrated by the situation of women in Muslim countries today. The status and rights of women are a major human rights concern in all parts of the world: women are consistently oppressed, discriminated against, and denied their rightful equality with men. Although the situation has recently improved in some developed countries, I believe that it is by no means satisfactory anywhere in the world today. The present focus on Muslim violations of the human rights of women does not mean that these are peculiar to the Muslim world.[100] As a Muslim, however, I am particularly concerned with the

99. *See, e.g.*, 32 INT'L COMM'N OF JURISTS REV. 19, 19–21 (1984) (a brief survey on the activities of the Women's Action Forum).

100. It is difficult to distinguish between Islamic, or rather Shari'a, factors and extra-Shari'a factors affecting the status and rights of women. The fact that women's human rights are violated in all parts of the world suggests that there are universal social, economic, and political factors contributing to the persistence of this state of affairs. Nevertheless, the articulation and operation of these factors varies from one culture or context to the next. In particular, the rationalization of discrimination against and denial of equality for women is based on the values and customs of the particular society. In the Muslim world, these values and customs are supposed to be Islamic or at least consistent with the dictates of Islam. It is therefore useful to discuss the Islamic dimension of the status and rights of women.

situation in the Muslim world and wish to contribute to its improvement.

The following discussion is organized in terms of the status and rights of Muslim women in the private sphere, particularly within the family, and in public fora, in relation to access to work and participation in public affairs. This classification is recommended for the Muslim context because the personal law aspects of Shari'a, family law and inheritance, have been applied much more consistently than the public law doctrines.[101] The status and rights of women in private life have always been significantly influenced by Shari'a regardless of the extent of Islamization of the public debate.

A. *Shari'a and the Human Rights of Women*

This part begins with a brief survey of general principles and rules of Shari'a which are likely to have a negative impact on the status and rights of Muslim women.[102] This includes general principles which affect the socialization of both men and women and the orientation of society at large as well as legal rules in the formal sense. The most important general principle of Shari'a influencing the status and rights of women is the notion of *qawama*. *Qawama* has its origin in verse 4:34 of the Qur'an: "Men have *qawama* [guardianship and authority] over women because of the advantage they [men] have over them [women] and because they [men] spend their property in supporting them [women]."[103] According to Shari'a interpretations of this verse, men as a group are the guardians of and superior to women as a group, and the men of a particular family are the guardians of and superior to the women of that family.[104]

This notion of general and specific *qawama* has had far reaching consequences for the status and rights of women in both the private and public domains. For example, Shari'a provides that women are disqualified from holding general public office, which involves the exercise of authority over men, because, in keeping with the verse

---

101. The private/public dichotomy, however, is an artificial distinction. The two spheres of life overlap and interact. The socialization and treatment of both men and women at home affect their role in public life and vice versa. While this classification can be used for analysis in the Muslim context, its limitations should be noted. It is advisable to look for both the private and public dimensions of a given Shari'a principle or rule rather than assume that it has only private or public implications.

102. For a more detailed discussion of these issues, see generally An-Na'im, *The Rights of Women and International Law in the Muslim Context*, *supra* note 11.

103. Holy Qur'an 190–91 (A. Ali trans. & commentary).

104. I. Kathiyr, 1 Mukthasar Tafsiyr Ibn Kathiyr 385 (M. Al-Ṣabuniy ed. 1400 a.h.) (Arabic).

4:34 of the Qur'an, men are entitled to exercise authority over women and not the reverse.[105]

Another general principle of Shari'a that has broad implications for the status and rights of Muslim women is the notion of *al-hijab*, the veil. This means more than requiring women to cover their bodies and faces in public. According to Shari'a interpretations of verses 24:31,[106] 33:33,[107] 33:53,[108] and 33:59[109] of the Qur'an, women are supposed to stay at home and not leave it except when required to by urgent necessity.[110] When they are permitted to venture beyond the home, they must do so with their bodies and faces covered. *Al-hijab* tends to reinforce women's inability to hold public office and restricts their access to public life. They are not supposed to participate in public life, because they must not mix with men even in public places.

In addition to these general limitations on the rights of women under Shari'a, there are a number of specific rules in private and public law that discriminate against women and highlight women's general inferiority and inequality.[111] In family law for example, men have the right to marry up to four wives and the power to exercise complete control over them during marriage, to the extent of punishing them

---

105. A. Al-Qurtubi, 5 Al-Jami Li Ahkam Al-Qur'an 169 (n.d.) (Arabic).

106. And say to the believing women that they should lower their gaze and guard their modesty; that they should not display their beauty and ornaments except what (must ordinarily) appear thereof; that they should draw their veil over their bosoms and not display their beauty except to their husbands, their fathers, their sons, their husband's sons, their brothers or their brother's sons, or their sister's sons or their women, or the slaves whom their right hand possess, or male servants free of physical needs, or small children who have no sense of shame of sex, and that they should not strike their feet in order to draw attention to their hidden ornaments. And O ye Believers! turn ye all together toward God, that ye may attain Bliss.

Holy Qur'an, *supra* note 103, at 904–5.

107. [O Consorts of the Prophet . . .] And stay quietly in your houses, and make not a dazzling display, like that of the former Times of Ignorance; and establish regular prayer, and give regular charity; and obey God and His Apostle. And God only wishes to remove all abomination from you, ye Members of the Family, and to make you pure and spotless.

Id. at 1115–16.

108. [O ye who believe . . .] And when ye ask (his ladies) [the Prophet's wives] for anything ye want, ask them from before [behind] a screen: that makes for greater purity for your hearts and for theirs.

Id. at 1124–25.

109. O Prophet! Tell thy wives and daughters, and the believing women, that they should cast their outer garments over their persons (when abroad): that is most convenient, that they should be known (as such) and not molested. And God is Oft-Forgiving, Most Merciful.

Id. at 1125–26.

110. Although some of these verses refer to the wives of the Prophet, they were taken to apply to all Muslim women.

111. For a general comparison between Shari'a and current standards of human rights in relation to the status and rights of women, see Tabandeh, *supra* note 37, at 35–67.

for disobedience if the men deem that to be necessary.[112] In contrast, the co-wives are supposed to submit to their husband's will and endure his punishments. While a husband is entitled to divorce any of his wives at will, a wife is not entitled to a divorce, except by judicial order on very specific and limited grounds.[113] Another private law feature of discrimination is found in the law of inheritance, where the general rule is that women are entitled to half the share of men.[114]

In addition to their general inferiority under the principle of *qawama* and lack of access to public life as a consequence of the notion of *al-hijab*, women are subjected to further specific limitations in the public domain. For instance, in the administration of justice, Shari'a holds women to be incompetent witnesses in serious criminal cases, regardless of their individual character and knowledge of the facts. In civil cases where a woman's testimony is accepted, it takes two women to make a single witness.[115] *Diya*, monetary compensation to be paid to victims of violent crimes or to their surviving kin, is less for female victims than it is for male victims.[116]

The private and public aspects of Shari'a overlap and interact.[117] The general principles of *qawama* and *al-hijab* operate at the public as well as the private levels. Public law discrimination against women emphasizes their inferiority at home. The inferior status and rights of women in private law justify discrimination against them in public life. These overlapping and interacting principles and rules play an extremely significant role in the socialization of both women and men. Notions of women's inferiority are deeply embedded in the character and attitudes of both women and men from early childhood.[118]

This does not mean that the whole of Shari'a has had a negative impact on the status and rights of women. Relatively early on, Shari'a granted women certain rights of equality which were not achieved by women in other legal systems until recently. For example, from the very beginning, Shari'a guaranteed a woman's independent legal per-

112. Polygamy is based on verse 4:3 of the Qur'an. The husband's power to chastise his wife to the extent of beating her is based on verse 4:34 of the Qur'an. *See* HOLY QUR'AN, *supra* note 103, at 179, 190–91.

113. *See talak* in SHORTER ENCYCLOPEDIA OF ISLAM, *supra* note 42, at 564–67.

114. Verses 4:11 and 4:176 of the Qur'an. *See* HOLY QUR'AN, *supra* note 103, at 181, 235–36.

115. This is based on verse 2:282 of the Qur'an. *See* HOLY QUR'AN, *supra* note 103, at 113–14.

116. A. AUDA, AL-TASHRI AL-JANA'IY AL-ISLAMIY paras. 155, 214 (n.d.) (Arabic).

117. *See supra* note 101.

118. *See, e.g.*, Vieille, *Iranian Women in Family Alliance and Sexual Politics*, in WOMEN IN THE MUSLIM WORLD 451 (Beck & Keddie eds. 1978) [hereinafter WOMEN IN THE MUSLIM WORLD]. *But cf.* Dwyer, *Women, Sufism, and Decision-Making in Moroccan Islam*, *id.* at 585 (suggesting that in the social reality of Sufi, Islamic mystic, traditions, women may have a stronger role than envisaged by Shari'a).

sonality to own and dispose of property in her own right on equal footing with men, and secured for women certain minimum rights in family law and inheritance long before other legal systems recognized similar rights.[119]

These theoretical rights under Shari'a, however, may not be realized in practice. Other Shari'a rules may hamper or inhibit women from exercising these rights in some societies. According to one author, "while legally recognized as 'economic persons' to whom property is transmitted, Muslim women are constrained from acting out economic roles because of other legal, as well as ideological, components of Muslim female status."[120] Customary practice in certain rural Muslim communities in Iran and Indonesia denies women their rightful inheritance under Shari'a.[121] While the strict application of Shari'a would improve the status and rights of women in comparison to customary practice in these situations, the position of women under Shari'a would nevertheless fall short of the standards set by international human rights instruments.[122]

This is Shari'a doctrine as it is understood by the vast majority of Muslims today. Significant possibilities exist for reform, but to undertake such reforms effectively, we must be clear on what Shari'a *is* rather than what it can or ought to be. Some Muslim feminists emphasize the positive aspects of Shari'a while overlooking the negative aspects. Others restrict their analysis to the Qur'an, and select only verses favoring the status of women while overlooking other parts and failing to take into account the ways in which the parts they select have been interpreted by the Shari'a jurists.[123] Neither approach is satisfactory. Shari'a is a complex and integrated whole and must be

---

119. *See generally* Smith, *Islam*, in WOMEN IN WORLD RELIGIONS 235 (A. Sharama ed. 1987).

120. Pastner, *The Status of Women and Property on a Baluchistan Oasis in Pakistan*, in WOMEN IN THE MUSLIM WORLD, *supra* note 118, at 434. Another author has noted that the financial activities of Saudi women take place behind the scenes, and often through the intermediary of hired male assistants. Furthermore, these activities were curtailed due to pressure to observe Shari'a more strictly after the seizure of the Grand Mosque of Mecca in 1979. *See* Ramazani, *Arab Women in the Gulf*, 39 MIDDLE E. J. 258, 260–61 (1985).

121. *See* Friedle, *State Ideology and Village Women*, in WOMEN AND REVOLUTION IN IRAN 217, 220 (G. Nashat ed. 1983) [hereinafter WOMEN AND REVOLUTION IN IRAN]; Cederroth, *Islam and Adat: Some Recent Changes in the Social Position of Women Among Sasak in Lombok*, in WOMEN IN ISLAMIC SOCIETIES 160, 164–66 (B. Utas ed. 1983).

122. Although these customary practices are inconsistent with the letter of Shari'a, they are reinforced by general notions of Shari'a that signify the inferiority of women and their subjection to men under the principle of *qawama*. Reform of these aspects of Shari'a through the reinterpretation of Qur'an and Sunna may therefore contribute to the eradication of those customary practices. The reformulation of Shari'a can then be used in specific educational programs and social policies designed to combat discriminatory practices in these Muslim communities.

123. For an example of this approach, see Hassan, *On Human Rights and the Qur'anic Perspectives*, 19 J. ECUMENICAL STUD. 52 (1982).

perceived as such. The status and rights of Muslim women are affected by the negative as well as the positive aspects of Shari'a. In fact, its negative aspects may receive greater emphasis than its positive aspects in some Muslim societies today. Moreover, Shari'a jurists have developed specific jurisprudential techniques which control and limit the prospects of reform within the framework of Shari'a. As will be explained in the final section on Islamic reform and human rights, modernist Muslims may need to challenge and change those techniques before they can implement significant reforms.

B. *Muslim Women at Home*

The human rights of Muslim women have been directly and continuously affected within the family by Shari'a, because its relevant aspects have remained in force under the legal systems of the vast majority of Muslim countries. This control which Shari'a exercises over the private realm of home and family is so entrenched, and its violation of human rights so clear, that it may explain in part why some Muslim countries refuse to ratify the relevant human rights instruments or at least entered reservations on their obligations under certain human rights treaties. For example, Egypt is one of the very few Muslim countries to have ratified the Convention on the Elimination of All Forms of Discrimination Against Women of 1979.[124] It entered, however, a reservation to Article 16[125] of the Convention which provides for the equality of men and women in all matters relating to marriage and family relations during the marriage and upon its dissolution. The Egyptian reservation specifically stated that since these matters were governed by Shari'a, Egypt had to derogate from its obligations under the Convention.[126]

The Shari'a personal law enforced in Iran is not significantly different from that prevailing in Sunni countries like Egypt except for the additional affront to the human dignity of women and the serious violation of their human rights caused by the institution of *mut'a*, or temporary marriage, peculiar to Shi'a jurisprudence.[127] According to this type of marriage, a man is entitled to take as many "temporary wives" as he can afford in addition to his four "permanent wives." In contrast to regular marriage which is contracted theoretically for life, *mut'a* marriage is contracted for a specific period of time, in terms of

124. Convention on the Elimination of All Forms of Discrimination Against Women, Dec. 18, 1979, G.A. Res. 34/180, 34 U.N. GAOR Supp. (No. 46) at 193, U.N. Doc. A/34/46 (1979).

125. *Id.* art. 16.

126. For the text of this Egyptian reservation, see INTERNATIONAL HUMAN RIGHTS INSTRUMENTS, *supra* note 8, at 220.13.

127. *See* SHORTER ENCYCLOPEDIA OF ISLAM, *supra* note 42, at 418–20.

years, months, days, or perhaps even hours. In addition to the discrimination and humiliation this type of "marriage" causes to the unfortunate temporary "wife," it demeans all women and degrades the institution of marriage itself. Despite these and many other extremely serious social and human rights implications of this type of "marriage," it is still practiced in Iran today.[128]

Some Muslim countries have introduced limited reforms in the family law field. These appear to be more likely to survive traditionalist and fundamentalist backlash than the Iranian ones discussed above, because of their modest nature. The 1979 amendments to the personal law of Egypt "were carefully formulated to forestall any unnecessary confrontation with conservative religious elements."[129] These amendments maintained the husband's rights of unilateral divorce and polygamy while seeking to balance those rights by some procedural and financial guarantees for the wife.[130] In Pakistan, the Muslim Family Laws Ordinance of 1961[131] introduced some reforms. Among other measures, it instituted a network of Arbitration Councils to deal with divorce, polygamy, and maintenance of wives. Now, the written permission of the Arbitration Council is required before a married man can take another wife.

These reforms are only small steps toward redressing human rights objections to the status and rights of women under Shari'a, and yet they are criticized by traditionalist and fundamentalist groups as un-Islamic. The repeal of the Iranian reforms and the threat of revision of the Egyptian and Pakistani reforms suggest to one author the need to use legitimate Islamic methodology in rendering such reforms.[132] I agree with this recommendation and add that the reforms must also go far enough to guarantee the full human rights of women in family and inheritance law.

---

128. Nashat, *Women in the Ideology of the Islamic Republic*, in WOMEN AND REVOLUTION IN IRAN, *supra* note 121, at 205–6.

The previous regime of the Shah introduced a number of limited improvements in the status and rights of women in Iran through the Family Protection Law of 1967 (amended in 1975). For example, the legislation required the consent of the first wife before a husband could take a second wife, and placed restrictions on the husband's right of unilateral divorce. For a discussion of these and other improvements see Bagley, *The Iranian Family Protection Law: A Milestone in the Advance of Women's Rights*, in IRAN AND ISLAM 47, 47–64 (C. Bosworth ed. 1971).

These limited gains have now been lost with the repeal of the Family Protection Law and the return of strict Shari'a provisions. *See generally* Higgins, *Wpmen in the Islamic Republic of Iran: Legal, Social, and Ideological Changes*, 10 J. WOMEN IN CULTURE AND SOC'Y 477 (1985).

129. Hussein, *Recent Amendments to Egypt's Personal Status Law*, in WOMEN AND THE FAMILY IN THE MIDDLE EAST, 229 (E. Fernea ed. 1985) [hereinafter WOMEN AND THE FAMILY IN THE MIDDLE EAST].

130. *Id.* at 231–32.

131. PLD 1961, CS 209; CP Mar. 3, 161.

132. J. ESPOSITO, WOMEN IN MUSLIM FAMILY LAW 131 (1982).

C. Muslim Women in Public Life

A similar and perhaps more drastic conflict exists between reformist and conservative trends in relation to the status and rights of women in the public domain. Unlike personal law matters, where Shari'a was never displaced by secular law, in most Muslim countries, constitutional, criminal, and other public law matters have come to be based on secular, mainly Western, legal concepts and institutions. Consequently, the struggle over Islamization of public law has been concerned with the reestablishment of Shari'a where it has been absent for decades, or at least since the creation of the modern Muslim nation states in the first half of the twentieth century. In terms of women's rights, the struggle shall determine whether women can keep the degree of equality and rights in public life they have achieved under secular constitutions and laws.

In Pakistan, for example, the 1973 Constitution dealt with fundamental questions in relation to the role of Islam in constitutional and other public affairs.[133] However, such issues are rarely finally resolved by constitutional provisions. In fact, constitutional guarantees clearly did little to settle questions pertaining to the status and rights of women in Pakistan.

Article 25(2) of the 1973 Constitution prohibits discrimination based solely on gender.[134] Article 27(1) outlaws discrimination against qualified candidates for federal service solely on the basis of gender. Among the Principles of State Policy, Article 34 states that: "Steps shall be taken to ensure full participation of women in all spheres of national life."[135] The 1973 Constitution also provides for universal adult suffrage and reserves a certain number of seats for women in the National Assembly and regional assemblies in addition to their right to compete for non-reserved seats. Unfortunately these provisions have been contested and their practical value diminished in a variety of ways.[136]

The Council of Islamic Ideology was one of the institutional mechanisms that tended to diminish the value of constitutional protections for women's rights. According to Article 230(1)(c) of the 1973 Constitution, this Council is authorized to "make recommendations as to

133. For a brief survey of the debate at the time, see Rahman, *Islam and the New Constitution of Pakistan*, VIII J. ASIAN & AFR. STUD. 190 (1973).

134. For the text of the 1973 Constitution of Pakistan, see CONSTITUTIONS OF COUNTRIES OF THE WORLD: PAKISTAN (Blaustein & Flanz eds. 1986) [hereinafter CONSTITUTIONS OF COUNTRIES OF THE WORLD].

135. *Id.* art. 34.

136. *See generally* Carroll, *Nizam-I-Islam: Processes and Conflicts in Pakistan's Programme of Islamisation, with Special Reference to the Position of Women*, 20 J. COMMONWEALTH & COMP. POL. 57 (1982).

the measures for bringing existing laws into conformity with the Injunctions of Islam and the stages by which such measures should be brought into effect."[137] This mandate was taken seriously throughout the Zia ul-Haq period during which the Council played an active role in the implementation of policies of Islamization.[138]

One component of the New Education Policy adopted by Zia's regime in 1978 was the progressive segregation of men and women in higher education and the establishment of separate women's universities. As one observer commented:

> Such an eventuality could not but have disastrous repercussions on both women's higher education and their career opportunities. At a time when women were breaking ground in new fields—for instance, engineering, town planning, architecture, aeronautics—a women's university could not possibly offer these subjects to the few pioneers then undertaking them in a co-educational institution.[139]

Pakistani women have been concerned with the implications of the policy of Islamization for their careers and successfully have protested against encroachments on their role in public life. Zia ul-Haq's regime did show some sensitivity to protests and demands by women's organizations. He appointed the first female cabinet secretary in Pakistan's history, and later appointed a female minister of state.[140] In 1979 he established a Women's Division within his cabinet whose activities included cosponsorship of a conference which recommended the elimination of stereotyping of women in textbooks, the projection of a more responsible and positive image of women in national life, and greater representation of women in educational administration and policy-making. In response to protests by the All Pakistan Women's Association and seventeen other women's groups against instructions by the Minister of Information restricting the appearance of female models in commercial advertising, Zia's regime declared that it "had no intention whatsoever to debar them [women] from taking an active part in national affairs."[141]

With the election of Benazir Bhutto as the first female Prime Minister of Pakistan, one can expect more action in support of women's

137. Constitutions of Countries of the World, *supra* note 134, art. 230(1)(c).
138. *See* Carroll, *supra* note 136, at 66.
139. *Id.* at 75. *See also* Hussain, *The Struggle of Women in the National Development of Pakistan*, in Muslim Women 198, 210 - 11 (F. Hussain ed. 1984).
140. *See* Carroll, *supra* note 136, at 82.
141. *Id.* at 83–84; Hussain, *supra* note 139, at 213–14.

rights in public life. Nevertheless, one must not underestimate the power of the proponents of Shari'a in Pakistan or any other Muslim country. Neither women's organizations nor political parties and politicians can afford to disregard or downplay the Islamic factor.[142] Numerous studies show that a variety of economic and social factors contribute to the current status and rights of women in the Muslim world, and to their own perceptions of and reactions to their situation.[143] But these studies also emphasize, in one way or another, the Islamic dimensions of these same factors.

The Islamization slogan appears to have aroused considerable excitement and enthusiasm in Pakistan. Even the Pakistan People's Party, presently in power after the death of Zia ul-Haq, has declared its commitment to Islamization policy and continues to compete with the Islamic parties in this regard. But there are problems, as one observer noted:

> The matter, however, becomes complicated and contentious when an attempt is made to translate the slogan into actual policies. Not much imagination is required to realise that the vision of an Islamic social order entertained by the Ulema [Ulama, traditional religious scholars] differs radically from that envisaged by educated and articulate women. But even Sunni politicians of the religious-orientated parties are by no means unanimous in their conception of an Islamic state.[144]

This comment applies throughout the Muslim world, including Iran where differences exist among Shi'a politicians. Educated women and other modernist segments of society may not be able to articulate their vision of an Islamic state in terms of Shari'a, because aspects of

---

142. *See, e.g.*, the analysis and evaluation of the All Pakistan Women's Association in Chipp, *The Modern Pakistani Woman in a Muslim Society*, in ASIAN WOMEN IN TRANSITION 204 (Chipp & Green eds. 1980). For a similar analysis of a group of Indonesian women organizations see Douglas, *Women in Indonesian Politics: The Myth of Functional Interest*, *id.* at 152.

143. On Egypt and Morocco see, *e.g.*, Maher, *Women and Social Change in Morocco*, in WOMEN IN THE MUSLIM WORLD, *supra* note 118, at 100; Davis, *Working Women in a Moroccan Village*, *id.* at 416; El-Messiri, *Self-Images of Traditional Urban Women in Cairo*, *id.* at 522. *See also* Rugh, *Women and Work: Strategies and Choices in a Lower-Class Quarter of Cairo*, in WOMEN AND THE FAMILY IN THE MIDDLE EAST, *supra* note 129, at 272; Hatem, *Egypt's Middle Class in Crisis: The Sexual Division of Labor*, 42 MIDDLE E. J. 407 (1988).

In relation to Iran see Friedle, *supra* note 121; Nashat, *supra* note 128; Bauer, *Poor Women and Social Consciousness in Revolutionary Iran*, in WOMEN AND REVOLUTION IN IRAN, *supra* note 121, at 141.

On the situation in Saudi Arabia see Ramazani, *supra* note 120; Allaghi & Almana, *Survey of Research on Women in the Arab Gulf Region*, in UNESCO, SOCIAL SCIENCE RESEARCH AND WOMEN IN THE ARAB WORLD 14 (1984).

144. Carroll, *supra* note 136, at 85.

Shari'a are incompatible with certain concepts and institutions which these groups take for granted, including the protection of all human rights. To the extent that efforts for the protection and promotion of human rights in the Muslim world must take into account the Islamic dimension of the political and sociological situation in Muslim countries, a modernist conception of Islam is needed.

V. ISLAMIC REFORM AND HUMAN RIGHTS

I have referred several times in this Article to the need for Islamic reform to protect and promote human rights in the Muslim world. Such reform must be *sufficient* to resolve human rights problems with Shari'a while maintaining *legitimacy* from the Islamic point of view. On the one hand, reform efforts which fall short of resolving the serious human rights problems indicated earlier may not be worth pursuing. On the other hand, it is futile to advocate reforms which are unlikely to be acceptable to Muslims as satisfying the religious criteria of Islamic reform.

Islamic reform needs must be based on the Qur'an and Sunna, the primary sources of Islam. Although Muslims believe that the Qur'an is the literal and final word of God, and Sunna are the traditions of his final Prophet, they also appreciate that these sources have to be understood and applied through human interpretation and action. As I have pointed out above,[145] these sources have been interpreted by the founding jurists of Shari'a and applied throughout Muslim history. Because those interpretations were developed by Muslim jurists in the past, it should be possible for modern Muslim jurists to advance alternative interpretations of the Qur'an and Sunna.

A. *An Adequate Reform Methodology*

I have elsewhere argued extensively for this position and advanced a specific reform methodology which I believe would achieve the necessary degree of reform.[146] The basic premise of my position, based on the work of the late Sudanese Muslim reformer *Ustadh* Mahmoud Mohamed Taha,[147] is that the Shari'a reflects a historically-conditioned interpretation of Islamic scriptures in the sense that the founding jurists had to understand those sources in accordance with their own social, economic, and political circumstances. In relation to the status and rights of women, for example, equality between men and women

145. *See supra* notes 12–28 and accompanying text.
146. *See generally* TOWARD AN ISLAMIC REFORMATION, *supra* note 11.
147. *See generally* M. TAHA, THE SECOND MESSAGE OF ISLAM (A. An-Na'im trans. 1987).

in the eighth and ninth centuries in the Middle East, or anywhere else at the time, would have been inconceivable and impracticable. It was therefore natural and indeed inevitable that Muslim jurists would understand the relevant texts of the Qur'an and Sunna as confirming rather than repudiating the realities of the day.

In interpreting the primary sources of Islam in their historical context, the founding jurists of Shari'a tended not only to understand the Qur'an and Sunna as confirming existing social attitudes and institutions, but also to emphasize certain texts and "enact" them into Shari'a while de-emphasizing other texts or interpreting them in ways consistent with what they believed to be the intent and purpose of the sources. Working with the same primary sources, modern Muslim jurists might shift emphasis from one class of texts to the other, and interpret the previously enacted texts in ways consistent with a new understanding of what is believed to be the intent and purpose of the sources. This new understanding would be informed by contemporary social, economic, and political circumstances in the same way that the "old" understanding on which Shari'a jurists acted was informed by the then prevailing circumstances. The new understanding would qualify for Islamic legitimacy, in my view, if it is based on specific texts in opposing the application of other texts, and can be shown to be in accordance with the Qur'an and Sunna as a whole.

For example, the general principle of *qawama*, the guardianship and authority of men over women under Shari'a, is based on verse 4:34 of the Qur'an quoted earlier.[148] This verse presents *qawama* as a consequence of two conditions: men's advantage over and financial support of women. The fact that men are generally physically stronger than most women is not relevant in modern times where the rule of law prevails over physical might. Moreover, modern circumstances are making the economic independence of women from men more readily realized and appreciated. In other words, neither of the conditions—advantages of physical might or earning power—set by verse 4:34 as the justification for the *qawama* of men over women is tenable today.

The fundamental position of the modern human rights movement is that all human beings are equal in worth and dignity, regardless of gender, religion, or race. This position can be substantiated by the Qur'an and other Islamic sources, as understood under the radically transformed circumstances of today. For example, in numerous verses the Qur'an speaks of honor and dignity for "humankind" and "children of Adam," without distinction as to race, color, gender, or religion.[149]

148. *See supra* text following note 103.

149. For instance, verse 17:70 speaks of how God "honoured the children of Adam." Yusuf

By drawing on those sources and being willing to set aside archaic and dated interpretations of other sources, such as the one previously given to verse 4:34 of the Qur'an, we can provide Islamic legitimacy for the full range of human rights for women.

Similarly, numerous verses of the Qur'an provide for freedom of choice and non-compulsion in religious belief and conscience.[150] These verses have been either de-emphasized as having been "overruled" by other verses which were understood to legitimize coercion, or "interpreted" in ways which permitted such coercion. For example, verse 9:29[151] of the Qur'an was taken as the foundation of the whole system of *dhimma*, and its consequent discrimination against non-Muslims.[152] Relying on those verses which extoll freedom of religion rather than those that legitimize religious coercion, one can argue now that the *dhimma* system should no longer be part of Islamic law and that complete equality should be assured regardless of religion or belief. The same argument can be used to abolish all negative legal consequences of apostasy as inconsistent with the Islamic principle of freedom of religion.[153]

Reference has been made to the possible need to challenge some jurisprudential techniques of Shari'a in order to implement the necessary degree of reform.[154] One of the main mechanisms for development and reform within the framework of Shari'a is *ijtihad*—independent juristic reasoning to provide for new principles and rules of Shari'a in situations on which the Qur'an and Sunna were silent. By virtue of its rationale and textual support, *ijtihad* was not supposed to be exercised in any matter governed by clear and categorical texts of Qur'an and/or Sunna because that would amount to substituting jur-

---

Ali translates the Arabic term "*baniy* Adam" as "the sons of Adam," *see* HOLY QUR'AN, *supra* note 103, at 714, although the word "*baniy*" means "children," both male and female. Yusuf Ali may have intended the word "sons" to include both sexes, but it is important to use a gender neutral term in this context. Verse 49:13 of the Qur'an may be translated as follows:

> O, humankind, We [God] have created you into male and female, and made you into peoples and tribes so that you may be acquainted [and cooperate] with each other; the most favored by God among you are those who are righteous and pious.

150. See, for example, verse 2:256 of the Qur'an which provides: "Let there be no compulsion in religion: Truth stands out clear from error . . . ." In verse 18:29 God instructs the Prophet: "Say, the Truth is from your Lord. Let him who will, believe, and let him who will, reject [it] . . . ." HOLY QUR'AN, *supra* note 103, at 103, 738.

151.
> Fight those who believe not in God and the Last Day, nor hold that forbidden which hath been forbidden by God and His Apostle, nor acknowledge the Religion of Truth, [even if they are] of the People of the Book [*Ahl al-kitab*], until they pay *Jizya* with willing submission, and feel themselves subdued.

HOLY QUR'AN, *supra* note 103, at 447.

152. *See supra* notes 42–51 and accompanying text on the *dhimma* system and its human rights implications.

153. *See generally* A. RAHMAN, PUNISHMENT OF APOSTASY IN ISLAM (1972) (a strong argument for abolishing the death penalty for apostasy in Islamic law).

154. *See supra* text following note 123.

istic reasoning for the fundamental sources of Islam.[155] According to the prevailing view in Shari'a, *ijtihad* should not be exercised even in matters settled through *ijma*, consensus.[156]

Some of the problematic aspects of Shari'a identified in this Article, however, are based on clear and categorical texts of Qur'an and Sunna. To achieve the necessary degree of reform, I would therefore suggest that the scope of *ijtihad* be expanded to enable modern Muslim jurists not only to change rules settled through *ijma*, but also to substitute previously enacted texts with other, more general, texts of Qur'an and Sunna despite the categorical nature of the prior texts.[157] This proposal is not as radical as it may seem because the proposed new rule would also be based on the Qur'an or Sunna, albeit on a new interpretation of the text. For example, the above-mentioned categorical verse 9:29 regulating the status of non-Muslims would be superseded by the more general verses providing for freedom of religion and inherent dignity of all human beings without distinction as to faith or belief.

I believe that the choice of texts to be implemented as modern Islamic Shari'a is systematic and not arbitrary; it is based on the timing and circumstances of revelation as well as the relationship of the text to the themes and objectives of Islam as a whole. Moreover, I maintain that the proposed reinterpretation is consistent with normal Arabic usage and apparent sense of the text. It is neither contrived nor strained. The ultimate test of legitimacy and efficacy is, of course, acceptance and implementation by Muslims throughout the world.

B. *Prospects for Acceptance and Likely Impact of the Proposed Reform*

In addition to this methodology's own Islamic legitimacy and cohesion, at least two main factors are likely to affect the acceptance and implementation of this or any other reform. It must be timely, addressing urgent concerns and issues facing Muslim societies, and it must be disseminated and discussed in Muslim countries. I believe that my proposal will be acceptable to Muslim peoples if offered in an effective and organized manner. Paradoxical as it may seem, I suspect that the proposal may face difficulties of dissemination and discussion precisely because it is timely.

This proposal is timely because Muslims throughout the world are sensitive to charges that their religious law and cultural traditions permit and legitimize human rights violations; hence the efforts of

155. *See* D. MacDonald, Development of Muslim Theology, Jurisprudence and Constitutional Theory 86 (1903); Vesey-Fitzgerald, *supra* note 16, at 93.

156. N. Coulson, *supra* note 17, at 60.

157. For a full explanation and substantiation of this position, see Toward an Islamic Reformation, *supra* note 11, at 17–33, 53–68.

contemporary Muslim authors to dispel such allegations.[158] Governments of Muslim countries, like many other governments, formally subscribe to international human rights instruments because, in my view, they find the human rights idea an important legitimizing force both at home and abroad. Moreover, as explained earlier, many emerging women's organizations and modernist forces are now asserting and articulating their demands for justice and equality in terms of international human rights standards.

Nevertheless, the proposed reform will probably be resisted because it challenges the vested interests of powerful forces in the Muslim world and may upset male-dominated traditional political and social institutions. These forces probably will try to restrict opportunities for a genuine consideration of this reform methodology. It is equally likely that they will attempt to obstruct its acceptance and implementation in the name of Islamic orthodoxy. Proponents of Shari'a will also resist it because it challenges their view of the good Muslim society and the ideal Islamic state.

Consequently, the acceptance and implementation of this reform methodology will involve a political struggle within Muslim nations as part of a larger general struggle for human rights. I would recommend this proposal to participants in that struggle who champion the cause of justice and equality for women and non-Muslims, and freedom of belief and expression in the Muslim world. Given the extreme importance of Islamic legitimacy in Muslim societies, I urge human rights advocates to claim the Islamic platform and not concede it to the traditionalist and fundamentalist forces in their societies. I would also invite outside supporters of Muslim human rights advocates to express their support with due sensitivity and genuine concern for Islamic legitimacy in the Muslim world.

As I have tried to show throughout this Article, the problematic aspects of Shari'a are not the sole underlying causes of human rights violations in the Muslim world. Other extra-Islamic structural and socio-economic factors also contribute to human rights problems. But the primary objectives of this Article have been: (1) to address the extent to which Shari'a-related factors contribute to human rights violations in the Muslim world; and (2) to propose a way of overcoming that particular dimension of the status of human rights in the Muslim world.

VI. CONCLUSION

This Article began with the general premise that human rights violations reflect the lack or weakness of cultural legitimacy of inter-

158. *See, e.g.*, Wafi, *supra* note 34; Hassan, *supra* note 123; Ishaque, *Human Rights in Islamic Law*, 12 INT'L COMM'N OF JURISTS REV. 30 (1974); Al-Faruqi, *Islam and Human Rights*, 27 ISLAMIC Q. 12 (1983); A. ZAHIR, HUQUQ AL-INSAN (1988) (Arabic).

national standards in a particular society. In accordance with this premise, because Shari'a, as the accepted version of the law of Islam, is inconsistent with certain human rights, those rights probably will be violated in the Muslim world, regardless of formal participation in international human rights instruments. This is likely to occur even if Shari'a is not constituted as the formal legal system of the country in question. As a religious and ethical code, Shari'a has far-reaching political and social influence, irrespective of its official legal status in Muslim countries. The evidence reviewed above from case studies of several Muslim countries illustrates Shari'a's extensive influence under very different cultural and legal conditions.

Therefore, because Muslim countries are more likely to honor those human rights standards which have Islamic legitimacy, human rights advocates should struggle to have their interpretations of the scriptural imperatives of Islam accepted as valid and appropriate for application today. Authority for this reinterpretive activity comes from the fact that contemporary majority perspectives on Shari'a are not necessarily the only valid interpretations of the scriptural imperatives of Islam, a fact which has been recognized by some modernist Muslim reformers.[159] Unfortunately, little has been done so far to develop a comprehensive reform methodology. In terms of human rights concerns there has been little effort to reconcile Islamic law with fundamental human rights, especially in relation to women and non-Muslims. Reform efforts have so far been confined to the family law area, and even there they have tended to be inadequate and open to reversal. A much more comprehensive and effective reform methodology is required to provide genuine and lasting Islamic legitimacy for human rights in the Muslim world.

In the final part of this Article, I have explained briefly what I believe to be an adequate Islamic reform methodology aimed at achieving greater legitimacy for human rights in the Muslim world. As indicated in that section, however, this methodology does not offer an easy or quick solution to all human rights problems. In fact, strong resistance can be expected not only from those with vested interest in the status quo, but also from some of the beneficiaries of the proposed reforms. For example, some educated women are Islamic fundamentalists. Nor do I suggest that reformulating Shari'a alone will alleviate all human rights violations. Economic and other factors and forces must also be addressed. Yet, the extent of observance of human rights standards in any country is affected by prevailing attitudes and conceptions regarding who is a human being entitled to the full range of

---

159. *See, e.g.*, F. Rahman, Islam and Modernity: Transformation of an Intellectual Tradition (1982); In Quest of an Islamic Humanism: Arabic and Islamic Studies in Memory of Mohamed Al-Nowaihi (A. Green ed. 1984).

human rights. In the Muslim context, these attitudes and conceptions are significantly influenced by commonly held views concerning what are the scriptural imperatives of Islam. Rethinking these scriptural imperatives is therefore one critical strategy for advancing human rights in Muslim countries. Human rights advocates have few allies in most parts of the world, including almost all Muslim countries. They need to enlist the support of powerful cultural and religious forces. Support will come if they look for it in an intelligent and sensitive manner.

[7]
Civil Rights in the Islamic Constitutional Tradition: Shared Ideals and Divergent Regimes*

INTRODUCTION

The basic premise of this paper is that, broadly speaking, human societies are entitled, and do in fact seek, to follow their own paths to self-determination in accordance with their world-views and visions of the public good.[1] Given the commonalities of human nature and environment,[2] paths to self-determination tend to intersect and overlap. This presents possibilities of both confrontation and cooperation among human societies. Without overlooking the fact that destructive confrontation continues to endanger human life and dignity, nor minimizing the role of international power relations in this regard, I believe that cooperation between societies on the basis of mutual respect and understanding is possible, indeed imperative.

In this light, and in accordance with the theme of this symposium (a decent respect for the opinion of humankind), I propose to contribute to the discourse of mutual respect and understanding by presenting an internal critique of civil rights in the Islamic constitu-

---

I am grateful to Tore Lindholm for his helpful comments and suggestions on an earlier draft of this paper.

1. The notion of societies as actors on a collective will can be problematic because it is often abused by despotic leaders who appropriate to themselves the exclusive right to speak and act for a given society as an organic whole. While being sensitive to this danger, I find it useful to speak of society in this figurative sense without losing sight of issues of internal power relations and political struggle over whose version of the society's world view prevails, or who determines what is in the public good. Although this is not the subject of the paper as such, these issues will be taken into account in the course of my discussion.

2. *See generally* CULTURE AND HUMAN NATURE: THEORETICAL PAPERS OF MELFORD E. SPIRO ch. 1 (B. Kilborne and L. Langness eds., 1987).

tional tradition in the modern context. I must emphasize from the outset that I am doing this out of the conviction that Muslim peoples have the right to conduct their constitutional and legal affairs in conformity with the principles of Islam. This right, however, is subject to the obligation of respecting the legitimate rights of all individuals and groups within Islamic countries. It is my task as a Muslim to seek ways of fulfilling this obligation from an Islamic point of view. The following internal critique is therefore intended to affirm, legitimate and effectuate the right of Muslims to self-determination in terms of an Islamic identity, including the application of Islamic law, and not to repudiate that right.

For the purposes of this paper, I define civil rights as the rights of the individual against the state and society at large, commonly referred to in human rights discourse as civil and political rights. These include rights of political participation, equality before the law, and freedom from discrimination on grounds such as race, religion or gender. I realize that this working definition may be too narrow or problematic in some contexts, but take it to be sufficient for the purposes of this paper, as determined by the framework of the symposium.[3]

In Western constitutional discourse, the terms "civil rights" and "civil liberties" are often used interchangeably, but "when they are differentiated the latter generally denotes the rights of *individuals*, while the former refers to the constitutional and legal status and treatment of *minority groups* that are marked off from the majority by race, religion, or national origin."[4] I do not wish to make this distinction here because it is not helpful for my analysis. As shown in section III below, women and non-Muslims are denied some civil liberties under historical formulations of Shari'a *because* of gender and religion.[5] Until these aspects of Shari'a are removed through Islamic reform as suggested below, it is misleading to maintain a distinction between civil rights and liberties. In any case, given the general interdependence between the two, it may not be meaningful to differentiate them, except under very specific

3. For a brief discussion of the question of individual rights and notions of communalism, see *infra* text at § I.B.

4. 3 MILTON R. KONVITZ, CIVIL RIGHTS, INTERNATIONAL ENCYCLOPEDIA OF THE SOCIAL SCIENCES 312 (David L. Sills ed. 1968).

5. Shari'a encompasses moral and pastoral theology, ethics, high spiritual aspiration, and detailed ritualistic and formal observances; it includes all aspects of public and private law, hygiene, and even courtesy and good manners.

On the development of the concept, see FAZLUR RAHMAN, ISLAM 101-09 (1979). For an explanation of the sources and development of this comprehensive system, see ABDULLAHI A. AN-NA'IM, TOWARD AN ISLAMIC REFORMATION: CIVIL LIBERTIES, HUMAN RIGHTS AND INTERNATIONAL LAW ch. 2 (1990) [hereinafter AN-NA'IM, TOWARD].

circumstances.[6]

The thesis of the paper is that various normative traditions may legitimately pursue different approaches to realizing the shared ideals of human dignity, liberty and well-being.[7] As appropriate means to legitimate ends, however, these approaches must remain open to criticism and reform in order to ensure and improve their practical ability to realize these ideals. I believe that effective reform can only be undertaken within the framework of each tradition and in accordance with its own internal criteria of legitimacy. This applies to the theoretical formulation of reform proposals, as well as to the political struggle for their implementation. Nevertheless, I submit that cross-cultural interaction can contribute to stimulating those theoretical formulations and to supporting the political struggle for their implementation. This must be done, however, with proper understanding of, and sensitivity to, the internal legitimacy and dynamics of the process of reform.

By focusing on Islamic constitutional theory and practice in this paper, I am not implying that this is the only available ideology or operative force pertaining to civil rights in the Muslim world today. Space does not permit a detailed explanation of the political situation in, or the constitutional and legal system of, individual Islamic countries. But I would, however, strongly emphasize that the beliefs and practices of contemporary Muslims, like those of other peoples in the world, reflect a wide range of ideological orientations and must continue to respond to many practical considerations and concerns. Despite the recent dramatic rise in what is commonly known as Islamic fundamentalism, the realities of the plural societies of the Muslim world, and of global political and economic relations, preclude the implementation of a totalitarian ideology, be it "Islamic" or otherwise.

---

6. Another reservation against using the term "civil liberties" is that it suggests an emphasis on "negative rights" as opposed to "positive rights"; that is, imposing restraints on the government without providing for its duty to provide economic and social rights. Although this view of civil liberties is changing, the "negative" association persists in popular usage.

It is meaningful to make this distinction in the American context because, although the basic civil liberties of Black Americans were constitutionally guaranteed since the end of slavery, their civil rights were violated for a long time. Serious civil rights issues remain in relation to women and racial minorities.

For a schematic description of civil liberties, including positive rights, see 3 Robert G. McCloskey, Civil Liberties, International Encyclopedia of the Social Sciences 307, 308 (David L. Sills ed. 1968).

7. In this paper, I assume that these are shared ideals without attempting to substantiate or argue fòr this assumption. It may be said that it is more appropriate to speak of "overlapping" rather than "shared" ideals because the latter term implies a conscious awareness of agreement on these ideals which may not be the case in practice. I prefer to use the term "shared" because I believe that, on reflection, such conscious awareness of agreement on these ideals can be identified within most human societies today.

Nevertheless, it is equally true that the *Islamic dimension* of the political, constitutional and legal situation in any predominantly Muslim country is, and will always be, extremely important. Thus, safeguarding and enhancing civil rights in Islamic societies requires an understanding of, and working with, the Islamic dimension of the internal legitimacy and dynamics of these rights in those societies. According to the rationale of Islamic discourse, the experience of the original Muslim communities of seventh century Arabia and the Middle East is the ultimate historical moment for Muslims up to the present day. This Islamic frame of reference is commonly believed to be central to political and constitutional discourse among millions of Muslims today, indeed to the legitimacy of government in a growing number of Islamic countries. It is therefore reasonable to assume that this Islamic frame of reference is integral to the moral justification of civil rights, and to the struggle for their protection in the modern context.

The key to conducting constructive discourse about civil rights in the Islamic constitutional tradition, I suggest, is the candid admission of the historical contradictions and ambivalence inherent to the subject itself, and an appreciation of the underlying causes thereof. I find this admission and appreciation to be essential for evolving a legitimate conception of civil rights in Islamic constitutional theory, and for implementing this concept in the modern states of the Muslim world.

In its origins and historical formulations, the Islamic constitutional tradition did not, and could not have, provided in detailed and institutional arrangements for the full range of civil rights in the modern sense of the term. A religious tradition originating in the Middle East of the seventh century could not have articulated and implemented a predominately secular constitutional concept emerging primarily from the political struggle in Europe and North America since the eighteenth century.[8] To maintain otherwise would involve a distortion of either the facts of Islamic constitutional history or the concept and principles of civil rights, if not both. This does not mean that there is no Islamic rationale for civil rights. In my view, a correct understanding of the nature and evolution of Islamic constitutional theory, and of the concept and principles of civil rights, will permit the development and imple-

8. It should be noted that the evolution of the modern concept of civil rights was not exclusively secular since the need for religious toleration and coexistence played an important role in the inception of the concept. *See generally* JOHN LOCKE, A LETTER CONCERNING TOLERATION (1955).

I am not discounting the importance of the antecedents and recent development of civil rights in other parts of the world. But it cannot be doubted, I believe, that the modern term derives from primarily Western intellectual and political developments over the last two hundred years.

mentation of a mutually supportive relationship between the two in modern Islamic societies.

In order to present and argue for this thesis in its proper context, it is helpful to begin by explaining the notion of the challenge of realizing the shared ideals of human dignity, liberty and well-being referred to earlier. In terms of the basic premise of the paper, I submit that these ideals should constitute the substance of the right to self-determination for all human societies. The ability to realize them should therefore be the criterion by which any ideology is evaluated and reformed, if need be, through the process of internal legitimation adopted here.

I. The Challenge of Realizing Shared Ideals

Subject to further clarification below, I wish to explain what I mean by the challenge of realizing shared ideals. In my view, the pursuit of the ideals of dignity, liberty and well-being is universal to all human societies. The matter is complicated, however, by the fact that perceptions of dignity, permissible limitations on liberty and the conditions believed to be conducive to well-being vary from one society to another. Even within the same society, these perceptions differ not only over time, but also at any given point in time as a result of the competing, if not conflicting, interests of various segments and groups within that society. In other words, the content and implications of these ideals are relative to, and contestable within, a given society in its specific historical context. Thus, the universality of these ideals is subject to the circumstances of political struggle and the dynamics of power relations within society at a given point in time. Each society is faced with the challenge of constantly specifying the meaning of these ideals for practical purposes, and of realizing them in the daily lives of its own members.

The term civil rights, as it is commonly used today, signifies a certain liberal and/or social democratic approach to realizing the ideals of dignity, liberty and well-being in the context of the modern nation-state. It presupposes the existence of this state and its institutions, and is intended to primarily protect the individual against encroachments by the state and its organs and officials. According to this view, as the model of the nation-state becomes universal [that is, as the entire world evolves toward state societies] so should this particular approach to civil rights become universally applicable, regardless of its liberal pedigree.[9] This reasoning would be valid, in my view, only if the proposed approach is appreciative

9. I am paraphrasing here the comments of Rhoda E. Howard in relation to human rights (which I believe apply to civil rights) *stated in*, HUMAN RIGHTS IN CROSS-CULTURAL PERSPECTIVES: A QUEST FOR CONSENSUS 81 (Abdullahi A. An-Na'im ed. 1992).

of, and sensitive to, global cultural diversity in relation to the precepts, institutions and mechanisms of civil rights. I would also emphasize that the need for a civil rights regime in a given state society must be legitimized and rooted in the local culture(s) of that society.

A. Purpose and Context of Civil Rights

As indicated earlier, my working definition of civil rights focuses on the rights of the individual to political participation, equality before the law and freedom from discrimination. The basic justification of these rights, in my view, is the universal principle of reciprocity. This principle, also known as the "Golden Rule," indicates that since every person should treat others as s/he would like to be treated by them, s/he should concede to them the same civil rights s/he claims for herself or himself.[10]

In practical terms, moreover, human experience to date has shown these rights to be necessary for economic and social development and justice, as well as for the proper functioning of political regimes.[11] As illustrated by the recent collapse of the totalitarian Marxist regimes in Eastern Europe and the Soviet Union, and the ensuing exposure of their corruption and inefficiency, civil rights provide vital safeguards for a valid process of determining and implementing policies which are best suited to serve the most widely held view of the public good. Even those whose view of the public good is not thereby implemented are best served by civil rights regimes because under them they would have a fair chance to achieve some degree of political power or otherwise influence policy in their favor. Where practice does not conform to this theory because power relations, economic interests and other factors distort and frustrate the process, the answer is surely more protection of civil rights, not their repudiation.

This common wisdom is also reflected in ideological and constitutional thinking throughout the world. Almost all constitutions in the world today incorporate these rights, and every political ideology claims their protection to be its immediate, or at least long term, objective. Even dictatorial regimes usually attempt to justify the abrogation or limitation of these rights as an "unavoidable temporary measure" in the interest of some alleged public good such as national security or economic development, and promise to restore them as soon as possible. It is true that such justifications are

---

10. For an elaboration on this principle as the justification of human rights, including civil rights, see AN-NA'IM, TOWARD, *supra* note 5, at 162-64.

11. *See generally* Rhoda E. Howard, *The Full-Belly Thesis: Should Economic Rights Take Priority over Civil and Political Rights? Evidence from Sub-Saharan Africa*, 5 HUM. RTS. Q. 467-90 (1983).

rarely, if ever, valid, and that the fulfillment of the promise to restore civil rights is sometimes postponed under one pretext or another. But the attempted justification and alleged pretext for postponement themselves show that the validity of civil rights cannot be openly denied even by those who violate them.

Reference has already been made to the importance of the context in determining a society's response to the challenge of realizing the ideals of dignity, liberty and well-being of its members. That is to say, the policies and practices of a society in this regard are influenced by historical, cultural, socio-economic and political factors and power relations at play in that society at a given point in time. This context influences a society's choice of a particular rights regime, or preference for a rights/duties approach that emphasizes communal interests over individual rights.

I would strongly emphasize, however, that this context itself is constantly changing through the interplay of internal struggle and external influences. The dynamics of internal cultural, socio-economic and political relations and shifts in power relations alter perceptions of what the shared ideals mean and how to implement those perceptions in practice. It should also be noted that the dominance of certain perceptions within a society does not mean that they are the only ones, or that dominated perceptions have no impact at all on public policy and practice. Often, apparently dominant perceptions maintain their political advantage by making "concessions" to other perceptions within society. Moreover, the culture as a whole usually offers its adherents a range of options or legitimate choices. These features of internal discourse may be referred to as "the ambivalence and contestability of culture."[12]

This internal discourse is constantly influenced by the society's external relations and dialogue(s) with other societies. Classes or groups within society who are dissatisfied with existing perceptions and norms will seek ways of changing or adjusting them in order to modify or replace the political or economic regime or priorities of their society with new proposals in pursuit of the shared ideals of dignity, liberty and well-being. In so doing, these classes or groups are influenced by what is happening in other societies; and may also enlist the support and assistance of external "allies" in their internal struggle. These two inter-related processes is what I call "the internal discourse" and "cross-cultural dialogue" of human/civil rights.[13]

---

12. *See Toward a Cross-Cultural Approach to Defining International Standards of Human Rights: The Meaning of Cruel, Inhuman and Degrading Treatment or Punishments*, HUMAN RIGHTS IN CROSS-CULTURAL PERSPECTIVES: A QUEST FOR CONSENSUS, *supra* note 9, at 19-27.

13. My thesis of cultural legitimacy of human rights, which applies to individual civil and political rights, is *explained in*, HUMAN RIGHTS IN CROSS-CUL-

B. *Communalism and Individual Rights*

It may be argued that, by focusing on the civil rights of individuals, I am overlooking the fact that some societies emphasize the "duties" of individuals to the community, rather than their rights against it. Given the basic premise of this paper that societies have the right to seek their own paths to self-determination, what if a society wishes to emphasize the public interest, as defined by collective or group rights, over individual civil rights? It is often asserted that Islamic cultures emphasize the importance of the public over the private good, and subordinate the rights of the individual to the interests of the community.[14] If (or to the extent that) this is true, does it mean that these cultures are not committed to *individual* civil rights? Would it be appropriate to seek to induce these cultures to change their attitudes and norms in order to share a commitment to individual civil rights?

Subject to further elaboration in the sections on Islamic constitutional theory and civil rights below, I believe that the following observations are relevant in response to these questions at this stage of my analysis. The assumed communalism of Islamic societies is plausible and acceptable only in traditional settings of small scale social and political organization based on kinship and ethnic networks of personal relationships. A purely, or even primarily, communalist conception of the relationship between the individual and the community/state is simply untenable under modern conditions of large scale and complex social and political relations.

As correctly stated by Ann Mayer, Muslim authors who assert traditional communalism in support of the argument that individual civil rights are inappropriate in the modern context of the Muslim world proceed from a false assumption to an unwarranted conclusion. First, they fail to appreciate that the model of communal solidarity is not distinctively Islamic, it "reflects the features commonly found in societies before the intrusions of industrialization and urbanization." Second, these authors jump from a description of the subordination of the individual that was widely accepted in traditional (including non-Islamic) societies, "to the unwarranted conclusion that Islamic doctrine calls for such subordination even in

---

TURAL PERSPECTIVES: A QUEST FOR CONSENSUS, *supra* note 9, at Intro., ch. 1 & Concl.; HUMAN RIGHTS IN AFRICA 159-79 (Abdullahi A. An-Na'im and Francis Deng eds., 1990).

14. This assertion is made by some Muslim writers without supporting it with specific evidence or detailed information. *See, e.g.*, M.F. Al-Nabhan, *The Learned Academy of Islamic Jurisprudence*, 1 ARAB L. Q. 391-92 (1986); A.K. Brohi, *The Nature of Islamic Law and the Concept of Human Rights*, HUMAN RIGHTS IN ISLAM, REPORT OF A SEMINAR HELD IN KUWAIT 48 (Int'l Commission of Jurists 1982); Abdul A. Said, *Precepts and Practice of Human Rights in Islam*, 1 UNIVERSAL HUM. RTS. 73, 74 & 77 (1979).

the drastically changed circumstances of contemporary states, where the power of the central government is immeasurably enhanced over what it was in the medieval era."[15]

Furthermore, it seems to me that the communalism thesis confuses the *ethics* of communal solidarity with the need for effective legal safeguards against the abuse of power and/or violation of rights. I believe that, generally speaking, the socialization processes of all human societies seek to instill in individuals a sense of obligation to the community and subordination of his or her private interest to that of the collectivity. Such socialization may be stronger or more effective in some societies than others, but this does not mean that legal safeguards for the rights of the individual are unnecessary. In my view, the rationale of this socialization process is that the rights and interests of the individual will be sufficiently protected through communal solidarity. Even when this is believed to be the norm rather than the exception, legal safeguards and remedies are essential for concrete cases or situations where individual rights are violated. In this way, I maintain that communalism and civil rights regimes are compatible, indeed complementary.

In light of my analysis so far, I now propose to briefly address the following questions: Should the process of adapting civil rights regimes, or adopting new ones, be totally relativist, in that each society should be left completely to its own internal standards and devices? Or should it be universalist in the sense of leading to a particular kind of regime for realizing the shared ideals of dignity, liberty and well-being, at least under a given set of circumstances? If the process is to be relativist, what should other societies do when they perceive serious deprivations or deviations from the shared ideals in the practice of a given society? If it is universalist, which society sets the standards for each set of circumstances, and why should other societies accept its judgment?

If it is cast in these terms, I would not know how to resolve the relativism/universalism dilemma. On the one hand, as a human being concerned with the fate of others and dependent on their concern for my fate, I worry about what societies might do to powerless or disadvantaged individuals and groups. Yet, I find it objectionable for one society to dictate or impose the standards to be implemented by other societies. But, in my view, the issue should not be presented as an either/or proposition in the first place. I would seek to resolve the relativist/universalist dilemma by promoting a model of cross-cultural interaction whereby one society may and

15. ANN E. MAYER, ISLAM & HUMAN RIGHTS: TRADITION AND POLITICS 62 (1991). For a similar critique of claims of African scholars that individual human rights are inappropriate in the African setting, see HUMAN RIGHTS IN AFRICA, *supra* note 13, at 159-83.

can influence the concept or content of the civil rights regime of another society, without dictating to it. This can be done, I suggest, through what I referred to earlier as cross-cultural dialogue, which, in turn, will feed into and support internal discourse within the culture or society in question.

In summary, my approach is premised on the following propositions about the nature, context and evolution of civil rights:

i. The universality of commitment to human dignity, liberty and well-being does not resolve the ambivalence and contestability of cultural norms and priorities because perceptions of these ideals and ways of realizing them vary from one society to another, as well as within the same society at a given point in time or over an extended period. The context in which these ideals are perceived and realized changes in response to internal and external factors. In adapting to changing circumstances, a particular society's conception and implementation of a modified or new regime is unlikely to conform to that of other societies because each society adapts in accordance with its own history and culture. While it might be possible to find parallel changes and adaption, it would be unrealistic to expect them to be identical, and misleading to present them as such.

ii. Culture is of paramount importance to civil rights in two ways: as the source of the concept and normative content of the particular civil rights regime, and as the context within which civil rights norms are interpreted and applied. The belief that individual civil rights should be respected and protected, as well as the specification of those rights, mechanisms and processes for their implementation, should emanate from the values and attitudes of the people concerned. To the extent that this is the case, civil rights may come to be respected and protected through the spontaneous behavior of the people and the natural functioning of their social and political institutions, with minimum controversy or coercive enforcement. Where (or to the extent that) this is not the case, it would still be possible, and in my view desirable, to strive to supplement or enhance the legitimacy and efficacy of civil rights within the culture in question. This should be primarily done through the process of internal cultural discourse, by utilizing and reconstructing normative resources in favor of greater respect and protection of civil rights. Such internal discourse can be supported through cross-cultural dialogue which is consistent with the guidelines suggested earlier.

iii. To the extent that individual civil rights of some segments of society are protected in traditional settings, that is achieved in informal and indirect ways, e.g., through the processes of mediation and consensus. But in those settings, equal protection is not usually accorded to disadvantaged groups or classes, such as women and religious or ethnic minorities. As the context changes (through, e.g., demographic changes, urbanization and the formalization of the structures and institutions of the state), there will probably be greater awareness of the inadequacy of traditional concepts of individual rights and the mechanism for their protection. Previously deprived groups or classes may begin to assert and struggle for their individual civil rights, and others may become dissatisfied with the scope of the civil rights they already have, demand more rights, and/or more appropriate enforcement mechanisms. All of this is likely to lead to the modification of the existing regime, or adoption of a new one. While influenced by the experiences of other societies, the modified or new regime will be peculiar to the society in question as the product of its history and culture.

iv. This does not mean that the process of adapting existing regimes or adopting new ones should be exclusively relative to the particular society. Each society should be concerned about the status of, and seek to influence events in favor of greater respect for, civil rights in other societies. By the same token, each society should remain open to reciprocal influence by other societies in this regard. Both aspects of this process of mutual support for civil rights must be done, however, with the utmost sensitivity and understanding of the internal dynamics of the evolution of civil rights in other societies in accordance with their own indigenous criteria of legitimacy.

II. Origins and Development of Islamic Constitutional Theory

In view of the vast geographic and demographic extent of the past and present Muslim world, and the tremendous richness and complexity of the Islamic tradition,[16] it is not possible to attempt here a comprehensive discussion of civil rights in Islamic constitutional thought. It may in fact be inaccurate to speak of a single Islamic constitutional tradition because there have been many distinctive juridical systems and political experiences over time and

16. Originating in Arabia around 610, Islam expanded to cover the whole Middle East within a few decades. During the next century, the Muslim world extended from Spain through North Africa and the Middle East into Northern India and beyond. Having lost Spain to Catholicism by the end of the fifteenth century, Islam is now the predominant religion in much of Africa and Asia. Depending on the criteria used in the classification, about thirty to forty countries in the world today identify themselves as Islamic countries populated by about one billion people. On the history and culture of the Muslim world, see generally The Cambridge History of Islam (P.M. Holt, et al. eds., 1970); Marshall G.S. Hodgson, The Venture of Islam (1974); Ira M. Lapidus, History of Islamic Societies (1988); Rahman, *supra* note 5.

place.[17] For the purposes of this paper, however, it will suffice to provide a brief theoretical survey of Islamic constitutional thought, its evolution, present status and the issues facing it in the Muslim world today. Against this background, I will focus on issues of civil rights in the modern context.

As indicated earlier, the Islamic frame of reference is commonly assumed to be the experience of the original Muslim communities of the seventh century, especially that of the community and state established by the Prophet in Medina, a town in western Arabia, around 622 and continued by the first generation of his followers (*sahaba*) for the next four decades.[18] Patterns of individual and collective behavior, models of political relationships and legal institutions commonly ascribed to that period continue to be held as the Islamic ideal to the present day. It is therefore reasonable to take the practice of the Medina community of 622-660 as the most authoritative source of Islamic constitutional theory, and its state as the ideal model.

While decrying deviations from that theory and model in the practice of subsequent generations, and seeking to justify and rationalize them with reference to the need to adapt to changing circumstances, present-day Muslims also greatly revere the jurisprudential and political thought of scholars and jurists of the first three centuries of Islam.[19] In fact, what is accepted today as authentic Shari'a is based on the work of those founding jurists as the authoritative transmitters and interpreters of the traditions of the earliest Muslim communities. It is therefore important to take this literature into account in tracing the development of Islamic constitutional theory. At another level, however, since Muslims must continue adapting to changing circumstances, previous patterns of adaptation are instructive in evaluating present patterns of individual and collective behavior, and in evolving Islamic political and legal institutions.

17. *See generally* KEMAL A. FARUKI, THE EVOLUTION OF ISLAMIC CONSTITUTIONAL THEORY AND PRACTICE FROM 610 TO 1926 (1971) [hereinafter FARUKI, EVOLUTION]; DUNCAN B. MACDONALD, DEVELOPMENT OF MUSLIM THEOLOGY, JURISPRUDENCE AND CONSTITUTIONAL THEORY (1972).

18. This stage of Islamic history is commonly known as the reign of the Four Right-guided Caliphs which ended by the death of Ali and coming of Mu'awya to power. Four years before his death in the year 690, Mu'awya secured the succession of his son, thereby setting the precedent of hereditary monarchy which was followed by the Umayyad, Abbasid and other dynasties for several centuries. T.W. ARNOLD, THE CALIPHATE 22ff (1966).

On the constitutional history and nature of the first Islamic state of Medina, see FARUKI, EVOLUTION, *supra* note 17, at 16-36; MOHAMED S. EL-AWA, ON THE POLITICAL SYSTEM OF THE ISLAMIC STATE 26-62 (1980).

19. *See generally* AHMAD HASAN, THE EARLY DEVELOPMENT OF ISLAMIC JURISPRUDENCE (1970); JOSEPH SCHACHT, THE ORIGINS OF MUHAMMADAN JURISPRUDENCE (1959).

A. The Constitutional Theory of the Medina State

It is somewhat a contradiction in terms to speak of the constitutional theory of the Medina state. The selection and powers of the ruler of that state, and the manner in which he exercised them, did not contemplate the institutions and processes of modern constitutionalism, such as effective limitations of powers through political and judicial accountability. It is still useful to review and evaluate the main features and principles of that state in constitutional terms because that state continues to be raised by powerful political forces as the model to be implemented by Islamic countries today.

Muslims, past and present, conceive of the Medina state as a religious state established and ruled by the Prophet Muhammad who, according to Muslim belief, was guided by Divine Will through revelation. In modern constitutional terms, the Prophet was the original sovereign and sole human source of law and political authority in the Medina state. Moreover, the subjects of that state are believed to have been the ultimate Muslim community of devout believers who were the embodiment of the ideal Islamic behavior under the immediate instruction and supervision of the Prophet himself. By definition, therefore, the exact model of the Medina state cannot be fully replicated. Yet, that model is supposed to forever provide Muslim communities with the concepts, institutions and mechanisms of government under Shari'a. What guidance can be drawn from the constitutional features of the Medina state as an Islamic model, and what are the concepts, institutions and mechanisms which should be implemented if that model is to be followed today?

The key constitutional features of the Medina state derive from the central role of the Prophet as the ultimate source of validity and legality, who was operating in the context of a traditional tribal society. In that setting, it was natural for the first Muslims to accept the complete unfettered political and legal authority of the Prophet as the patriarch of the community, especially since he was believed to be guided by divine revelation. Thus, it was simply inconceivable for the Prophet's political and legal powers to be restricted or challenged by any human agency.

Upon the Prophet's death, his successors (caliphs) were selected by a very small group of leading Muslims, or appointed by the preceding caliph, and then confirmed by the general Muslim population through a mass oath of allegiance known as *by'a*.[20] From the legal constitutional point of view, the caliph enjoyed absolute powers for life because, once *by'a* was given, there was no

20. ARNOLD, *supra* note 18, at 19-22; FARUKI, EVOLUTION, *supra* note 17, at 16-19.

mechanism for withdrawing or restricting it. This is illustrated by the fact that three (Umar, Uthman and Ali) of the four caliphs of the Medina state were assassinated. Due to the lack of the concept and mechanism of peaceful transfer of political power, the whole Muslim community was engulfed in civil war after the assassination of the third caliph, Uthman, and throughout the reign of Ali until his assassination and the establishment of the Umayyad dynasty by military force in 661. Thus, the Medina state lasted no more than thirty years after the Prophet's death, and ended in total civil war.[21]

Although the caliphs did not enjoy the Prophet's religious authority, they in fact exercised the full range of his political and legal powers.[22] In this way, the concept of absolute rule was entrenched by the lack of any legal mechanism for the accountability of ruler to the ruled. This is true, in my view, despite the existence of the notion of *shura* as an instrument of popular political participation. As I have explained elsewhere, both the textual sources and historical practice of *shura* made it an advisory function since the caliph had complete discretion whether or not to seek advice, on which matters, and was not bound by the advice given.[23] This does not mean that the notion of *shura* cannot be evolved into a modern Islamic constitutional principle whereby the government of the day will be representative of, and responsive to, the will of the governed. In fact, this is precisely the sort of development many Muslims are calling for today. To achieve this result, however, the concept must be clarified and disassociated from its limited historical usage.

It should be noted that I am concerned here with the lack of limitation of powers and accountability as legal concepts and institutions, rather than as anthropological phenomena. Space does not permit detailed analysis of the realities of political and social relations in the early Islamic era.[24] In any case, I do not find such an exercise particularly helpful in evaluating the implications of tradi-

---

21. For a brief survey of these events, see *id.* at 16-23.

22. Khalid M. Ishaque, *Al-Ahkam Al-Sultaniya: Laws of Government in Islam*, 4 ISLAMIC STUD. 293 (1970).

The caliphs were not original human legislators in the same sense the Prophet was before them because, as decreed by verse 33:40 of the Qur'an, divine revelation ceased with the Prophet's death. However, as the ultimate rulers of the community, the caliphs had the power to determine the authoritative interpretation of relevant texts of the Qur'an and Sunna as well as to exercise original law-making powers in matters not specifically covered by the Qur'an and Sunna. For an explanation of this point, see AN-NA'IM, TOWARD, *supra* note 5, at 77-78.

The Qur'an is the scripture which Muslims believe to be the final and conclusive divine revelation. It is cited in this paper by number of chapter, followed by number of verse. Sunna is the record of utterances and traditions attributed to the Prophet.

23. *Id.* at 78-80.

24. *See, e.g.*, LAPIDUS, *supra* note 16, at 11-53.

tional Islamic political theory as it applies in the modern context. This is due to the fact that the recent radical transformation of Islamic societies, and their local and international environments, make the patterns of political participation and power relations of the early Islamic era largely irrelevant, if not counter-productive. For example, to the extent that there was political participation in the sense of consensus and mediation to minimize conflict in a traditional setting, that practice did not normally include women and non-Muslims. In my view, neither is that traditional model of tribal participation appropriate for the state societies of today, nor is the exclusion of women and non-Muslims acceptable from a civil rights point of view.

B. Evolution and Present Status of Islamic Constitutional Theory

In view of the manner in which the Umayyad Dynasty was established in 661 and ruled the expanding Muslim empire until 750, that period of Islamic political history can only be described as secular. Whether in the direct appointment of a successor by the ruling calif, the administration of the state, adjudicating between competing Arab and non-Arab political forces, and so forth, the Umayyad caliphs pursued purely pragmatic secular politics. It is true that the caliphs utilized Islamic sentiments, particularly in the struggle against the external enemies, and performed the public functions of religious leaders, "but these were more gestures of practical politics than religious conviction."[25]

Despite the secular orientation of the Islamic state at the time, and perhaps because of it, that period witnessed the emergence of speculative or theoretical Shari'a jurisprudence. Denied effective political and judicial power, the *Ulama* (scholars and jurists) began to develop Shari'a as an ideal model of the comprehensive Islamic system.[26] Notwithstanding brief periods when the Ulama were allied with the rulers or were closely consulted by them, especially during the early Abbasid era,[27] the formative stages and subsequent development of Shari'a were characterized by a speculative theoretical orientation. The theory of Shari'a and practice of Muslims did coincide in some matters of daily administration of justice, especially in the fields of family law and inheritance, but not in political

25. FARUKI, EVOLUTION, *supra* note 17, at 28.

26. *Id.* at 29.

27. The Abbasids Dynasty was established in the year 750 after the overthrow of the Umayyads by military force. *Id.* at 32. To legitimize their revolt against the Umayyads, the Abbasids appealed to religious sentiments and asserted the primacy of Islam in the affairs of the state. *Id.* Nevertheless, their government "borrowed heavily from or was influenced by Sassanid ideas of an absolute monarch with super-human qualities." *Id.*

matters and affairs of the state.[28]

Thus, the dichotomy between the theory of Shari'a and Muslim practice through the ages is strongest in constitutional issues. This resulted in the emergence of two contradictory views of constitutional theory. The predominant view tended to make concessions to political expediency or "necessity" in the interest of maintaining the unity and cohesion of the Islamic state.[29] As long as the rulers maintained an acceptable level of commitment to Shari'a in other fields, Ulama of this group were willing to accept and rationalize the rulers' absolute political powers and emphasized the subjects' duty of obedience in order to avoid *fitna* (political upheaval and civil war).[30] According to this position, subjects should obey the ruler except when that would entail violation of Shari'a. But since this group of Ulama took an extremely restrictive view of when this might happen in concrete and practical terms, and rulers could always maintain that their policies were in fact consistent with Shari'a,[31] it was not possible to justify political opposition or dissent as such.[32] Even if the right to political opposition existed in theory, there was no mechanism for its lawful exercise in practice.[33]

The other, minority view, simply disregarded reality in favor of maintaining an ideal model in which rulers fully comply with the dictates of Shari'a as indicated to them by the Ulama, thereby securing the rights of all subjects.[34] By theorizing exclusively on what *ought* to be the case, this group of Ulama simply avoided the

28. *Id.* at 33-34; AN-NA'IM, TOWARD, *supra* note 5, at 31-33.

29. This dominant view was represented by Ulama such as al-Baqillani (d. 1012), al-Baghdadi (d. 1037), al-Mawardi (d. 1058), al-Ghazzali (d. 1111). For a review of the ideas of these Ulama see, FARUKI, EVOLUTION, *supra* note 17, at 43-52 and 56-66; ERWIN I.J. ROSENTHAL, POLITICAL THOUGHT IN MEDIEVAL ISLAM 27-61 (1958).

30. ARNOLD, *supra* note 18, at 48-50; FARUKI, EVOLUTION, *supra* note 17, at 35-36; H.A.R. GIBB, CONSTITUTIONAL ORGANIZATION, LAW IN THE MIDDLE EAST 14-16 (M. Khadduri and H. Liebesney eds., 1955).

31. As previously indicated, the ruler had an effective monopoly on what the position of Shari'a is on a given issue. AN-NA'IM, TOWARD, *supra* note 5, at 77-78. There was no independent arbiter, the equivalent of a modern Supreme Court, to adjudicate between the ruler of the day and the opponent of any of his policies or practices.

32. This is the dominant view in that branch of theoretical Shari'a dealing with constitutional matters and affairs, known as *al-siyasa al-shar'iya* (politics in accordance with Shari'a). On this branch of Shari'a, see N.J. COULSON, A HISTORY OF ISLAMIC LAW 129, 132-34, 147, 161, 172, & 184-85 (1964); JOSEPH SCHACHT, INTRODUCTION TO ISLAMIC LAW, 48-56 (1964).

33. M. Khadduri, *The Juridical Theory of the Islamic State*, 41 MUSLIM WORLD 184-85 (1951).

34. The primary example of this group of Ulama is Ibn Taymiyya. *See generally* OMAR FARRUKH, IBN TAYMIYYA ON PUBLIC AND PRIVATE LAW IN ISLAM OR PUBLIC POLICY IN ISLAMIC JURISPRUDENCE (1966); *see also* G.E VON GRUNEBAUM, ISLAM: ESSAYS IN THE NATURE AND GROWTH OF A CULTURAL TRADITION 68 (1955); MALCOLM H. KERR, ISLAMIC REFORM: THE POLITICAL AND LEGAL THEORIES OF MUHAMMAD ABDUH AND RASHID RIDA 220 (1966).

whole question of what happens when rulers fail to implement the ideal model. As observed by Coulson, the "supreme paradox, which leads to an outright nullification of this pious ideal, lies in the fact that the Shari'a fails to provide any guarantee that government will, in practice, assume this ideal form, and that, far from ensuring the existence of practical remedies against the ruler's abuse of his recognized powers, it [Shari'a] simply counsels acceptance of such abuse."[35]

While these inadequate views of the relationship between the individual and the state persist to the present day,[36] the realities of political and social power relations have been drastically transformed throughout the Muslim world.[37] As a result of the colonial intrusion of the late nineteenth century and other external influences as well as internal political and social developments,[38] the Muslim world is now constituted as separate independent nation states.[39] Western secular law has effectively displaced Shari'a in almost all of these states, especially in constitutional and public law matters.[40] Even countries like Saudi Arabia, which maintained Shari'a as their constitutional and legal systems, have more recently adopted some of the power structures and legal concepts of modern nation states.[41]

Despite these changes, the theoretical commitment to implement Shari'a has persisted throughout the Muslim world. This apparent paradox is explained by Anderson as follows:

> To a Muslim, it has always been a far more heinous sin to deny or question the divine revelation than to fail to obey it. So it seemed preferable to continue to pay lip-service to an inviolate Shari'a, as the only law of fundamental authority, and to excuse departure from much of it in practice by appealing to the doctrine of necessity (*darura*), rather than to make any attempt to adapt that law to the circumstances and needs of contemporary life.[42]

---

35. N.J. Coulson, *The State and the Individual in Islamic Law*, 6 INT'L & COMP. L. Q. 55-56 (1957).

36. *See* AN-NA'IM, TOWARD, *supra* note 5, at 94-97; MAYER, *supra* note 15, at 52-71.

37. *See* FARUKI, EVOLUTION, *supra* note 17, at 55-93 for a discussion on constitutional thinking and developments from the end of the Abbasid era (1258) to the Ottoman and Mughal period (1500-1700).

38. *See id.* at 112-200 for a review of developments within the Muslim world and reaction to the Western intrusion.

39. *See generally* JAMES PISCATORI, ISLAM IN A WORLD OF NATION-STATES (1986).

40. J.N.D. ANDERSON, LAW REFORM IN THE MUSLIM WORLD 1-2, 33 (1976); COULSON, *supra* note 32, at 161; HERBERT LIEBESNY, THE LAW OF THE NEAR AND MIDDLE EAST 56 (1975); .

41. Bryant W. Seaman, *Islamic Law and Modern Government: Saudi Arabia Supplements the Shari'a to Regulate Development*, 18 COLUM. J. TRANSNAT'L L. 413 (1980).

42. ANDERSON, *supra* note 40, at 36.

Although I believe that this explanation is valid, it is now clear that many Muslims feel that the logic of necessity is weakening as the political independence and economic prosperity of Muslim peoples increase in this age of self-determination. As illustrated by the dramatic rise of Islamic resurgence in most parts of the Muslim world, demands for the complete and immediate application of Shari'a are gaining in political power and influence.[43] To many Muslims, the issue is no longer whether or not to apply Shari'a, it is rather how to apply it in ways that are consistent with the national and international circumstances of today. I will briefly address this question in general constitutional terms before turning to its specific implications for civil rights.

C. *Islamic Constitutionalism in the Modern Context*

In light of the above analysis, it is clear that the fundamental challenge facing Islamic constitutional theory is how to transform the traditional concept of personal religious legitimacy of political power into conceptually and effectively limited institutional authority. As I will show in the next section, there are very serious civil rights objections to traditional formulations of Shari'a. But even if those objections are adequately redressed through Islamic law reform, the question remains: If Shari'a is supposed to be the guardian of rights, how will the "correct" view of Shari'a be identified and implemented in concrete situations?

The Iranian revolution of 1979 has clearly illustrated, in my view, the inadequacy of the traditional approach, even when there is the political will to implement it.[44] On the premise that the essential function of an Islamic state is to implement the will of God as expressed in Shari'a, it is reasoned that the most qualified Ulama should be constituted as guardians over the constitution to ensure that the state complies with the dictates of Shari'a.[45] This is the first and only modern application of the notion that the Ulama should act as the institutional guardian over the state (known in Arabic as *wilayat al-faqih*, *vilayat-i-faqih* in Farsi). As I have indicated elsewhere,[46] this notion reflects a deeper and more profound ambivalence in Islamic constitutional theory about the issue of sovereignty.

---

43. AN-NA'IM, TOWARD, *supra* note 5, at 2-4.

44. On the events and developments of the Iranian revolution, see SHAROUGH AKHAVI, IRAN: IMPLEMENTATION OF AN ISLAMIC STATE, ISLAM IN ASIA: POLITICS AND SOCIETY 32-40 (J. Esposito ed. 1987).

45. *See* the subtitle "The Mandate to the Just Clergy" and Articles 4 and 5 of the Iranian Constitution of 1979, *reprinted in* CONSTITUTIONS OF THE COUNTRIES OF THE WORLD 9 (Albert P. Blaustein and Gisbert H. Flanz eds., 1980).

46. AN-NA'IM, TOWARD, *supra* note 5, at 81-84.

The logic behind the Ulama's guardianship of the state is that, since Muslims attribute ultimate sovereignty to God, they must submit to the intermediate sovereignty of the Ulama as the human agents of divine sovereignty.[47] Even if one accepts the dubious proposition that a group of persons can act as the human agents of God, there is bound to be disagreement on who those persons are or ought to be. In any case, members of that group will disagree among themselves in carrying out that function. Both aspects of guardianship by the Ulama will therefore involve political considerations and processes. As illustrated by experience in Iran since the revolution,[48] the Ulama's guardianship of the state is nothing more or less than a fiction designed to hide the realities of political struggle for power. Given this state of affairs, the protection and promotion of civil rights become imperative in any modern state, be it openly secular or so-called Islamic.

While it may have somewhat different connotations or emphasis' in international law, constitutional law, political theory and so forth, sovereignty always signifies the highest governmental, legal or political authority in the state.[49] For analytical purposes, however, it may be helpful to distinguish between the sovereign of a given state and the bodies, organs or institutions to which that sovereign may delegate certain aspects or functions of sovereignty in specific circumstances. According to common Muslim belief, God is the Sovereign of any Islamic state.[50] For all practical purposes, however, it has always been recognized that there must be a human agent of the Divine Sovereign. All Muslims agree that the Prophet was the sole human agent of the Divine Sovereign during his lifetime, and there is perhaps common agreement that the caliphs of

---

47. This notion is not peculiar to Shi'i constitutional theory, but also seem to underlay the ideas of prominent Sunni Ulama, such as Ibn Taymiyya who enjoys great influence in Saudi Arabia and many other Islamic countries. The same logic would seem to apply in both cases: since the essential function of the state is to implement Shari'a, why not appoint the Ulama as guardians to ensure that the state fulfills its obligation?

48. The Iran model seeks to minimize the dangers and problems of disagreement among the Ulama by providing for a single person as the ultimate holder of the mandate of guardianship. But as can be seen in the express terms of Articles 5 and 107, the 1979 Constitution could not avoid providing for disagreement among the Ulama on the fundamental question of the selection of that person. Thus, the political nature of this "institution" remains in the selection of this uncrowned king, as well as in performance of his functions and dealings with the different organs of the state, his subsequent relationship with the Ulama, and so forth.

49. *See* FRANCIS W. COKER, *Sovereignty*, 14 ENCYCLOPEDIA OF THE SOCIAL SCIENCES 265 (Edwin R.A. Seligman ed. 1930); BERNARD CRICK, *Sovereignty*, 3 INTERNATIONAL ENCYCLOPEDIA OF THE SOCIAL SCIENCES 77 (David L. Sills ed. 1968); BLACK'S LAW DICTIONARY 1252 (1979).

50. This is the common understanding of one of the main themes of the Qur'an as expressed in, *e.g.*, verses 2:110, and 3:26-27. *See* H.A.R. GIBB, MOHAMMADANISM 39 (1955).

the Medina state were legitimate successors of the Prophet in that role.[51] But that does not answer the question of who is, or ought to be, the human sovereign today. More significantly, the experience of early Muslims provides little assistance on practical questions such as how the modern equivalent of the caliph is to be selected, whether and how he can be made accountable for his conduct today.[52]

Whether inspired by, or in response to, the Western notion of popular or people's sovereignty, some modern Muslim authors have suggested that the agent of divine sovereignty should be the whole *Umma* (the Muslim nation or community), rather than a single person or group of persons.[53] Provided the Umma is understood to include all the citizens of the state on completely equal terms, this idea can form the basis of a modern Islamic constitutional theory because it is fully consistent with both religious doctrine and the aspirations of Muslims for responsible representative government. As I will explain in the next section, however, this requires Islamic law reform to remove all features of inequality of women and non-Muslims under Shari'a.

A modern Islamic constitutional theory would also require the development of adequate mechanisms and institutions for the election and accountability of government, and other features of modern constitutionalism. As suggested earlier, this can be done through the development of the notion of *shura* into a binding principle of representative government rather than merely discretionary consultation.[54] Civil rights are needed not only in order to evolve and elaborate this modern concept of *shura*, but also for the proper implementation of the ensuing constitutional theory.

Finally, some reference must be made to the question of separation of religion and state, and its implications to a modern Islamic

51. MAJID KHADDURI, WAR AND PEACE IN THE LAW OF ISLAM 10 (1955).

52. The masculine pronoun is used to indicate that, according to the prevailing view of Shari'a, the ruler of an Islamic state should be a man. I do not share this view of Shari'a, but I must admit that, despite recent experience with the election of women Prime Ministers in the Islamic states of Pakistan and Bangladesh, masculinity remains a prerequisite for the head of an Islamic state in the minds of the vast majority of Muslims today.

53. *See generally* MUHAMMAD B. AL-MUTI'I, HAQIQAT AL-ISLAM WA USUL AL-HUKUM (ARABIC: THE TRUTH ABOUT ISLAM AND THE FOUNDATIONS OF GOVERNMENT, 1344 HIJRI); TAJ AL-DIN AL-NBAHANI, AL-DAWLA AL-ISLAMIYA (ARABIC: THE ISLAMIC STATE) 1952.

For a concise statement of this proposal in terms of representative constitutional government, see ABD AL-QADIR AUDA, AL ISLAM WA AWDA'UNA AL-SIYASIYYA (ARABIC: ISLAM AND OUR POLITICAL AFFAIRS 81-82 (1980)).

54. This development would require the reinterpretation of the relevant verses of the Qur'an, mainly 3:159 and 42:38, in accordance with a new principle of construction. *See* AN-NA'IM, TOWARD, *supra* note 5, at 52-68 for a proposal of such a principle of construction and its prospects today.

constitutional theory. In my view, it would be unrealistic, if not counter-productive, to expect Muslims to replicate the Western principle of separation of church and state. Neither Islamic doctrine nor the historical experience of Muslims would permit the evolution and implementation of the Western model in this regard.[55] Nevertheless, I also believe that the universality and centrality of Islam as a factor in the lives of Muslims does not preclude the evolution of a modern Islamic constitutional theory. To achieve this objective, however, it is necessary to undertake fundamental Islamic law reform to address the civil rights issues indicated below. I believe such reform to be entirely possible, indeed imperative, today.[56]

III. Civil Rights in Modern Islamic Constitutional Theory

Even if these issues of modern Islamic constitutional theory are resolved satisfactorily, there remain some serious specific civil rights problems with historical formulations of Shari'a at the theoretical level. I submit that the same modernist orientation and reform technique applied to the general constitutional questions raised above can also be employed to resolve these theoretical civil rights problems. In this section, I will present a brief survey of some of these problems, and then focus on the civil rights situation in present day Islamic countries.

A. *Shari'a and Civil Rights*

It must first be emphasized that, like English common law and other legal systems, the general rule of Shari'a is that people are guaranteed freedom of action (or inaction) unless, and only to the extent that, action (or inaction) is prohibited or restricted by the provisions of Shari'a itself.[57] In this sense, there are no theoretical limitations on civil rights under Shari'a except in specific cases, some of which are highlighted below. This apparently categorical general rule is rendered ambivalent and confusing by the diffused nature of Shari'a and great extent of disagreement among the Ulama who sometimes hold significantly different, if not diametrically opposed, views on the position of Shari'a on a given issue or

---

55. This view is shared by most Western scholars of Islam. *See, e.g.*, John L. Esposito, Voices of Resurgent Islam 3-5 (John L. Esposito ed., 1983); Bernard Lewis, *The Return of Islam*, Religion and Politics in the Middle East 9 (Michael Curtis ed. 1981); Danien Pipes, In the Path of God 4ff (1983); John Voll, *Renewal and Reform in Islamic History: Tajdid and Islam*, 32 (1983).

56. For a full explanation and substantiation of this position, see An-Na'im, Toward, *supra* note 5, at 69-100.

57. *See* Coulson, *supra* note 32, at 82-84; Hasan, *supra* note 19, at 34-39; Rahman, *supra* note 15, at 83-84.

situation.[58]

Muslims are therefore often uncertain about whether they have the right to act or refrain from action under Shari'a, and can consequently be manipulated in one way or another by rulers and their allies or supporters among the Ulama. Such manipulation is not only more likely in civil rights matters because that tends to serve the political interest of rulers, but is also more effective in view of Shari'a's emphasis on the subject's duty to obey the ruler in order to avoid political upheaval. As indicated earlier, this state of affairs makes it harder for political dissidents or opponents of the government of the day to justify their position from a Shari'a point of view.

Beside the generally inhibiting effect of this state of affairs on the civil rights of all citizens, women and non-Muslims are subjected to further restrictions under historical formulations of Shari'a. Briefly stated, the inequality of, or discrimination against, women and non-Muslims include the following features:[59]

Women: Verse 4:34 of the Qur'an has been taken to establish a general principle of men's guardianship (*qawama*) over women, thereby denying women the right to hold any public office involving the exercise of authority over men. While jurists differ in their views on the extent of denying women access to public office, none of them would grant women equality to men in this regard. By virtue of this general principle (together with certain specific provisions of the Qur'an and Sunna), women suffer much discrimination in family law, inheritance, and so forth.

Under the same general principle of qawama, and as a result of the interpretation commonly given to various verses of the Qur'an (e.g., 24:31 33:33, 53 and 59), Shari'a restricts the right of women to appear and speak in public or associate with men. Thus, although women have the same freedom of belief and opinion enjoyed by

58. COULSON, *supra* note 32, at 47-51; KEMAL A. FARUKI, ISLAMIC JURISPRUDENCE 166-94 (1975).

It has always been believed that it is improper to attempt to codify Shari'a because no view can be accepted as authoritative enough to be codified and enforced. In common Muslim belief, disagreement among the Ulama is greatly valued as a feature of flexibility and Divine grace, and individual Muslims should have freedom of choice among different views as a matter of conscience. SCHACHT, *supra* note 32, at 68 n.1.

59. I have explained and substantiated in detail these and other features of inequality and discrimination against women and non-Muslims under Shari'a in AN-NA'IM, TOWARD, *supra* note 5, at chs. 4, 5 & 7. *See also* Abdullahi A. An-Na'im, *The Rights of Women and International Law in the Muslim Context*, 9 WHITTIER L. REV. 491 (1987); *Religious Minorities and the Limits of Cultural Relativism*, 9 HUM. RTS. Q. 1 (1987).

For a detailed discussion of these issues in the broader context of human rights, see generally MAYER, *supra* note 15, at chs. 5-7.

men, their opportunity to exercise this right is greatly inhibited by restrictions on their access to the public domain.

Non-Muslims: According to the strict theory of Shari'a, non-Muslims are not entitled to remain within the territory of an Islamic state except under a special status of *dhimma*. This status guarantees them security of life and property, freedom of religion and communal autonomy subject to the jurisdiction of the Islamic state in public affairs. As such, non-Muslims are free to organize and conduct their private and communal affairs, but they have no right to hold any public office which involves the exercise of authority over Muslims.

Non-Muslims are also subjected to various types of discrimination in their dealings with Muslims. For example, whereas Muslims may propagate Islam among non-Muslims, and conversion to Islam should be actively encouraged by the state, non-Muslims have no right to propagate their faith, at least among Muslims, and conversion away from Islam is a capital offense under Shari'a.

Other examples of inequality and discrimination against women and non-Muslims can be cited, but my purpose here is to illustrate the sort of civil rights problems which will arise should Shari'a be applied today. Some advocates of Shari'a today point to reports of a few examples of participation by leading Muslim women, and the role of non-Muslims in the administration, as evidence of practical equality and non-discrimination. These, I submit, were the exceptions which prove the rule. Without going into questions about the historical accuracy of these reports and the level and extent of such participation, the fact remains that there was no legal and institutional basis for it under the strict rules of Shari'a.

Moreover, I submit that whatever political or sociological justifications may have existed in the past for these aspects of Shari'a, they are no longer valid in the context of the modern Islamic state. This view appears to be shared by the majority of Muslims today, as evidenced by the fact that the national constitutions of most Islamic states now provide for equality and prohibit discrimination on grounds of gender or religion. Many Islamic countries are also parties to international human rights treaties which require equality and non-discrimination. It is true that Islamic countries rarely live up to the level of their constitutional or international civil rights commitments, but that is a common failure of non-Islamic countries as well.

While emphasizing the need to understand and combat the underlying causes of this common failure, I find it significant that many Muslims around the world express commitment to the values of constitutionalism and civil rights. To assist these Muslims in honoring that commitment, I suggest the implementation of internal Islamic law reform in order to resolve the general constitutional issues raised earlier and to achieve complete equality for women and non-Muslims as a matter of Shari'a.[60] Such reform, I suggest, will contribute to the process of legitimizing and indigenizing the values of political participation, accountability and equality before the law, thereby enhancing the prospects of civil rights in Islamic societies. But this theoretical contribution can only be implemented in the context of the concrete circumstances of the Muslim world today.

B. *Civil Rights in the Present Muslim World*

As indicated in the Introduction, this paper's focus on issues of Islamic constitutional and civil rights theory should not be taken to imply that Islam is the only available ideology in the Muslim world. Muslims in fact subscribe to a wide range of ideological orientations, and their constitutional and legal systems must respond to issues and concerns shared by other developing nations. Although I believe that Islamic discourse is extremely important in any predominantly Muslim country today,[61] I must emphasize that it is by no means the only one even in those countries which claim a totally Islamic identity, be it of the traditional type such as that of Saudi Arabia, or of the revolutionary variety, as in the case of Iran.

Moreover, there is such a vast range of perceptions and practices of Islam among Muslim peoples, that one cannot speak of Islamic discourse as a common feature of these societies except at a very high level of abstraction and generalization. The role of Islam in political, constitutional and legal systems of Islamic countries should be seen as integral to the role of culture as the local setting underlying the social production of meaning.[62] While Islam as a culture has spread globally, it also became locally restricted, thereby producing vastly different perceptions and practices of the same religion.[63] "In other words, there is no universal Islam, but a

60. *See generally* AN-NA'IM, TOWARD, *supra* note 5, at ch. 3, for a detailed *Islamic* methodology of reform and its application to all issues of inequality and discrimination.

61. As evidenced by the size and depth of literature, the importance of Islam is appreciated by many scholars and observers of Islamic countries. The most recent works on the subject include: ISLAM AND THE POLITICAL ECONOMY OF MEANING: COMPARATIVE STUDIES OF MUSLIM DISCOURSE (William R. Roff ed. 1987); ISLAM, POLITICS AND SOCIAL MOVEMENTS (Edmund Burke, III and Ira Lapidus eds., 1988); HENRY MUNSON, JR., ISLAM AND REVOLUTION IN THE MIDDLE EAST (1988); *Islam and Politics*, 10 THIRD WORLD Q. 235 (1988).

62. CLIFFORD GEERTZ, INTERPRETATION OF CULTURE 193-233 (1973).

63. For an explanation and illustration of this phenomenon, see generally CLIFFORD GEERTZ, ISLAM OBSERVED: RELIGIOUS DEVELOPMENT IN MOROCCO AND INDONESIA (1971).

variety of local Islamic cultures."[64]

In light of these caveats on the limitations of the analysis of this paper, I now wish to focus on the realities of civil rights in Islamic countries. The countries of the present Muslim world are governed by a wide variety of regimes. At one end of the spectrum, there is the traditional absolute monarchies of Saudi Arabia and the Gulf states, limited or "constitutional" monarchies in Morocco and Jordan, and military/single party dictatorships, as in Iraq and Syria. While Iran presents the only example of an ideologically "Islamic" civilian government, the military dictatorship of the Sudan is generally believed to be also ideologically Islamic and perhaps preparing to follow the example of Iran. At the other end, some Islamic countries, such as Pakistan, Bangladesh and Malaysia, enjoy a reasonable, though somewhat precarious or temporary, degree of democratic constitutional government.

The vast majority of the governments of the Muslim world have very little regard for civil rights, but in most cases the rationale of this oppression is not observance of the teachings of Islam or the application of Shari'a as such. For example, the strongly secular regimes of Iraq and Syria are most notorious for their suppression of civil rights, and the ruling elite in Indonesia have consistently violated the civil rights of Islamic groups as well as those of communists and left wing activists. However, civil rights violations are expressly linked to an Islamic ideology in countries like Iran, the Sudan and Saudi Arabia. Both secular and theocratic types of regimes, however, often invoke "Islamic" arguments to legitimate their repressive policies in the name of political stability, national security and liberation and so forth.

Given the historical ambivalence of Shari'a on crucial constitutional issues and its violation of the civil rights of women and non-Muslims, coupled with the present circumstances of the politics of Islamization in some countries,[65] one can only conclude that the relationship between Shari'a and civil rights is rather negative. Nevertheless, recalling my earlier analysis of the contestability of culture, I believe that since Shari'a is an *historically conditioned* interpretation of Islamic sources, a modern reinterpretation is possible and desirable today. In this light, I maintain that Islam can and should still be used as a valuable cultural resource to legitimize and enhance civil rights in Islamic societies.

64. BASSAM TIBI, The European Tradition of Human Rights and the Culture of Islam, HUMAN RIGHTS IN AFRICA, *supra* note 13, at 104, 113.

65. *See, e.g., Religious Freedom in Egypt: Under the Shadow of the Dhimma System*, RELIGIOUS LIBERTY AND HUMAN RIGHTS IN NATIONS AND RELIGIONS, 43 (L. Swedler ed. 1986); Abdullahi A. An-Na'im, *Constitutionalism and Islamization in the Sudan*, 36 AFR. TODAY 11 (1989).

Despite the apparently poor status of civil rights in Islamic countries, I do not believe that the situation is hopeless. In the same countries, there are powerful modernist forces which are asserting their civil rights. I suggest that these forces can greatly enhance their position by enlisting Islamic support for their legitimate claims. This is both crucial because of the political and moral force of Islam in those countries, and possible to achieve by applying a modernist reinterpretation of Islamic sources.[66] In terms of the thesis of this paper, the struggle for civil rights in Islamic countries should utilize the processes of internal discourse and cross-cultural dialogue to realize the shared ideals of dignity, liberty and well-being for all.

IV. Conclusion: Cooperation in Realizing Shared Ideals

Finally, I wish to conclude with a summary of my thesis and offer some reflections on the theme of this symposium in light of the internal critique of the Islamic constitutional and civil rights tradition presented in this paper.

I argue that all human societies should strive to realize the shared ideals of human dignity, liberty and well-being. Different approaches to achieving this end may be justified by historical context and material, social and political circumstances of each society at any given point in time. For example, traditional societies tend to emphasize the public good over the private good, and to subordinate the rights of the individual to the interests of the community. This approach may well be more conducive to realizing human dignity, liberty and well-being in the historical context and circumstances of a particular society. But as the context and circumstances of that society change, it should adapt its approach accordingly, including the re-adjustment of the relationship between the individual and the community.

This does not indicate a deterministic evolutionary approach whereby "late" developing societies are simply following the path previously set by "advanced" societies. Each society should have its own manner of adaptation to changing circumstances and adjustment of the relationship between the individual and the community. On the other hand, cultural autonomy in this adaptation and adjustment process does not mean complete isolation from the influence of other societies. Such influence is usually unavoidable, and should be used constructively by reflecting due respect for, and sensitivity to, internal legitimacy and dynamics of change and reform in each society.

---

66. For a full statement and substantiation of this argument, see generally Abdullahi A. An-Na'im, *Human Rights in the Muslim World: Socio-Political Conditions and Scriptural Imperatives*, 3 Harv. Hum. Rts. J. 13 (1990).

While it is true that modern formulations of civil rights emerged from the Western liberal tradition, their underlying values of dignity, liberty and well-being are shared by Islamic societies. In adopting modern civil rights regimes, and adapting them to their own cultures and circumstances, Islamic societies are merely responding to the challenge of realizing ideals they already share in the modern context. This, however, is an exceedingly difficult and delicate task. It requires philosophical and conceptual clarity consistent with the criteria of internal cultural legitimacy; development of legal institutions, mechanisms and remedies; and the commitment of the political process to these goals and policies.

A decent respect to the opinion(s) of Muslim peoples means accepting their choice to retain the central role of Islam in their lives (if and to the extent that they wish to do so), and supporting them in evolving their own regimes of civil rights in that context. Muslims are entitled to pursue their own model(s) of constitutionalism and civil rights within the framework of an Islamic ideology. The negative relationship between Shari'a and civil rights should not lead to the conclusion that Muslims must abandon Islam and adopt a purely secular ideology in order to secure civil rights. Such a proposal is both objectionable to Muslims as a matter of principle, and unrealistic in practice.

Since Shari'a is simply a historically conditioned interpretation of Islamic sources, it should be possible to evolve an alternative interpretation which will legitimate and effectuate civil rights in the modern Muslim context. But the task of evolving and implementing this modern interpretation must be undertaken by Muslims working within their own cultural traditions. Others may support that internal discourse, but they should not try to preempt it by seeking to impose their own standards and models.

[8]
Human Rights in the Arab World: A Regional Perspective[1]

I. INTRODUCTION

The premise of this regional review and assessment of the human rights movement in the Arab world is that the wide variety of strategies for the effective and sustainable protection of these rights should always be determined and implemented in specific local, regional and global context. The paradox of self-regulation by the state in the definition and implementation of human rights standards, as briefly explained below, would emphasize the role of civil society. However, because both state and civil society tend to influence each other, either in favor or against the protection of human rights, through internal processes as well as external influence, these relationships should also be understood in local, regional and global contexts.

The challenge facing the advocates of the protection of human rights in any part of the world is how to promote positive aspects of these processes, and combat or minimize negative dimensions of these dynamic relationships. At all levels of analysis and action, one should seek to *combine* the best possible *immediate response* to specific problems with *long term strategies* for addressing the root causes and structural factors in the persistence of human rights violations. Because this combination can only be implemented through some sort of division of labor, it is necessary to coordinate the activities of local, regional and international actors according to an agreed framework.

---

1. I am profoundly grateful for the extensive research assistance of Essam El-Din Hassan, Research Director of the Hisham Mubarak Legal Center, Cairo, Egypt; and the helpful comments of Bahey Eldin Hassan, Emma Playfair, Clarisa Bencomo, and Ricky Goldstein. All the views and analysis presented here are my responsibility.

Throughout this regional review and assessment, I am particularly concerned with identifying and promoting ways of diminishing, and eventfully breaking what I call "human rights dependency." By this I mean the widely prevalent perception that *the governments of developing countries are more responsive to international pressure for the protection of human rights in their countries, than to the activities of local NGOs and other actors within their own societies.* Accordingly, international human rights NGOs tend to monitor human rights violations in developing countries, *with the indispensable help of local NGOs,* but publicize their findings mainly in Europe and North America in order to influence Western governments to pressure the governments of developing countries to protect human rights in their respective countries.[2] Moreover, local NGOs in developing countries also tend to depend on funding from, and seek publicity for their activities in, developing countries, instead of from and within their own countries or regions. In contrast, human rights are protected in developed countries by local NGOs, with the active support of their own local constituencies, and through activities addressed to their own governments and public opinion.

The complex web of "realistic" considerations which make this pattern of human rights activism unavoidable in the present context of the vast majority of developing countries are too obvious to warrant elaboration in the present limited space.[3] But it is equally clear, in my view, that this human rights dependency is extremely problematic for at least three main interrelated reasons.[4] First, it tends to perpetuate the public perception, in developing as well as developed countries, that the protection of human rights is a "Western" agenda rather than an internal priority of the

2. This and the following remarks are based on my personal experience as the Executive Director of Human Rights Watch/Africa from June 1993 to April 1995, and participation in the activities of several African and Arab human rights organizations. For example, I serve on the Board of Directors of the Institute for Human Rights and Development (based in Gambia), the Board of Trustees of the Cairo Institute for Human Rights Studies, the Advisory Council of the Arab Program for Human Rights Activists, and the Advisory Council of the Inter-African Network for Human Rights & Development (Afronet, based in Zambia). I was also a founding member of the Arab Working Group on Human Rights, from July 1997 until the Group terminated its activities in March 2001 due to operational difficulties.

For an overview and contact information of these and other NGOs in the Africa/Arab regions, *see* Marguerite Garling, *Building Bridges for Human Rights: Inter-African Initiatives in the Field of Human Rights, in* Interights (2001).

3. *See generally* Ted C. Lewellen, Dependency and Development: An Introduction to the Third World (1995) (discussing the complexities of human rights activism in developing countries).

4. Although the following remarks draw on my own experience with human rights organizations in developing countries, *supra* note 2, other human rights scholars have come to similar conclusions. *See, e.g.,* Claude E. Welch Jr., Protecting Human Rights in Africa: Strategies and Roles of Non-Governmental Organizations 301–14 (1995).

developing countries themselves. Second, NGOs in developing countries are not encouraged to seek the promotion of local political constituencies and funding sources within their own countries.

In addition to perpetuating perceptions of dependency, this reliance on Western political support and funding make NGOs in developing countries vulnerable to actual or potential governmental control of their "life-line," as illustrated by the case of Egypt discussed below. Third, both local and international NGOs are not accountable to the local societies of developing countries they claim to serve. While fully appreciating the profound need for international cooperation in diminishing the negative consequences of this complex and deeply entrenched web of multiple dependencies, I believe that effective and sustainable protection of human rights can only be achieved by each society for itself.

Accordingly, my emphasis in this essay is on national and regional NGOs as a means to diminishing human rights dependency. I am not calling for an end to, or even reduction of, international efforts to monitor and publicize violations in the region in order to "shame" Arab governments into greater compliance with human rights standards. On the contrary, I hope that such efforts will continue and increase in the future in view of the lack or weakness of local and regional human rights possibilities of protection and promotion of human rights within the Arab world, as explained below. But because international advocacy cannot be a substitute for work at the local and regional level, sufficient attention must be given to promoting local capacity. While strategies will necessarily vary according to context and over time, the constant objective of the international actors should always be greater cooperation in expanding the political and social "space" for local efforts and enhancing indigenous capacity for the protection of human rights.

Efforts to protect human rights are simply the present manifestation or expression of the constant struggle of persons and communities everywhere for realizing and maintaining human dignity and social justice in their respective contexts. This approach is now essential for the realization of the objectives of these ancient struggles in the present context of Arab societies because of the nature of the post-colonial state in this age of multi-faceted globalization. In my view, moral or philosophical justifications for the universality of human rights can be found in all major religious and cultural traditions of the world, which should be emphasized through an internal discourse within each tradition that also addresses those features of the religion or culture which are negative or hostile to human rights norms.[5] The

---

5. *See generally* HUMAN RIGHTS IN AFRICA: CROSS-CULTURAL PERSPECTIVES (Abdullahi Ahmed An-Na'im & Francis M. Deng eds., 1990); HUMAN RIGHTS IN CROSS-CULTURAL PERSPECTIVES: QUEST FOR CONSENSUS (Abdullahi Ahmed An-Na'im ed., 1992).

most obvious foundation of these rights is that they are necessary for protection of human dignity and achievement of social justice in the present context of the nation-state and global inter-state system. The basic fact of national politics and international relations is that, regardless of particularities of history, culture, political and social institutions, type of government, and so forth, all societies now live under specific forms of political organization commonly known as the nation-state, with particular powers and responsibilities at both the domestic and international level. This is not to say that all states are the same, as the underlying process of state-formation and operation tend to vary with the recent history and current context of each country. However, the essential features of states heighten the need to limit and regulate their powers. Ruling elites should not be allowed to use the structures and powers of the state, as they do in all Arab countries today, without the corresponding obligations.

For our purposes here in particular, whereas state sovereignty is commonly taken to mean exclusive domestic jurisdiction and the prerogative power to conduct international relations, it also raises corresponding obligations to respect and protect human rights. The autonomy and powers of the state to act or refrain from action are now conditioned by a variety of internal and external actors and factors which tend to interact within a framework of growing globalization. These include the dynamics of the processes of state-formation and demographic composition of the particular state, the role of competing political constituencies and social movements, economic and institutional resources, and regional and global geo-political and security considerations.[6] Consequently, human rights obligations should be discharged through a combination of internal efforts for legal and political accountability, on the one hand, and international cooperation and pressure, on the other. However, these external and internal spheres tend to interact and overlap, both in favor of as well as against the protection of human rights. It is important to understand this dynamic relationship precisely in order to more effectively pursue the possibilities of positive change, without taking a deterministic or naive view of the matter.

Mediation between competing concerns and perspectives within each polity has traditionally been regulated through constitutional norms and

---

6. Regarding human rights in the African context, which is similar to that of the Arab world in this regard, Welch observed:

> It would be presumptuous to place blame for the human rights abuses that have occurred on one factor alone. Rather, a combination of factors accounts for the problems in many states. Among these are historically searing colonial experiences, failures in the leadership of centralized governments, a high level of military involvement in politics, severe economic deprivations, cultural fragmentation, and weak regional means to promote and protect human rights. Lack of knowledge compounds the problems.

PROTECTING HUMAN RIGHTS IN AFRICA, *supra* note 4.

institutions as a framework for national politics, social policy, and economic life.[7] Moreover, principles of self-determination and national sovereignty under international law, as well as the realities of national politics and international relations, concede to the state exclusive control over their own territories and populations. Consequently, it is simply not possible to protect human rights in a practical and sustainable manner, without the consent and cooperation of the state in question. While "humanitarian intervention" can be justified in exceptional circumstances,[8] practical experience shows that the international community is neither able nor willing to replace the state in maintaining the long term legal, administrative, and other means for the protection of human rights in any part of the world. In any case, it is unacceptable from a human rights point of view for other states, whether acting unilaterally or multilaterally, to take control of a country in the name of the "good of its own people." After all, this is how European colonialism was rationalized in the past.[9] Therefore, one may wonder, what does the international dimension add to constitutional, legal, political and other means at the national level?

In my view, the *value added* of human rights is to provide an independent frame of reference, and practical mechanisms, for ensuring that governments do respect and protect the human rights of their citizens. Because horrific experiences have repeatedly shown that national governments cannot be trusted to maintain the necessary degree of protection for the rights of their own citizens, human rights were taken to be a matter of international concern under the Charter of the United Nations (UN), which provided for the protection of human rights as one of the purposes of the United Nations, under Article 1(3). Paradoxically, however, states continue to control the processes of defining and implementing human rights through international treaties and customary practice, as well as their domestic application within their own territories, as acknowledged by Article 2(7) of the UN Charter. Consequently, the question is how to achieve the international protection of human rights without violating national sovereignty, which is itself a collective human right under the first Article of the 1966 Covenants. It is not helpful to simply call for formal limitations on state sovereignty, because that is neither practically feasible nor necessarily good for the protection of human rights in the long term. As the practical

---

7. A discussion of the domestic constitutional/legal protection of human rights under the constitutions of Arab states is beyond the scope of this essay. *See, e.g.*, Fateh Azzam, Arab Constitutional Guarantees of Civil and Political Rights: A Comparative Analysis (1996).
8. *See, e.g.*, Fernando R. Teson, Humanitarian Intervention: An Inquiry Into Law and Morality (2d ed. 1997).
9. African peoples for example, were described as "not yet able to stand by themselves in the strenuous conditions of the modern world." John Iliffe, Africans: The History of a Continent 187 (1995). *See also* Roland E. Oliver, The African Experience 243 (2d ed. 1999).

expression of the fundamental human right to self-determination, strong sovereignty is both integral to the functioning of the present international order, and essential for the protection of national populations against exploitation and abuse by foreign powers and transnational corporations.

A more realistic and desirable approach, I suggest, is to seek to diminish the negative consequence of the paradox of self-regulation by the state through the infusion of the human rights ethos into the fabric of the state itself and the global context in which it operates. The protection of human rights should be the outcome of the free exercise of the right to self-determination, rather than an external imposition which violates that right. Accordingly, it is vitally important to understand *how the political will to uphold human rights is generated* within civil society, on the one hand, and *how to respond to civil society demands that are contrary to human rights norms*, on the other. At another level, it is also important to understand the nature of the state in its own context, the role of other internal and external actors, the economic dimensions, legitimate security concerns, and other *underlying causes* of human rights violations.

While neither comprehensive nor up to date in all respects, I hope that the following review and assessment of the Arab human rights movement will contribute to building consensus around a framework for cooperation among different segments of the international human rights movement through a clear contextual understanding of the possibilities and limitations of its regional components. The overview of developments in the next section should be seen in light of elements of both unity and diversity in the Arab world, as well as some political, economic, security and related factors in the recent history of the region as a whole, such as the Arab-Israeli conflict, Arab nationalism(s) and their legacies, and the political and social role of Islam. These contextual factors should also be taken into account in evaluating the main achievements, challenges and prospects of the Arab human rights movement.

II. AN OVERVIEW OF THE ARAB HUMAN RIGHTS MOVEMENT

In the following review of the main developments in the protection of human rights in the Arab world, I take this region to consist of all states members of the Arab League, because there is no alternative criterion of regional identification, despite the limitations of this one.[10] The first Article

10. The present membership of the League, in alphabetical order, is: Algeria, Bahrain, Djibouti, Egypt, Iraq, Jordan, Kuwait, Lebanon, Libya, Mauritania, Morocco, Oman, Palestine, Qatar, Saudi Arabia, Somalia, Sudan, Syria, Tunisia, United Arab Emirates, and Yemen.

of the Charter of the Arab League provides that it consists of the "independent Arab states" who have signed this Charter, and adds that every independent Arab state has the "right" to join the League by lodging an application with the Secretariat for consideration by the Council of the League.[11]

Because the Charter does not define what is an "Arab state," the matter is apparently decided in the complete discretion of pre-existing members of the League. Considering the list of the current twenty-one members, one can only conclude that inclusion or exclusion is decided by the concurrence of the wish of a state to join and of acceptance of the existing members. This may explain the membership of Djibouti and Somalia, though their populations do not speak Arabic or share a common culture with other members such as Lebanon or Iraq. In relation to the state-centric nature of international law under which human rights are supposed to be implemented, it is interesting to note that the Arab world, as defined by the membership of the Arab League, includes Palestine, although it is not formally recognized as a state, and Somalia, which has been a state without a government since 1992.

The Arab world is a region of sharp contrasts and wide diversity, ranging from Bahrain and Qatar, each with less than a million people in population, to Egypt, which has a population of 62 million. Among the Arab League members are some of the poorest countries in the world (Mauritania, Somalia, and Sudan), as well as some of the richest (Kuwait, Qatar, and the United Arab Emirates). There is also significant ethnic and cultural diversity within each member state, as well as among all of them as a group. Sudan is a member, even though the issue of Arab versus African national identity is one of the underlying causes of decades of civil war in that country.[12] While Islam is often assumed to be a major factor in the presumed unity of "Arab culture," there are some strong differences in the way it is understood and practiced in various parts of the region, especially in terms of its relationship to the state and public life, from Tunisia to Saudi Arabia, and from Somalia to Syria and Iraq. Sunni Islam is dominant in all the member states, except Bahrain where the Shi'a are the majority. The Shi'a may also be a majority in Iraq, and there are important Shi'a minorities in Lebanon, Saudi Arabia, and Syria. It should also be noted that Christians constitute significant percentages of the populations of Egypt, Lebanon, Palestine and Sudan.[13]

---

11. For the text of the Charter of the Arab League, see SA'ID SALIM AL-JUALIY, AL-MUNAZAMAT AL-DAWLIYAH WA AL-IQLIMIYAH (International and Regional Organizations) 189–94 (1997). Arabic sources are cited in this essay by the Arabic title and facts of publication in Latin alphabet, together with an English translation of the title.
12. *See generally* FRANCES M. DENG, WAR OF VISIONS: CONFLICT OF IDENTITIES IN THE SUDAN (1995).
13. *See* DAVID B. BARRETT ET AL., EDS., WORLD CHRISTIAN ENCYCLOPEDIA (2d ed. 2001).

The region is characterized by a similar diversity of recent histories, current political regimes, social conditions, and so forth. For instance, while Jordan, Lebanon, and Syria were part of the Ottoman Empire until its collapse after the First World War, Algeria suffered under total French colonialism for 130 years until independence in 1962. Egypt colonized Sudan from the 1820s until 1885, and again in partnership with Britain from 1898 to 1956. For much of this second period of the colonization of Sudan, known as the Anglo-Egyptian Condominium, Egypt itself was occupied by Britain as a "protectorate." Coastal parts of the Arabian peninsula experienced Ottoman and British occupations for varying periods.[14] These differences in recent history have had significant consequences not only for initial state-formation, but also for the forms of political institutions, administrative systems, state/civil society relations, and so forth, for each country to the present day.

The preceding remarks are not to suggest that problems of regional classification are peculiar to the Arab world, as similar points can be noted regarding any group of states who choose to identify as an alliance or unite for one purpose or another. It must also be emphasized that, despite the ambiguity of the criteria of membership in the Arab League, the Arab world is a clearly identifiable entity of a significant number of countries who choose to associate together and act collectively in some matters, for whatever reasons they may have. Rather, my purpose in highlighting these facts about the Arab world is to emphasize that the region should not be taken as a monolithic, uniform whole. A clear appreciation of the complexity of interests, as well as the diversity of factors and contexts, that condition the policy and practice of each Arab state, especially regarding the protection of human rights, is essential for any evaluation of performance and assessment of prospects. This is particularly true of such relevant considerations as the impact of the Arab-Israeli conflict, Arab nationalism(s), and political Islam on the current status and future prospects of the protection of human rights in this region. Generally speaking, since these factors have been cited as justification or explanation of human rights violations at various times in different Arab countries, they should be taken into account in any analysis of the current status, and assessment of future prospects.

Indications of serious and systematic concern with the protection of human rights in the Arab world, whether at the governmental, intergovernmental or civil society level, can be traced to the 1970s, probably due to the following factors.[15] First, at that time, the UN began to intensify

---

14. *See* Albert Hourani, A History of the Arab Peoples (1991).
15. Al-Ahrahm Center for Political and Strategic Studies, Al-Taqrir al-Istrategy al-Arabi 1995 327 (1996) [hereinafter Arab Strategic Report 1995].

its efforts to encourage governments to ratify the two International Human Rights Covenants of 1966. Second, the coming into force of those two Covenants in 1977 clearly indicated that human rights were a matter of important international concern, thereby prompting governments to commit to the protection of human rights in their national constitutions and through the ratification of international treaties. Third, and most importantly, the 1970s was a period of mounting appreciation *within Arab societies* of the high priority of democratization and human rights protection for their own internal best interest. The defeat of key Arab states by Israel in 1967 clearly demonstrated the total failure of claims or promises of giving national liberation, development, and social justice priority over genuine democratization and respect for the rule of law. In other words, it became increasingly clear to elite groups and the public at large that the benefits of liberation and development can only be achieved through democratization and protection of human rights.

Although my primary emphasis is on the work of NGOs, I will begin the following review of the main developments in the protection of human rights in the region with the activities of governments and the Arab League, because this is the framework within which civil society actors operate, and with which they interact. In presenting the following regional developments, I will also try to highlight their relationship to extra-regional aspects of the process, because all actors and factors in this field tend to influence, enable and/or constrain each other. While official action can either promote or retard civil society activism, the latter can also influence governments in certain ways.

A. Governmental Action

The beginnings of governmental concern about human rights were reflected in the ratification of the two Covenants by Syria and Tunisia in 1969, followed by Libya in 1970, and Iraq in 1971. Ratifications of these two Covenants continued to follow until they reached thirteen by the middle of 1999, when Algeria, Egypt, Jordan, Kuwait, Lebanon, Morocco, Somalia, Sudan, and Yemen ratified. Eleven Arab states have ratified the Convention for the Elimination of All Forms of Discrimination Against Women of 1979 (CEDAW): Algeria, Djibouti, Egypt, Iraq, Jordan, Kuwait, Lebanon, Libya, Morocco, Tunisia, and Yemen. The Convention Against Torture of 1984 has also been ratified by eleven Arab states: Algeria, Bahrain, Egypt, Jordan, Kuwait, Libya, Morocco, Saudi Arabia, Somalia, Tunisia, and Yemen.[16] Sudan has signed, but not yet ratified, this treaty.

16. For country reports under human rights treaties, see United Nations Human Rights Web site, Treaty Bodies Database, *available at* <http://www.un.hchr.ch.>.

On the other hand, however, at least one third of all Arab states have so far failed to ratify any of these basic human rights treaties. Moreover, even those who have a relatively good record of ratification continue to strongly resist compliance with the requirements of international supervision and accountability. For example, only three Arab states (Algeria, Libya, and Somalia) have ratified the Optional Protocol for the International Covenant on Civil and Political Rights, which enables victims to make individual complaints for violations of their human rights. Most of the states that have ratified CEDAW have entered reservations on some crucial provisions of this treaty that tend to undermine and, arguably, negate its basic purpose and content. Most of the Arab states which ratified the Torture Convention have not accepted the Convention's review mechanisms under Articles 20, 21, and 22, providing for the Committee's power to investigate charges of systematic torture, complaints from other states which have ratified this Convention, and individual complaints, respectively. Some Arab states also entered reservations on important provisions of the Convention. Saudi Arabia, for example, has entered reservations on Article 30, about arbitration and adjudication of differences between states parties to the Torture Convention, and Article 3, which precludes state parties from deporting, returning or delivery of any person to another state where he/she is likely to be subjected to torture.[17] Related developments, or lack thereof, include the fact that fourteen out of the twenty-six states throughout the world have failed to endorse the 1998 UN Declaration on the Rights of Human Rights Defenders.

In any case, those Arab states that did ratify major human rights treaties have not made serious amendments to their national legislation to make them consistent with their international obligations. Arab states are also failing to submit their periodic reports under those treaties. For example, half the Arab states that ratified the Civil and Political Rights Covenant failed to submit their reports on time, despite repeated reminders. Syria, for instance, was reminded 35 times to submit its second periodic report due in 1984, and the third report due in 1988. Egypt was four years late in submitting its second periodic report.[18] Generally speaking, and regardless of minor variations between them, it is clear that Arab states tend to be extremely reticent, often strongly suspicious, about any activity that even remotely pertains to the human rights field. The profound ambivalence of Arab states to the protection of human rights is clearly reflected in the aggressively hostile position of these governments towards human rights

17. *See generally* The Arab Organization for Human Rights, Huquq al-Insan fi al-Watan al-Arabi (1999) [hereinafter Human Rights in the Arab World].

18. Arab Strategic Report 1995, *supra* note 15, at 337–38.

NGOs, as elaborated below, through tactics ranging from total prohibition of their activities, harassment of activists, to cooption and undermining of these organizations from within.

Another type of development on the governmental side is the establishment of "governmental nongovernmental organizations," presumably to serve the government's political and public relations objectives, including response to international criticism of their human rights performance. Iraq took the lead in these efforts by establishing in 1970 its own "Iraqi Human Rights Organization" to promote the views of the Iraqi government on human rights in accordance with the revolutionary ideology of the Ba'th Party. In Egypt, an "Egyptian Human Rights Organization" was established in 1975 by persons closely associated with the late President Sadat, a fact that has raised serious concerns about its independence and credibility. In Tunisia, as tensions mounted between the government and the Tunisian League for Human Rights (an independent NGO), the authorities encouraged the establishment of another organization in May of 1987, to be known as "The Tunisian Society for Human Rights and Public Freedoms." Similarly, Libya allowed the establishment of the "Libyan Committee for Human Rights" to respond to charges of human rights violations, in addition to elaborate annual ceremonies for the "Ghadhafi Human Rights Award." The government of Sudan banned the Sudan Human Rights Organization (an independent NGO), and sought to replace it with its own organization under the same name.[19]

Some Arab governments have designated a "human rights department" within existing ministries, appointed a "human rights minister," or otherwise established human rights organizations or councils. Morocco, for example, established the "Advisory Council for Human Rights" in April 1990 by Royal Decree, and appointed a minister for human rights. In Tunisia, an advisory committee for the president was set up in January 1991, accompanied by the appointment of a first advisor to the president, to follow state policy in human rights matters. In addition to these organs, each of the Tunisian Ministers of Foreign Affairs, Interior, Justice, and Social Affairs has its own special human rights department. In Algeria, besides a human rights office within the Ministry of Justice, a position of minister of human rights was established in June 1991, but abolished in July 1992, following the establishment of a specialized governmental agency called "The National Monitor of Human Rights." Institutionalized governmental attention to human rights in Egypt took the form of a human rights department at the Ministry of Foreign Affairs and an office at the Attorney-General Chambers to receive and investigate complaints of human rights violations in the

19. *Id.* at 328–29.

country. The government of Lebanon established two organizations, the Constitutional Council to Ensure Conformity of Legislation with Constitutional Principles and the Parliamentary Human Rights Committee.[20] Oman appointed a human rights advisor, and human rights committees have also been set up in the legislative or advisory councils of Bahrain, Kuwait, and Yemen.

B. The Arab League[21]

Established in 1945, the Arab League did not show any interest in human rights until 1968, and it took another twenty-five years to adopt the Arab Charter of Human Rights in September 1994. In response to Resolution 2081 of the General Assembly of the UN, December 20, 1965, calling on member states and regional organizations to commemorate 1968 as "the year of human rights," in celebration of the twentieth anniversary of the UDHR, the Council of the Arab League set up two committees on the matter, through Resolutions 2259 of 12 December 1966 and 2304 of 18 March 1967. In light of the work of those two committees, the Council of the League adopted Resolution 2443 of September 3, 1968, establishing its Permanent Arab Human Rights Commission. The Secretariat of the League also convened the first Arab human conference in Beirut on December 2–10, 1968. In addition to resolutions condemning Israel and declaring solidarity with the Palestinian People, that conference called for Arab cooperation in the protection of human rights at the regional and international level, urged the implementation of the UDHR, and recommended the establishment of national human rights committees to cooperate with the League's Permanent Arab Commission for Human Rights.

By its Resolution of September 11, 1969, the Council of the Arab League charged its Permanent Arab Commission with the following functions: (1) to support joint Arab action in the field of human rights; (2) to endeavor to protect individual rights, while emphasizing the human rights dimensions of Arab concerns; and (3) to promote awareness among the Arab People about human rights and the need for their protection. Accordingly, the Commission drew a program of action at the regional and international levels consisting of the convening of seminars, celebration of the Arab Human Rights Day, cooperation with national committees (organi-

20. Iman Hassan, "Harakat Huquq al-Insan fi al-Watan al-Arabi: Dirasat Halat" (Human Rights in the Arab World: Some Case Studies of Lebanon, Tunisia and Egypt), *in* Qadayah Huquq al-Insan 75 (1999).

21. This review of the efforts of the Arab League is based on Nu'man Jalal, Jami'at al-Dual al-Arabiyah wa Huquq al-Insan 4–40 (1994) [hereinafter Arab League and Human Rights].

zations),[22] receiving reports from and offering advice to member states of the League regarding their human rights activities. At the international level, the Commission's activities were to consist of documentation of human rights violations by Israel to be analyzed in light of international human rights norms, participation in international conferences, and preparation of scholarly studies in the field.

The Permanent Arab Commission also adopted, on May 13, 1970, a recommendation to begin preparation of an Arab Declaration of Human Rights by a committee of experts to be established for that purpose. This committee convened from April 24 to July 10, 1971 and prepared a draft of the "Declaration on the Rights of Citizens of Arab States and Countries," consisting of 31 Articles covering civil and political rights as well as economic, social, and cultural rights. However, the committee received only nine responses from Arab states to its draft, varying between support, reservation, and total opposition. Consequently, that draft was discarded, and the matter was not considered again by the Council of the Arab League until the early 1990s. The Council took no action on human rights from 1971 to 1981, other than to continue the Permanent Commission, which was itself inactive except with regard to the rights of the Palestinian people.

The next phase of development at the regional level can be traced back to the seminar of 19–21 May 1979, convened by the Secretariat of the Arab Union of Jurists in Baghdad, Iraq. That seminar called for the rejuvenation of the Permanent Arab Commission, and produced a draft Arab treaty on human rights. For its part, the Arab League asked for preparation of a draft Arab Charter for Human Rights. A draft was examined by the Permanent Legal Commission and Permanent Human Rights Commission, and considered by the Council of the League, which decided on March 31, 1983 to refer the draft to the member states for their views. However, the whole matter was postponed again, pending the adoption of an Islamic Declaration on Human Rights and Duties by the Organization of Islamic Conference. This latter Declaration was finally adopted by the Islamic Ministerial Conference of August 1990, in Cairo, Egypt, as "The Cairo Declaration of Human Rights in Islam."

Another regional development to be noted here is the draft declaration, "Human and Peoples Rights in the Arab World," prepared in 1986 at a seminar convened in Syracusa, Italy, by experts from nine Arab countries, on the invitation of the International Institute of Higher Studies in Criminal Sciences. That draft was fully consistent with, and even expanded on,

---

22. Unfortunately, since the Arab Commission refused to grant observer status to any NGO without the approval of the state where the organization is based, those organizations which enjoy that status with the Commission tend to lack the independence and credibility of genuine human rights NGOs.

established international human rights standards. For example, the Syracusa draft made torture a criminal offense for which prosecutions cannot be barred by any statute of limitation, imposed limitations on the right of governments to declare a state of emergency, and included the right to a clean and healthy environment, in addition to rights to health care, social security, food, shelter, and education. The draft also provided in detail for strong mechanisms for the protection of human rights through the establishment of an Arab Human Rights Commission and Court. Unfortunately, though not surprisingly, that draft was never seriously considered by the Arab League or any national government.

The idea of the Arab Human Rights Charter was revived in the early 1990s. In 1992, the Legal and Human Rights Permanent Commissions of the Arab League examined and amended the draft in light of the responses of Arab governments. The two Commissions approved the draft by February 1993, and called on the Council of the League to adopt the Declaration before the convening of the International Human Rights Conference in Vienna that year. However, the Council postponed adoption to await further responses from member states. The Charter was finally considered and presumably adopted by the Council of the Arab League by Resolution 5437 of 15 September 1994.[23] That development was particularly surprising, not only because none of the seven states that had objected to the draft had changed its view,[24] but also because the Charter contained rights, such as the right to strike, prohibited in almost all Arab states.

The Arab Charter has not been ratified by a single Arab state since its adoption by the League. Even if widely ratified, it is unlikely to improve the protection of human rights in the region because of the serious weakness of its provisions, in comparison, for example, to those of the two International Covenants. For instance, the Charter's provisions for fair trial standards fall short of those set by the Civil and Political Rights Covenant, such as the right to appeal to a higher tribunal, including cases where the death penalty is imposed. The Charter also fails to provide for the right to political organization and participation, which is the core issue facing all efforts to promote democracy and protect human rights in the Arab world. Although Article 3 prohibits the denial of any of the fundamental human rights that are legally binding on member states by virtue of international treaties or custom, the Charter negates the value of this safeguard in Article 4, by providing that limitations or restrictions on all rights under the Charter can be imposed by law, if deemed necessary for the protection of national security and economy, public order, health, morals, and the rights of others.

23. For text of this Declaration, *see* 56 INT'L COMM'N JURISTS REV. 57 (1996).
24. The states which objected to the draft in 1992 were: Bahrain, Kuwait, Oman, Saudi Arabia, Sudan, United Arab Emirates, and Yemen.

This broad and vague exception opens the door for legislation and other measures that can undermine the totality of the rights provided for by the Arab Charter. Finally, the Charter is also weak on mechanisms for the implementation of the rights it recognizes, since the powers and competence of the committee of human rights experts it provides for are confined to examining reports submitted to it by states parties to the Charter, and reporting on them to the Permanent Commission of Human Rights of the Arab League.[25]

From the official point of view, a realistic assessment of the Arab Charter of Human Rights and its prospects was made by the Egyptian delegation during the Council deliberations over the draft. In calling for adoption of the draft, the spokesperson of the Egyptian delegation underplayed the significance of the Declaration, and described it as a regional shield against international pressures on Arab states in the field of human rights.[26] In a more positive sense, even that cynical attitude indicates official sensitivity to the power of the international human rights movement to force the Arab governments and their League to at least pretend compliance with internationally-recognized human rights standards. What will make this positive sense more realistic, in my view, is the role of NGOs.

C. Nongovernmental Organizations[27]

An initial question raised by an analysis of the role of NGOs in the Arab world is the proper characterization of some organizations. The question of characterization is partly a matter of the definition of a human rights NGOs, in the sense of whether the organization is confining its mandate and activities to "exclusively" human rights issues, as opposed to wider political or social policy questions. Another aspect of this ambiguity is whether the organization chooses to openly or deliberately identify itself as a "human rights" organization. Moreover, there can be disagreement about the characterization of professional organizations and trade unions whose mandate is related to human rights work, like lawyers and labor syndicates, civil rights committees of political parties, and human rights studies centers in some Arab universities. There can also be controversy about the

25. Human Rights in the Arab World, *supra* note 17, at 11–15.
26. Arab League and Human Rights, *supra* note 21, at 27–33.
27. The following review is drawn from: Issa Shivji & Hilmy Sha'rawi, Huquq al-Insan fi Afriqiya wa al-Watan al-Arabi (Human Rights in Africa and the Arab Homeland) (1994); Iman Hassan, The Human Rights Movement in the Arab World, Case-studies of Egypt, Lebanon and Tunisia 75–110; Ahmed Thabit, *The Human Rights Movement in the Arab World: Case-studies of Jordan, Palestine and Yemen*, *in* 4 Qadaiyah Huquq al-Insan 111–34 (1999); The Arab Strategic Report, *supra* note 15, at 331–34.

characterization of some groups and organizations operating in exile, usually as proxy for political parties and opposition parties that are unable to work within their own country. The primary concern here is that these types of actors may be more driven by the objectives and programs of the political organizations they represent than by human rights norms and principles as such. These ambiguities apply to the role of many national and regional organizations, such as national lawyers associations and the regional Arab Lawyers Union (ALU) or national journalist associations and the regional Union of Arab Journalists.

The beginning of human rights NGOs in the strict sense of the term, as truly independent organizations exclusively specializing in this field as defined by international standards, can be traced to the early 1970s. It should be noted here that my concern in this essay with an "exclusive human rights focus" in the mandate of NGOs does not mean that such "exclusivity" is either easy to achieve or desirable. On the contrary, it is extremely important that trade unions, professional associations, and all sorts of civil society organizations contribute to the protection and promotion of human rights within their respective mandates. In doing that, however, all NGOs should continuously reflect on whether their efforts are fully consistent with human rights principles. Since trade unions, professional associations, and so forth, cannot avoid being seen as substitutes for human rights NGOs as such, strategies for enhancing the protection of human rights in the region should seek to promote "specialized" capacity for the advocacy of human rights within each country and in the region in general.

As one would expect, the first specialized human rights NGOs began in those Arab countries that enjoyed a relative degree of political pluralism, or were at least receptive to civil society activism. Accordingly, the Moroccan Human Rights Organization was established in 1972, and the Tunisian League of Human Rights in 1977. In Egypt, branches of the Society of Supporters of Human Rights in both Cairo and Alexandria, were established in 1977 and granted official recognition. The Moroccan Association of Human Rights was established in 1979, but did not achieve official recognition until nine years later.

The next phase in this development came in the 1980s and was associated with the establishment of Arab Organization for Human Rights (AOHR) and the adoption of varying degrees of democratic and political reform by Arab governments for a variety of political reasons. The original initiative for the establishment of AOHR emerged in 1971, on the suggestion of the Iraqi Human Rights Organization. The idea was adopted and developed by the ALU, which set up a preparatory committee in 1973 to draft a charter and bylaws for a regional organization with national chapters. However, the founding conference, scheduled to convene in Beirut in

February 1974 did not materialize due to differences about the structure of the proposed organization. The idea was revived on the initiative of a group of Arab intellectuals who convened in Tunisia in April 1983 to discuss the crisis of democratization in the Arab world and concluded that the solution has to be through the protection of human rights. However, the founding conference of AOHR had to convene in Limassol, Cyprus, because it was not possible to hold it in any Arab country at the time. Moreover, although AOHR has located its General Secretariat in Cairo from the beginning, the Egyptian government has yet to officially recognize AOHR. The Egyptian government also refused to allow the AOHR to hold its first general meeting in 1986, but did permit the third meeting of 1993 to convene in Cairo.[28]

The Charter of AOHR charges the organization to endeavor to protect the human rights of all persons in accordance with the international standards, to seek to raise the awareness of the Arab peoples of their rights, and to cooperate with organizations and associations working in this field. To discharge this mandate, in 1987, AOHR began to publish its annual report on the status of human rights in the Arab world, a series of bulletins, and a biannual research journal. Moreover, AOHR collaborated with the ALU and the Tunisian League of Human Rights in establishing the Arab Institute of Human Rights in 1989, based in Tunis, Tunisia, charged with implementing various educational and public awareness programs in human rights, in addition to establishing a human rights documentation and resources center. In my view, however, the AOHR, as the umbrella organization, has failed to develop a comprehensive strategy for the movement as a whole, thereby forcing NGOs to seek independent coordination among themselves. The most recent illustration of this failure is the convening of the First International Conference of the Arab Human Rights Movement in Casablanca, Morocco, in April 1999, on the initiative of the Cairo Institute for Human Rights Studies, instead of under the auspices of the AOHR.

The mid 1980s also witnessed the emergence of several significant human rights NGOs and groups in various Arab countries as well as among Arab activists living outside the region, mainly in Western Europe. National organizations within the region include the Egyptian Organization for Human Rights, established in 1985 but still denied official registration by the Egyptian government,[29] and the Sudanese Human Rights Organization,

---

28. To emphasize the great personal risks Arab human rights activists have to endure, it should be noted here that Mansour Al-Kikhya, the Libyan opposition figure and member of the Board of Trustees of AOHR, "disappeared" after that meeting in Cairo, and his whereabouts have never been accounted for by either the Egyptian or Libyan authorities.
29. The Egyptian Organization was granted "tentative" approval for registration in 1999, under a new statute regulating non-governmental organizations (Law No. 153 of 1999). But formal registration will depend on the regulations to be issued under this statute.

also established in 1985 but operating from outside Sudan since the military coup of 1989. A third national human rights organization facing difficulties in official registration is the Kuwaiti Human Rights Organization. On the other hand, national organizations have been able to achieve official registration and operate within their respective countries since the late 1980s in Lebanon, Tunisia, Algeria, Morocco, Jordan, and Yemen.[30] Special consideration should be given to work of Palestinian human rights NGOs, pioneered by Al-Haq in the mid 1970s, which face particular difficulties as they are caught between the Israeli occupation and the Palestinian Authority.

Moreover, a remarkable proliferation of somewhat "specialized" human rights NGOs can be observed in Egypt where there are now more than ten organizations, in addition to those already noted. These organizations, in chronological order of their establishment, include: The Legal Research and Resource Center for Human Rights (1989), the Cairo Institute for Human Rights Studies (1993), Center of Issues Facing Egyptian Women (1994), Center for Legal Aid (1994), the Egyptian Center for Women's Rights (1996), the Land Center of Human Rights (1996—focusing on rights of farmers and farm-workers, and environmental issues), the Association for Democratic Development (1996), the Arab Center for the Independence of Judges and Lawyers (1997), Center for the Human Rights of Prisoners (1997), and the Regional Program for the Protection of Human Rights Activists (1997). Another type of organization is the Arab Working Group on Human Rights, which is a network of human rights activists and scholars first established in 1997 to work on the situation in Algeria, but is gradually expanding its mandate to other issues in the region at large, until it terminated itself in 2001 because of operational difficulties.

The case of Egypt raises a few general points to be noted here for discussion in the next section. First, most of the Egyptian organizations (some of which take a regional view of their mandate) had to establish themselves as civil companies/firms to avoid the pressures and limitations imposed by the previous Egyptian statute regulating civil society associations.

Second, the clear rise in the number of new organizations since 1993 is due to the fact that Egyptian human rights activists have abandoned their opposition to accepting foreign funding at that point in time. Unfortunately, these two opportunities have now been deliberately closed by the 1999 Egyptian law 153 on civic organizations. While creating excessive and inhibiting requirements for official registration under its own terms, this statute closed all other possibilities of legal operation under other forms of

30. This is the status of these organizations, as best as I can verify, at the time of writing. It should be noted that the legal status of any of them can change at any time, due to the political instability of their countries.

organization and granted the Minister of Social Affairs the authority to prevent any civic association from receiving foreign funding without having to give reasons for his decision.[31]

It is clear from the preceding review that the growth and development of human rights NGOs in the Arab world is largely restricted to the North African region, where the possibility of official registration is relatively better. But the effectiveness of human rights NGOs in this region tends to vary over time, due to various political, security and operational factors, as discussed in the next section of this essay. On the Asian side of the Arab world, except Jordan, Lebanon and Yemen, both secular and traditional Islamic governments have severely restricted the growth and development of human rights NGOs. The government of Syria, for example, has detained and sentenced to long terms of imprisonment the human rights activists who attempted to establish "committees for the defense of democracy and human rights" in the early 1990s. The government of Saudi Arabia detained the leaders of the Committee for the Defense of Legal Rights when it was announced in 1993, forcing it to operate from the United Kingdom.[32] Finally, in this sub-section, it is important to emphasize that the highly unstable politics of the region also encourage the manipulation of human rights organizations. As noted earlier, there are numerous entities among political opposition groups, usually operating outside their own countries, that claim a narrowly defined human rights mandate to serve their political objectives, while failing to observe human rights principles in other aspects of their activities. On the other hand, some governments are keen to "host" an exiled human rights organization whose agenda and activities are useful for undermining the government of their country of origin, and thereby promote the political interests of the host government. For example, Syria "hosts" an Iraqi committee for human rights, and Iraq does the same for a Syrian organization. Nevertheless, one cannot dismiss exiled human rights NGOs as necessarily illegitimate or ineffective. For instance, Bahraini organization (mainly in Denmark) and a Syrian one (mainly from Paris) are generally accepted by observers in the region as effective and legitimate human rights NGOs.

In conclusion of this review of the development of the Arab human rights movement, one can see the cup as "half full" or "half empty," but the question should be how to make it "more full" for the protection of human rights. A realistic and verifiable evaluation of the situation is difficult

31. Human Rights in the Arab World, *supra* note 17, at 13–16.
32. However, the commitment of this organization to the protection of rights as provided for by Islamic Law (Shari'a), without addressing conflicts between Shari'a and human rights norms, as explained in the next section, illustrate the difficulty of identifying a civil society organization as a human rights NGO.

because of lack of agreement on criteria for evaluating the effectiveness of the Arab human rights movement and how to apply it in practice for a specific time frame. For example, one can see the actual level of human rights violations as either rising or falling, depending on such factors as the availability of verifiable information or time frame of comparison. More reliable information is available on the North African part of the region because it is relatively more accessible to monitoring by internal and external observers than the West Asian part. But one would suspect that far more violations are occurring in the "closed" countries of the Arabian Peninsula where neither internal nor external monitoring is allowed. To the extent that there is an improvement in the human rights situation in one country or another at any given time, it does not necessarily follow that it is sustainable or can be attributed to one particular cause or another. In view of these difficulties, the tentative assessment offered in the next section is intended as a contribution to the development of conditions that are more conducive to the protection of human rights throughout the region, rather than an accurate and conclusive evaluation of the record of the Arab human rights movement as such.

III. AN ASSESSMENT

The following assessment of the main achievements, difficulties, and future prospects of the protection of human rights in the region is based on the view that the protection of human rights anywhere in the world is a process, not an "objective" that can be achieved once and for all. These remarks also assume that, while states have the international obligation and domestic jurisdiction to protect human rights on the ground, governments will not act accordingly without pressure from internal and external actors. Consequently, progress in the process of human rights protection is dependent on the ability of its advocates to constantly prompt governments into taking the necessary action, and hold them accountable for failure to do so. This, in turn, will depend on the ability of human rights advocates to generate and sustain sufficient political support, and to mobilize human and material resources, for their activities. In the final analysis, however, human rights cannot be protected in an effective and sustainable manner without developing an *internal* popular human rights culture and *local* human and material infrastructures necessary for consolidating achievements, responding to challenges, and realizing the prospects of greater success in the future. The following remarks are intended to contribute to the realization of these prerequisites for the protection of human rights in the Arab world.

The achievements of the Arab human rights movement can be seen to include: (1) exposing human rights violations at the national, regional, and international levels; (2) challenging the claims of Arab governments before the UN human rights treaty bodies and special rapporteurs, by providing information and publishing "shadow reports" for comparison with reports from governments; (3) establishing and sustaining a growing level of unbiased, non-partisan professionalism by defending the right of all persons and groups, regardless of the political affiliation or ideological orientation of victims of violation; (4) pressuring many governments into ratification of international human rights treaties, and establishing governmental organs and official positions devoted to human rights concerns; and (5) generally setting clear human rights standards of achievement for the performance of governments and opposition groups alike, as indicated by the high credibility accorded by both of these sides to reports of national and regional human rights NGOs. Some of the difficulties facing these organizations, discussed below, can also be seen as reflecting a level of credibility and success in their mission. For example, while the denial of official registration to Egyptian human rights NGOs, for up to ten years in some cases, is a human rights violation in itself, the ability of these organizations to operate openly in the country all this time clearly indicates a level of acceptance and credibility at the practical level.

Of particular significance to the objective of diminishing human rights dependency is the "graduation" and maturity of a second younger generation of activists who enjoy a higher level of technical competence and professional credibility than that of the founding first generation. One of the difficulties facing the movement was the common confusion between partisan political objectives and principled and professional human rights advocacy.[33] That weakness used to render human rights NGOs particularly vulnerable to being easily discredited, coopted, or infiltrated by the government and opposition groups alike for their own narrow political ends. As the reality or perception of partisan bias diminishes through the professional competence and credibility of the emerging generation of activists, the movement as a whole is becoming more secure against those earlier risks.

On the negative side, the Arab human rights movement suffers from a variety of internal and external problems, as well as broader difficulties which can be summarized as follows. On the internal side, there are problems associated with random establishment and structural weakness in the growth and development of some elements of the movement in different parts of the region, as reflected in the institutional inadequacy and lack of cooperation and coordination of activities among competing organizations. In Algeria and

33. Mohamed El Sayed Sai'd, *Al-Mashakil al-Dakhiliyah lil Haraka al-Arabiayh (Internal Problems of the Arab Human Rights Movement)*, 3 Rowaq Arabi 18–27 (July 1996).

Tunisia, for example, the remarkable strength of the 1980s is now replaced by weakness and confusion in the context of profound national political crisis. The efforts of some ideological factions to take exclusive control of the Egyptian Organization of Human Rights in 1994 by inflating membership for the meeting of its General Assembly in order to dominate the Board of Trustees, which was to be elected at that meeting, resulted in a prolonged crisis that paralyzed the organization for several years. The negative consequences of 1999 Law of Association for Egyptian NGOs are compounded and facilitated by the lack of unity and coordination among these organizations themselves. At the time of writing, some Egyptian organizations are rushing to register under the new statute, sometimes in violation of their internal institutional procedure, while others continue to resist the new regime altogether and campaign for the repeal of the statute. The effectiveness of the Sudan Human Rights Organization, operating in exile, is seriously hampered by competition over the leadership of the organization among various factions of the political opposition to the Islamic military regime of Sudan and internal problems among different elements of the movement.

External problems of the Arab human rights movement in its relationship to its general societal and intellectual environment are reflected in its inability to broaden its influence among civil society at large, thereby keeping itself relatively isolated among small groups of liberal intellectuals and activists. To diminish its political isolation, the movement must be able to develop a discourse that takes due account of the cultural and contextual specificity of the region without undermining the universality of human rights. A distinctively regional human rights discourse should, for example, address the problematic relationship between international standards of human rights and prevalent understandings of Islam in the region. A popular discourse should also seek to reconcile concerns about major regional issues, such as the Arab-Israeli conflict and the 1990–1991 Gulf War and its aftermath, on the one hand, and the protection of human rights of individual persons and groups in the context of those major regional crises. The movement must also find ways of coping with the extraordinary circumstances and crises experienced by countries like Algeria, Iraq, Sudan, and Yemen, where the very existence of society itself is threatened by civil war and/or external intervention.

While other internal and external problems can be cited, a more positive appreciation of the achievements of the Arab human rights movement, and understanding of the underlying causes of its failures, would follow from a realistic assessment of broader difficulties facing the movement throughout the region. These more general obstacles can be summarized as the following factors and processes, which should be seen as interactive and interdependent, rather than isolated or independent phenomena:

1. Arab human rights NGOs are consistently denied official registration and face systematic harassment by the majority of the governments of the region. This is true of traditionalist purportedly Islamic governments like those of the Gulf states and Saudi Arabia or so-called secular governments like those of Iraq, Syria and Libya. It remains to be seen whether the Egyptian government will honor its declared intention to permit full registration and legal operation for at least some human rights NGOs, but past experience in that country would lead one to be skeptical about the prospects of the government permitting genuinely professional and truly independent human rights activism in the country. It is also ironic that the Palestinian Authority has turned against the same human rights NGOs it found so useful during its struggle for recognition by Israel, and now deem them an unnecessary nuisance after the partial implementation of the Oslo Accord.[34]

Moreover, as illustrated by the crisis of the Tunisian League of Human Rights, formal legality can be only a cover for more fundamental frustration of the role of NGOs. In 1992, the Tunisian government amended the law to require human rights NGOs to open their membership to whoever wishes to apply, thereby forcing them to accept thousands of the political supporters of the government. When the League resisted this pressure in order to ensure genuine commitment to the principles of human rights advocacy among its members, the government "dissolved" the organization on 14 June 1992. After a year of international pressure, the government allowed the League to operate again, but with an artificially inflated membership which succeeded in replacing the leadership of the League during the General Assembly meeting of February 1994. Through that legalistic manipulation and "democratic" cooption, the Tunisian government managed to undermine the public credibility of the League.[35]

2. The consequences of unresolved conceptual difficulties of regional and international advocacy of human rights in general are particularly serious for the Arab human rights movement because of the colonial history and current profound crisis suffered by the region as a whole. For instance, the paradox is that, unlike conventional political action, the human rights

---

34. For example, in December 1998, the Palestinian Authority blocked the enactment of a law regulating the registration and operation of NGOs, which was passed by the Palestinian Legislative Council, and continues to harass local NGOs. *See* Khader Shkirat, *Al-Tahadiyat al-Jadidah li-Harakat Huquq al-Insan al-Philistiniyah* (*The New Challenges Facing the Palestinian Human Rights Movement*), *in* CHALLENGES 207–18 (Bahey El-Din Hassan, ed.) *See also*, *Indama Yasyru al-Dahiyaht Jaladan* (*Palestine: When the Victim Becomes the Executioner*), SAWASYAH BULLETIN 14–17 (Dec. 1996).

35. Munsif al-Marzouq, *Al-Muhima al-Sa'ba li Harakat Huquq al-Insan fi Tunis (Mission Impossible for the Human Rights Movement in Tunisia)*, *in* TAHADIYAT AL-HARAKA AL-ARABIYAH LI HUQUQ AL-INSAN (CHALLENGES FACING THE ARAB HUMAN RIGHTS MOVEMENT) 147–66 (Bahey El-Din Hassan ed., 1997).

movement relies on the moral force of its demands on governments and appeal for popular support. That is to say, the movement has to call for protection of human rights by the same authorities which violate those rights in the first place, and seek public support without being able to deliver on its claims. In more developed and stable regions of the world, the moral appeal of human rights is supported by a strong and active civil society which is aware of its own rights and able to effectively organize for their protection through political and legal action. In contrast, the nature and dynamics of the post-colonial state and weakness of civil society in the Arab world enable its governments to simply disregard moral appeals to human rights standards without any risk of political or legal accountability by their civil societies. No human rights movement anywhere in the world can achieve genuine and sustainable success unless the political and legal institutions of the country or region is capable of upholding the moral demands made by NGOs and civil society on the state. Paradoxically, the actual protection of human rights is needed for the long term process of creating and sustaining the ability of political and legal institutions to play this role. However, since social forces tend to seek immediate and concrete response to their demands, they will be attracted to strategies of more direct political action, instead of long term "investment" in the rule of law and protection of human rights.[36]

Another type of conceptual difficulty that is particularly troubling to the Arab human rights movement is how to deal with Islamist and other militant ideological groups which seek to manipulate the processes of democratization and protection of human rights in order to seize political power without genuine commitment to these values. On the one hand, a principled approach would insist on the protection of the human rights of these groups and their members, regardless of their "presumed intention" to repudiate democratic and human rights principles once they come to power. On the other hand, such an approach is not only dismissed as "unrealistic and naive" by security forces confronting violent Islamic groups, but is also resisted by some liberal intellectuals who are the actual or potential supporters of the human rights movement in the region. The latter group, who are ideologically opposed to the agenda of Islamic activists, tend to see the "excesses" of the security forces and other oppressive measures by the governments of the region as "the lesser of two evils," in comparison to what they expect at the hands of Islamists when they come to power.

These skeptical views can be supported in the Arab world by citing the example of Sudan, where the National Islamic Front (NIF) played the role of a "democratic" political party, and was even a partner in a coalition government until a few months before it was able to seize power by a

36. Sai'd, *supra* note 33, at 12–26.

military coup in June 1989. Immediately upon seizing the apparatus of the state, the NIF abolished the constitution, dissolved parliament and all other political parties, trade unions, professional associations, and banned every type or form of political opposition. In that light, it is not surprising that liberal intellectuals and human rights activists in Algeria expect a similar fate should Islamic groups come to power in that country. In this way, the Arab human rights movement is caught in a complex dilemma: uphold the human rights of all persons and groups as a matter of principle and regardless of the consequences, or qualify that commitment by some "realistic" considerations and thereby risk undermining the credibility of the moral imperative of human rights norms.

3. The deep sense of insecurity and profound distrust of the international community among Arab societies is a major obstacle facing popular acceptance of a human rights culture in the region. The roots of these "psychological" and material dimensions of the regional context of the Arab human rights movement go back to centuries of Ottoman and European domination, and decades of post-colonial Western hegemony, as more recently emphasized by the nature and development of the Arab-Israeli conflict and its devastating human costs for the Palestinian People since 1948, the year of the adoption of the UDHR. It is against this background that present Arab societies tend to "interpret" recent episodes in international relations, like the imposition of sanctions against Libya (1989 to 1999) and Iraq (1992 to present), ethnic cleansing in Bosnia, and the attack by the United States against Sudan in 1998. Both elite and popular public opinion compare the weak and ambivalent response of the international community to the Israeli invasion of Lebanon in 1982 and occupation of its territories in the south for eighteen years, to the massive response to the 1991 invasion of Kuwait by Iraq and sustained imposition of severe sanctions against Iraq since then. The Arab public wondered about Western support of Iraq during eight years of war with Iran, despite Iraq's gross and systematic violations of human rights and humanitarian law throughout that period, in contrast to Western determination to uphold international law at the cost of starving the people of Iraq and destroying a whole generation of their children so many years after Iraq was expelled from Kuwait.[37]

In this context, Arab elites from various shades of political, ideological, and intellectual perspectives are drawn to an agenda of strong self-identity

37. Bahey El-Din Hassan, "Mas'uliayat al-Gharb 'an Ta'athur al-Dahaul al-Dimogråty" (The Responsibility of the West for Hampering Democratic Transition) *Sawasyiah Bulletin*, issue no. 13 (Cairo Institute for Human Rights Studies, December 1996), at 3, 4; Neil Hicks, "Khitab Huquq al-Insan fi al-Alam al-Arabi" (Human Rights Discourse in the Arab World), 6 Rowaq Arabi (Apr. 1997), at 6–35; Bahey El-Din Hassan, Challenges Facing the Arab Human Rights Movement, op. cit., at 237–57.

and extreme hostility to "the West." From this perspective, they tend to see "settling the score" with the external enemy as a more compelling priority over democratization and protection of human rights at home. The inability of these elites to see that democratization and protection of human rights at home are in fact the best means for addressing the underlying causes of their difficulties with Western hegemony and double standards is itself part of the problem. Failure to appreciate that Arab governments and societies are also guilty of hegemony and double standards against religious and ethnic minorities within the region is also part of the problem. Unfortunately, pointing out these inconsistencies in the position of Arab societies regarding the "West" and the international community at large is not enough to change the dominant view among Arab elites and governments which tend to equate advocacy of human rights with service to the hegemonic agenda of Western powers. Accordingly, Arab human rights advocates are often represented in popular discourse as "traitors" for promoting an external imposition of Western values and institutions. As "the West" is taken in the region to be guilty of absolute and unconditional support of Israel and total and deliberate destruction of the people of Iraq, the identification of human rights with Western governments and societies is a major source of profound distrust of the advocacy of these rights in the region. This distrust is compounded by the reliance of Arab human rights NGOs on funding by Western governmental and private foundations.

4. Broader problems associated with the recent political and social history of the region also tend to undermine the cultural legitimacy of international human right standards and the modern international law from which they emerged. In this regard, the human rights movement can be seen as the latest phase of a long struggle with various issues of "modernization" since the early nineteenth century. Moreover, the combination of the lack of an internal philosophical or cultural justification for human rights principles, on the one hand, and the above-mentioned deep sense of insecurity and distrust of the international community, on the other, seems to focus the attention of the elites of the region upon a posture of confrontation with the "Western Other." This attitude tends to emphasize the priority of internal mobilization in confronting the neo-colonial hegemony of the West over issues of internal social and political transformation within the Arab world or its individual countries. This complex cultural difficulty is compounded by the general lack, or weakness, of traditions of civic activism in relation to the modern nation state, as distinguished from traditional forms of organization.[38]

5. Another aspect of the human rights dependency syndrome is the

38. Mohamed El Sayed Sai'd, "Da'wat Huquq al-Insan fe Siyaq al-Hala al-Thaqafiyah al-Rahinah" (The Cause of Human Rights in the Present Cultural Context), 6 Rowaq Arabi (Apr. 1997), at 48–59.

relationship between the Arab human rights movement and international human rights NGOs. On the one hand, as part of the international movement, the Arab movement reflects the current weakness of the former because of the shift in global power relations after the end of the Cold War. As briefly explained earlier, human rights have so far been protected primarily through economic and political pressure by Western governments on the governments of Arab and other developing countries, rather than through the internal activities of the civil societies of developing countries, as is the case in developed countries. In that scenario, the international movement was dependent on the dynamics of the Cold War competition in encouraging Western governments to pressure the governments of developing countries to protect human rights (read civil and political rights) of the populations of developing countries. However, because the current ambiguity of global power relations has diminished the ability of international NGOs to influence the foreign policy of Western governments in that regard, these governments are now less enthusiastic in upholding human rights demands as part of their political, security, and trade relations with developing countries.

Moreover, the influence of international NGOs has also been diminished by changes in the sources and pattern of human rights violations in developing countries. The notion that only states (and certain intergovernmental organizations like the UN) are subjects of international law means that non-state actors, such as violently militant Islamic groups and world and transnational corporations operating in the region cannot be held accountable for activities which would qualify as human rights violations if they were perpetrated by government officials. Yet, the activities of militant groups are cited by governments as justification for the need to "suspend" the protection of human rights in order to safeguard national and regional security. The legally binding force of international human rights law is perceived to be meaningless in the context of "collapsed states" like Somalia, or those undergoing civil war and severe civil strife like Algeria and Sudan. These and related factors have led to serious differences of opinion between the international and Arab human rights movements, and within the ranks of each side, regarding such issues as the legitimacy of "humanitarian intervention," imposition of economic sanctions or the use of "political conditionality" in economic aid and military assistance programs in the name of promoting the protection of human rights in developing countries.

Furthermore, the relationship between Western-based international human rights NGOs and the Arab human rights movement is also complicated by charges of a lack of coordination and cooperation, as well as perceptions of conflicting priorities.[39] While dependent on the cooperation

39. On this relationship and its implications, see Bahey El-Din Hassan, "Nahwa Isti'adat Zumam al-Mubadara" (Toward Retrieving the Initiative) 6 ROWAQ ARABI (Apr. 1997), at

of local and regional NGOs for access to credible information about human rights violations in Arab countries, international NGOs tend to focus their advocacy efforts almost exclusively on developed countries because that is "more effective" at pressuring the governments of developing countries in the short term, without regard to the long term need to enhance the capacity of local and regional NGOs and to expand and protect the "space" for local advocacy of human rights. While understandable from a narrow view of current conditions in Arab countries, this attitude tends to marginalize the Arab human rights movement and doom it to a position of permanent dependency on the initiatives and priorities of international NGOs.

This aspect of the human rights dependency syndrome is a clear reflection of economic, political, and technological dependencies of Arab countries on developed countries, due to historical and current violations of collective rights to self-determination and human development.[40] In some cases, the dependency relationship is complicated by strategic or security concerns. For example, while Saudi Arabia and the Gulf states are dependent on American technical and security support, Western dependence on the oil of those countries makes them less vulnerable to pressure by Western governments about their human rights performance. Egypt is heavily dependent on Western aid and technical assistance, but is also a key player in the Middle East peace process. Whatever the exact terms of the dependency may be, international human rights advocacy is compromised by foreign policy calculations of the governments of developed countries. In other words, the combination of selective use of human rights rhetoric and inconsistent practice of Western governments tends to undermine the moral authority of human rights activists in a region like the Arab world.

6. While human rights activists everywhere in the world are necessarily implicated in political controversy, because their objectives require changes in the policies and practice of governments, the Arab human rights movement suffers from excessive politicization due to several factors. First, the dominance of certain ideological groups at the initial stages of the AOHR alienated those of other political and philosophical orientations and undermined the credibility of this umbrella organization. As a consequence of this ideological bias and contestation, external political competition and rivalries tended to be reflected in the leadership and activities of AOHR, as well as several national member NGOs, like the Tunisian League and the Egyptian Organization for Human Rights. These ideological differences are

60–68; Fateh Azzam, "Tahwlat fi al-Alaqah bayn al-Munazamat al-Mahaliyah wa al-Dawliyah" (Transformations in the Relationship between Local and International Organizations), 3 Rowaq Arabi (July 1996), at 90–95.

40. *See generally*, Wilfred L. David, The Conversation of Economic Development: Historical Voices, Interpretations Reality (1997); Yusif A. Sayigh, Elusive Development to Self-reliance in the Arab Region (1991).

often reflected in profound disagreements within individual organizations, and among the leadership of the Arab human rights movement as a whole, about how to address major crises like the Iraqi invasion of Kuwait.

Another source of problematic politicization of the Arab human rights movement is the strong emergence of Islamic activism during the last two decades. Besides the dilemma raised by doubts about the genuine commitment of Islamic groups to democratic principles and human rights protection, the personal background of the secular Arab intellectuals who became leaders of human rights organization is not conducive to open dialogue with the leaders of the Islamic groups. Yet these leaders of human rights organizations find it difficult to openly challenge calls by Islamic groups for the application of Islamic Law (Shari'a) for fear of being branded as "anti-Islamic" despite the obvious fundamental contradictions between Shari'a principles and international human rights norms on such issues as the rights of women, non-Muslims, and freedom of belief among Muslims.[41]

7. The institutional weakness of Arab human rights organizations is closely associated with all the above-mentioned factors, especially the lack of official recognition and general harassment of activists by official organs of the state, and by non-official ideological and religious groups. Additional causes of institutional weakness are the inadequacy of organizational and administrative skills among human rights activists and the tendency to use populist methods in the absence of sustainable professionalism. While these problems are more evident in some organizations than others, they do affect the internal cohesion of the Arab human rights movement as a whole, and its ability to constitute a united front in the face of so many internal and external challenges and difficulties.[42] Another operational difficulty is the inability of the Arab movement to develop strategies of negotiation with governments, as supported by grass-roots mobilization of local constituencies,[43] thereby allowing external advocates to come and play that role. This is one aspect of human rights dependency that can only be addressed from within the ranks of the Arab human rights movement.

These difficulties and problems are being addressed by some segments of the Arab human rights movement.[44] As noted earlier, the failure of the

41. On these and other conflicts between Shari'a and international human rights standards, see generally, Abdullahi Ahmed An-Na'im, Toward an Islamic Reformation: Civil Liberties, Human Rights and International Law (1990).

42. Sai'd, *supra* note 33, at 12–27.

43. Hanny Megally, "Azmat Hawyah: Hal Balaghat al-Haraka al-Arabiyah Sinn al-Rush" (A Crisis of Identity: Did the Arab Human Rights Movement Achieve Maturity?), 3 Rowaq Arabi 74–79 (July 1996).

44. Bahey El-Din Hassan, "*Nahwa Istrategiya Munsajimah li Harakat Huquq al-Insan*" (Toward a Coherent Strategy for the Arab Human Rights Movement), Rowaq Arabi (July 1996), at 46–63; and the working papers by Hanny Megally and Bahey El-Din Hassan, presented at the First International Conference of the Arab Human Rights Movement, Casablanca, Morocco, 22–25 Apr. 1999.

AOHR to provide regional leadership in this regard is being redressed by others. The Cairo Institute for Human Rights Studies convened the First International Conference of the Arab Human Rights Movement in Casablanca in April 1999, and the Second Conference, which convened in Cairo in October 2000. The Casablanca Declaration, adopted by that First Conference, reviewed the internal and external context of the Arab human rights movement, and set its responsibilities in relation to most of the issues raised in the assessment presented in this essay.[45] The second conference focused on issues of human rights education and public awareness.

IV. CONCLUDING REMARKS

The preceding review and analysis of the emergence and development of the protection of human rights in the Arab world clearly indicates remarkable growth since the mid 1980s. This review also highlights the limitations and problems of these efforts. Consequently, the current status of the protection of human rights in the region is somewhat mixed, and can go either way in the future, depending on which strategies are followed or not at this stage. On the one hand, there are more than 50 human rights NGOs in the region, working in the fields of monitoring and advocacy, consciousness raising, education, training, research and scholarship, legal aid and adjudication, and rehabilitation of victims of violations. On the other hand, the 1990s has been marked by serious decline in the level of democratization and protection of human rights in countries that had earlier shown good promise in this regard, namely, Algeria, Egypt, Jordan, Sudan, Tunisia, and Yemen. In these and most of the other countries of the region, gross and systemic human rights violations have continued to mount, while the ratification of human rights treaties have not been honored by the necessary degree of conformity with international norms or compliance with the requirements of implementation mechanisms.

Recent measures taken by some governments to restrict freedoms of expression and association, like the Jordan statute on publications of July 1998 and the Egyptian law 153 of 1999 on civic associations, are of particular concern because of their implications for the role of local NGOs in the protection of human rights. In my view, these seriously regressive recent developments do not negate the significant achievements of the Arab human rights, especially when viewed in light of the difficult conditions under which they have been achieved. However, as suggested earlier, since

45. The full text in English of the Casablanca Declaration of the Arab Human Rights Movement is published by the Cairo Institute for Human Rights Studies, and reprinted in 17 Neth. Q. Hum. Rts. 363–69 (Sept. 1999).

the situation in general can be seen as a cup "half full" or "half empty," the question should be how to make it "more full" for the protection of human rights.

The brief elaboration in the preceding section of this essay of the obstacles and problems of the Arab human rights movement already indicates what needs to be done in both the short and long term. For example, in relation to point 1, one can call for the simplification of registration procedure for human rights NGOs, ending of harassment of activists, and so forth. From an analysis of the relationship between local and international NGOs (point 5), one can "imagine" ways of increasing cooperation and mutual respect between the two sets of organizations. Similar suggestions can be made to address excessive politicization (point 6) and institutional weakness (point 7). Other types of obstacles would clearly require longer term, broader, and more extensive and complex strategies of action, like issues of regional insecurity and distrust of the international community (point 3), or questions of cultural legitimacy of human rights standards (point 4). However, this sort of approach to "recommendation" is not very helpful, because these sets of difficulties are so interactive and interdependent that none can be addressed in isolation from the others. This sort of proposed strategies can also be seen as simplistic and naive.

As briefly explained in the Introduction of this essay, the protection of human rights in the Arab world requires the progressive diminishing of dependency, while continuing to enhance and promote international cooperation. Local and global civil society has a crucial role to play in the protection of human rights everywhere, but the goal of civil society and other actors should always be to diminish dependency by enhancing indigenous protection of human rights. Accordingly, international cooperation must be based on a principled commitment to *parity and mutual respect*, despite clear differentials in power relations and realities of Western hegemony.

To be clear, I am not in the least opposed to international protection of human rights as such, whether through the efforts of other governments, inter-governmental organizations, or international NGOs. On the contrary, I see all appropriate forms of international cooperation as imperative for the protection of human rights in any part of the world. Because the actual protection of human rights can only be realized through the agency of the state in question, international concern and action will always remain necessary simply because the state, which is the primary violator of these rights, cannot be trusted to protect them effectively. Moreover, the citizens of an oppressive state are necessarily less able to protect their own rights than those of states which are more respectful of these norms. But I am calling for combination of short term response to violations, through immediate action by the international community, with strategies to gradually diminish dependency on these external efforts in the long term. In other words, international protection efforts should include strategies for strengthening local capacity in this regard because the external imposition of measures is neither feasible, sustainable, nor acceptable as the primary means of protection of human rights on the ground. Fortunately, there is already awareness of the need for this combination of immediate response and longer term efforts to promote local capacity within the region, and some tentative efforts in this regard.

Ultimately, the challenge is how to be "visionary yet realistic," because there are no "magic solutions" that can materialize immediately for any of the obstacles and problems facing the protection of human rights in the Arab world. Because one has to take the world as it is, not as one would like it to be, strategies for promoting the protection of human rights must take into account the deep-rooted nature of the problems in devising *incremental* solutions that address immediate short term needs, while seeking to achieve long term ends. The primary objective of *diminishing* (not immediate termination of) human rights dependency cannot be achieved without strengthening civil society in general, and the Arab human rights movement in particular. This approach clearly indicates priority to *internal* initiatives. Yet the present weakness of Arab civil society and the human rights movement is due to deep-rooted and entrenched structural and cultural factors that cannot be changed in the immediate future. Nevertheless, in addressing the immediate consequences of these obstacles, ways must also be found to "invest" in long term and more sustainable solutions.

[9]
Human Rights and Islamic Identity in France and Uzbekistan: Mediation of the Local and Global[1]

INTRODUCTION

This discussion of current expressions of Islamic identity in Western Europe and Central Asia is part of my wider and continuing concern with issues of cultural transformation in Islamic societies and communities. The relevance

---

1. This paper was written under the auspices of the Faculty Seminar of the Halle Institute for Global Studies of Emory University. I am grateful to the Institute for supporting my research, including a visit to Uzbekistan in May 1998, and to the Ford Foundation for partial financial assistance for a second visit to Uzbekistan in December 1998.

I also gratefully acknowledge the indispensable help of Ms. Aizada A. Khalimbetova, who facilitated all aspects of my first visit, arranged for all interviews and informal discussions, and provided comprehensive translation throughout my stay. I thank the many colleagues who generously shared with me their insights regarding the situation in Uzbekistan during both visits, and Ms. Yael Fletcher of the Department of History, Emory University, for her thorough research assistance on France.

My special appreciation goes to my research assistant, Ms. Svetlana Peshkova of the Candler School of Theology, Emory University, who provided essential research as well as Russian/English translation and oral interpretation throughout the preparation of this paper.

and implications of a human rights paradigm for these issues in apparently different parts of the world are explored herein. This choice is explained below. The theoretical position I will argue is that the application of a human rights paradigm to the processes of cultural transformation draws on the interdependence of culturalist notions of contingency and global mutual influence, on the one hand, and positivist ideas of rights and their institutional expression, on the other. In the last section, I suggest that the human rights paradigm can play this role only to the extent that it both includes different perspectives and is capable of mitigating the negative consequences of differentials in power relations in the processes of globalization.

By the term "human rights paradigm," I mean the articulation and application of the same norms to every human being everywhere, a standard that presupposes the validity of cross-cultural moral judgment and requires systematic efforts to influence state policy and practice in matters that were previously deemed to be subject to the exclusive domestic jurisdiction of the state.[2] At a time when the world was just emerging from the horrors of the Second World War, the Charter of the United Nations of 1945 and the Universal Declaration of Human Rights of 1948 emphasized the idea that, in the interest of protecting human dignity, states should accord all persons, subject to their domestic jurisdiction, certain rights and freedoms. The basic idea is that, whereas the state traditionally determined the normative and institutional framework for matters such as citizenship and its implications, that framework is now partially defined by the human rights paradigm which is articulated and implemented by a variety of governmental, intergovernmental, and nongovernmental actors from all parts of the world, including vulnerable groups like women and immigrants.

As discussed later, the human rights paradigm is premised on a paradox. On the one hand, the normative and institutional arrangements it mandates are supposed to be produced and sanctioned by processes beyond the

2. This premise of the modern human rights movement found its first and most authoritative expressions in the Charter of the United Nations of 1945 and in the Universal Declaration of Human Rights of 1948, which was subsequently elaborated in numerous international human rights treaties. The tension between national sovereignty and the application of international human rights standards was reflected in the UN Charter itself and continues seriously to limit the practical implementation of these standards. Nevertheless, it is clear by now that this premise has been established beyond dispute through developments within the global UN system, the regional systems of Europe, the Americas, and Africa, and national and international nongovernmental human rights organizations.

For extensive materials on, and discussion of, a wide range of issues in this field, see generally, International Human Rights in Context: Law, Politics, Morals (Henry J. Steiner & Philip Alston eds., 1996); and International Human Rights Law & Practice: Cases, Treaties and Materials (Francisco Forrest Martin et al. eds., 1997).

exclusive control of the state and local communities. On the other hand, this paradigm also concedes to the state and local communities a crucial role in the interpretation and implementation of human rights norms.

The focus herein is the role of the human rights paradigm in the dynamics of the formation and transformation of Islamic identity in France and Uzbekistan today. In France, this process is taking place for a small minority living in physical diaspora of place or space, while in Uzbekistan it is happening for a clear majority in terms of what may be called "a diaspora of time or displaced memory." Despite differences in their historical experiences and specific present context, both types of complex Muslim communities face the question of the relationship between Islam and the state. As I will emphasize, however, this relationship should not be seen simply in terms of acceptance or rejection of secularism as the complete separation of religion and the state.

While the situations in France and Uzbekistan are quite different in many respects, I see them as raising similar tensions between the dynamic of cultural transformation and the adequacy and legitimacy of institutional arrangements for pluralism and multiculturalism within each country. Yet, the clear differences between the two situations are useful for drawing at least some tentative general conclusions from this comparative analysis. For example, if one can identify some similarities about the relevance and implications of a human rights paradigm for Islamic modernist initiatives in different regions (in this case, Western Europe and Central Asia), that might be helpful in understanding corresponding processes taking place in other parts of the world. In other words, discussing these two situations in comparative terms may contribute to a better understanding of the relationship between identity formation and institutional change at a global, as well as national or regional, level. Furthermore, while each case must always be studied on its own terms for the most reliable conclusions, general reflections from such comparative analysis can inform and guide specific country studies.

Local Muslim communities in France are currently negotiating with the wider national French identity and culture about the meaning and relevance of their Islamic identity in the context of a highly developed and effective national and regional European human rights framework. That context also includes continuing relations with Muslim communities elsewhere, from local and national communities in the immigrants' countries of origin (like Algeria and Turkey) to the global theological and/or ideological networks of a universal Islamic community (*ummah*). Major sites of contestation within France itself, to be highlighted below, include education, religion, language, political participation, and immigration policies. The issues are also ultimately about the relationship between "citizenship" and "nationality" in a country like France as it moves toward greater European unity.[3]

Uzbekistan is struggling with the meaning and relevance of an Islamic identity in the context of a post-Soviet-state society that is only beginning to discover the possibilities and benefits of a human rights framework. The ruling elites of the Soviet era claim to have transformed themselves and their political institutions to meet the demands of democratic governance and free-market economy in the context of the Organization for Security and Cooperation in Europe (OSCE). At the same time, they are also resorting to Islam as a source of national identity while attempting to limit the ideological and geopolitical consequences of that choice. Unable to control the terms of both forms of transition, the ruling elites tend to turn to old Soviet-style tactics to suppress political opposition and avoid accountability for their policies and practice.

Current scholarship on the regions in question tends to examine issues of identity in broader socio-political terms, focusing on implications for domestic politics or regional and international geopolitical and security considerations. While these perspectives are useful for my purposes here, I am more concerned with how a human rights paradigm can contribute to the successful and sustainable mediation of issues of identity and citizenship—and with the institutional expression of that process in apparently different circumstances: a small Muslim minority in Western Europe and a clear majority in Central Asia. The main question that I am raising regarding these two situations is whether a human rights paradigm, both as an external normative and institutional framework and as a popular discourse for political mobilization, has a useful role to play in these transformative processes.

In the case of France, membership in the European as well as the United Nations human rights systems can influence French domestic definition and practice of notions of citizenship and rights beyond the traditional confines of French nationality. In other words, the French political and legal system is required by the human rights paradigm to secure certain minimum rights for Muslims permanently living in France despite the fact that they do not fit the historical profile of French nationality. Similarly, the post-Soviet state of

3. Until 1993, most children born in France to immigrant parents automatically became French nationals on reaching the age of majority, but this is no longer the case. The position of Algerian immigrants was rather different, depending on whether or not they were born before Algeria's independence in 1962, and remains largely untouched by the 1993 changes in the French nationality code. *See* ALEC G. HARGREAVES, IMMIGRATION, "RACE" AND ETHNICITY IN CONTEMPORARY FRANCE 135 (1995).

Uzbekistan is driven by the economic, political, and security concerns of its new context to seek international legitimacy through democratization and the protection of human rights at home. But, given the nature of the state and society of Uzbekistan, the question is whether the ruling elites will succeed in achieving the benefits of international legitimacy without serious challenge to their hold on political power or loss in their economic and social privilege. As discussed below, the outcome of such efforts at any given time will depend on a variety of factors, including the ability of civil society to hold the government accountable to democratic and human rights principles.

To the extent that people accept that a human rights paradigm is useful for achieving stronger political participation and more social justice, that paradigm becomes an integral part of the processes of cultural transformation. Yet, the validity of this paradigm may not be acceptable to many Muslim activists who perceive an inherent tension between Islamic cultures and the universality of human rights. Nevertheless, those activists and the constituencies they represent may have to adopt human rights as a shared frame of meaning in order to effectuate their own claims to Islamic identity, whether as a majority or minority in a given state. In other words, Muslims in France and Uzbekistan *may have to modify aspects of their understanding of what an Islamic identity means in the process of claiming that identity in the modern context.*

In order for the universalist human rights project of the second half of the twentieth century to succeed, I suggest, it needs to engage possibilities of internal discourse and cross-cultural dialogue in promoting its own normative legitimacy as well as its political and legal efficacy.[4] An internal discourse is needed for cultivating and fostering an indigenous human rights culture against other competing perceptions of the values and institutions of a given culture. A cross-cultural dialogue is necessary for mitigating differentials in power relations in the present context of economic and technological globalization. Without such adjustments, globalization will simply be used to perpetuate the exploitative and hegemonic policies of developed countries over developing countries. The combination of the two processes, I am proposing, ensures greater participation in the definition and implementation of human rights norms which will thereby enjoy stronger legitimacy among different cultures of the world.

This is not to say, however, that a human rights paradigm is either independent from socio-political and economic factors, or sufficient by

4. Human Rights in Africa: Cross-Cultural Perspectives (Abdullahi Ahmed An-Na'im & Francis M. Deng eds., 1990); Abdullahi A. An-Na'im, Human Rights in Cross-Cultural Perspectives: Quest for Consensus (1992).

itself for overcoming all difficulties of the relationship between identities and institutions, whether in Europe, Central Asia, or elsewhere. Rather, I am suggesting a model for understanding this relationship in the broader context of different societies. In my view, a human rights paradigm is a particularly useful framework for analyzing the relationship between identity and institutional change because its claim to set universal norms challenges all sides in the identity negotiation process. By setting specialized standards for the rights of particularly vulnerable groups like women, children, and religious or ethnic minorities, as well as general norms which apply to the population at large, the human rights paradigm promotes social change in certain directions. At the same time, all persons and groups seeking to benefit from this paradigm must accept and act upon its dual premise of the universality of its norms and the accountability of the state. Given the growing moral and political, as well as legal, importance of human rights in national politics and international relations, states can no longer afford to ignore the practical implications of this paradigm. By the same token, moreover, governments and civil-society actors are increasingly finding it necessary and beneficial to participate in the specification and institutionalized implementation of human rights norms. Governments prefer to contribute to defining the terms of their obligations, while civil-society actors seek to ensure broader and more effective protection of their rights.

I wish to emphasize that I am not claiming that the role of the human rights paradigm in the mediation of religious/cultural—(in this paper Islamic)—identity is already fully utilized or even appreciated. Although I would like to see that happen more systematically and deliberately, the immediate objective of this paper is to examine the present situation of Islamic communities in France and Uzbekistan to see whether and how the human rights paradigm is playing (or can play) this role in those settings. To this end, I will begin with some clarification of the nature and process of identity formation and transformation, then examine the situation in France and Uzbekistan, and conclude with some reflections and suggestions for further research along the lines indicated here.

IDENTITY FORMATION AND TRANSFORMATION

While the term identity is commonly taken to indicate something that is clearly defined, stable, and fixed, I share the view that people structure their lives by an unanchored, open, and self-generating pattern of meaning and value. In other words, I see identity formation and transformation as a dynamic process rather than an immutable condition.

Individuals construct meaning and value with the aid of cultural codes shared by particular groups. Personal identity is in this sense inseparable from—though not necessarily reducible to—socio-cultural identity. It is not uncommon for a person to switch between codes. By the same token, he or she moves between a variety of socio-cultural identities.[5]

Cultural codes include "primordial attachments" such as language and religious affiliations, which are learned or formed at an early age, as well as new codes learned later in life. Moreover, code-switching can be done in an "instrumentalist" or calculated manner, sometimes to achieve different objectives than those envisaged by the original codes. For example, Muslim workers in France may adopt an "Islamic stance" not only out of conviction but also as a strategy for dealing with French authorities under certain circumstances.[6] In Uzbekistan, "during the Soviet era many individuals apparently claimed 'Uzbek' nationality due to pressure, as a matter of convenience, or as a category which promised better opportunities than identification with other groups."[7]

While there is never an "identity-vacuum"—since we all have some identity at any given time—(though our consciousness of it may vary)—persons and communities do engage in identity formulation and transformation processes in interaction with other persons and communities. Moreover, each set of processes and interactions combines elements of adjusted and/or retrieved preexisting identities, together with newly-created or situation-specific identities. For example, for one to be a Muslim in a specific context includes what being a Muslim has meant to that person in the past, which necessarily includes negotiation with others about that meaning, as well as the purpose of Islamic identity in the situation at hand. One's understanding of what it means to be a Muslim includes, though of course is not fully identical to, understandings by others, yet all these different meanings of identity contribute to its constant formation and transformation. In other words, the determination of identity at any given point in time is a product of the actors, context, and purpose, as well as whatever normative or behavioral content different actors associate with the identity in question.

An important aspect of this process that is likely to be overlooked in the rhetoric of cultural self-determination is the need for acceptance or recognition of the assumed or claimed identity by others.[8] Although the

5. Hargreaves, *supra* note 3, at 94.
6. Making Muslim Space in North America and Europe 86–87 (Barbara Daly Metcalf ed., 1996).
7. William Fierman, *Political Development in Uzbekistan: Democratization? in* Conflict, Cleavage, and Change in Central Asia and the Caucasus 363 (Karen Dawisha & Bruce Parrott eds., 1997).
8. Mike Featherstone, *Localism, Globalism, and Cultural Identity, in* Global, Local: Cultural Production and the Transnational Imaginary, 46–77 (Rob Wilson & Wimal Dissanayake eds., 1996).

primary focus of identity formation and transformation appears to be internal self-identification, the success of the whole process is dependent on the response of the external "other" against whom an independent identity is being asserted. In a country like France, a Muslim person or community asserting an Islamic identity for some communal concerns—regarding education, for example—would need the acknowledgment of that claim by the relevant authorities of the state and larger society. An assertion of an Islamic identity for political or social objectives in a country like Uzbekistan would need to be accepted both by the wider society and by state authorities in order to achieve its purpose. Yet, none of us has much control over the characterization of our identities by others. Consequently, not only is the outcome of the process of negotiation of identities contingent at any given point, but it can also change over time because of factors that may be perceived to be external or irrelevant to a supposedly "identity-defining" process. For example, civil war in neighboring Tajikistan, especially to the extent that it involves conflict over the relationship between Islam and the state, is bound to influence the formation and transformation of Islamic identity in Uzbekistan.

It is therefore misleading to speak of an isolated or self-contained, identity-defining process leading to a specific, predictable, and permanent outcome for the parties concerned. It is true that some stages and/or factors in the process can be more significant than others, depending on the relationship between the actors, context, and purpose. But the point I wish to emphasize here is the contingent nature of the process and its constantly shifting and interacting outcomes. As Mike Featherstone put it:

> The unwillingness of migrants to passively inculcate the dominant cultural mythology of the nation or locality raises issues of multiculturalism and the fragmentation of identity. In some cases this provoked intensified and extremist nationalist reactions, for example, the racist campaigns of Le Pen in France. . . . This can lead to a complex series of reactions on the part of the immigrants. For some ethnic groups this entails a retreat into the culture of origin . . . or into fundamentalist religions from the home country. For others this may entail the construction of complex counterethnicities. . . . For yet others the prospect of a unified single identity may be impossible and illusory as they move between various identities.[9]

It is also important to note the variety of overlapping identities that persons and communities tend to have at the same time. Given the unavoidable religious, cultural, or ethnic diversity of any modern society, and the variety of political, professional, and other affiliations of individual persons in each

9. *Id.* at 66.

community, one should not speak of an Islamic identity in isolation of the other types and forms of identity held or upheld by the same communities or persons. For example, a local community may identify with one community through shared affiliation with a particular Islamic Sufi (mystic) or theological tradition, with another community in terms of ethnicity, and with yet a third community because of common economic interests. A person may at one level identify as a member of a Muslim community (with consequent Sufi, theological, ethnic, and other possible affiliations with other Muslim communities), while at another level his or her membership in a professional trade union and/or political party may bring him or her to identify with others of different religious or ethnic identities. This matrix of actors and factors should remain central to our methodological and theoretical reflection.

To summarize, the concept of identity itself can be broadly or narrowly defined, depending on the actors, context, and purpose. It is often a code for moral and political discourse or a proxy for a wide variety of declared and undeclared agendas. As a working definition, I use the term to refer to the meaning and anticipated consequences of interaction between the ways persons or communities define themselves, and the ways they are defined by others. Given the contingency of the process and multiplicity of identities (social, religious, political, professional, and so forth) that all persons and communities have at any given time, it is necessary to specify the actors, context, and purpose of the identity-formation process one wishes to discuss. In this light, it is important to note the following about France and Uzbekistan.

As indicated earlier, the vast majority of Muslims in France can be seen as living in a state of diaspora, or physical displacement, but this characterization should be qualified in intercommunal as well as intergenerational terms. It is true that some commonalities are likely to emerge among various Muslim communities in France who are engaged in identity negotiation locally, while at the same time interacting with other Muslim societies through global institutions and media.[10] Nevertheless, one must be careful in making generalized claims about the meaning and consequences of this physical diaspora. Factors that can influence the dynamics of Islamic identity include different perceptions of that identity at the place of origin (in Algeria, Turkey, and so forth), whether it was urban or rural, as well as conditions and timing of migration to France, and experiences since arrival, both with other Muslims and the wider French society. Similarly, various generations of Muslims, whether or not born and raised in France, are likely to have different perceptions of Islamic identity, though not necessarily in

10. Metcalf ed., *supra* note 6, at 2.

predictable ways. While one may expect French-born Muslims to internalize the cultural codes of French society through school and social interaction,[11] some of them may in fact develop a more distinctive or pronounced Islamic identity than their parents, who may have sought greater and faster integration. The dynamics of identity for the members of each generation are likely to be conditioned in different ways by the experiences of the preceding generation as well as their own.

More generally, the public expression of Islamic identity for all generations is shaped by such factors as the context of the wider society, the size and composition of the Muslim community, the Muslims' legal status in the country, and assumptions about the relationship between religion and the state in France.[12] But again, it is difficult to predict the precise outcome of different combinations of these factors. For example, ethno-religious discrimination may either stimulate development of an Islamic identity or encourage assimilation with the dominant culture.[13] Furthermore, the redefinition and reappropriation of Islamic identity in a new context should not be seen as alternative processes in which "the old and new cultures are fixed, and that change results from the pieces being added and subtracted. Instead, new cultural and institutional expressions are being created using the symbols and institutions of the received tradition."[14]

Muslims of Uzbekistan can be seen as inhabiting a temporal diaspora of displaced memory as they seek to recall a historical, pre-Soviet understanding of an Islamic identity of which they had no personal experience. The process of negotiation of an Islamic identity in cases like Uzbekistan today can also be understood in terms of the reconstruction of that historical identity while attempting to retrieve it. While there is always reconstruction in retrieval of preexisting identities, the outcome of the process is probably more uncertain when memory is claimed to extend several centuries into the past. In this context, there are bound to be competing visions of the past, none of which quite fits the present or necessarily fulfills the needs of those seeking to retrieve the past identity. This is because what is believed to have happened in the past, to the extent it is factually true, was the product of the perceptions and action of a people reacting to their own specific conditions and within the wider context of their relationship with other people around them at that time. All of this is now being filtered through the constructed "memory" of today's Muslims of Uzbekistan in relation to their present context.

---

11. HARGREAVES, *supra* note 3, at 95.
12. Metcalf ed., *supra* note 6, at 12; W.A.R. SHADID & P.S. VAN KONINGSVELD, RELIGIOUS FREEDOM AND THE POSITION OF ISLAM IN WESTERN EUROPE: OPPORTUNITIES AND OBSTACLES IN THE ACQUISITION OF EQUAL RIGHTS 13 (1995).
13. Metcalf ed., *supra* note 6, at 12, 86.
14. *Id.* at 7.

Thus, a past identity would have to be reconstructed in order to serve the social or political purposes for which it is invoked by a people living in the present time. Such reconstruction and retrieval would involve, for example, a deliberate articulation by ruling elites or leaders of social movements of specific criteria by which the utility and authenticity of presumed past events may be assessed, certain aspects of the past emphasized, and other aspects deemphasized. Ruling elites and leaders of social movements also tend to define local, regional, and/or global conditions to fit the reconstructed identity they seek to retrieve and install in the consciousness of the population or groups they seek to influence. Past conditions of religious or ethnic composition of the community may be misrepresented, manipulated, or interpreted in particular ways to legitimize and substantiate the claims being made by those actors. For example, a past community may be claimed to have been more religiously conscious or ethnically homogeneous than it really was in order to support claims about what the present should or can be. In all of this, elites and leaders of social movements will, of course, use all the political, educational, institutional, media, and any other resources they can muster in the service of their reconstruction and retrieval project.

In the case of Uzbekistan today, this process can be clearly illustrated by the way Timur Link (1336–1406) was selected as the central figure in the reconstruction and retrieval of an Uzbek identity. Although the region as a whole had a long and prosperous history for many centuries, before the coming of Islam during the seventh–eighth century, and although that earlier history also inspired outstanding intellectual and theological achievements, President Islam Karimov has instead chosen the so-called "Timurids Renaissance" of the fifteenth and first half of sixteenth centuries as the focus of building a national identity for modern Uzbekistan. It is that particular episode of the history of the region that is now emphasized in school curricula, and highlighted by the media. In personal interviews that I conducted during a visit to Tashkent in May 1998, professors of political science and sociology, educated for decades in Marxist-Leninist philosophy of historical materialism, quoted and discussed "the Code of Timur" as the ultimate scheme of political and social organization.

There are clearly many elements and complex dynamics of Islamic identity in France and Uzbekistan today; and there is room for reasonable disagreement about the meaning of the elements and working of the process through which they are mediated in one place or another. It is not my purpose to uphold one choice as more legitimate or desirable or to discredit another. Rather, the point I am emphasizing is that *conscious choices* about the nature and implications of Islamic identity today are being made and actively promoted, whether by members of minority local Muslim communities in France or on behalf of a national Muslim majority in Uzbekistan. It would therefore seem to follow that *alternative* choices can also be made and promoted within the framework of internal cultural discourse and cross-cultural dialogue as indicated earlier. Looking at France first, how are these choices being made, by whom and to what extent?

ISLAMIC IDENTITY, NATIONALITY, AND CITIZENSHIP IN FRANCE

Some Muslim scholars, like the late Fazlur Rahman and Zaki Badawi, have suggested that Islamic renewal may come from Muslims in the West. Badawi is reported to have added that the most profound formulations will come from France, where Muslims will be challenged by the hardness of life, the deeply held convictions of Republican secularism, and the depth of racism.[15] It has also been suggested that France's self-image as a country with a universal message embodied in the French Revolution's Declaration of the Rights of Man and of the Citizen, makes it harder for the French to accept the idea that an immigrant group can pose a sociological challenge. Yet, this attachment to the human rights ideal may come into conflict with the powerful French self-image as a unitary, homogeneous, and centralized nation-state. It is assumed that all citizens have not only equal rights but also the same cultural background and education; i.e., the French "melting pot" should make everyone exclusively French.[16]

However, the influx of North and West African, Turkish, and other clearly "un-French" immigrants makes it clear that this traditional French perception of the unity of nationality and citizenship is no longer tenable. What role, if any, can human rights as a normative and institutional framework play in the mediation of the relationship between nationality and citizenship? My argument here is that since the human rights paradigm precludes the coerced assimilation of migrant populations into French culture and nationality in the traditional sense, it forces an adjustment of dominant understandings of what it means to be French. But because this is a two-way process, immigrant Muslims will also have to adjust their understandings of what it means to be Muslim precisely in order to be able to claim an Islamic identity in France. In this new environment, education and language have become sites of contestation and mediation of French nationality and Republican secularism, on the one hand, and Islamic identity, on the other. This process is unfolding within the framework of multicultural citizenship as mandated by the principles of equality and nondiscrimination under the European human rights system.

15. *Id.* at 19.
16. Ronald Koven, *The French Melting Pot: Preventing Boil-Over*, FRANCE TODAY 11 (Fall 1991).

To begin on a demographic note, with an estimated following of four to five million people, Islam is often described as the second largest religion in France, after Catholicism. Muslims in France have largely come from North Africa and, to a lesser degree, French West Africa.[17] Turkey has also been a source of somewhat late but not insubstantial labor migration to France since the early 1970s.[18] It should be noted, however, that in the absence of official registration of religious affiliation, such demographic information is mainly based on estimates. Moreover, these estimates do not indicate which form or degree of Islamic religious attachment, if at all, various individuals have. Nor do they permit even an approximate estimation of the theological or political views of this diverse Muslim population. Whatever demographic information is available about Muslims, it should also be understood in the context both of immigration from Italy, Portugal, Spain, and sub-Saharan Africa, and of French citizens born in France of foreign parents, because the presence of these other immigrants clearly influences the situation of Muslim immigrants.[19]

Immigrant Muslims have lived in France for decades, but they have become the focus of attention in public discourse and political rhetoric since the 1980s due to the emergence of certain domestic issues within France, in addition, international terrorist attacks involving Muslim activists, and family reunification policies. While terrorist attacks by a handful of Muslims are taken as substantiating negative stereotypes about Islam and all Muslims, the coming of family members to join their relatives in France is seen as a drain on public resources and social services. These and related factors appear to have led to perceptions of an "Islamic threat" to French cultural identity, political institutions, or legal order. It is important to emphasize here, however, that much of the debate about issues such as polygamy, circumcision of girls, disrespect for Western legal order, or questions of language and religious education, is based on some assumptions and negative stereotyping, rather than empirical research.[20] For example, according to Ronald Koven, Jacques Chirac, the Gaullist Party leader, then Mayor of Paris and subsequently Prime Minister and President of France, said that he constantly hears outraged comments like those of "the French worker who sees on the same floor of his low-rent housing complex a man with his three or four wives and twenty-odd kids who gets

---

17. Metcalf ed., *supra* note 6, at 1.
18. Jorgen S. Nielsen, Muslims in Western Europe 9 (2d ed. 1995) (1992).
19. As one author noted: "A myth has evolved that the assimilation of millions of Italians, Spaniards and Poles was smooth because they shared with the French the same Catholic religion and European culture. The historical reality is that none of those groups were easily integrated: Italians in the South of France, for instance, were massacred at the turn of the century." Koven, *supra* note 16, at 11–13.
20. Shadid & Van Koningsveld, *supra* note 12, at 2–5.

$8000 or $9000 a month in family welfare payments without working. If you add in the noise and the smell, the French worker goes crazy." After emphasizing this statement, Koven adds: "No actual examples of such a family could be found. There are officially 268 polygamous marriages in France, accepted after a court ruling that marriages legally contracted abroad cannot be rejected by the French authorities."[21] But the fact that official figures on polygamy and welfare flatly contradict such statements from the highest levels of political leadership is immaterial to those with whom the stereotype resonates most strongly.

Within such a context, one can appreciate the importance for Muslims in France of informal mutual support systems as wider social networks drawing on cultural practices of immigrants from the same village or region. These networks are often supplemented by formally constituted associations pursuing welfare, cultural, and sometimes political objectives. Given their important role, it is not surprising that countries of origin as well as the French government continue to exert significant influence over voluntary associations because of the dependence of associations on subsidies from either or both governments. Countries of origin tend to attempt to control such activities for fear of their consequences or implications in their own country, as illustrated by the Algerian government's effort to combat the activities of the Islamic Salvation Front (better known by the French acronym, FIS) in France. On the other hand, the primary purpose of funding provided by the French Ministry of Social Affairs is to support the state project of integrating immigrants and their descendants into French society. Consequently, such subsidies tend to assist those voluntary associations whose activities are conductive to integration, but not if they are driven by separatist ambitions.[22]

Muslim immigrants to France have tended to come from working class and village backgrounds. They are largely poorly skilled and unskilled workers who have tried to duplicate their village environments in their newly adopted countries. Moreover, because the educational and organizational levels of these communities are low, there have been serious communication problems where they have interacted with the host communities.[23] Under these conditions, schools have become an important site of construction and contestation of identity as the immigrants seek to balance the conflicting needs of securing a better education for their children and preserving their Islamic and ethnic identities. The interplay of education, religion, and language can therefore be a useful prism for examining the

21. Koven, *supra* note 16, at 13.
22. Hargreaves, *supra* note 3, at 88–89.
23. Ziauddin Sardar, *Racism, Identity and Muslims in the West, in* Muslim Minorities in the West 1 (Sayed Z. Abedin & Ziauddin Sardar eds., 1995).

role of a human rights paradigm in the mediation of Islamic identity in France.

Regardless of nationality, children in France are required to attend school from age six to sixteen, but the majority of children enter school younger because of the generous nursery school provisions. Immigrants also have the theoretical possibility of setting up their own schools, but in practice most of them have neither the economic means nor the organizational skills to do so. For most children of immigrant parents, the free-of-charge French state education is the only practical option. French law allows for some possibilities for religious education on a confessional basis on public school premises upon the request of parents. Though this is supposed to happen at the expense of parents, the law officially permits public authorities to subsidize these forms of additional optional education. Moreover, "factual information" about Islam is included in the official history syllabus, and some state schools include some aspects of Islam as part of intercultural educational programs.[24]

Since the middle of the 1970s, the French government has allowed countries of origin to provide, at their own expense, instruction in "homeland languages and cultures" within French primary schools. A few immigrant parents take advantage of this policy to supplement state education with extracurricular classes, and some countries of origin (like Algeria and Morocco) provide qualified teachers for such activities.[25] But such classes last no more than three hours a week, and the language taught could be quite different from the child's mother tongue. For example, North African children are taught the standardized version of Arabic which has little in common with the dialects spoken by their parents. The Berbers, who constitute a substantial portion of North Africans in France, may speak no Arabic at home, but there is no state-funded instruction in their own language because their countries of origin (Algeria and Morocco) are trying to suppress the Berber language and culture in favor of Arabic.[26]

It is in this general context of schools as sites of contestation of religious and cultural identity that the so-called "head-scarf affair" arose, mainly since the late 1980s. Several factors contributed to the timing and intensity of debates over the wearing of the head-scarf at public schools, but the issue is commonly framed in terms of the compatibility of Islam with the laical traditions of the French Republic.[27] While these traditions are believed to prohibit wearing any kind of symbol of religious affiliation at any French

24. Shadid & Van Koningsveld, *supra* note 12, at 113.
25. Hargreaves, *supra* note 3, at 89–90.
26. *Id.* at 101–02.
27. Nielsen, *supra* note 18, at 164–66.

public school, the actual situation in the schools themselves had reflected some diversity of practice for several decades. For example, in some schools, the principle of laicity was taken to require wearing a formal uniform, but in other schools the wearing of certain tokens of Christian or Jewish affiliation (like the cross, the Star of David, and the yarmulke) was allowed. In other words, both restrictive and permissive understandings of the French official ethos coexisted for some time, and conflict did not arise until the appearance of the Islamic scarf.[28]

As a result of several confrontations over whether students were allowed to wear a head-scarf at public schools, the Minister of National Education consulted the Council of State, which rejected the restrictive interpretation of laicity. In its advice of 27 November 1989, the Council stated that consideration of the Constitution and laws of France and of the international human rights treaties it had ratified, indicates that:

> the wearing of tokens by pupils by which they wish to express their affiliation to a religion, is not in itself incompatible with the principle of laicity, in as far as it constitutes the exercising of their right to freedom of opinion and to the manifestation of religious beliefs. . . . [But] this liberty would not permit pupils to flaunt, in a conspicuous fashion, symbols of religious affiliation which, by their very nature, by the conditions under which they are worn individually or collectively, by their ostentatious character or by the claims they lay, would constitute an act of pressure, provocation, proselytism or propaganda, [and thus] would infringe upon the dignity or the liberty of the said pupils or of other members of the educational community, endanger their health or their security, obstruct the course of the educational activities and the educational role of the teachers, or, finally, disrupt the order of things at the institution or the normal functioning of the public service.[29]

The Council of State concluded that an internal code of conduct for school should ensure that wearing tokens of religious affiliation should conform with (1) respect for the principles of laicity and pluralism; (2) the duty of tolerance and respect for the person and conviction of others; and (3) the obligation of every student to participate in all educational activities (including sports and practical training as in laboratories and workshops). The instructions issued by the Minister of National Education in accordance with these guidelines from the Council of State also provided for dialogue between the school authorities and students and their parents in case of conflict. If after a reasonable period of time the issue is not resolved, the rules of laicity will have to prevail.

However, conflicts over the interpretation and application of these

---

28. SHADID & VAN KONINGSVELD, *supra* note 12, at 88–89.
29. *Id.* at 89–90.

principles continued to arise under different sets of ministerial instructions.[30] Disagreement also persisted regarding the precise circumstances, significance, and consequences of the various incidents and debates about the head-scarf issue. After a review of several incidents, studies, opinion polls, and media treatments of the issue, Hargreaves concludes that most Muslim immigrants and their descendants have adapted to the framework of law governing religious practices in France.[31] However, this does not mean that the mechanical process of acculturation has led to the abandonment of their religious faith, or that they have become entirely assimilated into preexisting cultural norms. Instead, according to Hargreaves, "in the field of religion, as in other cultural spheres, immigrants and their descendants are forging new syntheses combining elements drawn from their pre-migratory heritage with a commitment to the overarching norms governing social intercourse in France."[32]

Such tensions between immigrant groups and their adopted country are, of course, old and common throughout the world. There may also be much similarity among the types of policies and practices usually adopted in the mediation of these conflicts in many societies, especially those which share the same basic ideological or cultural orientation, as is becoming increasingly the case in Western Europe today. The question that I am raising here is whether and to what extent the human rights paradigm is changing the terms and dynamics of this process for the immigrant groups, the host state, and society at large. I will return to these and related issues after the following brief review of some relevant issues in Uzbekistan today.

ISLAM AND THE POLITICS OF TRANSFORMATION IN UZBEKISTAN

Since little is commonly known about Uzbekistan because much of its affairs have been obscured by centuries of marginalization, Russian colonialism, and Soviet/Russian domination, I begin this section with a brief review of the history and present situation in this country in the broader context of Central Asia. Against this background, I shall focus on the role of Islam in the social and political transformation of the country in the post-Soviet era, while highlighting some features that may be relevant to an assessment of the possibilities and limitations of using the human rights paradigm in mediating Islamic identity in that country.

30. *Id.* at 90–92.
31. Hargreaves, *supra* note 3, at 125–31.
32. *Id.* at 131.

Background and Present Political Context

The history of the region commonly known today as Central Asia spans more than two thousand years and several civilizations. For the last three centuries, however, the region's fortunes have changed from being the location of great wealth and importance as the crossroads of commerce (the Great Silk Road), where leading centers of learning and scientific exploration flourished and influenced the course of development throughout the pre-modern world, to decline and marginalization. Prior to the coming of Islam in the seventh and eighth centuries, Zoroastrianism (which emerged in the territory of present-day Uzbekistan), Buddhism, and Christianity were the dominant religions of the region. Through several centuries of gradual Islamization, initially in urban centers (Samarkand and Bukhara) and slowly among nomadic tribes, Central Asia became a leading center for scientific and intellectual developments (al-Khorezmi, Beruni, and ibn Sina [Avicenna]), architecture and artisanship, technological progress, paper production, and abundance of grain.

The renaissance of the fifteenth and sixteenth centuries, after the devastation of the Mongol invasion, began with the unification of the Turko-Mongol tribes and the cultural-economic integration of the region under Timur (1336–1405), who also developed an advanced system of administration and common set of legal norms (Code of Timur) for his empire. But by the sixteenth century, the region lost its global strategic economic importance as alternative trade routes were established by the emerging European maritime powers, resulting in the increasing isolation of the region for the next three centuries.

The modern history of Central Asia (also known as Turkestan) can be traced back to gradual colonization since the late eighteenth century by Tsarist Russia, culminating in its total incorporation into the Russian Empire between 1890–1917. With its limited objectives in the region, Tsarist Russian colonialism practiced some form of indirect rule from Moscow, preserving the titular sovereignty of the Emir of Bukhara and the Khan of Khiva and generally exercising minimal interference with traditional power structures and cultural institutions. Nevertheless, that phase of Russian colonialism was a powerful force for change in the region, introducing railroads, new markets, irrigation projects, and European forms of education.[33]

With the collapse of the Tsarist Empire in 1917, Central Asia had a brief opportunity for independence, but the Soviet Union prevailed by the early 1920s and divided the region for the first time into five Soviet national republics (Turkmen 1924, Uzbek 1924, Tajik 1929, Kazakh 1936, and

33. Shirin Akiner, Central Asia: Conflict or Stability and Development? 5 (1997).

Kirgiz 1936) which eventually became fully sovereign states by the early 1990s.[34] Among the various ideological, economic, and other elements of the rationale of the Soviet policies of division and forced population relocation within and from outside the region, was a desire to neutralize ethnicity and Islam as the two common denominators most likely to unite Central Asians against control from Moscow. Without engaging in an evaluation or debate about the rationale or efficacy of those policies,[35] I wish to note an apparent paradox in this situation. It is true that the Soviet Union did not collapse because of any religious uprising, whether Islamic or Christian. At the same time, and for whatever reasons, a strong undercurrent of transnational unity of Turkestan (Central Asian) and Islamic identity has clearly survived to varying degrees within the region *precisely because of the ability of regional unity and Islamic identity to adapt to changing conditions.*

This paradox is reflected in the fact that instead of immediately claiming independence when the Soviet Union collapsed in 1990, the communist rulers of the five Central Asian republics waited for the adoption of the New Union Constitution of August 1991, which would have shifted more powers from the federal government to the republics. But after the failed coup d'état of 1991 in Moscow, the Central Asian leaders opted for complete independence with all the trappings of sovereignty under international law. Accordingly, these Republics have now adopted their own national constitutions[36] and have become members of the United Nations and intergovernmental organizations such as the Conference (recently renamed Organization) for Security and Cooperation in Europe, the World Bank, and the International Monetary Fund (IMF). All these developments are significant for my analysis, as indicated below, but one should not assume that these new global connections will necessarily significantly diminish the role of

---

34. On this process, its rationale, and its consequences, see Edward A. Allworth, The Modern Uzbeks: From the Fourteenth Century to the Present: A Cultural History ch. 12 (1990).
35. After discussing Soviet efforts to suppress Islam in the region, Keller concluded:

> The Bolsheviks failed to replace Islam with Marxism-Leninism in Central Asia for many reasons. They put themselves in an impossible position by assuming that religion could be separated from other components of identity, and they failed to take into account the lasting power of ancient customs and rituals. They failed to heed the warnings of Sultan Galieve, who was correct in predicting that Muslims would never trust a system run by Russians that did not give them equal power in government. Finally, when propaganda and education did not have their predicted effects, the Soviets resorted to using violence to destroy Islam, a tactic which also completely obliterated any hopes of converting Muslims.

Shoshana Keller, *Religion of an Atheist State: The Attempt to Supplant Islam with Marxism-Leninism in Soviet Central Asia*, Advanced Study Center Working Paper Series, 7, at 29–30 (International Institute, University of Michigan, 1997–98).

36. The dates of adoption of national constitutions were as follows: Turkmenistan in May 1992, Ubekistan in December 1992, Kazakstan in January 1993, Kyrgyzstan in May 1993, and Tajikistan in November 1994.

Russia in the affairs of each of the five republics, and in Central Asia as a whole.

The Russian/Soviet factor has of course been foundational for these republics and crucial in their bilateral and regional relations.[37] In addition to the impact of Tsarist colonialism on the region as a whole, the Soviet boundaries of what were then called "the national republics," and the social engineering policies of the Soviet Union have effectively determined the territories and populations of the present republics, with little regard for ethnic, linguistic, religious, or other components of nationality in the European sense.[38] On the other hand, however, the Soviet Union also "dramatically raised literacy rates in Uzbekistan, achieved universal primary education, and brought secondary and higher education to large segments of the population."[39] It is too early to assess the degree to which Russia has inherited the economic, political, educational, cultural, and other aspects of the role of the Soviet Union in each of the now-independent republics and the region in general. However, it is reasonable to assume that much of that will continue for the foreseeable future because of structural and practical reasons, such as trade networks, common language (Russian), and currency services.[40]

Moreover, I suggest, the role of Russia as a permanent member of the UN Security Council, as well as its influence throughout the United Nations and European systems and in international relations in general, will also continue to be critical for the near future of Central Asia. The Cold War may be over in terms of superpower confrontation, but it seems to have been replaced by a strong respect among the old rivals for their respective so-called "spheres of influence," especially the western hemisphere for the United States, and Central Asia and the Balkans for Russia. As indicated in

37. Akiner, *supra* note 33, at 6–7.
38. The composition of the population of each of the republics has changed several times, both during the Soviet era and since independence. For a detailed demographic review for each of the now-independent republics, as of the mid-1990s, see *id.* at 19–37. Given the present state of uncertainty and transition, it is not surprising that there is some variation in the information provided by different sources. For example, Akiner provides the following percentage figures for the ethnic composition of Uzbekistan: Uzbek 71.4 percent, Russian 8.3 percent, Tajik 4.1 percent, Kazak 0.9 percent, Korean 0.9 percent (see *id.* at 32). The *Encyclopedia Britannica Yearbook*, on the other hand, gives the following significantly different percentage figures for Uzbekistan: Uzbek 75.8 percent, Russian 6.0 percent, Tajik 4.8 percent, Kazak 4.1 percent, Kyrgyz 0.9 percent, Ukranian 0.6 percent, Turkmen 0.6 percent, other 7.2 percent. This source also estimates religious affiliation in 1997 as follows: Muslims (overwhelmingly Sunni) 88.0 percent, Russian Orthodox 1.0 percent, other (mostly nonreligious) 11.0 percent. *See* Britannica Book of the Year 740 (1998).
39. Fierman, *supra* note 7, at 365.
40. Akiner, *supra* note 33, at 9–10.

the next section, such considerations can have significant consequences for the operation of the human rights paradigm.

Islam Karimov, the president of Uzbekistan at the time of writing, is one of the Central Asian leaders who managed to hold on to power through the transition to independence—from being the first secretary of the Communist Party of the republic under the Soviet Union to the president of the independent republic.[41] Following formal independence on 1 September 1991, Karimov won the first multiparty presidential elections in December of that year. After several legal, administrative, and political developments that enabled Karimov to consolidate his hold on power, the first parliament (Oliy Majlis) was elected in December 1994/January 1995. Karimov's People's Democratic Party (PDP which is essentially Uzbekistan's branch of the Soviet Communist Party)[42] is in firm control of the parliament, supported by legally registered and supposedly autonomous parties, like the Progress of the Homeland Party and Adalat Social Democratic Party. In its first session, the parliament voted to hold a referendum to extend the president's term to the year 2000 instead of ending it in 1997. According to official reports, "99.6 percent of the electorate was said to have participated, with an overwhelming 99.4 percent approving."[43]

But for our purposes, social movements and other modes of popular political expression are significant regardless of their "official" status in the country. During the gradual collapse of the Soviet Union, *Birlik* (Unity) was founded (under the leadership of Abdurakhim Pulatov) in November 1988 as the first social/political movement in Uzbekistan. Birlik led a campaign to have Uzbek declared the official state language, something that happened in 1989.[44] Initially, this movement consisted of a coalition that included the Islamic Renaissance Party, the Green Party, the Tomaris Women's Association, and the Organization of Free Youth of Uzbekistan. However, the lines within and between all these groups during and soon after independence were vague and constantly changing; some groups existed more on paper than in fact, others split or joined forces with other organizations, and some individuals were simultaneously members of more than one organization.[45] Birlik sought to continue its work on civil rights and environmental protection, but with less success, and soon broke up into hostile factions after its failure to gain official registration for the presidential elections of 1991.

Other informal groups/opposition parties include Erk (Freedom), which grew out of Birlik in 1988 to stress the priority of independence over

41. Fierman, *supra* note 7, at 368–69.
42. *Id.* at 380.
43. *Id.* at 392.
44. *Id.* at 367.
45. *Id.* at 370–71.

establishment of democracy. Erk attempted to participate in postindependence politics, but its founding leader, Mohammed Salih, was defeated in the 1991 presidential elections, resigned from the parliament in July 1992, and has lived in forced exile since April 1993. The Islamic Renaissance Party (IRP) also sought to register in 1990 and 1991, without success. It is interesting to note for our purposes here that IRP declared that:

> it would operate by constitutional methods and it openly condemned the practice of terrorism, extremism, and all forms of discrimination. It also advocated equality between believers and non-believers. Its "Islamic" inclination manifested itself in such proposals as support for religious education and scholarship, introduction of "the economic principles of Islam," and reinforcement of women's roles as mothers and preservers of "the home and hearth."[46]

The point I wish to emphasize here is that, considering the transitional period as a whole up to the present time, it is difficult to avoid the conclusion that the government of President Karimov is unwilling to allow any meaningful opposition, whether Islamic or secular, to organize into informal groups or aspiring political parties. For present purposes, it is important to note that such political oppression continues under the guise of "democratically enacted" legislation like the law to protect the honor and dignity of the president, and the law on public associations, the law on the mass media, and the law on freedom of conscience and religious organizations, all adopted in 1991.[47] Freedom of the press was controlled by administrative measures, such as the state control of paper supply and printing facilities, and by legislation like the 1993 law to protect state secrets. Karimov also consolidated his personal hold on power through "the close integration of the PDP and the state, other semi-official institutions, and their ability to command resources."[48]

Several years later, for the same basic reason and under the guise of the same laws, nongovernmental organizations like the Human Rights Society of Uzbekistan are facing similar difficulties in registering officially so that they can function openly and legally.[49] In contrast, the Committee for the Protection of Human Rights has achieved official registration. But in Uzbekistan, as in many other countries, the fine line between advocacy of human rights and political opposition in the wider sense is difficult to observe because the latter is often partially motivated by concerns about the former. Governments usually either suppress human rights organizations because politicians are also confused about the matter or deliberately

46. *Id.* at 375.
47. *Id.* at 375–77.
48. *Id.* at 389.
49. *Id.* at 387.

emphasize the confusion in order to discredit human rights organizations and rationalize their suppression. For example, some may argue that the Human Rights Society of Uzbekistan is facing difficulties because it is headed by Abdoumannob Polatov, the brother of the exiled leader of Birlik, Abdurahim Polatov. On the other hand, there is suspicion that the Committee for the Protection of Human Rights was allowed to register and operate legally "even though it had not yet adopted its statutes,"[50] precisely because it was not really independent from the government, despite its reported success in investigating some human rights violations.

The preceding brief review of the political context reiterates a sadly familiar story of manipulation by ruling elites in order to hold on to power in postindependence situations in other parts of the world, and can be seen as the continuation of Soviet-style politics. For our purposes here, however, it is important to note the underlying dynamics of the balance between coercion and popular legitimacy. "Whereas coercion obliges citizens to follow rules because they have no other rational choice, legitimacy fosters voluntary compliance."[51] President Karimov's successful use of coercion does not mean that he is not also trying to promote the legitimacy of his regime. He has clearly deployed a variety of strategies in pursuit of legitimacy; he has both glorified Uzbek identity and assured non-Uzbek people of their rights as equal citizens, pursued economic development, and stressed the need to preserve peace and political stability. The civil war in neighboring Tajikistan is commonly seen as a stern warning of the risks of ethnic and religious strife. Of particular interest is the Uzbek government's ambivalence toward a public role for Islam—support when Islam serves as a vehicle for national pride, but opposition when it is perceived to be undermining the official view of the state.[52] After an extensive review of postindependence politics, Fierman concluded that President Karimov has been careful to show great deference to Islam, identifying it as an integral part of Uzbek culture, while insisting that Uzbekistan is a secular state. According to Fierman:

> To date this approach has not evoked mass dissatisfaction among Uzbekistan's Muslims . . . [but] under certain economic and social conditions, Islam could become the symbolic standard for opposition; . . . [it] has the potential to bring closer together a broad spectrum of opposition forces which would otherwise be divided along regional, nationality [ethnicity], and linguistic lines.[53]

---

50. *Id.* at 385–87.
51. *Id.* at 360.
52. Olivier Roy, *The Ties That Bind*, 27 Index on Censorship (Mar./Apr. 1998).
53. Fierman, *supra* note 7, at 394.

As briefly explained later, this assessment reveals a situation that is remarkably similar to what has happened after independence in other parts of the Muslim world, especially in North Africa and the Middle East. I would not presume to offer predictions about the precise combination of economic and social conditions that might promote the Islamization of politics or politicization of Islam in Uzbekistan. Instead, my purpose is simply to highlight this aspect of Islam in the country as part of the present context of the formation and transformation of identity.

Islam and Culture

Just as observers of other parts of the world disagree about the role of religion in public life, so they dispute the role of Islam in different parts of Central Asia.[54] There is little agreement even about the significance of possible indicators, such as a rise in level of ritual practice, dress, and lifestyle (e.g., use of the veil for women and open consumption alcohol or pork by Muslims).[55] But, the key to a proper understanding of the nature and role of Islam in the region is to appreciate its organic relationship to traditional customary norms and practices (*adat*) at different levels of community. In noting this organic nature of Islam in the societies of this region (as, I believe, in all Islamic societies), I am rejecting the notion of an abstract, pristine "Islam" that is supposed to exist outside human history.[56] In reviewing seven books on Islam in Central Asia, Jo-Ann Gross explained:

---

54. In a recent seminar in the region, intellectuals and officials from the various countries of Central Asia expressed a wide range of opinions on the role of Islam in their respective countries and the region as a whole. Some saw Islam as a positive force in the growth of national self-awareness and argued that the relation between Islam and politics will happen; others asserted that for Central Asia, the experience of the Arabic countries and the Muslim East is more relevant than that of Japan, the West, or Russia. To some participants, Islamic fundamentalism should not be seen as a negative development; others emphasized that the principle of Islamic democracy needs to be connected with the liberal democracy of Europe, but that this connection needs to be backed up by the Islamic doctrine (based on the Qur'an) which is open to free liberal interpretation. There was also much disagreement about Islam's position on democracy and women's issues and about the relevance or prospects of the so-called Iranian or Turkish models. *See Central Asia: Religion and Society*, Proceedings of a Seminar in Tashkent, Uzbekistan, 6 CENTRAL ASIA J. 7–19 (Alexander Dzhumaev ed., 1997) [in Russian].
55. CENTRAL ASIA: CONFLICT, RESOLUTION AND CHANGE (The Center for Political and Strategic Studies, Roald Z. Sagdeev & Susan Eisenhower eds., with Douglas A.R. Goudie & Heather Parrish Schmitt (assoc. eds.), 1995). The text is posted at <http://www.cpss.org/casiabk/intro.txt>.
56. On this view, see, e.g., *The Study of Islam in Local Context*, 17 CONTRIBUTIONS TO ASIAN STUDIES 1–16 (1982), Marilyn Robinson Waldman, *Tradition as a Modality of Change: Islamic Examples*, 25 HISTORY OF RELIGIONS 318–40 (1986).

> Plaguing the view of and attitude toward the study of Islam in Central Asia has been the tendency to measure Islamic beliefs and values against a "normative" standard of doctrinal Islam. Traditional beliefs and practices are often perceived as primitive survivals, while the assimilation and synthesis of Islamic values within the indigenous worldview are seen as "nominal" Islam and popular forms of religiosity (Sufism, veneration of the family of the Prophet, tomb visitation, for example) as merely the external veneer lightly masking deeper pre-Islamic religious practices and values. The dichotomous notion of a clear-cut common core of Islamic tradition and an opposing set of "localized" Islamic practices and beliefs is, as all of the studies under review illustrate, a methodologically unsound approach to the study of Islam in Central Asia or any other region.[57]

After discussing mutual influence between Islam and traditional beliefs, and fusion of *shari'ah* and *adat,* Dzhabbarov concluded that it is time now (after independence) for the revival of national values including *shari'ah* and *adat.*[58] He then added that these resources "need to be used reasonably" through the careful drafting and enactment of laws, and implementation of policies, that are characteristic and reflective of all of the recent processes of renewal, and the goal of future progress.[59] The latter part of this conclusion would probably resonate strongly with the governments of the republics, which are apparently apprehensive of the political role of Islam and seek to restrict the few emerging Islamic parties that have sought to put religious ideas into political life.[60]

It is often suggested that Uzbek identity survived Soviet social engineering through adherence to the above-mentioned integration of Islam and local culture. The social institution of *mahalla* (a local community center of public life), especially in urban settings, remained the site of a whole range

57. Jo-Ann Gross, *Islamic Central Asia: Approaches to Religiosity and Community,* 24 Religious Stud. Rev. 353 (1998).
58. Shari'ah is the normative system of Islam, which prescribes the religious way of life. Its subject matter ranges from general ethical norms, legal principles, to religious ritual practices. Adat are the customary or traditional cultural norms and practices of local communities.
59. Sandzhar Dzhabbarov, Shariat, Semeinoe I Obychnoe Pravo V Uzbekistane: Istoriia I Sovremennost' 120 (1996) (*Shari'ah, Family, and Customary Law in Uzbekistan: History and Present-Day Reality*). Tashkent, Uzbekistan: The Academy of Science of Uzbekistan, Muminov Institute of Philosophy and Law.
60. During the 1 May 1998 session in which the parliament of Uzbekistan (Oliy Majlis) passed a law imposing new restrictions on religious groups, President Islam Karimov is reported to have spoken out harshly against the Wahhabis, accusing them of seeking to turn Uzbekistan into a second Tajikistan by "killing officials [and destroying] food factories, powers stations, and other strategic installations." Karimov is reported to have added that "such people must be shot in the head. If necessary, I'll shoot them myself, if you lack the resolve." *See* 10 Human Rights Watch, Republic of Uzbekistan. Crackdown in the Farghona Valley: Arbitrary Arrests and Religious Discrimination 3–6 (May 1998).

of social relations in daily life. Events such as weddings, funerals, and birthdays are celebrated at the local *mahalla* with the exchange of gifts. This exchange of goods and services helps reinforce personal loyalty to the local community by adding a dimension of economic benefits to the familiar basis of social relations. Through the Islamic practice of *waqf* (religious endowment), the Uzbeks managed to maintain private philanthropic institutions for the preservation of their buildings and artifacts. Islam was so interwoven with all aspects of individual and collective identity that it is said to be the other side of the same coin.[61] Even attitudes and practices that were apparently by-products of forced adaptation to an outside impetus, carry the unifying force of Islam that served both to shape and to sustain a distinct culture.[62]

The dynamics of the role of Islam are likely to change in the near future due to somewhat contradictory internal and external factors. To begin with, the collapse of the Soviet agency for supervision of Islamic affairs, the Muslim Spiritual Board of Central Asia and Kazakstan (MSBC) under Gorbachev in 1989, opened the way for separate development in each republic. Whereas the Chair of MSBC was an Uzbek based in Tashkent, each of the other four republics has now opted for its own religious authorities. The role of Islam in public life is therefore now evolving separately, in response to such factors as Middle Eastern funding for establishment of mosques and Islamic educational institutions, and theological education and training in the Middle East. The so-called Turkish factor is also likely to have different, and perhaps contradictory, consequences in different republics.[63] On the one hand, some claim that Turkey presents the Central Asian republics with a model for an Islamic society living in a secular state. On the other hand, given the persistence of Islamic political activism in Turkey itself, the Turkish connection may reinforce rather than diminish the influence of Middle Eastern and South Asian Islamic organizations on Central Asia in general. Another paradoxical dynamic may come from calls by Muslims and Orthodox Christian

61. Gross, *supra* note 57, at 354. *See also*, Martha Brill Olcott, *Central Asia's Islamic Awakening*, Current History, Apr. 1994, at 150–54; and Jonathan Steele, *Uzbeks Return From Communism to God and Mammon*, The Guardian (London), 18 Mar. 1992, at 5.
62. Allworth, *supra* note 34, at 208.
63. The Kazakh, Kyrgyz, Turkmen, and Uzbekis are ethnically Turkic, while the Tajiks are of Persian origin. One would therefore expect a Turkic Sunni influence to be higher among the first four ethnic groups, and their respective republics, while the Iranian Shi'a factor is unlikely to be seen outside Tajikistan. But as can be appreciated from the fact that more than 35 percent of all Tajiks at the time of Soviet division of the region (1924/1929) were included in Uzbekistan, international boundaries do not necessarily mean ethnic or religious homogeneity for each of the Central Asian republics.

authorities for favoring "traditional religions" in their joint opposition to increasingly active and open proselytization by Western Protestant churches. Such calls may have unintended political consequences or serve wider social and ideological objectives. All these and related complex factors are of course interacting with internal perceptions of different segments of the population, especially women as noted below, regarding the role of Islam. Generally speaking, therefore, the dynamics of the role of Islam appear to be in a state of flux and open to different outcomes.

Moreover, there are other aspects of Uzbek identity that may be relevant to our concern about the role of the human rights paradigm in the country. For example, some analyses indicate a "rise of exclusive ethnic nationalism and xenophobia."[64] There are also elements of tension within the population associated with ethnic discrimination (against the Tajik or Russian minority), Uzbek chauvinism, linguistic and cultural differences, as well as variations in local conditions. For example, as one author noted:

> in Namangan in the Ferghana Valley, veiling for women, the ban on alcohol and other Islamic practices are strictly enforced by "religious patrols" in the streets, [whereas] in the less militant atmosphere of Uzbekistan's cities, a rise in visible adherence to Islam and voluntary Islamic education among women can be seen in the increased attendance in religious schools.[65]

There are also indications of growing attention to religious matters among different groups of women: "Poor girls in Tashkent gain social status through study of the Qur'an, while older middle-class women seek to expand their role in cultural life, regarding Islamic law as something an educated person is supposed to know."[66]

It is important for our purposes here to note that there is growing awareness of the important role of women's organizations, not only with regard to the status of women and general human rights concerns, but also in promoting and sustaining economic liberation and political stability in a multi-ethnic society. These organizations are seen as the mediators of the paradox and ambiguity of the position of women in the country, caught between tradition in the family and community, on the one hand, and the promises of progressive ideology of the Soviet era.[67] As can be expected,

---

64. Security Politics in the Commonwealth of Independent States: The Southern Belt 119–20 (Medhi Mozaffari ed., 1997).
65. Nikplai Andreyev, *Central Asia Looks Towards the East,* 39 New Times Int'l 19–22, at 19 (1992).
66. Nadezhda Konstantinova, *Girls Read the Koran,* 4 New Times Int'l 4, 11–13, at 12 (1993).
67. Ihtibor Sultaniva, Istoriko-politologicheskii vzgliad na razvitie zhenskikh organizatsii v Respublike Uzbekistan (A Historical-Politological View of the Development of Women's Organizations in the Republic of Uzbekistan), University of World Economy and Diplomacy, Tashkent, Uzbekistan (forthcoming) (on file with the author) [in Russian].

however, there are clear variations in the attitudes of the women of Uzbekistan regarding the role of Islam and tradition in their lives today, reflecting differentials in economic and social, educational, and other factors between rural and urban segments of the population, as well as within the urban centers.[68] While some are opposed to what they see as regression in gender relations and return of women to their traditional roles of housewife,[69] others are not sure of the benefits of past claims of liberation and equality. As one author characterized the preindependence experience in this regard:

> Soviet policies did not, in fact, succeed in replacing traditional Islamic values and institutions, especially in rural areas, but merely created a parallel system where only integration into Soviet institutions received social rewards. The longer term disservice of Soviet policies on the question of women may have been to create an association between authoritarianism and the concept of women's emancipation. This association may inadvertently encourage or legitimize restrictions on women's existing rights in the name of a revival of indigenous culture. However, such interpretations will undoubtedly be contested and challenged by Uzbek scholars who are reevaluating the contributions of jadidist [an Islam reform social movement] reformers of the turn of the century in a new light, and investigating the local roots of Muslim reformism and its enlightened agenda for women. The equal rights accorded to women in civic law have little bearing on customary practice, especially for the rural majority.[70]

A HUMAN RIGHTS FRAME OF REFERENCE

In light of the preceding brief review of some relevant aspects of the present situation in Uzbekistan today, and the earlier review of the issues facing the Muslim minority in France, I will now consider a possible role of the human rights paradigm in the transformation of Islamic identity in these two countries.

From the outset, I wish to emphasize that to propose a human rights frame of reference for the mediation of Islamic identity in France and Uzbekistan is not to suggest that this paradigm can provide an independent, comprehensive, and final resolution in this regard. In addition to the

68. M. Tokhakhodjaeva, *The Oriental Woman: What Doors Are Open For Her?* 17 The Central Asian Post, 4 May 1998, at 4.
69. Zhenshchiny: Vybor v mire traditsii i peremen (Women: Choice in a World of Traditions and Changes); Bishkek, Kirgizstan: Goskonsern "Akil" 23 (Z. Agbagisheva et al. eds., 1996).
70. Social Policy and Economic Transformation in Uzbekistan, UN Development Programme and International Labor 134–35 (Keith Griffin et al. ed., 1995).

difficulties of the human rights paradigm indicated below, a fundamental limitation of the paradigm as a whole is that, at best, it can only be part of the answer and only to the specific, discrete matters it addresses. The human rights paradigm can neither by itself address the underlying structural causes of human rights violations around the world nor be a substitute for a range of political, social, and economic action at the national and international level in response to the spiritual, emotional, and other needs and concerns of human beings. It should also be recalled here that the formation and transformation of identity (whether on religious, ethnic, or other basis) *is a dynamic and continuous process* rather than an event or status to be realized or achieved once and for all. As emphasized earlier, the outcome of this process at any given time is *necessarily contingent* on the interaction of a variety of actors and factors in the particular context. Therefore, my proposal that the human rights paradigm might play a useful role in this process must be based on a clear understanding of the limitations, as well as the possibilities, of this paradigm. I will begin this last section with a brief realistic assessment of the human rights paradigm before considering its possible relevance as a frame of reference for the mediation of Islamic identity in France and Uzbekistan.

As noted earlier, I use the term "human rights paradigm" to mean the articulation and application of the same norms to every human being everywhere, which presupposes acceptance of the validity of cross-cultural moral judgment and requires systematic efforts to influence state policy and practice in matters that were previously deemed to be subject to the exclusive domestic jurisdiction of the state. The underlying assumption of this paradigm is that the rights it proclaims are due to every human being by virtue of his or her humanity, and without distinction on grounds such as race, gender, religion or belief, social status, or political opinion. This conception immediately raises questions about the process through which these norms are identified and articulated. How inclusive has this process been (or can it be) of different cultural and ideological perspectives around the world without losing its utility as the "common standard of achievement" envisaged in the Preamble of the 1948 Universal Declaration of Human Rights? The basic dilemma here is that the inclusion of some perspectives may be inconsistent with the ideals of equality and justice that this paradigm seeks to achieve, yet the exclusion of such perspectives may undermine the legitimacy and acceptance of the human rights paradigm itself among those who hold those perspectives. This is what is commonly referred to as the debate over the universality and cultural/ideological relativity of human rights.

Without engaging in this debate here, I wish to emphasize the following points. First, problems with the universality of human rights arise in every major cultural tradition or ideology in the world today, and not only in

Islamic, East Asian, or other non-Western societies.[71] Whereas Islamic societies are commonly known to have problems with regard to the principles of equality and nondiscrimination on grounds of gender or religion in particular, Western liberal societies also find it difficult to accept that economic, social, and cultural rights are actually human rights.[72] In this light, the universality of human rights must be deliberately cultivated and promoted, and cannot be taken for granted in any context or seen as globally accepted by proclamation in international documents. The approach I recommend in this regard is first to appreciate the difficulty of global normative agreement and then to work through internal discourse within each culture, and through cross-cultural dialogue, to promote an overlapping consensus on fundamental human rights norms.[73]

I have also referred earlier to the paradox of relying on states to articulate and implement international standards that are designed to limit or regulate what a state may do within its own domestic jurisdiction. As part of international law, human rights norms are laid down by states, either as a matter of customary international law (which requires consistent practice by states out of a sense of legal obligation) or through the ratification of specific treaties. Moreover, since international law itself is founded on traditional notions of sovereignty and noninterference in the domestic affairs of other states, the task of practical interpretation and implementation of international human rights standards has to be entrusted to the national institutions and processes of each country.[74] Thus, according to the theory of the human rights paradigm, the prerogative power of states to determine the normative and institutional framework for matters such as citizenship and its implications, is supposed to be limited by relevant international human rights norms. In practice, however, states not only control the process by which international human rights standards are set in the first place, but are

---

71. There is an extensive and rapidly growing literature in this field. For a good overview, see, e.g., Steiner & Alston, *supra* note 2, at 166–328. On the so-called Asian values debate, see THE EAST ASIAN CHALLENGE FOR HUMAN RIGHTS (Joanne R. Bauer & Daniel A. Bell eds., 1999).

72. This point is clearly illustrated by the way in which the European human rights system treats different groups of rights. Whereas civil and political rights are categorically stated in the European Convention for the Protection of Human Rights and Fundamental Freedoms of 1950 and in its subsequent Protocols, economic, social, and cultural rights were addressed much more tentatively and gradually through various nonbinding charters and policy documents. *See* Steiner & Alston eds., *supra* note 2, at 580–81. It is true that some of these rights are in fact respected to varying degrees at different times in Western Europe and North America, but that is usually done as a matter of policy or outcome of the political process rather than because these rights are accepted as human rights.

73. AN-NA'IM & DENG eds., *supra* note 4; AN-NA'IM, *supra* note 4.

74. Steiner & Alston eds., *supra* note 2, at 117–65.

also entrusted with the practical interpretation and implementation of those standards within their own territories.

Another type of consideration regarding the human rights paradigm at the domestic level relates to the need for structural, institutional, and political support for effective implementation, both in the sense of general protection and promotion and in providing remedies in cases of violations. The domestic application of human rights standards presupposes such elements of structural and institutional capacity as the proper functioning of administrative agencies, an independent and credible judiciary, legally and politically accountable police and other law enforcement agencies. Political support is necessary not only for the allocation of sufficient resources for these elements to operate effectively, but also for the actual working of these structures and institutions. For example, for the judiciary to be independent and credible, the government and its officials must be prepared to comply with judicial directives. The political and legal accountability of the law enforcement agencies require the ability and determination to enforce regulatory regimes, an institutional culture within the agencies themselves that promotes cooperation with such regimes, and general public awareness of, and willingness to use, available resources. Moreover, such elements of structural and institutional capacity at the domestic level are not only difficult to realize and sustain in practice, but also probably most problematic where they are most needed. That is, more human rights violations tend to occur in countries where the necessary structural, institutional, and political conditions for the effective protection and promotion of those rights are lacking or insufficient.[75]

However, since these types of problems also arise in relation to the implementation of domestic constitutional rights, similar strategies to those that sustain constitutional rights can perhaps be deployed to promote the effective application of the human rights paradigm beyond what the state may be willing or prepared to do if left on its own. In the same way that constitutional rights are sustained by civil society's demands for their protection, an international civil society is emerging globally to demand protection of human rights. Due to the activism of civil society around the world, the human rights paradigm has become such a powerful legitimizing force in national politics and international relations that no government in any part of the world today would openly reject or defy its dictates.[76]

75. For a discussion of some of these issues in the African context, see Abdullahi A. An-Na'im, *The Legal Protection of Human Rights in Africa: Doing More with Less, in* Human Rights: Concepts, Contests, Contingencies (Austin Sarat & Thomas Sarat eds., forthcoming Apr. 2001).

76. For a similar call in relation to feminist issues, see, e.g., Saskia Sassen, Globalization and its Discontents 95–97 (1998).

Governments will of course deny that they have committed human rights violations or claim that they are striving to comply with those norms to the best extent permitted by their local circumstances. They will try to get the benefits of international legitimacy without the "inconvenience" of compliance with human rights standards, but that is true of constitutional rights in any domestic setting, even in the most developed and stable societies. In the same way that the claims of governments are not taken at face value in the latter case, global civil society activism is pressing for more compliance with human rights norms for legitimacy to be conceded to governments around the world.

For example, the parliament of Uzbekistan established the Institute for Monitoring of the Applicable Legislation, which was organized according to a decree of the Cabinet of Ministers.[77] The main objectives of the Institute include: studying existing legislation and its correspondence with international norms in the sphere of human rights; working out proposals on bringing the legislation of Uzbekistan into conformity with international norms and standards in the sphere of democracy and human rights; working out proposals on applying international legal norms in the sphere of human rights into the existing legislation of Uzbekistan and in law enforcement practice; and preparing proposals aimed at development of cooperation with institutes and international organizations in sphere of monitoring of human rights in Uzbekistan. Human rights are also integrated into the working machinery of the Institute to regulate how the Institute is to interact with committees of Oliy Majlis, and so forth. It is significant for our purposes here that the parliament and government of Uzbekistan find it important to claim such a high level of commitment to human rights, regardless of the real intentions behind such measure. However, this commitment can have practical consequences only to the extent that local and global civil society keep pressing for compliance with a declared policy of the state.

In this light, it is clear that the willingness and ability of communities to use the human rights paradigm is crucial for the ability of this paradigm to influence the course of events on the ground. Willingness and ability to use the human rights paradigm, as is also the case with constitutional rights, are separate but related factors. People may be willing to use this paradigm but be unable to do so because of the structural, institutional, and political limitations indicated above. While efforts to minimize the impact of such limitations can be seen as part of the objectives of using a human rights paradigm, no change in people's ability to use this paradigm can be

77. Decree No. 322-1 by the Oliy Majlis (3 Dec. 1996); Decree No. 29 of the Cabinet of Ministers (15 Feb. 1997).

expected if they are either indifferent or hostile to the paradigm in the first place. In other words, conditions affecting the ability to use the human rights paradigm presuppose the willingness to use it, though the latter by itself does not mean that there are no problems with the former. What factors and processes affect this dynamics of willingness and ability to use the human rights paradigm effectively for the Muslim minority in France (physical diaspora) and the disoriented Muslim majority in Uzbekistan (temporal diaspora)?

In the case of countries like France, the situation seems to be conditioned both by the racism of the wider societies and by the "siege mentality" of Muslim communities in those settings.[78] Muslims are victims of racism and discrimination on grounds not only of color and ethnicity but also of religion and culture: "Muslim minorities are seen not only as distinct and different but also as a threat to the national way of life."[79] The ethnic concept of the nation as a people of common descent, linked together by kinship ties, vernacular language, customs, and tradition, does not permit the inclusion of "alien" or "foreign" cultures. This is particularly true in France, it seems, because of persistent negative stereotyping and demonization of Islam and Muslims in the media, popular culture and political rhetoric. For their part, Muslim minorities in Western countries like France tend to construct purely self-referential criteria for their religious identity, portraying themselves as a noble and morally superior people who have total monopoly on truth. This sense of religious superiority and moral arrogance becomes justification for isolationism on the Muslim minority side, a tendency not to participate in the public and political life of the wider society. These attitudes and isolationism, in turn, tend to provoke resentment and hostility among the non-Muslim majority, thereby perpetuating disadvantages of the Muslim minority.[80]

A complicating factor is that most immigrant Muslims tend to assume that time stopped when they left their country of origin, not realizing that even that country has changed radically from the way they "remember it" to have been. Accordingly, they often articulate their religion and worldview in terms of a traditionalism that no longer exists, even in their country of origin.[81] This is happening at a time when they need more openness to adaptation, and flexibility in the identification and reconciliation of important differences between the two cultures to the benefit of both. It is also

78. *See generally, e.g.*, Muslim Minorities in the West (Syed Z. Abedin & Ziauddin Sardar eds., 1995).
79. Sardar, *supra* note 23, at 4.
80. Featherstone, *supra* note 8, at 47–68; Sardar, *supra* note 23, at 9–10.
81. Sardar, *supra* note 23, at 11; Margaret E. Pickles, *Muslim Immigration Stress in Australia, in* Muslim Minorities in the West 106–16 (Sayed Z. Abedin & Ziauddin Sardar eds., 1995).

important for Muslims to act out of a sense of secure minority identity and strong group identification. However, that is unlikely when Muslims perceive serious threats to their communal cultural autonomy or are worried about total loss of Muslim identity through assimilation into the wider society.[82] Moreover, openness and flexibility by the Muslim minority require a willingness by the host Western society to confront the sources of racism and prejudice in their own cultures and policies.[83]

The distance between these polarities of racism of the French majority culture and siege mentality of the Muslim minority can be negotiated through the human rights paradigm, which brings a framework of cultural self-determination into the context of the premise and rationale of the secular, pluralistic nation-state. Thus, defenders and opponents of the right to wear head-scarves in public seek to invoke what they see as normative French values. Those values now include human rights norms at the international and regional European levels. While the international human rights system is stronger on norm-setting than practical implementation, the European system is highly developed and effective on the implementation of its own norms. The normative contents of the two systems tend to overlap, but the European system uses clearer and more categorical terms in defining its human rights norms. More significantly, the European system of which France is a part provides for the right of individual persons to petition the European Court of Human Rights for remedy or redress for human rights violations.[84]

As they seek to safeguard their Islamic identity (within the framework of the right to cultural self-determination), some Muslims participate in the emerging networks of solidarity that can contribute to the changing context of the state today and to the creation of transnational networks of every kind. The "claims" on space are thus complex and not exhausted by either ties to the homeland or participation in France, though both are important factors.[85] But the common framework of these emerging networks must also include the human rights paradigm if the networks' claims are to be taken seriously by the domestic French and wider European systems. While an exclusively Islamic frame of reference will probably be confronted with an exclusively French one, the human rights paradigm offers the possibility of common ground between these competing ethnic and cultural claims. Consequently, Muslims in France must formulate their demands for entitlement

---

82. Theodore Pulcini, *Values Conflict among American Muslim Youth, in* Muslim Minorities in the West 178–203 (Syed Z. Abedin & Ziauddin Sardar eds., 1995).
83. Sardar, *supra* note 23, at 15.
84. Donna Gomien, Short Guide to the European Convention on Human Rights, 137–50 (France: Council of Europe, 1998).
85. Metcalf ed., *supra* note 6, at 16.

to Islamic identity as well as full citizenship in human rights terms, rather than the supposedly exclusively Islamic terms of the countries of their origins. In order to do so effectively, they would have to transform their perceptions of Islamic identity to include the underlying values of the human rights paradigm.

Despite significant differences in normative and institutional contexts and in the dynamics of social and cultural conditions, I suggest that a similar dynamic will probably develop in Uzbekistan because of the above-mentioned moral and political force of the human rights paradigm. Soon after independence, the government of Uzbekistan declared its commitment to the Universal Declaration of Human Rights and ratified the major treaties, in addition to the incorporation of these norms in its own constitution.[86] As illustrated by the establishment of the Institute for Monitoring of the Applicable Legislation, the government has also taken steps to institutionalize its declared commitment. These internal steps are reinforced by regional and international dynamics, especially in view of Uzbekistan's membership of the OSCE.[87] To note these developments is not to say that they should be taken at face value or to assume that they will automatically transform the human rights situation in the country. Rather, the point is that they create a conducive environment for the assertion of human rights norms in Uzbekistan in relation to formation and transformation of Islamic identity, provided those making such claims declare their own commitment to the human rights paradigm.

In emphasizing the need for Muslims to adopt a human rights paradigm (including its norms and institutions and its popular advocacy) in order more effectively to assert their Islamic identity, I wish to highlight two points. First, as a general theoretical matter, I see this as a clear example of how the processes of formation and transformation of identities are now conditioned by global, as well as local, factors and dynamics. Both the identity-asserting entity, whether in individual or communal terms, and other actors in the process must now engage in this mediation of the local and global. Second, with regard to Islamic societies in particular, the issue is how Islamic identity is now conditioned by what many Muslims regard as external, some would claim un-Islamic, notions of equality and nondiscrimination on grounds of gender and religion. Without going into a discussion of the relationship between Islam and human rights—something I have done in detail elsewhere[88]—it is clear to me that Muslims can

86. *See* Human Rights Watch, *supra* note 60, at 15.

87. Akiner, *supra* note 33, at 38–39.

88. *See generally*, Abdullahi Ahmed An-Na'im, Toward an Islamic Reformation: Civil Liberties, Human Rights and International Law (1990). In relation to the human rights of women in particular, see Abdullahi Ahmed An-Na'im, *Human Rights in the Muslim World: Socio-Political Conditions and Scriptural Imperatives*, 3 Harv. Hum. Rts. J. 13–52 (1990).

reconcile this apparent paradox by seriously engaging in the universal human rights paradigm. It may appear paradoxical to say that Muslims, or any other religious or ethnic group for that matter, will have to accept the incorporation of an external normative system, namely, universal human rights standards and institutions, into their own identity in order to claim that identity. However, the paradox is resolved or mediated to the extent that Muslims are active actors in (not merely subjects of) the articulation, interpretation, and implementation of human rights. The human rights paradigm is necessary for the formation and transformation of Islamic identity. Muslims have a choice in either rejecting this imperative paradigm as "alien" to their cultures or accepting it as integral to those cultures in today's interdependent world.

[10]
'The Best of Times' and 'the Worst of Times': Human Agency and Human Rights in Islamic Societies

[1]

Introduction

The premise of this article is that there are good reasons for 'pragmatic optimism' about human rights in all Islamic societies, precisely because they are experiencing multiple and profound crises of unprecedented scale and magnitude. In my view, this is a source of hope for possibilities of positive transformation in all aspects of life, including the human rights field. I am not, of course, suggesting that the present multiple crises are *as such* the basis of hope or causes of transformation. Rather, my claim is that these crises are effectively challenging and transforming deeply entrenched assumptions about Islam and Muslims, undermining traditional social institutions and political structures, within Islamic societies, and their relationships to other societies. These crises are opening new opportunities for creative human agency, which is the ability of people to take control of their own lives and realize their own objectives, thereby becoming the source and cause of transformation I mean. That is, the 'best of times' *can* therefore materialize out of the 'worst of times' through the human agency of persons, acting individually, collectively or institutionally. But outcomes are contingent upon what Muslims and others make of these opportunities, hence the qualification of my optimism as pragmatic, drawing on realistic prospects in the real world to inspire appropriate action, rather than simply assuming that respect for human rights will necessarily improve as a matter of course.

In fact, it seems to me, except for natural disasters and the like which operate at a different level, nothing happens in human relationships, whether good or bad, except through the agency of some person or groups acting or failing to act. But the human agency of all of us, Muslims and non-Muslims alike, is inherently interactive with that of other people, its outcomes are contingent on what else is happening in the world around us. So, to emphasize, the role of Muslims in fully contributing to the global joint-venture of protecting and promoting human rights at home and abroad includes their collaboration with others in that regard. Since human rights are by definition universal in concept and application as the equal rights of all human beings everywhere, all societies must also take this paradigm equally seriously. The same crises that are prompting the human agency of Muslims are also relevant to other societies, thereby creating a more conducive environment for global collaboration in this field.

Before turning to elaborate on this premise and subject, I will give a brief explanation of my perceived connection between Islam and human rights that will hopefully introduce the rationale of my focus on the human agency of Muslims themselves. But first, to anticipate what may appear like a logically prior question of why this focus on Islam or Islamic societies in the first place, my answer is that because I am a Muslim scholar and advocate of human rights. Such inquiry is, in

2

my view, legitimate, indeed necessary, for all scholars and/or advocates of human rights, each regarding his or her own religion or ideology. The cross-cultural dialogue that can promote consensus around the concept and content of human rights as universal standards requires each of us to play our role in relation to our own societies. It is only by critically examining the status of human rights within our own religious and cultural traditions that we can demand of others to do the same regarding their traditions.[1]

Moreover, one should be concerned about human rights in Islamic societies in general in view of the fact that Muslims are estimated at 19.6% of the total world population,[2] living in every continent and region, and constituting the clear majority of the population in 44 states, a quarter of the total membership of the United Nations. That is, they represent too large a proportion of the field to be overlooked by any systematic study or monitoring of the status of human rights around the world.

But does this assume too strong a connection between religion and human rights in general, whereby Muslims (and other believers) are expected to act as such in relation to human rights? Asserting the relevance and importance of the question does not explain *how* can one speak of 'Islam' as the religion of this large and tremendously diverse group, on the one hand, and of human rights, whether as a set of moral or ethical norms or part of international law, as a presumably secular legal system, on the other. In other words, what does my suggested relationship between Islam and human rights mean in practice?

In my view, the question can be meaningful only when it is about Muslims not Islam, Christians, not Christianity, Hindus not Hinduism, and so forth, because it would then be the same general question of how do human beings everywhere negotiate the relationships between their religious beliefs and human rights. That is, the question is always about people's understanding and practice of their religion, not the religion itself as an abstract notion, and about human rights as a living and evolving body of principles and rule, not as a theoretical concept. Whether regarding religion or human rights, reference to states, countries or international organizations like the United Nations is really to people who control the state apparatus, inhabit a country or work through international institutions. Whether institutions and organizations are religious, political or diplomatic, the question about their relationship to human rights is always about how people negotiate power, justice, and pragmatic self-interest, at home and abroad. Such negotiations always take place in specific historical contexts, and in

---

[1] See, generally, Abdullahi Ahmed An-Na'im, editor, *Human Rights in Cross-Cultural Perspectives: Quest for Consensus*. Philadelphia, PA: University of Pennsylvania Press, 1992.

[2] CIA, *The World Fact Book*, http://www.cia.gov/cia/publications/factbook/geos/xx.html; *select* World (viewed July 30 2004.

response to the particular experiences of believers and unbelievers living together. Each religion or ideology is relevant to those who believe in it, but only in the specific meaning and context of their daily lives and not in an abstract, de-contextualized sense.

This contextual framing of the issue is necessary for focusing on Muslims as human beings and societies in their internal and external relationships like all other people and societies. But since the question here is about what difference does being Muslim or Islamic make to the status of human rights in general or specific time and place, I am thus concerned here with the Islamic traditions (in the plural, to indicate its diversity) as well as with the humanity of Muslims. In other words, unless I am claiming that all religions and philosophies have the same relationship to human rights, the implication of the subject of this article is that there is something distinctive about being Muslim, as opposed to being Christian, Hindu, Marxist or Buddhist in that regard.

However, I am not suggesting that all Muslims understand and practice Islam in the exact identical way, and share the same understanding and attitudes about human rights from that perspective. That diversity testifies to the impact of contextual and historical factors in theological or legal development of the Islamic traditions, being Muslim or Islamic did not in fact have the same meaning in different places or over time. In fact, I argue that it is logically impossible for that to ever be the case. The reality and permanence of difference among all human beings, Muslims and non-Muslim alike, is expressly affirmed in the Qur'an in, for example, Chapter 10 verse 93;[3] Chapter 11 verses 118-119;[4] Chapter 32 verse 25;[5] and Chapter 45 verse 17.[6] That is one reason why the protection of such human rights like freedom of belief, opinion and expression, is imperative from an Islamic point of view in order to protect the rights of Muslims to be believers in their own way, without risks to life and livelihood.[7] In other words, without the existence of the right to disbelieve, there is no possibility of any genuine belief, including religious belief.

Granted such protection of freedom of religion and belief for Muslims and non-Muslims alike, the question remains how to reconcile religious belief with

---

[3] "...certainly thy Lord will judge between them as to the divisions amongst them on the Day of Judgment".

[4] "If thy Lord had so willed, He could have made mankind One People, but they will not cease to dispute..."

[5] "Verily, thy Lord will judge between them on the Day of Judgment, in the matters wherein they differ".

[6] "...Verily, thy Lord will judge between them on the Day of Judgment as to those matters in which they differed".

[7] Abdullahi Ahmed An-Na'im, "Islamic Foundations of Religious Human Rights," in John Witte, Jr., and Johan D. van der Vyver, editors, *Religious Human Rights in Global Perspectives: Religious Perspectives*. The Hague: Martinus Nijhoff Publishers, 1996, pp. 337-359.

4

human rights doctrine. In relation to Islam in particular, the fact that specific verses in the Qur'an are taken to authorize or require certain actions, regarding the rights of women or non-Muslims, for instance, does not explain why some Muslims choose to act on one understanding of such verses, while others act or fail to act on a different understanding, or have a different relationship to the text altogether. My response to this question is that such choices are the product of the human agency of believers, not the inherent, sole or eternal meaning or necessary implications of Islam as such, independent of all material conditions under which Muslims live and interact with others. From this perspective, the attitudes and practice of Muslims in these matters can change in favor of the equal human rights of women and non-Muslims through internal debate within present Islamic societies.

In practice, the manner in which Muslims are likely to interact with human rights will be conditioned by such factors as what other societies are doing about the same issues, and the orientation, motivation or objectives of various actors on all sides. For instance, Muslims' responses are likely to be affected by whether they perceive that they are required to 'prove' their allegiance to the human rights paradigm while others are not expected or required to do so. Muslims are more likely to resist commitment to these rights when they are presented as being alone in struggling with the principle, while the commitment of other cultural or religious traditions is taken for granted. Another set of factors that can influence positions has to do with power relations and institutions: how inclusive is the international law that is supposed to provide the legal framework for human rights? Does it sufficiently respect the sovereignty of Muslims, with due regard for their concerns about security and development? That is, are all peoples, including Muslims, genuine *subjects* of international law, or merely its 'object', whereby international law is defined and applied by powerful Western countries to control other peoples and exploit their resources, as happened during the colonial period? How do the realities of power relations operate within the United Nations and other international organizations? In view of these concerns about historical exclusion and present hegemony, about reciprocal treatment and mutual hostility or suspicion, how and by whom is the information about the attitudes and practice of various societies regarding human rights collected and assessed?

The Worse of Times and the Best of Times

I have equally strongly condemned, from the start, both the terrorist attacks of September 11, 2001 and the unilateral military retaliation by the United States.[8]

---

[8] See, for example, Abdullahi Ahmed An-Na'im, "Upholding International Legality against Islamic and American *Jihad,*" in Ken Booth and Tim Dunne, *Worlds in Collision: Terror and the Future of Global Order*. Houndmills, England: Palgrave Macmillan, 2002, pp. 162-171.

5

But I also believe that the more damaging in the long term is the grossly disproportionate aggressive foreign policy of the United States ever since, especially its 'failed colonization of Iraq' since March 2003. That occupation, in my view, has been a colonial venture because colonialism, by definition, is the usurpation of the sovereignty of a people by military conquest without legal justification. This reckless and unaccountable invasion and occupation was neither justified by self-defense principles nor authorized by the Security Council of the United Nations. As such, the failed colonization of Iraq constitutes a fundamental repudiation of the very basis of international legality and regression to the lawlessness of 'might is right' of the colonial era. In other words, I am not only condemning this action as illegal and immoral, but also see it as a negation of the *possibility* of the rule of law in international relations – there is no international law when powerful nations appropriate to themselves the right to invade and occupy other countries for whatever reasons they deem fit, without even a national debate of the legality of such action. Living in the United States during the period leading up to the invasion of Iraq in March 2003, and closely following the 'decision-making process' at the time, I am convinced that the question of the legality of invasion as a matter of international law was not even discussed.

The fact that the United States was joined by Britain, the previous colonial power of Iraq after the collapse of the Ottoman Empire by the end of the First World War, confirms the colonial nature of the occupation, rather than confer legality on an inherently illegal act. Also, the participation of other countries mainly in response to bribes or coercion by the United States only expands the membership of the criminal conspiracy. After all, it was at the Berlin Conference of 1884-85 that a gang of Western powers agreed to partition African regions among themselves.[9] By the same token of which that criminal conspiracy did not make colonialism legal by any definition of 'international law' that Africans can accept, the illegal and utterly counter-productive invasion of Iraq since March 2003 represents a regression to 19th century colonialism at the dawn of the 21st century.

But that was only part of the global foreign policy of the United States that seriously undermined international legality and human rights throughout the

[9] At that 'diplomatic conference' of November 1884-February 1885 Western powers with so-called 'interests in Africa' (Britain, France, Germany, Portugal, The Netherlands, Belgium, Spain and the United States) agreed on matters of trade and transport in the Congo region, and procedures to claim new coastal areas in Africa. In effect, the conference initiated a rush to grab as much colonies as possible, until the whole continent was colonized over the following twenty years, except Ethiopia.

world. As former President Jimmy Carter of the United States described it on the first anniversary of the terrorist attacks:

> We have ignored or condoned abuses in nations that support our anti-terrorism effort, while detaining American citizens as 'enemy combatants,' incarcerating them secretly and indefinitely without their being charged with any crime or having the right to legal counsel. This policy has been condemned by the federal courts, but the Justice Department seems adamant, and the issue is still in doubt. Several hundred captured Taliban soldiers remain imprisoned at Guantanamo Bay under the same circumstances, with the defense secretary declaring that they would not be released even if they were someday tried and found to be innocent. These actions are similar to those of abusive regimes that historically have been condemned by American presidents.[10]

At the same time, however, there were many positive developments, like the massive protests by citizens of the United States, United Kingdom and their allies like Spain and Italy, against the invasion of Iraq even before it started, and the subsequent official national inquiries that proved the fallacy of the reasons given for the war. But the most significant fact, it seems to me, is that the United States and Britain had to resort to the same United Nations they had by-passed in the rush to war in order to negotiate vacating the dubious position of being 'occupying powers' and returning sovereignty to a native Iraqi government by the end of June 2004, without achieving any of the declared objectives of the invasion. Thus, the neo-colonial ambitions of these two countries were defeated by a combination of protest by their own citizens and other European citizens, wide-spread international condemnation and armed resistance by Iraqis. It may still take a long time for peace, stability and democratic development to be realized in Iraq, but it is now categorically clear that international legality and cooperation are the only viable way forward in that regard. Colonialism and its pretentious claim to 'democratize Iraq', in this instance, have been effectively and conclusively repudiated thereby giving the whole of humanity a positive outcome from a negative initiative. But regression is possible, hence the need for even stronger emphasis on the protection of and respect for human rights to enable people everywhere to pre-empt such reckless adventures in the future and hold their perpetrators accountable.

On the other side of the coin, however, we Muslims have so far failed to respond effectively enough to the responsibilities of sovereignty. Since colonialism is initially a consequence of the weakness of colonized societies,

[10] *Washington Post*, of September 5, 2002, at p. A31:

though it also contributes to that over time, its effective and sustainable termination requires enhancing the genuine sovereignty and independence of formerly colonized societies. After all, freedom is always earned, never granted, and is sustained through constant vigilance to safeguard it.

A critical part of that process in the present global context is to confront terrorism within our own societies, as it is ultimately a challenge to our human decency and responsibility for what we do, or is done on our behalf or in our name, with our approval or acquiescence. Terrorism could not exist or thrive as it does at present if we have not somehow supported or encouraged it, at least by our indifference to the broader phenomenon of political violence and its underlying causes. The degree of our individual and collective responsibility and failure vary according to our locations and what we can do in combating the culture of violence and lawless retaliation in our own societies, but each should look for his or her share, and what we can do about it. Too much of our effort is squandered in futile apologia for Islam as a religion, or our societies as oppressed and marginalized.

It is commonly said that the term 'terrorism' is too relative to be defined clearly, that one man's terrorism is another man's freedom fighter. I think that this is an apologetic fallacy: terrorism can simply be defined as the use of indiscriminate and arbitrary violence in pursuit of political objectives, without being concerned for the safety of innocent by-standers. My definition of the term does not make any distinction between so-called state and non-state or private actors. If the officials of any state use violence in this manner, they do not deserve any protection or special allowance because of their affiliation with a state. While this definition, including its application to state-actors, is theoretically clear and coherent, the difficulty may be in employing it consistently in all cases, regardless of our sympathies with the cause in which terrorist acts are committed. Moreover, the ability of perpetrators to use terrorist acts, and the willingness of the wider population to tolerate such behavior, indicates an underlying disregard for the safety and well-being of others.

Confronting terrorism would therefore include combating this underlying culture of political violence, as well as the immediate causes and consequences of the use of arbitrary and indiscriminate violence in furtherance of political ends, whatever they may be or however we may feel about them. In the final analysis, I am completely convinced that no cause is worth advancing through terrorism. For Islamic societies in particular, I believe that we must repudiate any alleged religious rationale for political violence and terrorism, which is the subject of conflicting views in the historical Islamic traditions.[11] As I am suggesting in

[11] Abdullahi Ahmed An-Na'im, "Islamic Ambivalence to Political Violence: Islamic Law and International Terrorism," *German Yearbook of International Law*, vol. 31, 1988, pp. 307-336.

8

relation to human rights, Muslims must exercise their human agency in choosing peaceful co-existence and mediation of conflict over the arbitrary and indiscriminate use of violence to achieve political objectives.

Despite the 'worst of times' scenario outlined above, this is also the 'best of times' for a positive engagement of international legality and peaceful co-existence. Among the many lessons and insights that can be drawn by all societies from the atrocities of September 11 is what I call our shared human vulnerability - the recognition that all human beings everywhere are vulnerable to arbitrary violence. The conceit of any of us, Muslims and non-Muslims alike, in thinking that we are not as vulnerable as everybody else is really part of the problem because it makes us less sensitive to the suffering of others. The more we appreciate our shared, universal, human vulnerability, in all its different and varied forms and manifestations, the more we can respond to the challenge of terrorism and all other forms of political violence, whoever the perpetrator happens to be, as well as to poverty, disease and other evils in general. The same insight of shared human vulnerability also emphasizes the urgency of protecting the human rights of all people, everywhere, as any of us can be a victim or perpetrator of violations.

But this multifaceted, universally shared vulnerability of human beings everywhere can be really counter-productive when it is manipulated to grant governments excessive powers 'to protect us,' as has happened in the United States with the so-called Patriot Act of 2001. It is not even possible to know or predict how many people will be affected by official abuse of power under this pretext because of the secrecy and lack of accountability for these powers in the name of combating terrorism. What is ironic is that limitations of human resources and time constraints are bound to undermine the efficacy of this approach to national security, however extensive and powerful the apparatus may have become. Sooner or later, normal human complacency will creep in, opening new possibilities for terrorists to strike again. The contradictory and self-defeating nature of this illusion of security, without any regard to the requirements of justice, are so obvious that it is hard to believe that intelligent, rational people are doing this for the alleged declared objectives.

Another lesson of September 11 in my view is the futility of lawless unilateral retaliation at the presumed source of harm, without addressing the underlying causes that prompt the perpetrators, or which they take as justifying their actions, and persuade others to condone or facilitate violence in any given situation. It is true that a hardcore group of religious/ideological extremists like those who perpetrated the terrorist attacks of September 11, or national chauvinists like those who are driving the militaristic American response, will probably harbor aggressive designs, whatever others may do or fail to do. But it is also clear that such hardcore elements cannot act on their aggressive designs without the support, or at least acquiescence, of a much larger number of people who can be persuaded to withhold their support and cooperation with the hardcore few, if the grievances or concerns of that wider constituency are addressed. Neither the terrorist attacks nor the American retaliation could have happened without the support of a wider constituency on each side, a much wider circle of complicity for having justified, condoned or facilitated those acts of violence. This complicity includes justifying or condoning the specific action in question, permitting the continuation of injustices that seem to motivate the actors, or failing to ensure the establishment of a credible system of accountability according to due process of the law.

Any appropriate response to violence or other danger must therefore be firmly grounded in a clear and profound appreciation of the multifaceted, universally shared vulnerability of all human beings everywhere, instead of the illusion that any of us can escape it by fortifications, pre-emptive or retaliatory violence, accumulation of wealth or exploitation of others. This point is dramatically made by the crude methods in which the atrocities of September 11 were perpetrated in the heartland of the most powerful and prosperous nation in the world today. An appreciation of the full range of our shared vulnerability as human beings everywhere will indicate different modes of response to various sources of violence and danger. But the most effective and sustainable response must include addressing the underlying grievances that drive people to the desperation of terrorism, because some will always resort to that response as long as the injustice persists.

The preceding remarks emphasize both the opportunities and risks of the present global environment, and particularly that we must do our part in order to be able to demand the same of others. It is not possible to elaborate further on these complex issues here, but my underlying premise of pragmatic optimism is that, given the realities of the world as it is, what can each one of us do to improve on the situation. Without in the least being naïve or simplistic about those realities, the question for me is how can we all take our own initiatives and pursue our own agenda, instead of helplessly lamenting injustice, poverty or human rights violations. I will now turn to further reflections about Islam and human rights in particular in light of the earlier clarification of the relevance and importance of this connection today.

Islam and Human Rights

To be clear on the point, in raising this question I am not suggesting that Islam is either fully supportive or inherently antagonistic to human rights. Rather, as indicated earlier, the relationship is open to engagement and transformation precisely because it is contingent on an interactive web of internal and external factors and forces. Like other major religious and cultural traditions, Islam

10

provides a basis for upholding human rights and dignity through its own account of what it means to be human. But these dimensions of the Islamic traditions (in the plural) should be seen as open to critical reflection and reformulation among the believers themselves, because of the inherent and permanent diversity of the tradition itself. There are not only similarities as well as variations in perceptions and practices of human rights and dignity among Muslims and Islamic societies, but also possibilities of change in relevant attitudes and practices. By the same token, however, outcomes can either be positive or negative from a human rights perspective.

The human rights framework is commonly perceived to be a universal secular vision of what it means to be human, and a call for the urgency and necessity of protecting the innate rights of all human beings everywhere in the world. The mistaken view that this perception of human rights has nothing to do with the Islamic traditions, if not actually being contrary to them, is largely due to the fact that the present articulation of the human rights framework arose out of the experiences of Western societies. To suggest that human rights are 'Western' is a contradiction in terms, because that means they cannot be universal, which is their essential quality as the equal rights of all human beings. That is, these rights have to belong to all cultural and religious, including Islamic, traditions if they are to be human rights at all. Moreover, these rights are needed by Muslims for protection against abuses and excesses of the powers of the state that gave rise to Western articulations of these rights. Since the same model of European territorial-state has become 'universalized' through colonialism, and remains the dominant form of political organization throughout the world, the human rights framework that has evolved in response to that reality is now equally relevant everywhere.

However, while I believe that this view 'ought' to be generally accepted and acted upon as one of the main foundations of the universality of human rights, it is also clear that this is not the case at present. A common objection in my experience is how can the human rights framework claim to be universally valid and applicable without taking into account the permanent and profound cultural and religious diversity of human societies around the world. But to me the question is how can we Muslims, together with all other societies, make this happen, instead of complaining that it is not done by others for us. My own approach would therefore emphasize a proactive *process* for promoting consensus around the concept and content of human rights through the human agency of all actors, rather than expect it to emerge on its own. In relation to the subject of this article in particular, the process also includes 'negotiating' the complex and contingent relationship between Islam and human rights, as it plays out in each social context. I have attempted to elaborate a specific methodology from an Islamic perspective, especially in *Toward an Islamic Reformation* (1990), but would also consider any alternative approach that can effectively address the following parameters of that process of negotiation.

First, some elements of the historical Islamic traditions, like other major religious traditions, are not readily consistent with the key human rights principle of non-discrimination, especially regarding the rights of women and non-Muslims. This difficulty is compounded by the common perception that these aspects of what is known as *Shari`ah* are inviolable because they are divinely ordained. This apparent incompatibility is emphasized by a perception of the human rights framework as necessarily and exclusively based on a secular universal vision of humanity.

At the same time, this tension must be mediated because it is critical for the binding force and practical efficacy of human rights everywhere, and not only in Islamic societies, as noted earlier. With Muslims constituting a fifth of the total world population, excluding them from the universal validity and application of human rights would really undermine them everywhere. Since there is no reliable international mechanism for enforcing human rights standards against the will of national governments, human rights advocates need to motivate the general populations of territorial states to pressure their own government to ratify and enforce human rights treaties. The way this is done in various social, cultural and religious settings is relevant to what can happen in other societies.

In Islamic societies, efforts to legitimize and effectuate human rights through social movements need to include effective responses to counter arguments that governments are likely to use in resisting such pressures which limit and constrain their own powers. The allegation that human rights are an anti-Islamic Western imposition is a clear example of this sort of pretext, used by ruling elite to escape responsibility for violating the rights of Muslims as well as non-Muslims. In other words, to mobilize public opinion and motivate civil society organizations in their own societies, human rights scholars and advocates in Islamic societies must understand how to transform the relationship between these rights and local cultures, political context, economic factors, and so forth. This process calls for the sort of questioning of deeply entrenched assumptions about Islam and Muslims, and challenging of social institutions and uprooting of political structures that is now facilitated by the current global environment as suggested at the beginning of this article.

For instance, I believe that the dichotomy between the religious and secular is often exaggerated to suggest an inherent incompatibility of the two, though they are in fact interdependent. For example, Muslims believe that the Qur'an is the literal and final word of God, and *Sunnah* (traditions of the Prophet) is the second divinely inspired source of Islam. But both sources have no meaning and relevance in the daily lives of believers and their communities except through human understanding and behavior. The Qur'an was revealed in

12

Arabic, which is a human language that evolved in its own specific historical context, and many verses of the Qur'an were addressing specific situations in the daily lives of early Muslims at that time (610 to 632 CE) in their local context of western Arabia. *Sunnah* also had to respond to the immediate concerns arising in that context, in addition to broader matters. Thus, human agency was integral to the process of revelation, interpretation and daily practice from the very beginning of Islam, initially of the Prophet, and subsequently generations of Muslims who adhered to the Qur'an and *Sunnah* according to their own understanding in their respective historical context and daily experiences.

It is therefore clear that a sharp distinction between the religious and secular is misleading. Religious precepts necessarily respond to the secular concerns, and have practical relevance only through their acceptance and application by the believers in their daily lives. In other words, religious doctrine is necessarily implicated in the secular, and the secular is perceived by believers to be regulated by religious doctrine. This does not mean that there is no transcendental dimension to Islam for believers. Rather, it is simply to say that the practical relevance and utility of the social order of Islam are contingent upon human understanding and practice, which testifies to its ability to provide for the practical needs of its adherents. This point is critical for the theological basis of the relationship between Islam and human rights today.

In conclusion, these are the best of times and the worst of times for Muslims, with infinite possibilities in either direction, dependent on the way we all use or abuse our human agency. These are the worst of times as we continue to be the object of imperial aggression and neo-colonization, suffering with other peoples around the world the worst violations of our individual and collective human rights at the hands of our own governments and through the excesses of global capitalism. They are also the best of times because the present crises enable us to transcend the limitations of our traditional assumptions about Islam and Muslims, to challenge and transform our social and political institutions. The possibilities of human agency are infinite, and the rest is up to all of us, everywhere, and whatever our religious, ideological and/cultural affiliations may be.

Part Three

Some Topical Issues in Islam and Human Rights Discourse

[11]
The Islamic Law of Apostasy and its Modern Applicability: A Case from the Sudan

On 18 January, 1985, the Sudanese Muslim reformer, *Ustadh* (revered teacher) Mahmoud Muhammad Taha, was executed in Khartoum, Sudan. Specified at the criminal trial were charges of offenses against the state under the Sudan Penal Code, 1983, and the State Security Act, 1973. In separate actions, The Special Court of Appeal and former President Nimeiri confirmed conviction and sentence, however, not only for the secular charges specified at the criminal trial but also for the *Shari'a* religious offense of apostasy—the renunciation of Islam by a person known to have been a Muslim.

The entire episode brought to the surface questions about President Nimeiri's attempts to govern the Sudan by imposing traditional *Shari'a* religious law. In the case of the execution of *Ustadh* Mahmoud, this involved silencing an outspoken critic. But Nimeiri's introduction of the *Shari'a* into civil contexts seemed also generally aimed at other segments of the political opposition. Questions of the bizarre legal and judicial proceedings attending this complex episode also arise, and will be discussed in due course.

However legal chicanery and political motivation may have figured in *Ustadh* Mahmoud's execution, even larger issues are at stake. *Ustadh* Mahmoud's case has implications for universal human rights and civil liberties. The real importance of *Ustadh* Mahmoud's trial and execution is in the questions it raises about the place of the *Shari'a* in the modern world. Especially important is the relation between sincere Muslim belief and compliance with laws purporting to be derived from that belief. In the *Shari'a* principle of apostasy, the tension between faith and legalism is most obvious. The candid admission of this element of religious intolerance in *Shari'a* is an essential prerequisite for the success of any attempt to secure complete respect for freedom of religion. The author hopes to undertake the major task of contributing to the building of the theological, philosophical and legal case for religious freedom in Islam at a later stage. Meanwhile, this preliminary treatment of the issues may be useful as an early caution to those contemplating the enforcement of the totality of *Shari'a* law. They seem to have chosen this course of action out of religious conviction or political expediency without being aware of the full implications of such policy.

To understand the case of *Ustadh* Mahmoud, however, it is necessary to give a brief account of the legal and constitutional background and the process of Islamization undertaken by former President Nimeiri in 1983. The basic features of Sudan's constitutional and legal system prior to Nimeiri's Islamization was not unlike that of many other Muslim countries where similar Islamization is likely to take place. Current constitutional and legal safeguards in force in their own countries should not lead Muslims to believe that they are immune from facing the consequences of the *Shari'a* law of apostasy and other related concepts. What happened in the Sudan can happen in any other Muslim country today.

LEGAL AND CONSTITUTIONAL BACKGROUND

The Sudan was ruled by a Turco-Egyptian administration throughout most of the 19th century until it was liberated by the indigenous religio-nationalist movement of Muhammad Ahmad al-Madhi in 1884. Britain joined Egypt in the successful campaign to recover possession of the Sudan in 1898. As the dominant power, Britain was by far the stronger partner, and managed to rule the Sudan with very little Egyptian participation until the Sudanese took over after Independence in 1956.

During the Anglo-Egyptian Condominium, as the colonial partnership was called; and throughout the national rule since Independence, the Sudan has been administered under three concurrent systems of law, namely, the overall official system, herein termed the general territorial law, the customary laws of the various tribal groups, and Islamic *Shari'a* Law.[1]

Although the general territorial law has so far been more dominant, local customs, or what may be called customary laws, are the oldest and most widely practised of the three legal systems. The indigenous Sudanese tribes and peoples have been settling their disputes in accordance with their local customs for centuries before the advent of Islam and the rise of modern colonialism that brought the British to Egypt and the Sudan. Moreover, the manner in which Islam came into the country, with Muslim migrant tribes and *Sufi* (Muslim mystic) religious leaders, meant that the Sudanese knew and practised what may be described as popular Islam long before any official legal administration was attempted by the Turco-Egyptian administration during the 19th century.[2] Some principles of Islamic law itself were no doubt adapted and incorporated into the native customary law.[3]

The Anglo-Egyptian administration began to regulate the administration of customary law, in accordance with the colonial policy of decentralization, in the early 1920s. A number of Ordinances, culminating in the Chief's Courts Ordinance and the Native Courts Ordinance of 1931 and 1932, respectively, attempted to regulate the jurisdiction, personnel and basic procedure of the customary law courts. These Ordinances were subsequently revised and consolidated into a single enactment: The People's Local Courts Act, 1977.

The general territorial law consists of a large body of legislation enacted by the various types of legislatures the country had over the past 80 years. The reception of principles of English common law began with the enactment of the Penal Code, the Code of Criminal Procedure and the Civil Justice Ordinance around the turn of the century. All three basic Codes, and subsequent enactments regulating the various spheres of Sudanese civil and commercial life, were based on English law as applied in other parts of the British Empire. Active adaptation and reception continued throughout the codominium through the judicial work of English lawyers appointed as judges and judicial officers.[4] When systematic legal training for Sudanese was undertaken on a regular basis in 1936, it was done by English lawyers using English textbooks and material.

Thus, when independence was achieved in 1956, the Sudan Judiciary was firmly established in the techniques and traditions of English common law. Although an increasingly poor replica,[5] the Sudanese legal profession continued its nominal adherence to the common law tradition up to 1983. This general territorial law, based on principles of English common law as adapted and sudanized through generations of revisions and re-enactments,[6] governed civil and criminal matters in the towns and more accessible countryside of northern and central Sudan. Over the rest of the country customary law prevailed.

Islamic *Shari'a* law, on the other hand, has been confined to the area of family law and inheritance for Muslims since the beginning of the Anglo-Egyptian administration.[7] Marriage, divorce, child custody and succession for Muslims remain under the jurisdiction of *Shari'a* courts.[8] Although the Judiciary was supposed to have been unified under the provisions of the 1973 Constitution and the Judiciary Acts since 1973,[9] the Civil and *Shari'a* Divisions of the Judiciary have remained divided by much more than formal administrative considerations. They belong to totally distinct and irreconcilable legal traditions, namely English common law and Islamic *Shari'a* law. Although applied to the same population, the two legal systems are a world apart in terms of substance, literature and techniques. The anomaly is often emphasized in the debate over radical legal reform in the Sudan.

All three legal systems, however, have always been implemented within the context of a secular constituional framework. The Anglo-Egyptian Condominium administration pursued secular colonial policies that maintained a very strict separation of religion and state.[10] In December 1955, the Sudanese

Parliament, set up under the Self-Government Statute of 1953, adopted that Statute as the country's first constitution. It was called the 'Transitional' Constitution because it was adopted hurriedly in order to achieve full independence, with a view of enacting the 'Permanent' Constitution at a later stage.[11] The Transitional Constitution provided for liberal parliamentary democratic government and guaranteed freedoms of thought, belief and expression, etc.

The Transitional Constitution was abolished by the coup d'état of 17 November, 1958, only to be re-enacted, with some slight amendments, on the overthrow of military rule in October 1964. Another *coup d'état,* on 25 May, 1969, abolished the Transitional Constitution once again. The May Regime, as the regime established by that coup came to be known, enacted its own constitution, called the 'Permanent' Constitution of 1973. This 1973 Constitution was also a secular document, providing for some of the democratic rights and freedoms, including religious freedom, within a one-party state. President Nimeiri ruled the Sudan under that constitution until his overthrow on 6 April, 1985. The major political parties,[12] in partnership with the Armed Forces this time, have now adopted another 'Transitional' constitution on 10 October, 1985, to be applied until another 'Permanent' constitution is drafted and enacted by the Constituent Assembly which was elected in April 1986.

Although both the 1956 and 1973 Constitutions established a secular state, and the legal system as a whole retained its essentially secular, common law orientation until 1983, the question of Islamization has always been a major issue in Sudanese political and constitutional debate since Independence. On the one hand, all the major, northern political parties at least paid lip-service to the policy of implementing Islamic Shari'a Law to replace the pre-existing 'colonial and alien laws'. The southern parties, on the other hand, represented their non-Muslim constituents' objection to the implementation of Shari'a.[13] The Muslim majority almost prevailed twice, once in 1958 and again in 1968, when draft 'Islamic' constitutions were about to be enacted, thereby making *Shari'a* not only the main source of legislation, but also the criterion by which the legality of all legislation and judicial practice was to be judged. Both attempts were aborted by *coup d'état*, and nothing concrete was done to enforce *Shari'a* outside the area of personal law for Muslims until the recent efforts of former President Nimeiri.

Following his 'National reconciliation' with his political opponents in 1977, President Nimeiri set up a committee for the revision of Sudanese laws in order to bring them into conformity with *Shari'a* Law. The Committee produced seven draft bills purporting to bring Sudanese laws into conformity with *Shari'a* in matters such as prohibitions of alcohol, gambling and *riba* (usury) and the imposition of the *hadd* (prescribed penalty of amputation of the hand) for theft, and the voluntary regulation of *zakah* (religious tax on Muslims). The most significant draft bill, *'Usol alahkam al-qad'iah* (the Sources of Judicial

Decisions) purported to make Islamic *Shari'a* law applicable in all matters not provided for by specific and explicit Sudanese legislation. Moreover, the draft bill made *Shari'a* applicable to the interpretation and enforcement of existing legislation and created a presumption of compatibility and consistency of all existing and future legislation with the principles of *Shari'a* . Any piece of legislation was to be deemed invalid to the extent it was incompatible or inconsistent with *Shari'a* . It was presumably intended to introduce subsequent legislation to enact *Shari'a* principles in place of legislation found to be inconsistent with *Shari'a* .

President Nimeiri did not seem at first particularly keen to implement the program devised by the Committee for the Islamization of the Sudanese legal system. During the first five years of the Committee's existence, the Regime enacted only one of the seven draft bills,[14] and did not undertake the revisions and repeal of legislation deemed to be inconsistent with *Shari'a* law. He did, however, encourage the implementation of the so-called Islamic banking system by granting 'Feisal Islamic Bank' significant tax and other operational advantages over the first five years of its existence in the Sudan. Therefore, it came as a complete surprise, even to his own Islamic fundamentalist allies, when President Nimeiri suddenly declared his intention in August 1983 to transform the Sudan into an Islamic republic.[15]

THE PROCESS OF ISLAMIZATION

A committee of three lawyers was set up inside the Presidential Headquarters sometime in July–August 1983, and entrusted with the task of transforming the Sudanese legal system into 'an Islamic' one. By the first week of August, the committee started producing the draft bills which President Nimeiri enacted into Provisional Republican Orders having the force of law subject to confirmation by the People's Assembly under Article 106 of the 1973 Constitution. When the People's Assembly reconvened in November 1983, the President put before it the eight Provisional Republican Orders he had enacted over the previous two months. They included a full Penal Code, Code of Criminal Procedure, Civil Procedure Act and a Judiciary Act. The Assembly passed all eight Orders, without debate, in two morning sessions in its first week of business. Other Provisional orders followed in 1983 and early 1984, covering a wide range of legislative subjects, and were all approved by the Assembly without much debate.[16] The most significant enactments of that period include the Sources of Judicial Decisions Act, one of the bills drafted by Dr At-Turabi's Committee of 1977, *Zakah* and Taxation Act and the extensive Civil Transactions Act which purported to regulate every aspect of civil liability and commercial and property law.

When it became apparent to President Nimeiri that some aspects of the new legal order were inconsistent with the 1973 Constitution then in force, he proposed to the People's Assembly in June 1984 amendments of the Constitution which were so extensive that they were in effect a fresh 'Islamic' constitution. During the debates over this 'new' constitution, it became clear that the Assembly was unlikely to pass it with the necessary two-thirds majority.[17] The President then decided to postpone 'debate' over the amendments, and they were never reintroduced. In that way, the 1973 Constitution remained intact until it was abolished by the April 1985 *coup d'état* which overthrew President Nimeiri and replaced him with a civilian–military coalition. The conflict between the Constitution and Nimeiri's 'Islamic' laws remained unresolved because the Supreme Court, established under the same 'Islamic' laws, rejected on procedural grounds the few constitutional challenges mounted against those laws.[18] These laws which remained in force after Nimeiri's overthrow, are also inconsistent with the 1985 Constitution. The transitional government of 1985–86 left the issue to be settled by the parliament to be elected in April 1986. Despite its apparent commitment to repeal these laws, the new government which took office by the end of April 1986 has not yet acted on the matter.

With the successful completion of the legislative task, the President and his staff turned to implementation. The Judiciary and other branches of government were obviously not doing enough to enforce the 'Islamic' laws. To rectify that state of affairs, the President decided to inject some 'Islamic' spirit and motivation into the judicial and executive organs by declaring a state of emergency on 29 April, 1984. Article 111 of the Constitution enabled the President to 'take the necessary measures . . . which may include the suspension of all or any of the freedoms and rights guaranteed by this Constitution', except the right to resort to the Courts. All measures taken by the President under the provisions of this Article 111 were to have the force of law.

The President issued the State of Emergency Regulations of 1984, under which he granted the Army and other security forces extensive powers of arrest and search and established the State of Emergency Courts and Prosecution machinery. This so-called 'prompt-justice' courts system dispensed with some of the basic requirements for judicial appointments and fair trial procedure guaranteed by the Constitution. These extraordinary measures were certainly effective in dramatically increasing the number of convictions under the 1983 'Islamic' Penal Code, which seemed to be the sole criterion employed by the Regime for judging the success of the 'Islamic Legislative Revolution' of 1983–84. Public floggings and amputations for alleged violations of the 'Islamic' Code were extensively publicized by the state-owned media.

Despite its success in raising the level of criminal law enforcement, the State of Emergency was too expensive to maintain for long. Beside the financial burden of maintaining the security forces in a state of full alert, the continuation of the State of Emergency contradicted the President's claims that the country was undergoing genuine voluntary and profound religious transformation. As he still needed the 'Islamic' law enforcement advantages of the State of Emergency, the President sought to maintain the machinery he had devised for the enforcement of the criminal law after the abolition of the State of Emergency in September of 1984.

The primary tool for achieving that objective was the Judiciary Act of 1984 which repealed and replaced the 'Islamic' Judiciary Act of 1983.[19] The new Act increased the President's power to appoint and deploy judges and set up special courts and appoint special prosecutors to enforce the 'prompt' justice of the 'Islamic' Code. The Act provided for the establishment of 'special' criminal courts to be manned by judges who may be appointed by the President of the Republic personally, regardless of whether they satisfied normal requirements for judicial appointment.[20] A new post of State Minister for Criminal Affairs was established within the Attorney-General's Chambers to supervise and conduct prosecutions before the 'special' criminal courts. The Act also gave the President the power to appoint a specific judge or a special court to try a specific case or accused person, to appoint any person to any judicial office, including membership of the Court of Appeal and the Supreme Court, regardless of requirements and qualifications specified by the Act itself for appointment to each level of judicial office.[21]

Using his powers under this Act, and by means of issuing Presidential Decrees which were immune, by virtue of Articles 81 and 82 of the Constitution, from challenge before any authority on any grounds whatsoever,[22] the President established a special system of criminal courts, to be served by a special system of prosecution machinery. Cases before those courts were to be tried in accordance with special summary procedure. Appeals and revisions were to go before the special Court of Criminal Appeals, also set up by the President and manned by three judges who also had their own special criminal trial courts. As the three judges sat in the most crucial and active trial courts in the capital, Khartoum, they often sat on appeal or revision over cases they had tried themselves! One of these three judges was also a member of the Supreme Court which considered constitutional challenges to proceedings before the special criminal trial courts. In at least one major case, the same judge was sitting as a trial judge and on the Supreme Court Panel which considered a constitutional challenge to the legality of the trial proceedings.[23]

Such was the state of the administration of criminal justice when *Ustadh* Mahmoud Muhammad Taha was released from 19 months of political detention without charge or trial, on 19 December, 1984. In retrospect, it would almost seem like an elaborate scheme specifically designed to entrap and eliminate a single man. He was the only political prisoner to be executed through the system. The immediate collapse of this judicial system after Taha's execution seems to reflect its internal contradictions and inability to function as a real legal instrument. Who was this man, and why did he have to be killed in this way?

ALL IN THE CAUSE OF ISLAMIC REVIVAL

Ustadh Mahmoud was one of the founders, and the first leader of the Sudanese Republican Party in October 1945. The Party worked for the complete independence of the Sudan from Egyptian as well as British control, and the establishment of a Sudanese republic, hence the Party's name.[24]

Ustadh Mahmoud, an engineer by profession, was jailed twice by the British colonial administration in 1946 for his political activities. During his second term of imprisonment, which extended two years, he started to develop his conception of Islamic revival through the evolution of certain aspects of Islamic *Shari'a* law. He continued his endeavor, based on the personal worship practices of the Prophet,[25] after his release from prison in 1948 until he mastered the theory of the comprehensive and universal level of Islamic ideology which he continued to articulate and propagate from 1951 until his death in 1985.

According to this theory, Islam was originally offered in Mecca in eastern Arabia from around A.D. 610 to 622 in terms of freedom of choice (*ismah*) and personal responsibility for such choice. Numerous verses of the Qur'an at that stage emphasized this freedom and personal responsibility.[26] Equality of all human beings regardless of sex or religion would have followed if those texts were made the basis of the law, but that was not to be in the 7th century. When it was shown in practice that the Arabs were not mature enough to appreciate and live in accordance with those superior principles, and they conspired to kill the Prophet, the offer of freedom and responsibility was withdrawn. Compulsion (*ikrah*) and guardianship were imposed following the Prophet's migration to Medina, another town in eastern Arabia. Qur'anic verses establishing *jihad*, holy war to spread the faith, and discrimination against non-Muslims and women were revealed in this second stage.[27] The Prophet elaborated upon these principles and made them the basis of the law, *Shari'a*, of the new polity of Muslims. Muslim jurists undertook the processes of tabulation and rationalization of the *Shari'a* over the following three centuries. The earlier texts of the Meccan stage that were inconsistent with the Law as enacted in Medina were deemed to have been repealed or abrogated from the legal point of view. They remained part of the Qu'ran and traditions of the Prophet and as such were revered by all Muslims, but only as ethical standards that enjoy moral authority without being legally binding. This was assumed by all Muslim jurists and scholars to be the final state of affairs. *Ustadh* Mahmoud, however, thought otherwise. He argued that the repeal or abrogation of the earlier Meccan texts were merely a postponement until the appropriate circumstances for their enforcement arose. He maintained that the abrogation should be related to its rationale, namely the socioeconomic and political conditions prevailing in Arabia at the time. With the radical transformation of these conditions in Modern times, Islamic Law should respond by enacting the verses of freedom of choice and personal responsibility in order to establish the principles of freedom and equality which should be the basis of the *Shari'a* of today. In other words, he advocated the development of a modern Islamic *Shari'a* law from the basic Islamic sources to meet the needs and aspirations of today.

The Republican Party was transformed in the early 1950s into an organization for the propagation of this new conception of Islam. The group was never really a political party in the usual sense of the term. The organization, for example, never contested any election or sought power through any other means. It concentrated, instead, on the re-education and enlightenment of the people through public lectures, debates, pamphlets, books, etc. The group maintained a strict policy of nonviolent, open and direct popular action.

Ustadh Mahmoud and his followers were opposed to the immediate implementation of traditional Islamic *Shari'a* law. They called, instead, for the radical revision of certain aspects of *Shari'a* law, and the re-education and remolding of individual Muslims in accordance with the moral values and ethics of Islam before any attempt at the implementation of Islamic *Shari'a* law. They proposed the establishment of a socialist,[28] democratic state, where complete equality between men and women, Muslims and non-Muslims would prevail. Their opposition to the immediate implementation of the totality of traditional *Shari'a* incurred them the severe and often violent hostility of the 'Moslem Brothers' and other Islamic fundamentalist groups.[29]

In May 1983, the Republicans issued a pamphlet criticizing the Sudanese Chief of State Security, who also happened to be the First Vice-President of the Republic, for his failure to check the incitement to religious hatred and abetment of sectarian violence that was being conducted in some mosques and through the state-controlled media. The Vice-President retaliated by arresting and detaining *Ustadh* Mahmoud and about 50 of his followers, without charge or trial, for more than 18 months.[30] The detention of the Republican leadership continued from May–June 1983 to 19 December, 1984. While they were in detention, President Nimeiri introduced the so-called Islamic Laws of 1983–84.

The Republicans started their campaign against the 'Islamic Laws' in March 1984, while their leadership was still under political detention, by issuing a booklet and several pamphlets explaining how those laws not only violated the Sudanese Constitution and distorted fundamental Islamic principles but also contravened elementary principles of the very *Shari'a* law they purported to implement.[31] The Republicans also instituted three constitutional suits before the Supreme Court on the grounds that those laws discriminated against women and non-Muslims and violated specific provisions of the Sudan Constitution. The Supreme Court, which had been re-constituted under the same laws, dismissed the suits on the ground that the Republicans had no standing to bring them because they were not personally aggrieved by those laws. On 25 December 1984, within one week of the release of *Ustadh* Mahmoud and his leading disciples, the Republicans issued a leaflet calling for the repeal of what they described as the 'September 1983 Laws', a peaceful settlement of the conflict in Southern Sudan,[32] and the provision of opportunities for popular enlightenment and public debate throughout the country in order to achieve proper Islamic revival.

During the last week of December 1984, members of the group were arrested and charged, this time with the minor offense of inciting disturbance of the peace, but the Minister for Criminal Affairs suddenly intervened and promoted the charges to the capital offenses of undermining the Constitution and waging war against the State, and two other offenses against the State. *Ustadh* Mahmoud was himself arrested on 5 January, 1985 and brought to trial with four of his disciples, who just happened to be arrested in the same district as himself, on 7 January.[33] All five of them were convicted and sentenced to death the next day, 8 January, after two brief sessions of under one hour each. The special Criminal Court of Appeal, also constituted under the 'September 1983 laws', confirmed the conviction and sentence on all five accused five days later. On 17 January, President Nimeiri gave his final approval for the immediate execution of *Ustadh* Mahmoud, and granted the other four a reprieve of three days to repent and recant or else be executed. They recanted and were spared.

Ustadh Mahmoud and his co-accused boycotted the Court on the ground that it was constituted under laws which, in their view, violated and distorted *Shari'a* and Islam itself, and were designed to terrorize and humiliate the people.[34] They also challenged the technical competence and moral integrity of the judges enforcing those laws because they allowed themselves to be manipulated by the executive branch of government in humiliating and oppressing its political opponents. The five accused considered the trial to be nothing but a political ploy and treated it as such.

In this way, *Ustadh* Mahmoud sought to revive Islam and interpret it in a more egalitarian and tolerant way than that he felt prevailed under traditional Islamic *Shari'a* law. His own death was the ultimate act in the advocacy of his vision and conception of what he used to call the Second Message of Islam. As indicated above, he believed that the repeal of certain restrictive and discriminatory aspects of traditional *Shari'a* and their replacement by alternative Islamic principles is more appropriate to the needs and capabilities of modern humanity. Such alternative principles, as he continued to explain and demonstrate for over 30 years, would be the Islamic *Shari'a* law of today because they are derived from the same basic Islamic sources in response to the challenges and problems of modern society.

Rather than advocate secularism, *Ustadh* Mahmoud suggested an Islamic way out of the problems raised by some aspects of traditional *Shari'a*, such as questions of the civil and political rights of all the subjects of an Islamic state, including women and non-Muslims. He called for the establishment of a more just Islamic socialist economic order, where all citizens would have their basic needs satisfied as of right, and not by way of charity. He also strove to distinguish his conception of democracy and socialism from the prevailing notions of liberal democracy and Marxist socialism.[35]

A POLITICAL TRIAL

The whole episode was fraught with procedural and substantive errors which compromised the proper aims of a judicial system. On the face of it, the prosecution was itself unconstitutional on several counts in the light of the Permanent Constitution of the Republic of Sudan of 1973—the constitution in force at the time. It violated the freedoms of thought, belief and expression guaranteed by Articles 47 and 48 of the Constitution. Since—incredibly—no attempt was made at the trial to show how the accused's conduct constituted the offenses charged, one may be justified in concluding that the charges under the Penal Code and State Security Act were merely a pretext for bringing *Ustadh* Mahmoud to the court in order to try him for his political activities and his opposition to the implementation of *Shari'a*. Such opposition was deemed to amount to a repudiation of the faith, technically known as apostasy. The initial arrest and police interrogation of the accused were all done under the state security offenses and nothing was said of apostasy. But when Presidential sanction for the trial was obtained,[36] the State Minister for Criminal Affairs added Section 458(3) of the Penal Code and Section 3 of the Sources of Judicial Decisions Act. Both provisions were introduced for the first time in 1983 as part of 'the September 1983 law'. The combined effect of the two sections purports to authorize the courts to impose Islamic penal provisions, and *hadd* penalities in particular, regardless of the lack of legislative provisions penalizing the particular conduct under Sudanese law. These sections were later on utilized by the Court of Criminal Appeal in confirming the convictions and sentences for apostasy although the trial court made no mention of this charge, and despite the fact that the two sections clearly violated Article 70 of the Sudan Constitution of 1973.[36a]

The accused were charged with several offenses against the state, pleaded not guilty and then boycotted the Court for the reasons indicated above. The case for the prosecution consisted of a single witness, the police officer who interviewed the accused. This witness simply read out the statements made by the accused to the police admitting full responsibility for the leaflet. The leaflet itself was the only prosecution exhibit. Nothing was said or presented at the trial on the writings or views of the accused on the wider issues of Islamic law reform or Islamic revival. These writings and views were introduced by the Special Court of Appeal on its own motion and made the basis of conviction for apostasy as we shall see below.

There was no case presented for the defense because of the boycott, but it must be noted here that the accused pleaded not guilty and boycotted a trial on state security offenses and not a trial for apostasy. Although convicting all of the accused for the state security offenses he specifically named, the Trial Judge stated that the death sentence would not be carried out if the accused were to repent and recant at any time before execution. As the notion of stay of execution on the grounds of repentance and recanting of one's beliefs or views is completely alien to Sudanese criminal law, the Judge must have had the *Shari'a* offense of apostasy in mind although he refused to mention it, presumably because of the obvious constitutional objections.

Again, and although the Trial Judge failed to discuss any of the ingredients of the offenses against the state with which the accused were supposed to have been charged and convicted, he emphasized in his judgment those aspects of the leaflet that hinted at the accused's conception of Islamic revival and their belief in the need for Islamic law reform. The judge took judicial notice of those views and beliefs, i.e. assumed the correctness of his own statement of the position without adducing evidence in court on the matter, and ruled that the accused's views and beliefs would cause upheaval if allowed to be publically propagated. This is the rationale for punishing religious and ideological dissent in traditional Islamic *Shari'a*. In other words, he was in fact convicting the accused of apostasy while citing provisions of the Penal Code to make it appear as if the convictions were for regular offenses against the state. This clearly violates the requirements of a fair trial provided for under Article 64 of the Constitution.

The judgment of the special Court of Criminal Appeal was at least candid in openly raising the question of apostasy, although it dealt with it in an unsatisfactory manner. The Court of Appeal started by noting the problem raised by convicting the accused under the specific sections of the Penal Code, while allowing them time to repent and recant, thereby gaining stay of execution. The Court of Appeal then proceeded to 'rectify' the decision of the Trial Court by raising the two questions: is apostasy punishable under Sudanese law, and if yes, did the conduct of the accused amount to apostasy as defined in Islamic law sources? The Court answered both questions in the affirmative, and proceeded to confirm the conviction and sentence of all five accused for apostasy as well as the state security offenses with which they were originally charged. According to the Court of Appeal, *Ustadh* Mahmoud was to be executed immediately, without opportunity to repent and recant, because he had persisted in advocating his 'heretical' views for many years and refused to heed judicial and other pronouncements. He was, moreover, to be denied burial with Muslim rites, and his property was to be forfeited upon his death. The other four convicts were allowed one month to repent and recant and re-embrace Islam or else be executed. All Republicans, i.e. the followers of

Ustadh, were declared by the Court of Appeal to be apostates, to be treated as such in all matters and transactions. Their books, pamphlets and other publications were to be confiscated and destroyed, and all future publications and circulation of such material was banned together with any other activities of the Republicans. This judgment of the special Court of Appeal was then submitted to the President of the Republic for final confirmation.

Since the accused were never formally charged with apostasy, they, naturally, offered no defense against it. Even the prosecution did not present any evidence in support of apostasy! It was the Court of Appeal which took it upon itself to specify and try apostasy for the first time at the confirmation of proceedings stage. In the absence of the accused, and without representation for either side, the Court of Appeal produced its own interpretation of the views and theories of the accused. In convicting *Ustadh* Mahmoud of apostasy the Court relied almost exclusively on two grounds: a ruling by a *Shari'a* Court in Khartoum on 18 November, 1968, and the extra-judicial announcements of foreign institutions declaring the apostasy of *Ustadh* Mahmoud.

As to the first ground, the decision of the *Shari'a* Court was completely null and void because that Court lacked jurisdiction over questions of apostasy as such.[37] The cause of action itself was unconstitutional in the light of the 1956 Constitution, as amended in 1964, which was in force in 1968. The defendant, *Ustadh* Mahmoud was therefore entitled to refuse to attend the 1968 trial, and he in fact simply disregarded its outcome. There was nothing the plaintiffs could do to compel his attendance or enforce the judgment of the Court. How could, therefore, the judgment of one court in a civil cause of action, rendered in the absence of the defendant and without any jurisdiction, be a basis for a criminal conviction by a different court 17 years later?

The Court of Appeal then proceeded to cite the opinions of two foreign institutions, namely the Muslim World League and the Egyptian Azhar University, to the effect that these institutions held *Ustadh* Mahmoud to be an apostate and advised the Sudanese authorities to treat him as such. It is obvious that such 'opinions' have no weight in a court of law, especially since they were not adduced in evidence by the prosecution in a way that enable the accused or their counsel to cross-examine the experts on their claims to have the competence to make that judgment, and the grounds on which it was based.

The unjudicial reasoning of the Court of Appeal is also reflected in the manner in which the Court dismissed legal objections to the imposition of the death sentence on *Ustadh* Mahmoud. Section 247 of the Code of Criminal Procedure, 1983, one of the 'Islamic' laws themselves, prohibits the imposition of the death penalty on any person over 70 years of age. *Ustadh* Mahmoud was 76 years old at the time. The Court of Appeal simply dismissed this provision as inapplicable to Islamic *hadd* offenses, i.e. offenses for which *Shari'a* sets a specific unalterable punishment, since no law may be interpreted in contravention of

Shari'a. There was, however, no legal basis for that claim in relation to the Code of Criminal Procedure 1983.[38]

Having dismissed Section 247 in this arbitrary way in relation to the so-called *hadd* offense of apostasy, the Court of Appeal immediately proceeded to confirm the conviction and sentence under the Penal Code and the State Security Act, expressly describing them as non-*hadd* offenses. Even if Section 247 of the Code of Criminal Procedure did not apply to apostasy, it surely applied to the ordinary criminal offenses under the Penal Code and the State Security Act. It would therefore seem that the Court of Appeal was keen to confirm the death sentence, irrespective of legal objections.

President Nimeiri cited religious and political reasons for confirming the convictions and sentences on all five accused. He ordered the immediate execution of *Ustadh* Mahmoud, and reduced the period allowed for recantation by the other four accused, from the one month allowed by the Court to three days only. The President simply quoted claim after claim of alleged heretical views and beliefs of the accused, without bothering to cite or adduce any specific reference to the sources of such allegations in the writings and utterances of the accused. He also cited evidence of the emerging opposition of the group headed by *Ustadh* Mahmoud, the Republicans, to his regime in support of the view that the group was really a political organization and not an intellectual group.

Although the President's speech made no explicit mention of apostasy, and confirmed the convictions under specific sections of the Penal Code and State Security Act, all his arguments and reasons related to apostasy rather than any other offense. *Ustadh* Mahmoud was thus executed for an offense for which no one could be legally tried under Sudanese law in force at the time—an offense of which he was not personally guilty in any case, since he was not an apostate but rather a non-violent Muslim scholar and reformer who happened to hold views on Islamic revival that were at variance with those held by the government of the day. In the absence of any other rational explanation, one is forced to conclude that *Ustadh* Mahmoud was sacrificed in the cause of maintaining President Nimeiri's personal drive for Islamization, whatever the real motives behind that drive may have been. *Ustadh* Mahmoud was killed in order to frighten others who might have been contemplating criticism or opposition to Nimeiri's policies in general, and his Islamization policy in particular.[38a]

TRADITIONAL ISLAMIC LAW OF APOSTASY

President Nimeiri's motives and methods are not in issue here—even though one can argue that he exploited various religious or philosophical precepts in a bid to perpetuate his stay in power. What is at issue is the fact that the traditional Islamic law of apostasy is not only liable to be abused, but that it is also inherently in contradiction with more universally accepted standards of constitutional civil liberties and international human rights. The case of *Ustadh* Mahmoud in the Sudan cannot, unfortunately, be dismissed as an isolated and curious example of despotic and oppressive brutality. Notwithstanding President Nimeiri's manipulation of Sudanese law, it is in fact genuine traditional Islamic law of apostasy that confronts Muslims all over the world with very real and fundamental questions. Before reviewing some of the human rights and civil liberties implications of apostasy, and considering some possible answers, it may be necessary to point out the legal bases of the offense and its consequences under traditional Islamic law.

Islamic law has two primary sources, the Qur'an and *Sunna*, the traditions of the Prophet. The agreement of the learned as representing the body of believers (*Ijma'a*) and derivation of legal principles by analogy (*Qiyas*) are subsidiary sources, resorted to either to settle arguments on the interpretation of Qur'an and *Sunna*, or to provide for situations not covered by the two primary sources.

The Qur'an deals with apostasy in several verses: e.g. chapter 4, verse 90; chapter 5, verse 59 and chapter 16, verse 108. None of these verses expressly provide for the penalty for apostasy in this life, but they all condemn the apostate in very harsh and unequivocal terms. The punishment of apostasy in *Shari'a* is based on *Sunna*. It is reported, for example, that the Prophet said: 'The blood of a fellow Muslim should never be shed except in three cases: That of the adulterer, the murderer and whoever foresakes the religion of Islam'.[39] It is also reported that the Prophet, peace be upon him, said: 'Whosoever changes his religion, kill him'.

On the bases of these *Sunna*, and standard commentaries on the Qur'an, traditional Islamic schools of jurisprudence are unanimous in holding that apostasy is punishable by death, although they differ on such questions as to whether to execute the sentence immediately or grant the apostate a reprieve of a few days in order to allow him time to reflect and reconsider his position in the hope that he may recant and re-embrace Islam, thereby saving his life as well as his soul.[40] There is also disagreement on whether a female apostate is to be killed or merely imprisoned until she returns to the faith. Her offense is not regarded by any school or jurist to be of less magnitude, the disagreement merely relates to whether the appropriate punishment is death or life imprisonment.

Other traditions cited in commentary and jurisprudence (*fiqh*) books in the context of apostasy may raise problems of interpretation as they tend to cover a more serious situation than mere passive apostasy. It is reported, for example, that a band of Arabs, from 'Ukl tribe came to the Prophet in Medina and announced their embrace of Islam. When they were later taken ill, they asked the Prophet for medicine, and he advised them to go outside the town to live with the Muslim herdsmen, and drink the milk and urine of their camels. When they recovered, the eight Arabs apostasized, killed the herdsmen and drove off with the camels. The Prophet ordered their capture and slow death and dismemberment. This extremely harsh punishment may be explained by a number of factors peculiar to this specific case. The offense itself, to begin with, was not merely passive apostasy but also robbery and murder, the former warranting the penalty of death and dismemberment as a *hadd* offense, i.e. one for which specific penalty is specified, while the latter is punishable by the *qassas* penalty for murder, which is death. There were also considerations of state security to be taken into account in the light of prevailing nomadic customs and practices of 7th century Arabia.[41]

If apostasy as an offense punishable with death was based solely on this last cited tradition, it may be argued that the Prophet was penalizing those Arabs for the multiplicity of aggravated offenses they committed, and not merely for passive apostasy. The offense and its punishment are based on the much stronger and more explicit authority of the two *Sunna* cited above and the *ijma'* of all leading Muslim jurists and schools.

A number of other drastic civil law consequences follow upon a finding of apostasy.[42] The legal effects of all the acts of an apostate are suspended pending his repentance or death. His right to dispose of his property, for example, is immediately held to be in abeyance (*mawqof*) until he either repents or is executed, or dies if he had escaped punishment. If he repents and returns to Islam, on the one hand, all his property rights are restored, including the right to dispose of it in the usual ways. If he dies an apostate, on the other hand, his estate falls to the Public Treasury. An apostate also lacks the capacity to himself inherit from others. A marriage contract is immediately dissolved (*faskh*) upon the apostasy of either spouse.[43]

These are the basic generally agreed criminal and civil law consequences of apostasy under traditional Islamic *Shari'a* Law. How does that Law determine apostasy? What is the test for identifying an apostate who is to suffer those consequences?

An apostate, one who is held to have turned away from Islam (*murtadd*), is a Muslim by birth or conversion who has renounced Islam, regardless of whether or not he subsequently embraced another faith. He is held to have done so if he expressed unbelief by words or deeds, whether explicitly or by necessary implication.[44] The test commonly applied is whether he has repudiated what is 'necessarily' known to be part of the Islamic Religion, presumably as determined by the judge or court. It is only natural that jurists differ on whether or not certain instances or cases are covered by this test,[45] but the following examples are clearly beyond dispute. A person who is known to have been a Muslim and then converted to Christianity or any other religion, or simply declared himself to have become atheist or agnostic, is the most obvious example. Even a Muslim who does not openly declare himself to have become an atheist, but is known to be a Marxist, for example, may be held an apostate because Marxism is believed by most Muslim jurists to be incompatible with Islam.[46] Other generally agreed examples include Muslims who join the Ahmadi sect or the *Baha'i* faith because of the belief of these groups that Muhammad, peace be upon him, is not the final Prophet.[47] Members of these two religious traditions are in fact persecuted, sometimes prosecuted, in Iran and Pakistan, for example, because of their religious beliefs. Very recent examples of specific cases of persons treated as apostates on such grounds are reported within the most developed Muslim countries.[48]

A controversial application of the principle of apostasy is to be found in the area of the duty to implement Islamic *Shari'a* law today. Some jurists and scholars argue that the literal meaning of some Qur'anic texts indicate that any Muslim who refuses to judge or be judged by *Shari'a* law is an apostate.[49] While not disputing the basic premise of this principle, some modern scholars, however, insist that such rejection of *Shari'a* must arise out of the belief that non-Islamic rules are better and more just than Islamic rules.[50] This has recently been a serious political issue in some Muslim countries,[51] and continues to be the almost irresistible argument of the fundamentalists who demand the immediate implementation of the totality of *Shari'a*. It places the burden on the secularists to argue against the implementation of *Shari'a* without falling into the trap of apostasy. A secularist would either have to admit the validity and justice of *Shari'a* and thereby abandon his opposition to its implementation, or reject it as inappropriate and unjust and accept the consequences of being declared an apostate.

APOSTASY AND RELIGIOUS FREEDOM TODAY

The inescapable conclusion of the above review of traditional Islamic *Shari'a* law of apostasy is that it is inconsistent with modern notions of religious freedom, an internationally acknowledged basic human right and generally accepted fundamental civil liberty guaranteed by most constitutions throughout the world.

Modern Muslim jurists and scholars have responded to this charge in a variety of ways. Some proponents of *Shari'a* simply claim that *Shari'a* is beyond defense or justification, it being an article of faith with 'good' Muslims that anything that is inconsistent with *Shari'a* is necessarily wrong and bad.[52] Others make an attempt to justify the law of apostasy on the ground that it amounts to high treason, and is therefore punished as such.[53] They maintain that Islam is not only a religion, but also a social and political order. An apostate repudiates the very basis of this society, and ceases to hold allegiance to it. As such, he is most probably going to engage in hostile subversive activities. According to this argument, an apostate is killed in order to protect the Islamic polity, an extreme preventive measure. This line of reasoning may be acceptable to some Muslims but it can never be convincing to non-Muslims, or even Muslims who expect to have rational objective justification for such basic policy decisions.

Another equally unconvincing line of argument seeks to limit the scope of religious freedom by excluding the freedom to change one's religion or belief.[54] For one thing, this is an integral part of the freedom of thought, conscience and religion as defined by Article 18 of the Universal Declaration of Human Rights and Article 18 of the International Covenant on Civil and Political Rights.[55] That was only logical because the freedom to change religion or belief is essential to any notion of religious freedom. The Muslims themselves would demand this dimension of freedom for those wishing to convert to Islam, how can they argue for its denial to those wishing to repudiate their faith in Islam? It appears that it was this compelling logic which forced all the Muslim states who are members of the United Nations to accept such freedom in the recently adopted Declaration on the Elimination of Intolerance and Discrimination Based on Religion or Belief.[55a] It is true that they objected to identical language,[56] but the phrase they did accept amounts to the same thing. Article 1(1) states that the right to freedom of thought, conscience and religion 'include freedom to have a religion or whatever belief of his choice'. Other Articles of the same Declaration provided for more specific rights and freedoms in this regard, such as the guarantee against coercion which would impair the freedom to have a religion or belief of his choice, and protection against discrimination on grounds of religion or other beliefs.

A more plausible line of reasoning is taken by another group of modernist Muslim scholars who seek to change the traditional Islamic *Shari'a* law of apostasy. There are those, for example, who argue that apostasy should not be punished with death unless it was accompanied by a threat to the Islamic state.[57] According to the logic of this argument, the apostasy of the person should be an irrelevant consideration, the offense being treason or other appropriate offense against the state. Such offenses can be defined and enforced within the ordinary criminal law of the land, without making any reference to the religious beliefs of the accused person. When stated in these terms, we find that this argument lacks legal and theological foundation in *Shari'a* law which is primarily concerned with the question of religious belief, with the notion of treason or offense against the state coming as a much delayed attempt at rationalization.

Another difficulty with this approach is that it is limited to trying to restrict the imposition of the death penalty for passive apostasy, and has nothing to say in relation to the civil law consequences of apostasy indicated above. Moreover, since these arguments are limited to questioning the legal basis for imposing the death penalty for apostasy under *Shari'a*, and do not seek to establish a positive right to change one's religion or faith, they admit that adverse consequences may follow upon apostasy. This is inconsistent with freedom of religion.

The modernist Muslim scholars who adopt this line of reasoning seem to feel the political need to operate within the framework of traditional *Shari'a* in the hope of gaining quicker and wider acceptance for their views. This position would drastically limit the scope of their endeavor because it implies submission to the strict canons of construction and derivation of legal rules (*'usol al fiqh*) applied by the jurists of traditional *Shari'a*. The most serious difficulty they face is the cardinal principle of *Shari'a* that there can be no exercise of rational juristic reasoning (*ijtihad*) in any matter covered by an explicit text of Qur'an or *Sunna*. In view of this principle, it may not even be possible to avoid the death penalty for passive apostasy because it is based on the very explicit *Sunna* quoted above.[58]

A NEW APPROACH

It is precisely in response to these difficulties and limitations of reform within the framework of traditional *Shari'a* that *Ustadh* Mahmoud Muhammad Taha strove to perfect his novel reform technique outlined above. As applied to the present problem, namely the inconsistency between *Shari'a* law of apostasy and the modern principle of freedom of religion and belief, the principle of Evolution of Islamic *Shari'a*, *tatwir at-tashri' al-Islami*, as he used to call his approach, may be summarized as follows.

As noted above, Islam was originally offered in Mecca, around A.D. 610 to 622, through the principle of freedom of choice and voluntary conversion (*ismah*). Qur'anic texts of this class are often cited as evidence of religious freedom and tolerance in *Shari'a* law.[59] This is misleading, however, because the legal principles of *Shari'a* were not based on this class of texts. Legally binding principles were in fact based on the repeal or abrogation (*naskh*), in legal terms, and the enactment of the texts of compulsion (*ikrah*) revealed subsequently in Medina following the Prophet's migration to that town around A.D. 622.[60] This basic shift, which was manifested in the principles of *Shari'a* providing for *jihad*, and discrimination against non-Muslims, is summarized in the *Sunna* in which the Prophet, outlined his future policy as follows: 'I have been instructed to fight people until they accept that there is no god except God, and that Muhammad is the Messenger of God [i.e. the Islamic affirmation of faith] and undertake the prayers and payment of *Zakah* [i.e. Islamic worship practices]. Once they do that, they become secure in life and property except for just cause [i.e. in accordance with due process of law], and I leave their sincerity to be judged by God'.

It is therefore clear that the legally binding principles of *Shari'a* were not based on the texts of freedom of choice, but rather on the texts of compulsion and *jihad*. The former group of texts, which were in fact revealed earlier in Mecca, remained part of the Qur'an and Islamic traditions, albeit not part of the legally binding law.[61] *Ustadh* Mahmoud started with the premise that the repeal of those texts was actually a postponement and not final abrogation.[62] He then suggested that Muslims should now enact those texts and repeal, again in legal terms only, the texts of compulsion and *jihad*. It is important to note that he was only concerned with legal efficacy, and the repeal of texts in this sense does not tamper with the sanctity of the Qur'an or deny any of its texts.[63] *Ustadh* Mahmoud simply maintained that the Qur'an was designed to provide the Muslims with a comprehensive source of guidance and instruction. The Muslims should apply themselves to that source in order to derive their law, the modern *Shari'a*, in the same way the Muslims of 7th century Arabia and the Middle East applied themselves to that fundamental source and developed their law, which has been handed down to us as historical *Shari'a*.

This technique of shifting legal efficacy from one class of texts to another may also be employed in other areas of Islamic law, thereby evolving *Shari'a* in relation to the status and rights of women, and other questions of economic, social and political reform.[64] This approach involves the radical revision and reformulation of the techniques for deriving legal rules from basic Islamic sources (*'usol al-fiqh*). To remove all the criminal and civil law consequences of apostasy, for example, it is necessary to practise rational juristic reasoning (*ijtihad*) throughout a wide range of legal principles, including those derived from explicit Qur'an and *Sunna* texts. This is not possible within the framework of traditional *Shari'a* because the traditional rules for derivation of legal principles from basic sources (*'usol al-fiqh*) will not permit *ijtihad* in matters governed by explicit texts. It takes a juridical revolution to evolve *Shari'a* and not merely reform it, thereby removing all features of compulsion and infringements of religious freedom in the fullest and widest sense of this basic human right.

CONCLUSION

This preliminary study demonstrates that the *Shari'a* law of apostasy violates freedom of religion because it penalizes a Muslim who renounces his faith in Islam. According to the prevailing view, apostasy is punishable by death. Several negative civil law consequences also follow upon a finding of apostasy. It is true that some modern Muslim scholars have argued against the death penalty for apostasy, while others have tried to restrict the death penalty to apostasy when combined with active rebellion. With all due respect to the effort put into the argumentation of both positions, it is still inconsistent with religious freedom to maintain the negative civil law consequences of apostasy.

The only Muslim author who has argued convincingly for the abolition of *all* civil as well as criminal law consequences of apostasy, in my view, is the late

Sudanese reformer *Ustadh* Mahmoud Muhammad Taha. To establish complete freedom of religion within Islamic law, argued *Ustadh* Mahmoud, Muslims must be prepared to base this aspect of Islamic law on a group of texts of Qur'an and *Sunna* that has hitherto been deemed to have been repealed or abrogated by the operative texts that discriminate against non-Muslims and penalizes apostasy.

This technique is clearly revolutionary, but it seems to be the only way for removing all the legal basis for discrimination on grounds of religion or belief. Some Muslims may maintain that it is not necessary to abolish such discrimination because this is the proper and fair way to treat non-Muslims and apostates. Arguments based on the principle of freedom of religion are unlikely to influence this class of Muslims. For those Muslims who feel the need to abolish legal discrimination as bases for protecting freedom of religion and enhancing tolerance, the technique suggested by *Ustadh* Mahmoud deserves serious consideration.

NOTES

The first draft of this article was prepared at Columbia University, New York City, under a generous grant from The Ford Foundation. I am grateful for the many helpful comments and suggestions offered by Professors William Alford, Henry McGee and Phillip Trimble of the UCLA School of Law.

I wish to dedicate this discussion to *Ustadh* Mahmoud Muhammad Taha, the Sudanese Muslim reformer whose execution is discussed in this article. His exceptional courage and superior moral stature, his vision and support, have helped many Muslims both to see certain problems and to speak clearly of them.

1 For a survey of the working of these three systems see C. Thompson, 'The Sources of Law in the New Nations of Africa: A Case Study of the Republic of the Sudan', *1966 Wisconsin Law Review* 1146.

2 Islamic Law was applied informally by the people as part of their customs long before the Turco-Egyptian administration introduced official courts in the 19th century.

3 Abu Rannat, 'The Relationship between Islamic Law and Customary Law in the Sudan', *Journal of African Law*, 1960, **9**.

4 The process of reception and its circumstances are discussed in detail in Z. Mustafa, *The Common Law in the Sudan* (Clarendon Press, Oxford, 1971).

5 See id. chapter IX on the operational difficulties that seem to have led to this result.

6 Major revisions and re-enactments of the main codes and statutes were undertaken in 1925, 1941, 1955 and 1974.,

7 N. J. Anderson, *Islamic Law in Africa* (Her Majesty's Stationery Office, London, 1955), pp. 301–321.

8 For aspects of Islamic and non-Islamic personal law in the Sudan, see C. O. Farran, *Matrimonial Laws of the Sudan* (Butterworth, London 1963).

9 The Judiciary Act was amended several times, and re-enacted twice during the 1970s and early 1980s before the enactment of the so-called Islamic Judiciary Act of 1983.

10 It seems that the colonial administration was very sensitive to the dangers of religiopolitical movements such as that of al-Mahdi which ousted the previous Turco-Egyptian administration in 1884. The new administration was therefore careful to maintain a balance between respect for the religious feelings of the population and the exclusion of religion from legal and political processes.

11 M. 'Abd Al-Rahim, *Imperalism and Nationalism in the Sudan* (Oxford University Press, 1969), pp. 226–227.

12 The traditional political parties, such as the *Umma* (Mahdists) and Democratic Unionists, etc., were revived after the overthrow of President Nimeiri who had banned them for 16 years, since the *coup* of 1969.

13 Southern Sudan is predominantly non-Muslim in contrast to the predominantly Muslim northern part of the country.

14 The least controversial bill, the one providing for the regulation of the voluntary collection and distribution of *zakah*, Muslim religious alms, as a charity and not obligatory tax, was selected for enactment during that period.

15 President Nimeiri's regime was always under attack by Muslim fundamentalists who demanded the immediate and total implementation of Shari'a in the Sudan. The regime tried to accommodate and contain the fundamentalists under the 'National Reconciliation' policy adopted in 1977. As the pressure continued, President Nimeiri seemed to have decided to implement *Shari'a* on apparently his own initiative, thereby taking political credit for the move.

16 Although Article 106 of the 1973 Constitution clearly provided for legislation by Provisional Republican Orders as exceptional procedure to be used 'at any time when the People's Assembly is not in session or in cases of importance and urgency . . . ', President Nimeiri used this method to pass all the so-called Islamic Laws of 1983–84, even when the Assembly was in session and quite available. Extensive and highly technical legislation, such as the *Zakah* and Taxation Act and the Civil Transactions Act, were all enacted by Provisional Orders and subsequently confirmed by the Assembly with very little debate. The apparent effect of enactment as a Provisional Order is to make it extremely difficult for the Assembly to reject the bill as that would amount to direct confrontation with the President of the Republic. It must be noted in this connection that Article 108 of the same Constitution authorized the President to dissolve the Assembly if he 'considers that the public interest and the circumstances necessitate new elections . . . ' The President did in fact utilize this power more than once. The only People's Assembly that refused to confirm the President's Provisional Orders was dissolved soon after it took that decision in 1979.

17 It seems that the Assembly felt that the amendments were too drastic, transforming the nature of the Regime itself, and maybe costing the Members of the Assembly their political base. Many Members knew that they would not be re-elected if Sudan was transformed into an 'Islamic Republic.' Another factor that may have contributed to the defeat of the constitutional amendments was the position taken by the Members from Southern Sudan. These non-Muslim Members of the People's Assembly walked out in protest when the Provisional Orders enacting the so-called 'Islamic' Laws were being confirmed by the Assembly in November 1983. They changed their tactics in confronting the proposed amendments of the Constitution by staying and forcefully arguing against their adoption.

18 Three constitutional suits brought by several Republicans, followers of *Ustadh* Mahmoud, were all dismissed by the Supreme Court on the ground that the applicants had no 'standing' to bring the suits, i.e. they were not personally aggrieved by the legislation which they challenged as unconstitutional. The Court neither defined 'standing' nor attempted to show how the principle applied to the plaintiffs.

19 In accordance with the policy of total Islamization, the Government adopted the Islamic *Hijri* calendar to replace the Western Gregorian calendar previously used. The second Judiciary Act was therefore called the Judiciary Act 1405 Hjri, i.e. 1984.

20 Section 16(1) of the Judiciary Act 1984 authorized the President of the Republic to establish 'special' criminal courts for the national capital, while Section 16(2) authorized the Chief Justice to do the same in the provinces. Section 17 to 19 specified the 'special' procedural rules applicable to the 'special' criminal courts. Section 29(b), as explained in the following footnote, provided for the President of the Republic's power to appoint *any* person to *any* judicial position, regardless of qualifications and other requirements.

21 According to Section 29(b) of the Judiciary Act of 1984, the President of the Republic may, on the recommendation of the High Judiciary Council, appoint *any* person to *any* judicial position irrespective of the conditions set out in Sections 23 to 26 for appointment to various ranks of judicial office. The requirement of recommendation by the High Judiciary Council provided no real safeguard because the President of the Republic was not only the President of the High Judiciary Council, but he also appointed and dismissed the other members of the Council at will.

22 These two articles were amended in 1975 in order to confer on Presidential Orders and Decrees such immunity.

23 This case involved the trial of an Indian merchant named Lalitt, who was resident and doing business in the Sudan, for certain business practices, some of which were not penalized by Sudanese law in force at the time. The constitutional challenge raised by defense counsel was dismissed by a Panel of the Supreme Court of which the trial judge, al-Makashfi Taha al-Kabashi, was a member.

24 In the 1940s, some of the Sudanese nationalists were working for the evacuation of British forces and administrators so that the Sudan may unite with Egypt. Others were seeking independence with very close ties with Britain. The Republican Party was formed to oppose both strategies and demand immediate total independence.

25 *Ustadh* Mahmoud insisted that his ideas were based on deep religious insights acquired during his profound spiritual experience, and not as a result of purely rational intellectual endeavor. This is important for the religious authenticity of his views in accordance with the mystic approach he had subscribed to throughout his adult life.

26 See, for example, the Qur'an chapter 16, verse 125; chapter 18, verse 29; chapter 49, verse 13 and chapter 2, verse 228.

27 See, for example, the Qur'an chapter 9, verses 5 and 29; and chapter 4, verse 34.

28 Although he supported socialist economic development, *Ustadh* Mahmoud was strongly anti-Marxist. He objected to Marxism's atheism, and accused it of failing to achieve socialism.

29 The Muslim Brothers' fundamentalist movement originated in Egypt around 1928. It spread into Sudan in the late 1940s and early 1950s when it was being persecuted in Egypt. Although there are other fundamentalist groups in Sudan, the Muslims Brothers are by far the strongest and best organized group. On the Muslim Brothers generally see, for example, R. Mitchell, *The Society of the Muslim Brothers* (Oxford University Press, 1969).

30 Five Republicans, including four women, were released after nine months. A group of Republican students were also arrested and released after six months of detention. Detention orders were issued and periodically renewed under Section 22 of the State Security Act 1973 (as amended in 1975). Section 22 authorized detention without trial only for one who 'is about to commit or is likely to commit any of the offenses under this (State Security) Act', i.e. specified offenses against the state. The Republicans were neither 'about to commit' nor 'likely to commit' such offenses as they were actively supporting the Regime at the time. In the pamphlet which constituted the immediate cause of their detention, the Republicans declared their support for the Regime and argued that their criticism of the First Vice-President's failure to curb fundamentalism and religious fanaticism was intended to prevent a take-over of power by those forces. The Republicans were denied access to the courts to pursue their complaints of illegal arrest by being physically prevented from appearing before the court as required by Sudanese Code of Criminal Procedure, Section 156.

31 The pamphlet argued that the laws violated the general precepts of Islam as a religion as well as violating the specific provisions of *Shari'a* as a law. To illustrate the second point, they cited the omission of the requirement that theft must be from a securely enclosed place in order to warrant the penalty of amputation. The omission of this requirement under Section 320 of the 'Islamic' Penal Code greatly increased the incidence of amputation by allowing it to be enforced to a much wider class of offenses than originally intended by *Shari'a*.

32 Civil war had resumed in 1982 in Southern Sudan, following President Nimeiri's violation of the Addis Ababa Agreement of 1972, which ended the first civil war. By first redividing the Southern Region and then subsequently unilaterally imposing Islamic *Shari'a* law, President Nimeiri acted against the letter as well as the spirit of that Agreement.

33 *Ustadh* Mahmoud was arrested and tried in Omdurman, across the White Nile from Khartoum. Other Republicans were arrested and charged with the same combination of offenses in other parts of the Capital, Khartoum, and in other towns of northern, eastern and central Sudan. All charges against the other Republicans were subsequently dropped following the execution of *Ustadh* Mahmoud. Over three hundred Republicans who were detained without charge around the same time were also released over the two weeks following the execution.

34 Each of the accused made a short statement explaining his reasons for refusing to 'co-operate' with the Court, and then remained silent for the duration of the trial, refusing to answer questions or present any defense.

35 *Ustadh* Mahmoud was critical of injustices of the capitalist liberal tradition as well as the atheism and oppression of totalitarian Marxist-Leninism. He published about 30 books and many newspaper and magazine articles. He also lectured and debated in many Sudanese towns and cities for over 20 years. His followers, the Republicans, also published hundreds of pamphlets, booklets and articles and

traveled all over the Sudan distributing their literature, holding debates and giving public lectures on their methodology for Islamic Law reform.

36 The specific sanction of the President of the Republic is required for prosecutions of certain offenses against the state under Section 147 of the Code of Criminal Procudure 1983.

36a Article to guarantee against the imposition of criminal punishment in the absense of pre-existing penal provisions in Sudanese law.

37 The jurisdiction of *Shari'a* Courts was then determined by the Sudan Mohammedan Law Courts (Amendment) Act 1961, which limited such jurisdiction to 'questions regarding marriage, divorce, guardianship of minors or family relationships provided that the marriage to which the question related was concluded in accordance to Mohammedan Law . . . ', *wakfs*, gifts and succession amongst Moslems or parties who submitted to the jurisdiction of the Court. The *Shari'a* Court had no jurisdiction over apostasy as such. See C. O. Farran, *Matrimonial Laws of the Sudan*, pp. 230–234.

38 The Code makes no exceptions of *hadd* or any other offenses. There was also no provision anywhere to the effect that *Shari'a* principles are superior to other legislation or raising a presumption of consistency with *Shari'a*.

38a Following the overthrow of former President Nimeiri in April 1985, the daughter of *Ustadh* Mahmoud and one of his co-accused instituted a constitutional suit before the Supreme Court (S.C./Const. S./2/1406, i.e. 1986) to have the judgment against *Ustadh* Mahmoud and his co-accused set aside as null and void. The petition, dated 25 February, 1986, cited a wide range of constitutional and procedural objections. On 17 April, the Attorney General, acting as counsel for the Government, directly admitted the case for the applicants and stated before the Supreme Court that he had nothing to say in defense of that trial which was totally illegal. The Supreme Court, however, asked for a more detailed itemized response to the applicants' petition. As of the date of the publication of this article, the Supreme Court has not yet ruled on the substantive issues. In view of the direct and complete admission by the Government's attorney it is difficult to see how the Supreme Court can avoid giving judgment for the applicants. Nevertheless, as this Article demonstrates, one should not readily expect rational legality to prevail in a Muslim country when principles of *Shari'a* are being challenged. Moreover, even if the Supreme Court should nullify this particular trial and exonerate *Ustadh* Mahmoud, the problems with the *Shari'a* law of apostasy discussed in this article shall remain unless and until they are treated authoritatively by the Muslims themselves acting from within the religious tradition.

39 According to some sources, the *Sunna* adds, ' . . . foresakes (or abandons) his religion and separate himself from the community'. This element of rejection of the community is seized upon by those who argue that mere passive apostasy, without threatening the Islamic state, is not punishable by death. The first *Sunna*, and the numerous sources that report this second *Sunna* without the additional factor seem to reduce the credibility of this restrictive interpretation.

40 Ibn Rushd Al Qartabi, *2 Badyet-Al-Mujtahid*, 383. See Peters and Devries, 'Apostasy in Islam', *XVII Die Welt des Islams*, 1 at 5 *et seq.* (1976–77).

41 This incident is usually cited by treatises on the meaning of the Qur'an as an illustration of the capital offense provided for under chapter 5, verse 33 (i.e. *fasad fi al-ard*).

42 Procedural requirements for a fair trail of the issue can easily be added in the modern context although they may not have been a part of the traditional literature on the subject.

43 Peters and Devries, *supra* note 40, at 7–9, and sources they cited in their footnote 15 on page 7.

44 Id. at 2–4.

45 See Nu'man 'Abd Al-Razid Al-Samarr'i, *Ahkam Al-Murtad Fi Al-Shari'a Al-Islamyya*, 116 (1968).

46 Peters and Devries, *supra* note 40, report at page 11 an authoritative legal opinion (*fatwa*) by a committee of al-Azhar (Islamic University in Cairo, Egypt) to the effect that a marriage concluded with a known communist man from a Muslim family would be null and void, as he must be considered an apostate.

47 Id. at 10–11, and authoritative legal opinions from various Muslim countries cited there.

48 *Human Rights Internet Reporter*, 10, 3 & 4 (January–April 1985), quoted on page 406 a statement of the American Coptic Association, Christians of Egypt, U.S.A. (29 March, 1985) reporting the decision of an Egyptian Administrative Court which ruled that the *Baha'i* marriage is invalid, even if both parties are *Baha'is*.

49 Qur'an chapter 5, verse 44.

50 See Mahmoud Shaltut, *Al-Fatawa, Dirasah Li-Mushkilat Al-Muslim Al-Mu'Asir Fi Hayatih Al-Yawmiyah Wa-Al-Ammah*, 37–9 (1969) 6 Mohamed 'Abduh and Mohamed Rashid Ridda, *Tafsir Al-Manar*, 405 *et seq.*

51 Peters and DeVries, *supra* note 40, at 12 quoted an example from Tunisia in the 1930s when Tunisians who adopted French Nationality, and as such became subject to French law, were regarded as apostates by other Tunisians who demanded that such apostates should not be buried in Muslim cemeteries.

52 'Abd Al-Mota'al Al-Saidi, *Al-Hurriyyah Al-Diniyyah Fi Al-Islam* (Religious Freedom in Islam) (undated) 56–64 and 74–88.

53 There are several versions of this argument. See. for example, 'Abd Al-Qadir 'Awdah, *1 At-Tashri Aj-Jina'y Al-Islami* (Islamic Criminal Legislation) 536; and Mohamed Al-Ghazali, *Hoqoq Al-Insan Bayn Ta'Alim Al-Islam Wa-I'Lan Al-Omam Al-Mottahidah* (Human Rights between Islamic Principles and the United Nations' Declaration) 102–103 (1963).

54 For examples of this reasoning, see Samuel Zwemer, *The Law Of Apostasy In Islam* (Marshall, London, 1924) 45: and Wafi, 'Human Rights in Islam', 11 *Islamic Quarterly* 64–65 (1967).

55 All Muslim countries have by now adopted the United Nation's (U.N.) Universal Declaration of Human Rights, 1948. Even Saudi Arabia which abstained when the U.N. voted on the Declaration in December 1948, has now adopted the Declaration through subsequent conduct in the U.N. In any case, religious freedom may now be regarded as part of customary international law, and as such, binding on all states regardless of treaty obligation. Several Muslim countries, moreover, are parties to the International Covenant on Civil and Political Rights of 1966, a legally binding treaty which guarantees religious freedom.

55a This Declaration was adopted by the General Assembly of the U.N. on 18 January, 1982. U.N. GAOR Supp. (No. 51), U.N. Doc. A/RES/36/55 (1982).

56 Muslim states always had difficulty with the inclusion of the right to change one's religion, even at the time when the Universal Declaration of Human Rights was adopted in 1948. See Nehemiah Robinson, *The Universal Declaration of Human*

Rights (Institute of Jewish Affairs, New York, 1958), 128–129. The fact that they have always had to concede and support the international instruments on this point demonstrates the untenability of the Islamic traditional law of apostasy.

57 5 Mohamed 'Abduh and Mohamed Rahid Ridda, *Tafsir Al-Manar*, 327; Mahmoud Shaltut, *Al-Islam 'Aqidah Wa Shari'a* 292–293; and Al-Saidi, *supra* note 52. See also Mohamed S. El-Awa, *Punishment in Islam* (American Trust Publications, Indianapolis, 1982) pp. 49 *et seq.*

58 The argument advanced by some jurists and scholars that these *Sunna* cannot abrogate Qur'anic rule against the death penalty for passive apostasy summarized by Peters and Devries, *supra* note 40 at 14–15, is based on the false assumption that there is such a Qur'anic rule against the death penalty. The verses used in this argument (i.e. Qur'an chapter 4, verses 89–90 and chapter 2, verse 256) have already been rules by Muslim jurisprudence to have been repealed or abrogated (by Qur'an chapter 9, verse 5 and 29).

59 See, for example, Qur'an Chapter 16, verse 125 and chapter 18, verse 29.

60 Qur'an, chapter 9, verse 5, was in fact made the bases of legally binding principles, thereby abrogating, from the legal point of view, all the verses of *ismah*, i.e. freedom of choice. The concept of *jihad*, holy war to propagate the faith, and the status of non-Muslims, based on the Qur'an chapter 9, verses 5 and 29, many *Sunna*, and the practice of the Prophet as well as the practice of leading companions of the Prophet, are all inconsistent with freedom of religion.

61 Muslim jurists set out the so-called *'ayat wa-'ahadith al-'ahkam*, i.e. the verses and *Sunna* of legal binding rules, in a class of their own. The rest of the Qur'an and *Sunna* and other traditions are revered, and may be even observed in practice, but only as moral and ethical standards and not as legally binding rules. In relation to religious freedom, for example, it is generally regarded as advisable to practise persuasion and peaceful means, but if they fail, then resort must be had to compulsion and *jihad*.

62 The meaning of Qur'an chapter 2, verse 106, may be translated as follows: 'Whenever We (God) abrogate any verse or postpone it, We replace it with a better verse or a similar one, do you not know that God is able to do everything?' *Ustadh* Mahmoud cites this verse in support of his argument that abrogation is merely enactment of the more appropriate verse of the Qur'an and the postponement of the inappropriate one until its time comes.

63 It is an article of faith for a Muslim to affirm that the whole of the Qur'an is the literal and final revelation of God. Debate as to the meaning of the Qur'an and the legal implications of its verses is legitimate *ijtihad*, i.e. exercise of rational legalistic reasoning, open to all Moslems. Some Muslim jurists argue that only a few highly qualified individuals may practise *ijtihad*. This may be true, but who is qualified to certify others as competent *mujtahds*, i.e. competent to practise this function? The competence to practise *ijtihad* is clearly related to the quality of the end result, both of which, it is submitted, will have to be judged by Moslems at large and should not be allowed to be monopolized by any institution or group of people.

64 For a brief discussion of these wider implications of the work of *Ustadh* Mahmoud, see El Naiem, 'A Modern Approach to Human Rights in Islam: Foundations and Implications for Africa', in *Human Rights And Development in Africa*, 75 (C. Welch and R. Meltzer, eds, 1984).

ABDULLAHI AHMED AN-NA'IM was Head of the Department of Public Law at the University of Khartoum. Since 1985, he has been Visiting Professor at the School of Law, Univesity of California, Los Angeles, lecturing in comparative and Islamic law.

School of Law, UCLA, Los Angeles, CA 90024, U.S.A.

[12] Religious Minorities under Islamic Law and the Limits of Cultural Relativism*

Non-Muslim minorities within an Islamic state do not enjoy rights equal to those of the Muslim majority. Some apologist Muslim writers have tended to misrepresent *Shari'ah,* the historical religious law of the Muslims, in order to minimize the seriousness of discrimination against non-Muslims. Such an approach is futile not only because the misrepresentation can easily be exposed, but also because current public opinion is unwilling to tolerate any degree or form of discrimination on grounds of religion or belief. On a practical level, although most of the constitutions of modern Muslim states guarantee against religious discrimination, most of these constitutions also authorize the application of *Shari'ah*. As such, these constitutions sanction discrimination against religious minorities. This is inconsistent with the constitutions' own terms. The existence of such contradictions, and the underlying tensions they reflect, call for urgent and candid discussion of this problem. Moreover, the constitutions of some Muslim countries, such as Iran, have already openly approved of discrimination on grounds of religion.[1] If the current trend towards what is commonly known as Islamic fundamentalism continues, it may not be long before other Muslim countries follow suit.

It may therefore be appropriate to try to anticipate possible arguments which may be used to justify or rationalize the inferior status of religious minorities under *Shari'ah*. A direct fundamentalist approach may argue, for example, that Muslims are entitled to treat their own religious minorities in this way in accordance with the established norms of Islamic culture. By

---

* A draft of this article was prepared under a grant from the Ford Foundation and presented at the Seventh Annual International Human Rights Symposium and Research Conference, Columbia University, New York, on 12 June 1986.

1. The Constitution of the Islamic Republic of Iran, Articles 12 to 14, clearly authorizes discrimination on grounds of religion. A. P. Blaustein and G. H. Flanz, vol. VII, *Constitutions of the Countries of the World* (Dobbs Ferry, New York: Oceana Publications).

analogy to the national sovereignty argument raised by some countries against what they regard to be interference in their domestic affairs,[2] fundamentalist Muslims may claim Islamic sovereignty. Such argument, in my view, can no longer be used to rebut charges of human rights violations, at least in relation to basic universally accepted group and individual rights. In the same way that, for example, the status of the black majority is not the exclusive domestic concern of the Republic of South Africa, the status of religious minorities is not the exclusive concern of any national or cultural tradition. As we shall see below, this much has clearly been established by the international community.

To avoid confusing the issues, however, we must be clear on the proper role of cultural autonomy, emphasized in anthropological literature as cultural relativism, in relation to human rights. Otherwise, the legitimacy of cultural relativism will be abused to justify norms and policies in clear violation of the valid objectives of cultural relativism itself.

THE HUMAN RIGHTS CRISIS

Thirty-seven years after the adoption of the Universal Declaration of Human Rights in 1948, ten years after the coming into force of the human rights Covenants,[3] and despite the adoption of regional documents in three continents,[4] many observers are wondering whether these international and regional documents will ever achieve their purported objectives. Independent monitoring organizations such as Amnesty International and publications such as the Human Rights Internet Reporter continue to report massive and gross violations of human rights throughout the world. It is therefore imperative to investigate ways of resolving the present crisis and revitalize the international human rights movement.

2. The sovereignty argument in relation to human rights has come to be associated with the Soviet position. See, for example, F. Przetacznik, "The Socialist Concept of Human Rights: Its Philosophical Background and Political Justification," *Revue belge de droit International* 13 (1977): 238.
3. International Covenant on Economic, Social and Cultural Rights, *opened for signature* 19 December 1966, *entered into force* 3 January 1976, G.A. Res. 2200A, 21 GAOR Supp. (No. 16) at 49, U.N. Doc. A/6316; International Covenant on Civil and Political Rights, *opened for signature* 19 December 1966, *entered into force* 23 March 1976, G.A. Res. 2200A, 21 GAOR Supp. (No. 16) at 52, U.N. Doc. A/6316 (1966).
4. The first of the regional documents was the European Convention for the Protection of Human Rights and Fundamental Freedoms, *signed* 4 November 1950, *entered into force* 3 September 1953, 213 U.N.T.S. 222 (1950). The next document was the American Convention on Human Rights, *signed* 22 November 1969, *entered into force* 18 July 1978, O.A.S.T.S. No. 36, at 1, O.A.S. Off. Rec. OEA/Ser. L/V/11.23, doc. 21, rev. 6 (English 1979). The latest is the African Charter on Human and Peoples' Rights, *adopted* 27 June 1981, O.A.S. Doc. CAB/LEG/67/3 rev. 5, *reprinted in* 21 I.L.M. 58 (1982). It came into force 21 October 1986. "Banjul Charter Comes into Force," *Human Rights Internet Reporter* 11 (Sept. 1986): 46.

At one level of analysis it may be argued that human rights advocates were too optimistic in assuming that the adoption of general standards formulated in terms of legally binding treaties would automatically transform state practice. The analogy between domestic law and international law may have been carried too far too soon. It takes more than normative formulation in terms of positive law, even in the domestic context, to achieve compliance. The international and regional documents have no doubt achieved some improvement in the situation. Beside developing consensus on, and awareness of, a set of standards for judging state practice, these documents have also greatly influenced the drafting of state constitutions, especially those of newly emerging states. To that extent, the international human rights standards have influenced the content and practice of civil liberties in these states.[5] But since massive violations continue to occur throughout the world, we need to look further at the necessary prerequisites for greater compliance with norms.

At a deeper level of analysis it would seem that culturally rooted norms stand the best chance of compliance. We would therefore need to enhance the legitimacy of the human rights standards by rooting them in the various cultural traditions of the world. This is necessary, in my view, not only for the tactical reason of denying violators the pretext of claiming that they need not comply with some of the international norms because these norms are alien and unrepresentative of their own cultural values, but also as a matter of principle. It is true that the pretext is often belied by the fact that these states have not only failed to advance their own cultural alternatives but also duplicated the same international standards in their own constitutions and regional documents. Nevertheless, I suggest that the implementation of the international human rights standards will improve if they can be shown to be the natural and legitimate evolution of the cultural tradition of the particular community.

Given their Western liberal origins and the actual historical development of the current international human rights standards, it may not be completely plausible to argue that these rights have existed in their precise present formulation within the cultural traditions of most historical civilizations.[6] The genesis of the same norms, I believe, can be found in almost all major cultural traditions. It may take some innovative reinterpretation of traditional norms to bring them into complete accord with the present

5. It is not assumed here that constitutional guarantees are fully observed in practice, but they certainly reflect, to some extent, political realities and the general perception of rights deserving formal protection. The very fact that the country's elites selected the rights of religious minorities to be safeguarded in the constitution is significant even if their practice does not conform to constitutional theory. Such guarantees also provide strong legal support for the demands of the beneficiaries, whether individuals or groups.

6. See Jack Donnelly, "Human Rights and Human Dignity: An Analytic Critique of non-Western Conceptions of Human Rights," *American Political Science Review* 76 (1982): 303.

formulation of the international standards, but the essence of these standards is already present. This is particularly true of the Islamic tradition, as I have attempted to show elsewhere.[7]

Cultural considerations are also important in another sense. Given the dynamic and evolutionary nature of human rights, different cultural traditions may contribute positively by raising new areas of concern, adding more rights, and generally informing the interpretation and application of the accepted norms. This dynamic and evolutionary nature of human rights has already been demonstrated by the contribution of socialist and developing countries in relation to social, economic, and cultural rights.

The involvement of the various cultural traditions is, therefore, vital for developing existing rights, adding new ones, and informing their interpretation and application as well as improving compliance with international human rights standards. To emphasize the need for cultural contribution and legitimacy in this way, however, does not mean that we should concede the claim of extreme cultural relativism that there are no universal standards of human rights. To do so would defeat the purpose of cultural relativism itself, which seeks to uphold and protect the dignity and integrity of all human beings regardless of sex, race, religion, or belief.

CULTURAL RELATIVISM AND HUMAN RIGHTS

The insights of cultural relativism have made a positive contribution to intercultural understanding, mutual respect, tolerance, and cooperation between the peoples of the world.[8] Briefly stated, the cultural relativist position is that "[j]udgments are based on experience, and experience is interpreted by each individual in terms of his [or her] own enculturation."[9] This process of enculturation, i.e., the thorough socialization of the individual in accordance with the norms and values of his or her own culture, is a necessary and vital requisite for individual and collective survival and development. The resultant ethnocentricity, the belief that one's own way of life is to be preferred to all others, often degenerates into negative por-

7. See Abdullahi Ahmed El Naiem (now written An-Na'im), "A Modern Approach to Human Rights in Islam: Foundations and Implications for Africa," in C. E. Welch and R. I. Meltzer, *Human Rights and Development in Africa* (Albany: State University of New York Press, 1984).
8. The specific focus of this article does not permit dwelling on the concept of cultural relativism as such. For information on the subject, in addition to the writings of Professor Melville J. Herskovits cited in note 9 below, the reader may refer to the classic statement of the principle in Ruth Benedict, *Patterns of Culture* (Boston: Houghton Mifflin Co., 1934). For a very recent treatment of the topic see Marcus and Fischer, *Anthropology as Cultural Critique* (Chicago: University of Chicago Press, 1986).
9. Melville J. Herskovits, *Cultural Relativism, Perspectives in Cultural Pluralism,* ed. Frances Herskovits (New York: Random House, 1972), 15.

trayals and hostility towards alien cultures and a tendency to dominate and dictate to other people how they should live their lives.

Cultural relativism is primarily concerned with checking and correcting this tendency and cultivating mutual respect, tolerance, and cooperation through emphasizing the worth of many ways of life and affirming the values of each culture. As expressed by Professor Herskovits, one of the founders and leading proponents of cultural relativism, "to say that we have a right to expect conformity to the code of our day for ourselves does not imply that we need expect, much less impose, conformity to our code on persons who live by other codes."[10]

The cultural relativists are therefore opposed to claims of absolute criterion of values, i.e., that any given set of values should be the absolute criterion for judging the validity of the values of other cultures. This does not mean that they reject all universal criteria. The relativists do in fact accept universal systems, which are "those least common denominators to be extracted from the range of variation that all phenomena of the natural or cultural world manifest."[11] In this way, the cultural relativist position is clearly consistent with the emergence of universal standards, including universal standards of human rights.

Writing with reference to world peace, Herskovits suggested that the following four principles be advanced to shape attitudes and inform policy.

I. Recognition that different peoples often achieve identical ends by different means.

II. Identification of the functional unities that underlie the differences in form which are to be observed in different modes of belief and behavior found among the peoples of the world.

III. Clear definition of the values and goals of all parties so that each is aware of the values and goals of the other parties.

IV. Building on these differing patterns to achieve common ends, accepting the right of choice among peaceful alternatives for all people.[12]

The same principles, in my view, can be adapted to shape attitudes and inform policy in relation to human rights. The last clause of the fourth principle would, of course, be rephrased to read "accepting the right of all people to choose among alternatives equally respectful of human rights." The rights to life, liberty, and dignity for every individual person or group of people within each cultural setting are, I submit, universal norms accepted by all cultures. All cultures are entitled to a measure of freedom of choice as to how to safeguard these rights in the cultures' own context. At the same time, no culture, I suggest, should be allowed to violate these basic universal human rights.

---

10. Ibid., 33.
11. Ibid., 32, 55–59.
12. Ibid., 95–96.

Rights to life, liberty, and dignity are, of course, used in the generic sense because they have now been elaborated and formulated into several specific rights in the various international and regional documents as well as the national constitutions of most states. The least common denominators to be extracted from these sources can be taken to be the universal standards. Insofar as they reflect international agreement or consensus on a particular set of rights, these sources at least make a *prima facie* case for the existence of the minimum individual and collective human rights, say, of religious minorities. Making a *prima facie* case should suffice to shift the burden of proof from the proponents to the opponents of the universality of these rights. Before discussing the possible cultural relativist argument against the rights of religious minorities, it may be helpful to briefly state the universalist position.

THE UNIVERSAL RIGHTS OF RELIGIOUS MINORITIES

The general principle of the rights of members of religious minorities is to be found first in the guarantee against discrimination on grounds of religion or faith.[13] All the relevant international human rights documents and national constitutions consistently and explicitly provide for this fundamental principle. Article 55(c) of the United Nations Charter, a treaty binding all the Muslim countries of the world,[14] commits the United Nations to promote "universal respect for, and observance of, human rights and fundamental freedoms for all without distinction as to race, sex, language or religion." All members of the United Nations, including the Muslim countries, pledge themselves by virtue of Article 56 of the Charter "to take joint and separate action in cooperation with the Organization [UN] for the achievement of the purposes set forth in Article 55."

The first major action taken in fulfillment of this pledge was the adoption of the Universal Declaration of Human Rights on 10 December 1948.[15] After reaffirming in Article 1 that "[a]ll human beings are born free and equal in dignity and rights," the Declaration proceeds to state the following fundamental principle in Article 2:

13. The international human rights documents, especially the earlier ones, tend to speak of the rights of the individual. The issue of individual versus collective rights is not relevant to the present discussion because the rights of members of religious groups include the right of the individual person to belong to and participate in the activities of the group.
14. The term Muslim country can be problematic. In this article the term refers to those countries with a clear Muslim majority even if the country does not identify itself as an Islamic state in the constitutional sense. All these countries are members of the United Nations and as such parties to its Charter as a treaty.
15. G.A. Res. 217 A (III), U.N. Doc. A/810, at 71 (1948).

> Everyone is entitled to all the rights and freedoms set forth in this Declaration, without distinction of any kind, such as race, colour, sex, language, religion, political or other opinion, national or social origin, property, birth or other status.

The Declaration's extensive catalog of fundamental human rights is subject to the general limitations allowed by Articles 29 and 30 which are, themselves, consistent with the principle of nondiscrimination. Article 29(2) permits only those "limitations as are determined by law solely for the purpose of securing due recognition and respect for the rights and freedoms of others and of meeting the just requirements of morality, public order and the general welfare in a democratic society." More significant for our purposes is the text of Article 30 which reads as follows:

> Nothing in this Declaration may be interpreted as implying for any State, group or person any right to engage in any activity or to perform any act aimed at the destruction of any of the rights and freedoms set forth herein.

The Universal Declaration of Human Rights was adopted by the unanimous agreement of the General Assembly of the United Nations with Saudi Arabia, South Africa, and the Soviet bloc abstaining. The Soviet bloc has since confirmed the Declaration in a number of international instruments,[16] while Saudi Arabia and South Africa continue to abstain. Far from derogating from the universality of the principles of the Declaration, the Saudi abstention, ostensibly based on Islamic religious grounds, in fact demonstrates the equal untenability of discrimination on grounds of either race, in the case of South Africa, or religion, in the case of Saudi Arabia.[17]

To reinforce the moral and political impact of the Universal Declaration, the General Assembly of the United Nations has since adopted several treaties, including the Covenant on Economic, Social and Cultural Rights and the Covenant on Civil and Political Rights.[18] Both Covenants have been ratified by many Muslim countries. Article 2 of both Covenants states the fundamental nondiscrimination principle in legally binding terms.[19] In this way the principle of nondiscrimination on grounds of reli-

---

16. The U.S.S.R. and other East European countries have ratified the International Convention on the Elimination of All Forms of Racial Discrimination, *opened for signature* 21 December 1965, *entered into force* 4 January 1969, 660 U.N.T.S. 195 (1969); G.A. Res. 2106 A (XX), 20 U.N. GAOR Supp. (No. 4), U.N. Doc. A/6014 (1965), and the International Covenants, note 3 above. All three instruments adopted the Universal Declaration, note 15 above, in their preambles.
17. In other words, Saudi Arabia's allegedly Islamic abstention from joining the international comsensus on universal human rights standards is similar to South Africa's racist abstention.
18. International Covenants, note 3 above.
19. Ibid. Article 2(2) of the Covenant on Economic, Social and Cultural Rights binds states parties "to guarantee" while Article 2 of the Covenant on Civil and Political Rights binds the states parties "to respect and to ensure" the rights "enunciated" and "recognized" in the

gion has the sanction of legally binding international treaties. Since those Muslim countries which failed to ratify these Covenants have included in their own national constitutions the fundamental principle of nondiscrimination on grounds of religion, as we shall see below, it can safely be assumed that their failure to ratify was not intended to challenge the universality of this principle.

The second general source of the rights of members of religious minorities is to be found in Article 18 of both the Universal Declaration and the Covenant on Civil and Political Rights, namely the right of everyone to freedom of thought, conscience, and religion. In its more detailed formulation under the Covenant on Civil and Political Rights, the right "include[s] freedom to have or to adopt a religion or belief of his choice, and freedom, either individually or in community with others and in public or private, to manifest his religion or belief in worship, observance, practice and teaching." The same Article also provides that "[n]o one shall be subject to coercion which would impair his freedom to have or to adopt a religion or belief of his choice."

In debates over this Article since 1948, and debates over the more recent Declaration on the Elimination of All Forms of Intolerance and of Discrimination Based on Religion or Belief,[20] Muslim countries have concentrated on the difficulty they face in accepting the right to change one's religion.[21] But strict compliance with *Shari'ah,* the historical Muslim religious law, would raise difficulties with most components of the principle of freedom of religion and the rights of religious minorities.[22] It is, therefore, very significant that Muslim countries have elected to support the same principles of religious freedom and rights of religious minorities in their own national constitutions. The same principles have also received the support of those Muslim countries which are members of the Organization of African Unity, and have accepted Africa's own Charter on Human and

Covenants. The slight difference in the drafting of the two Articles seems to be due to the nature of the rights and has no significance to the principle of freedom from discrimination on grounds of religion. Because of the limitations in human and material resources necessary to implement state obligations under the Covenant on Economic, Social and Cultural Rights, the states parties were allowed by Article 2(1) to achieve progressively the full realization of these rights. This is, in my view, the reason behind the difference in formulation, which does not reflect on the substance of the fundamental principle of nondiscrimination on grounds of religion.

20. *Adopted* 18 January 1982, G.A. Res. 55, U.N. GAOR Supp. (No. 51), U.N. Doc. A/RES/36/55 (1982).

21. One difficulty facing Muslim countries is that it is a capital offense under Islamic law for a Muslim to repudiate his faith in Islam. See, for example, An-Na'im, "The Islamic Law of Apostasy and its Modern Applicability: A Case from the Sudan," *Religion* 16 (1986): forthcoming.

22. Some of these difficulties will be discussed in the next section of this article. See further El Naiem, note 7 above, and Abdullahi An-Na'im, "The Elusive Islamic Constitution: The Sudanese Experience," *Orient* 26 (1985): 329.

Peoples' Rights.[23] Article 2 of this charter guarantees against discrimination on grounds of, *inter alia,* religion, while Article 8 safeguards freedom of conscience and religion.

Space does not permit full analysis of the relevant constitutional provisions. It is sufficient for our purposes here to note that the principles of nondiscrimination and religious freedom and the rights of religious minorities enjoy constitutional sanction in the vast majority of Muslim states today.[24] Since the modern Muslim world has expressed such support for the rights of religious minorities at both the national and international levels, can we accept this commitment at face value and consider the question settled once and for all? The answer is, unfortunately, in the negative because although the formal legal systems of these countries do not openly authorize discrimination on grounds of religion, such discrimination does in fact exist.[25] The question cannot be considered settled until it is settled at the Islamic cultural level. What are the Islamic cultural impediments to the full and effective safeguard of the rights of religious minorities and how can they be removed? Unless and until these rights are culturally rooted, formal commitment does not guarantee full compliance. Moreover, if the countercultural norms are allowed to remain valid and operative, they will undermine the existing formal commitment and threaten to eradicate its limited gains instead of enhancing and expanding the universal norms and informing their interpretation and application. In other words, current Islamic cultural relativism seems to threaten the two main positive features of cultural relativism indicated above.

Although cultural norms are a complex phenomenon that cannot be attributed to a single cause, the religious factor seems to be a major formative force. To the extent that it shapes and/or is shaped by other socioeconomic and political forces, religion can be one of the ways of understanding the dynamics of cultural norm formation and development. This is particularly true, I suggest, of Islamic cultures where religious norms pur-

23. African Charter, note 4 above. Egypt, Gambia, Guinea, Niger, Senegal, Sierra Leone, and Tunisia have fully ratified the Charter, while Mauritania, Somalia, Sudan, and Libya have signed but not yet ratified.

24. The wide ideological and political variety of the Muslim countries make systematic analysis and broad generalizations a lengthy and difficult process. To illustrate the commitment of these countries to the principles of nondiscrimination and religious freedom, reference may be made to the following examples: Algeria arts. 39 and 44; Guinea arts. 6 and 8; Indonesia art. 29; Jordan arts. 6, 14, and 15; Kuwait arts. 29 and 35; Mali arts. 6, 14, and 16; Mauritania arts. 1 and 2; Somalia arts. 6 and 31; Syria arts. 25(3) and 26. For English translations of these and other constitutions of Muslim countries see Blaustein and Flanz, note 1 above.

25. See Abdullahi An-Na'im, "Religious Freedom in Egypt: Under the Shadow of the Islamic *Dhimma* System," in *Religious Liberty and Human Rights in Nations and in Religions,* ed. Leonard Swidler (Philadelphia: Ecumenical Press, and New York: Hippocrene Books, 1986), 45, and Khalid Duran, "Religious Liberty and Human Rights in the Sudan," in ibid., 61.

port to have the binding force of positive legal principles and rules. To adopt a religio-legal approach is not to deny the validity of other approaches and analyses. Such an approach, however, is helpful, especially in the Mulsim context, because of the historic and contemporary role of Islam in these societies. It is, therefore, important to know not only what *Shari'ah* has to say on religious minorities, but also why the law was formulated in that way.

RELIGIOUS MINORITIES UNDER *SHARI'AH*

A cultural relativist argument for Islamic fundamentalism would start with the assumption that if the status of non-Muslims under *Shari'ah* is inferior, then this is the way it should be. It would be heretical for a Muslim who believes that *Shari'ah* is the final and ultimate formulation of the law of God to maintain that any aspect of that law is open to revision and reformulation by mere mortal and fallible human beings. To do so is to allow human beings to correct what God has decreed.

If this were the case, there would be very little, if anything, to be said to Muslims at the religious level. Fortunately, this is not the case, I suggest, because *Shari'ah* was not the totality of the word of God. As indicated by the way Islamic sources were interpreted to develop *Shari'ah*, it is obvious that *Shari'ah* is in fact no more than the understanding of the early Muslims of the sources of Islam.[26] That understanding, as will be shown below, must have been, and was in fact, influenced by the early Muslims' experience and perception of their world.

Given the then prevailing violent tribal rivalry and severe social and gender discrimination, the early Muslims in fact improved on contemporary practice by restricting non-gender discrimination to religion and reducing the severity of discrimination against women. To do that, the early jurists emphasized those aspects of the Islamic sources which justified and supported such religious discrimination. Those particular aspects were developed at a time when the fundamental sources of Islam, namely *Qur'ān* and *Sunnah*,[27] were specifically addressing the concrete problems of an Islamic state in seventh century Arabia.[28] As long as the problems persisted and the answers remained valid for the following centuries, it was natural and proper for *Shari'ah* to remain the way it was. Now that the problems have changed, and the historical answers ceased to be valid, I maintain,

26. For a general survey of the origins and development of *Shari'ah* see N. Coulson, *A History of Islamic Law* (Edinburgh: Edinburgh University Press, 1964).
27. According to Muslim belief, the *Qur'ān* is the literal and final word of God while *Sunnah* is the record of what the Prophet is believed to have said and done.
28. The distinction between the different stages of Islam, and implications of that distinction for our present purposes, are explained in the text accompanying note 41 below.

new answers must be developed out of the *Qur'ān* and *Sunnah*. This would be the Islamic *Shari'ah* for today. Before indicating one way in which modern Muslims can build on this analysis to resolve the problem of the rights of religious minorities from within the Islamic context, let us first outline *Shari'ah's* position on non-Muslim minorities.

Shari'ah classifies the subjects of an Islamic state into three main religious categories:[29] Muslims; People of the Book, being non-Muslims who believe in one of the heavenly revealed scriptures, mainly Christians and Jews; and Unbelievers, being non-Muslims who do not believe in one of the heavenly revealed scriptures. Muslim males are the only full citizens of an Islamic state.[30] People of the Book may be granted some rights of citizens if they submit to Muslim sovereignty under what is known as a compact of *dhimmh*, a charter of rights and duties with the Islamic state. Unbelievers are not even entitled to this option of limited citizenship except under temporary *āmān*, safe conduct.

The compact of *dhimmh* entitles the particular community of People of the Book to security of the person and property, freedom to practice their own religion, and a degree of internal community autonomy to conduct their personal private affairs in accordance with their religious law and customs. *Dhimmis*, members of these communities, may continue to enjoy these rights as long as they conform to the terms of their compact with the Muslim state. The most important constant feature of these compacts was the payment of *jizyh*, a poll-tax paid as tribute and symbol of submission to Muslim rule.[31]

According to the theory of *Shari'ah*, *dhimmis* are not allowed to participate in the public affairs of an Islamic state. They are not allowed to hold any position of authority over Muslims although Muslims may, and do, hold such positions over *dhimmis*. *Dhimmis* may practice their religion in private, but they are not allowed to proselytize or preach their faith in public. A *dhimmi* is allowed and even encouraged to embrace Islam while a Muslim may never abandon Islam.[32]

As to Unbelievers, *Shari'ah* does not contemplate their permanent resi-

29. The following survey is based on a variety of primary Arabic sources such as Abū Yūsuf, *Kitab al-Kharaj* (Cairo: *al-Matba'h al-Salafiyya*, 1382 *Hijri*) translated by A. Ben Shemesh as *Taxation in Islam*, vol. III (Leiden: E. J. Brill, 1969); Ibn Qayyim al-Jawẓīyah, *Aḥkam Ahl Al-Dhimmah* (Damascus: *Matba'h Jami'ah Dimashq*, 1961). For concise and accurate statement of *Shari'ah* rules for non-Muslims see generally M. Khadduri, *War and Peace in the Law of Islam* (Baltimore: The Johns Hopkins Press, 1955). See also generally H. A. R. Gibb and J. H. Kramers, Shorter *Encyclopaedia of Islam* (Leiden: E. J. Brill, 1953) s.v. "*Ahl al-Kitab*," 16–17, "*Dhimma*," 75–76, "*Dizya*," 91–92, "*Kafir*," 205–206, and "*Shirk*," 542–544.

30. The further distinction between Muslim men and women, and its human rights implications, are not discussed in this article. On this issue see El Naiem, note 7 above.

31. See sources cited in note 29 above; Daniel C. Dennett, *Conversion and the Poll Tax in Early Islam* (Cambridge: Harvard University Press, 1950).

32. As indicated in note 21 above, it is a capital offense for a Muslim to convert to any other faith or otherwise repudiate his faith in Islam. A number of other legal consequences also

dence, let alone partial citizenship of an Islamic state. Unbelievers are to be killed on sight unless they are granted temporary *āmān,* safe conduct, by the Muslims.[33] If an Unbeliever is granted such *āmān,* then his or her rights and duties are determined by the terms of the *āmān.* Once it has lapsed or been revoked, they become *harbis,* at war with the Muslims. As such, they have no permanent and general sanctity of life or property.

When we apply these *Shari'ah* principles to a modern nation-state, such as the Sudan, we find that the human rights implications are very serious indeed. For the non-Muslim Sudanese, about one-third of the population, the immediate options are to become Muslims, *dhimmis* if they happen to be People of the Book, or become *harbis* to be killed on sight unless they are allowed temporary *āmān.*

If the *Shari'ah* legislation enacted in 1983–1984 is to be enforced strictly, Sudanese *dhimmis* would, therefore, be second-class citizens in their own country.[34] In exchange for the privilege of being defended by the Muslims, the *dhimmis* of the Sudan would be, legally speaking, disqualified from holding general executive or judicial office and denied full participation in the political process for the government of their own country. If *Shari'ah* legislation is enforced, "unbelievers" among the Sudanese would not be allowed even these "privileges" of partial citizenship.[35]

These modern implications of strict *Shari'ah* may be seen today in Khomeini's Iran which purports to be governed in accordance with these principles. The 1979 Constitution of the Islamic Republic of Iran reflects an

---

follow upon apostasy. See An-Na'im, "The Islamic Law of Apostasy," note 21 above, and Rudolph Peters and Gert J. J. De Vries, "Apostasy in Islam," *IVII Die Welt des Islams* (1976–1977), 1.

33. Chapter 9 verse 5 of the *Qur'ān* is translated by Abdullah Yusuf Ali in *The Holy Qur'ān* (Qatar National Printing Press, undated), 439, as follows:

> But when the forbidden months (the four months of Grace in the Arabic-Muslim calendar) are past, then fight and slay the Pagans wherever ye find them, and seize them, beleaguer them, and lie in wait for them in every stratagem (of war); but if they repent, and establish regular prayers and practise regular charity, then open the way for them: For God is Oft-Forgiving, Most Merciful.

Āmān or safe conduct was originally intended to be temporary, but as the Muslim domain expanded and it became necessary to accommodate communities of Unbelievers, the Muslims gradually relaxed the definition of *dhimmh* to include these communities. The strict *Shari'ah* rule, however, remains that only People of the Book, mainly Christians and Jews, may be offered a compact of *dhimmh.* See the *Qur'ān* chapter 9 verse 29. On Islamic juridicial controversy regarding the precise status of Unbelievers, see Al-Shāfi'ī, *Al-Risāla,* translated by Majid Khadduri as *Islamic Jurisprudence: Shāfi'ī's Risāla* (Baltimore: The Johns Hopkins Press, 1961), 58–59, 265–266; Al-Shaybānī, *Siyar,* translated by Majid Khadduri as *The Islamic Law of Nations: Shaybānī's Siyar* (Baltimore: The Johns Hopkins Press, 1966), 142–154, 224, 275–283; Muhammad Hamidullah, *The Muslim Conduct of State,* rev. 3d ed. (Lahore: Sh. M. Ashraf, 1953), 106–122, 322–331.

34. This is the strict implication of the application of *Shari'ah* as enacted into Sudanese law in 1983–1984. The enforcement of *Shari'ah* legislation, however, is being resisted by non-Muslim Sudanese, mainly in the southern part of the country.

35. Unbelievers are of course defined by *Shari'ah* regardless of how the individual or group regard their own religious belief. The criterion is not belief in God as such, but rather such belief as is acceptable to *Shari'ah.*

explicit view of these limitations from the particular *Shi'ah* sectarian perspective. Article 12 of the Constitution declares the *Twelvers Shi'ah* sect to be the official and dominant faith in Iran, but tolerates Muslims of other denominations. According to Article 13, Zoroastrians, Jews, and Christians are "recognized minorities who, *within the limits of the law,* are free to perform their own religious rites, and who, *in matters relating to their personal affairs and teachings,* may act in accordance with their religion."[36] Although the Constitution does not expressly say so, the obvious implication of these provisions is that nonrecognized minorities, including the *Bahá'ís* and other Unbelievers, are not even entitled to these rights.[37]

Article 14 of the Iranian Constitution does provide for the treatment of non-Muslims, presumably the "recognized minorities," in accordance with "the dictates of virtue and Islamic justice" and with "honor to their human rights." But the Article adds the sinister proviso that "[t]his principle will be applicable only to those who do not become involved *in conspiracies and activities which are anti-Islamic or are against the Islamic Republic of Iran.*"[38] Since it is up to the state to determine when a person is so involved, every non-Muslim risks being denied treatment in accordance with "virtue, Islamic justice and honor to human rights" at the discretion of the state.

These constitutional manifestations of *Shari'ah* are obviously radically inconsistent with the universal human rights of religious minorities outlined above. The Iranian Constitution may be more explicit, but the risk of similar radical inconsistency exists under all constitutions of Muslim countries, such as Algeria, Kuwait, Somalia, and Syria, which declare Islam to be the official religion of the state, and especially those that make *Shari'ah* "a main source of legislation."[39] The ambivalence of these constitutions is illustrated by the contradictory provision of Article 2 of the Constitution of Mauritania, for example, which states that "[t]he Muslim religion is the religion of the Mauritanian people. The Republic shall guarantee to all freedom of conscience and the right to practice their religion."[40] One may well wonder what the guarantee of liberty of conscience means when *Shari'ah,* the

36. Constitution of Iran, note 1 above. Emphasis added.
37. For documentation of the persecution of Bahá'ís in Iran see G. Nash, *Iran's Secret Pogrom, The Conspiracy to Wipe-Out the Bahá'ís* (Suffolk: Neville Spearman, 1982) and Douglas Martin, *The Persecution of the Bahá'ís of Iran, 1844–1984* (The Association of Bahá'í Studies, 1984). Although the Bahá'ís have been persecuted in Iran from the mid-nineteenth century, the motivation and justification of their persecution have always ostensibly been "Islamic" as they are regarded as apostates from Islam.
38. Constitution of Iran, note 1 above. Emphasis added.
39. See Article 3 of the Algerian Constitution and Article 3(a) of the Somali Constitution which make Islam the state religion. Article 2 of the Kuwaiti Constitution and Article 3 of the Syrian Constitution specifically provide that *Shari'ah* "is a main source of legislation." Blaustein and Flanz, note 1 above. The majority of the constitutions of Muslim countries make Islam the state religion, while some of them add the specific provision that *Shari'ah* is a main source of legislation.
40. A. J. Peaslee, *Constitutions of Nations,* vol. I (the Hague, Netherlands: Martinus Nijhoff, 1974), 503.

religious law of Islam that is constitutionally sanctioned as the religion of the people, severely restricts liberty of conscience and formally discriminates on grounds of religion.

In view of this extremely serious ambivalence, it becomes imperative that the precise implications of religious liberty and the rights of religious minorities be authoritatively discussed and settled within the Islamic tradition. The Muslims are not to be allowed to treat religious minorities in this way because they believe that their own religious law authorizes them to do so. Otherwise, we would have to accept not only similar mistreatment of Muslim minorities in non-Islamic states, but also the complete negation of all the achievements of the domestic civil liberties and international human rights movements. If this type of argument is allowed, all forms and degrees of human rights violations, including torture and even genocide, may be rationalized or justified with reference to alleged religious or cultural codes or norms.

Cultural relativism can never be allowed to go this far. This cannot be justified today even if the above-mentioned principles of *Shari'ah* represent Islam's final word on non-Muslims. I do not believe, moreover, that these principles of *Shari'ah* are Islam's final word. I do believe that Islamic *Shari'ah* can be reformed from the fundamental sources of Islam to fully accommodate and even contribute to the further development of the current universal standards. In the following section I outline one way in which *Shari'ah* can be brought into full accord with universal human rights.

AN APPROACH TO MODERN *SHARI'AH*

To identify the roots of discrimination against non-Muslims and other similar problems, and to pave the way to their solution, we need to emphasize the basic distinction between Islam itself, as derived from the totality of its sources, and the actual historical experience of the Muslims which tended to emphasize certain aspects of Islam. The experience of the Muslims, like that of any other people, was shaped by the operative economic, social, and political forces at any given point of Muslim history. These same forces, however, were influenced by, and in turn influenced, Muslim religious law, the *Shari'ah*. At a deeper level of analysis one should look at the dynamics of the interaction between these existentialistic factors and the formal law. This fascinating study is not, however, the subject of this article. It is nevertheless important to note for our purposes here the complexity and interdependence of these two sets of factors because in this process lie both the modern problem and its answer.

The systematic analysis of the nature and actual development of *Shari'ah* clearly establishes the obvious fact that *Shari'ah* is not the whole of

Islam but rather the early Muslims' understanding of the sources of Islam. The basic sources of Islam are the *Qur'ān* and *Sunnah* (the living example of the Prophet's own life in accordance with the *Qur'ān*). When we look more closely at the process by which these two basic sources were used to develop *Shari'ah* we find the following significant facts.

First, the *Qur'ān* itself was revealed in two distinct but overlapping stages, the earlier stage of Mecca between 610 and 622, and the latter stage of Medina between 622 and 632.[41] The existence of these two stages is beyond dispute because the text of the *Qur'ān* itself indicates which chapters and verses were revealed in Mecca and which were revealed in Medina. Also beyond dispute is the clear difference in the nature and content of the two sets of revelations. While the earlier texts tended to be of general religious and moral content, the latter texts were clearly more specific and legalistic. This difference in the nature and content of revelation reflects the difference in the nature of the Muslim society and the role of the Prophet in the two stages. Following the statement of the basic underlying religious and moral norms of the Mecca stage, the Prophet set about establishing the first Muslim political state in Medina. In this way the *Qur'ān* in theory, and the Prophet in practice, had to respond to the concrete realities of establishing an Islamic state in seventh century Arabia. This process did not need to exhaust the whole of the religious and moral principles of Islam as established in the Mecca stage.[42] Seen in this light, the Medina model of the Islamic state was obviously a specific model in response to a concrete situation.

The second significant fact is that while the text of the *Qur'ān* was largely recorded during the Prophet's own lifetime and finally and authoritatively written by the time of his third successor, the *Khaliffa* Osman,[43] the *Sunnah* was not recorded until well into the second and third centuries of Islam. Through an elaborate process of authentication and selection, Muslim jurists established what they believed to be the true *Sunnah* of the Prophet by the third century of Islam. The majority of Muslims today accept those records as valid, although controversy continues as to the au-

41. Mecca is the Prophet's hometown in western Arabia where he started to receive and preach the *Qur'ān*. As a result of continued and mounting persecution of his followers, culminating in a conspiracy to kill the Prophet himself, he migrated with his followers to Medina, another town in western Arabia, in 622.

42. *Ayat al-ahkam*, the verses employed to develop *Shari'ah*, do not exceed one hundred, or at most five hundred, out of a total of over six thousand verses in the *Qur'ān*. The difference in the number of legal verses is due to differences in the criteria employed in identifying these verses.

43. Parts of the texts of the *Qur'ān* were written during the Prophet's own lifetime, but most of it was memorized by the Muslims themselves. The record of the whole *Qur'ān*, prepared during the reign of Osman, the third *Khaliffa* or successor to the Prophet, is now accepted by all Muslims to be the authentic text of the *Qur'ān*.

thenticity of some marginal traditions.[44] The importance of noting this problem in relation to the second sacred source of Islam is not to raise doubt as to the authenticity of the recorded *Sunnah* but rather to appreciate that the process of authentication and selection itself must have been affected by the limitations of both the transmitters and the collectors.[45] The transmitters must have tended to remember those aspects of the *Sunnah* which they understood best while the collectors must have tended to accept those aspects which seemed to be confirmed by their own perception of Muslim reality. The understanding of the transmitters as well as the acceptance by the collectors were in this way influenced by their own experience and circumstances. It would, therefore, follow that we should understand the available texts of authentic *Sunnah* in light of the actual process of its authentication and collection.

The third significant fact is that the *Shari'ah,* as a body of positive law, was developed by Muslim jurists in the second and third century of Islam. The raw material out of which *Shari'ah* was constructed was not, therefore, the pure *Qur'ān* and *Sunnah,* but rather the *Qur'ān* and *Sunnah* as already understood and practiced by generations of Muslims. Muslims are now agreed that the sources of *Shari'ah* are not only the *Qur'ān* and *Sunnah,* but also include *ijmā',* consensus, and *qiās,* analogy. The *ijtihad,* independent juristic reasoning, of the leading companions of the Prophet and the early jurists, has thus become a formative force in the construction of *Shari'ah.*

To note these facts is not to imply that *Shari'ah,* as perceived in its own historical context, was distorted or misrepresented by the early jurists. On the contrary, it is my firm conviction that *Shari'ah* has developed in the only way it should, and could possibly, have developed in that historical context. *Shari'ah* is the law of Islam for the Muslim community and must, therefore, be stated and interpreted by the Muslims themselves. The early jurists, in my view, did an excellent job and succeeded in serving the needs and aspirations of their community for centuries. By the same token, however, it should be open to modern Muslim jurists to state and interpret the

---

44. Mainstream Muslims, commonly known as *Sunnis,* accept the records of leading *Sunnah* collectors such as Bukhari and Muslim, as the true text of the *Sunnah* of the Prophet. *Shi'ah* Muslims and the followers of minor and other largely extinct schools of Islamic jurisprudence tend to emphasize other collections of *Sunnah.*

45. The main collectors of *Sunnah,* the Prophet's words and deeds, were *ibn Hanbal,* who died in 855 A.D.; *Bukhari,* who died in 869; *Muslim,* who died in 874; *ibn Majah,* who died in 886; *Abu Dawd,* who died in 888; *Tormozi,* who died in 892; and *Nasa'y,* who died in 915. When we note that the Prophet, whose *Sunnah* these jurists recorded for the first time, died in 632 A.D., we can appreciate that what they collected and recorded existed as oral tradition for at least two hundred years. The jurists employed sophisticated techniques for checking the credibility of the transmitters of the oral tradition of *Sunnah* and corroborating their reports. The collectors rejected what they believed to have been fabricated or uncorroborated and classified what they did include in terms of their own criteria of the strength or weakness of the chain of reporting and other corroborative evidence.

law for their contemporaries even if such statement and interpretation were to be, in some respects, different from the inherited wisdom.

I say in some respects because I do not conceive of all aspects of *Shari'ah* as open to restatement and reinterpretation. Belief in the *Qur'ān* as the final and literal word of God and faith in the Prophet Mohammed as the final prophet remain the essential prerequisites of being a Muslim. The prescribed worship rituals such as prayer and fasting, known as the five pillars of Islam, remain valid and binding on every Muslim. What is open to restatement and reinterpretation, I submit, are the social and political aspects of *Shari'ah*. Since both the social and physical environments have changed enormously from the time *Shari'ah* was developed, the law must also change in response to new circumstances. The basic requirement of such law reform is that it must be based on Islam's fundamental sources, namely the *Qur'ān* and *Sunnah*. Otherwise, the proposed reforms would be secular and not religious.

In light of this analysis, my thesis in relation to religious minorities in the Muslim context is as follows:

1. The status of non-Muslim religious minorities under *Shari'ah* is not consistent with current universal standards of human rights.

2. The current state of affairs cannot be justified on claims of Islamic cultural relativism. Muslims are not free to treat their religious minorities as they please unless and until the Muslim cultural norms are consistent with the relevant universal standards.

3. It is not only possible, but also imperative, that the status of non-Muslims under *Shari'ah* be reformed from within the fundamental sources of Islam, namely the *Qur'ān* and *Sunnah*. Such reform would at once be both Islamic and fully consistent with universal human rights standards.

These propositions and the analysis on which they are based are founded on the work of the late Sudanese Muslim reformer *Ustadh* Mahmoud Mohammed Taha.[46] *Ustadh* Mahmoud suggested that the fundamental and universal message of Islam is to be found in the *Qur'ān* and *Sunnah* texts of the earlier stage of Mecca. According to this Muslim reformer,

46. *Ustadh* Mahmoud has written extensively in Arabic. The English translation of his main book, *The Second Message of Islam*, prepared by the present author, will be published by Syracuse University Press in the spring of 1987. *Ustadh Mahmoud* was executed by former President Nimieri of Sudan for his opposition of what he regarded to be premature and arbitrary application of *Shari'ah* in the Sudan in 1983–1984. *Ustadh* Mahmoud maintained that *Shari'ah* must be reformed along the lines he suggested before it can be applied today. On the circumstances of the trial and execution of *Ustadh* Mahmoud see An-Na'im, note 21 above.

those texts were not enacted into law and did not provide the basis of the first Islamic state of Medina because the concrete socioeconomic and political circumstances of seventh century Arabia did not permit their practical implementation. Those earlier sources, argued *Ustadh* Mahmoud, were not lost forever but rather postponed until such time as it would be possible to enact them into law. Citing *Qur'ānic* verses of the Meccan era which support complete freedom of choice and prohibit any degree of coercion of non-Muslims,[47] he concluded that the modern law of Islam, modern *Shari'ah,* should not authorize discrimination against non-Muslims in any degree, shape, or form. In this way, all citizens of a modern Islamic state must enjoy full rights of citizenship, regardless of religion or belief.

As far as one can see from the available Muslim literature, the specific nethodology proposed by *Ustadh* Mahmoud seems to be the most viable and effective way of achieving complete respect for the rights of religious minorities under Islamic law. Needless to say, one is equally open to accept any other methodology which is capable of achieving the same results. The object of modern Islamic law reform should be to remove all discrimination against non-Muslims and legally guarantee complete freedom of conscience and belief. Any reform methodology that can achieve this objective is welcome.

CONCLUSION

The international human rights movement has succeeded in establishing universal human rights standards for religious minorities based on moral as well as pragmatic arguments. Faced with these arguments, modern Muslim countries have had to participate in the formulation and adoption of these standards, not only at the international level, but also at the regional and national levels. Nevertheless, extremely serious tensions exist between these standards and the Muslims' historic religious law, *Shari'ah*. Since the Muslims cannot, and should not be allowed to, justify discrimination against and persecution of non-Muslims on the basis of Islamic cultural norms, the Muslims themselves must seek ways of reconciling *Shari'ah* with fundamental human rights.

The choice of the particular methodology for achieving this result must be left to the discretion of the Muslims themselves. A cultural relativist position on this aspect of the problem is, in my view, valid and acceptable. I would argue, however, that no cultural relativist argument may be allowed to justify derogation from the basic obligation to uphold and protect the full human rights of religious minorities, within the Islamic or any other cultural context.

---

47. Such verses include chapter 16 verse 125 and chapter 18 verse 29, *Qur'ān*, note 33 above.

[13]
The Rights of Women and International Law in the Muslim Context*

The religious nature of Islamic Law (Shari'a), makes it difficult for Muslims to appear critical of that law. They tend to regard the specific jurisprudential interpretations and formulations of Shari'a as divine and heavenly as the sources of Islam itself, namely the *Qur'an* and *Sunna*.[1] Whether in relation to the rights of women, or any other aspect of Shari'a, a Muslim cannot be comfortable in his or her criticism of the establishment formulations of Shari'a and, more importantly, expect other Muslims to accept and act upon such criticism, depends on whether, he or she can base the criticism on some provisions of the *Qur'an* and *Sunna*.

For Muslims, the debate and controversy over the interpretation and implications of texts of *Qur'an* and *Sunna* are acceptable, if not expected, although the intolerance of some Muslims may cause those

---

* Faculty of Law, University of Khartoum, Sudan. Visiting Professor of Law, UCLA, 1985-87. I am grateful to Professor Nancy Galleger of the Department of History, University of California at Santa Barbara, for reading a draft of this article and making helpful suggestions and comments.

1. The *Qur'an* is the Arabic text of what Muslims believe to be the literal and final word of God as revealed to the Prophet Muhammad between 610 and 632 A.D.

Sunna are the records of what the prophet is believed to have said and done in the interpretation and application of Islam.

The *Qur'an* was recorded shortly after the Prophet's death and its Arabic text is accepted by all Muslims as authetic and beyond dispute. *Sunna*, however, was not collected and recorded until the second and third centuries of Islam, eight and ninth centuries A.D. Certain records of *Sunna*, such as those of Bukhari (died 869 A.D.) and Muslim (died 874 A.D.) are accepted by Muslims in general as containing authentic (*sahih*) *Sunna*. Nevertheless, controversy continues among the Muslims as to the authenticity of some *Sunna* reports and the relationship between the *Qur'an* and *Sunna*. It is not settled, for example, to what extent *Sunna* may restrict or otherwise affect the interpretation of some of the verses of the *Qur'an*. These jurisprudential and methodological questions can be relevant to the reform of Shari'a in relation to the rights of women suggested in this article.

holding unorthodox views to suffer for their opinions.[2] Complete secularism, however, is unacceptable to the majority of Muslims. Muslims believe that they have a very clear and definite obligation to conduct every aspect of their public, as well as private, life in accordance with principles of the *Qur'an* and *Sunna*.[3] While subscribing to this sense of religious obligation as a matter of principle, and appreciating the political fact that this sense of obligation is shared by the vast majority of Muslims throughout the world, one may nevertheless question the appropriateness of the modern application of certain historical formulations of Shari'a. The obligation to maintain the religious law, I submit, does not necessarily mean the application of Shari'a in its historical formulations.[4]

This article discusses some aspects of the relationship between Shari'a and current international standards on the rights of women. The article starts with a statement of the main relevant principles of Shari'a on the rights of women not only because of the historical role of Shari'a but also in view of the likely re-establishment of Shari'a in the public domain. This trend, however, is unlikely to have free field because of the impact of secularization in recent Muslim history. Following a brief assessment of the interaction between secularization and re-Islamization in the sense of the application of Shari'a, the article proceeds to consider the role of international law on the rights of women in the Muslim world. In conclusion, the article proposes an approach to the rights of Muslim women, combining traditional and modern forces in order to promote the rights of women in a coherent and realistic fashion.

---

2. Although the Prophet is reported to have said that the differences of opinion among the Muslims is a blessing from God, and despite the existence of a wide range of schools of Islamic jurisprudence, often with differences of the opinion within the same school, proponents of unorthodox interpretations of the sources are sometimes charged with apostasy (heresy) punishable with death. For a discussion of the recent trial and execution of a Muslim scholar because of his unorthodox views, including a call for the reform of Shari'a in relation to the rights of women, *see* A. An-Na'im, *The Islamic Law of Apostasy and its Modern Applicability: A Case from the Sudan*, 16 *Religion* 197 (1986).

3. The *Qur'an* 5:44-47. 24:51 and many other verses require the Muslims to conduct all their public and private affairs in accordance with what was revealed by God and decreed by the Prophet.

4. The religious obligations is to the sources, the *Qur'an* and *Sunna*, and not to their historical interpretation by Muslim jurists. The technique for reinterpretation of the *Qur'an* and *Sunna* in order reconcile Islamic law with the full range of human rights, including the rights of women, to which I personally subscribe, is the one advanced by the late Sudanese Muslim reformer *Ustadh* Mahmoud Mohamed Taha. For an authoritative statement of his theory, see the English translation of his book, THE SECOND MESSAGE OF ISLAM (A. An-Na'im trans. 1987).

Although reference will be made to the need for reform of Shari'a on the rights of women, and to a specific proposal to achieve such reform, this subject will not be considered in detail for two reasons. First, this is an internal debate for the Muslims to conduct and settle among themselves. Second, such reform involves consideration of alternative approaches and technical matters which may not be of interest to the readers of this article. The need for such reform, and the existence of proposals to realize it in practice, must nevertheless be noted here.

THE THEORY OF THE RIGHTS OF WOMEN IN SHARI'A

The Muslim world is a vast geographical area, extending from west and north Africa, through the Middle East and the southern Soviet Union to Indonesia. According to generally accepted estimates, there are approximately 837-million Muslims in the world today.[5] As can be expected, the vast spread of Muslim lands and the tremendous diversity of their cultural and ethic composition have affected the interpretation and application of Islam.[6]

Since its initial phenomenal expansion within the first few decades of its existance, Islam has tended to incorporate and assimilate the social customs and institutions of the various regions and communities which converted to Islam.[7] As Shari'a was gradually developed as a comprehensive system of law and a way of life over the first three centuries of Islam, around the eighth to the ninth centuries A.D.,[8] it was supposed to be used as the criterion for screening and admitting, or

5. MUSLIM PEOPLES, A WORLD ETHNOGRAPHIC SURVEY, xxi (R. Weeks, ed. 1984) [hereinafter cited as WEEKS, MUSLIM PEOPLES]. See also C. Geertz, ISLAM OBSERVED: RELIGIOUS DEVELOPMENT IN MOROCCO AND INDONESIA (1968).

6. For current manifestations of the different cultural perspectives on the interpretation and application of Islam, see the articles on various Muslim peoples in WEEKS, MUSLIM PEOPLES.

7. On the expansion of Islam and assimilation and Islamization of various cultures, see generally CARL BROCKELMAN, HISTORY OF THE ISLAMIC PEOPLES (J. Carmichael and M. Perlmann trans. 1960) and REUBEN LEVY, THE SOCIAL STRUCTURE OF ISLAM (1969).

8. On the history and Development of Shari'a see generally N.J. COULSON, A HISTORY OF ISLAMIC LAW (1964). The major jurists, and the schools of thought (Madhahb) they established, tended to be concentrated in the main urban centers of Arabia, southern Iraq, Syria and Egypt before spreading throughout the Muslim world in subsequent centuries.

rejecting, local custom and social institutions.[9] Although a purist may conceive of this process in terms of a preexisting and fully intregrated body of Shari'a influencing and validating local customs and institutions, I would agree with the more realistic view which perceives the process as a dynamic process of interaction between Islamic principles and endogenous norms and practices. Local customs, attitudes and institutions have naturally influenced the interpretation and application of Shari'a as law in the particular region, as well as being themselves influenced by Islam and its Shari'a law.

Disentangling and distinguishing the "pure" Shari'a from local custom may be a fascinating subject for some, while others may declare this to be an impossible task. Fortunately, we need not undertake this difficult, if not impossible, task for our present purposes.[10] What needs to be emphasized here is that there is a body of general principles and detailed rules which the Muslims as a whole accept as the authoritative statement of Shari'a.[11] In particular, the prevailing conceptions of Shari'a are either the law of the land or at least very influential in the formulation and maintenance of certain attitudes and policies with regard to the rights of women. It is for this reason that we have to take Shari'a into account as a very important consideration in assessing the current position and future porspects of the rights of women in the Muslim world.

Although it is difficult to generalize, in view of the wide cultural diversity of the Muslim peoples and the extensive scope of Shari'a,[12]

---

9. Coulson in A HISTORY OF ISLAMIC LAW, *id.* at 38, descibes the process of Islamization as follows:

"[T]he starting point was the review of local practice, legal and popular, in the light of their principles of conduct enshrined in the *Qur'an*. Institutions and activities were individually considered, then approved or rejected according to whether they measured up or fell short of these criteria."

10. The difficulty or impossibility of this task is due to two problems. First, there is the problem of the lack of verifiable information on the pre-Islamic customs of the Islamized peoples. Second, since Shari'a took two to three centuries to evolve as a comprehensive system of law, it would be extremely difficult, if not impossible, to determine the precise point in time when Islamization took place. A people and their customs may have been influenced by Islamic norms for generations prior to the formulation of Shari'a as legal rules and principles or prior to its formal application in the particular region.

11. Subject to some differences between the established schools of Islamic jurisprudence adhered to in the various regions of the Muslim world, Shari'a signifies an identifiable and generally agreed upon main principle of law and ethics accepted by all Muslims.

12. Shari'a provides for codes of ethics, social interaction and a positive legal system. It regulates the full range of human activities, from religious rituals, social manners and political institutions and relationships, to positive legal rules in civil, commercial, criminal and family law matters. Generalizations on such a comprehensive scale for the extremely wide diversity of Muslim cultural traditions is obviously difficult. Reference to principles and rules relevant to the

one can confidently assert that Shari'a has had, and for a very long time, a positive impact on the rights of women.[13] From its very beginning in the seventh century, Shari'a guaranteed all Muslim women an independent legal personality, including the capacity to hold and dispose of property in their own right, a specific share in inheritance, access to education (provided it is conducted in facilities seperate from men) and some participation in public life.[14] At the family law level, for example, Shari'a restricted polygamy and guaranteed a wife's right to maintenance and decent treatment.[15] It also provides for the right to judicial divorce, on certain specific grounds.[16] This level of achievement may not appear impressive by some modern standards, but it has meant very signficant improvements in women's rights when viewed in historical perspective.[17] Shari'a on the rights of women, I would suggest, compares very favorably with any other legal system until the nineteenth century.

A historical perspective, however, is a poor excuse for the current inferior status of women under Shari'a when compared to other contemporary legal systems or when judged by the emerging international standards. Although the Muslim women's legal personality is complete in theory,[18] their access to opportunities for making that personality meaningful are rather restricted. Gender segregation and requirements of the veil and confinement to the home, as a general

rights of women will therefore be confined to the most fundamental principles which are accepted as binding by the vast majority of Muslims.

13. It is not suggested here that the position of women in pre-Islamic Arabia was uniform or necessarily bad in every respect. There is clear evidence of some recognition and relatively good status for some women prior to the coming of Islam. *See, generally*, L. SABAGH, AL-MAR'A FI AL-TARIKH AL-'ARABI (WOMEN IN ARAB HISTORY — IN ARABIC) (1975). What is suggested, however, is that women in pre-Islamic Arabia generally had a status inferior to that of men. In particular, women suffered from a number of legal and social institutions which Islam sought to redress. *See*, for example, Fazlur Rahman, "Status of Women in the *Qur'an*" in WOMEN AND REVOLUTION IN IRAN 37 (G. NASHAT ED., 1983). The improvements introduced by Shari'a should therefore be seen in relation to the general status of women, and with reference to the specific problems addressed by Shari'a in that context.

14. *See generally*, AMEER ALI, THE SPIRIT OF ISLAM, 222-57 (1922).

15. JOHN ESPOSITO, WOMEN IN MUSLIM FAMILY LAW, CHAPTER 3 (1982).

16. M. El Arousi, *Judicial Dissolution of Marriage*, 7 *Journal of Islamic and Comparative Law* 13, (1977).

17. LEVY, THE SOCIAL STRUCTURE OF ISLAM, *supra* note 7 at 91-96; R. Smith, Kinship and Marriage in Early Arabia, 92-94 (1939).

18. While all the major schools of Islamic jurisprudence accept the right of women to hold and dispose of property in their own right, the Maliki school, currently prevailing in West Africa, denies unmarried women capacity to conclude contracts and restricts the right of married women to dispose of their own property. See NOEL J. COULSON, COMMERICAL LAW IN THE GULF STATES, THE ISLAMIC LEGAL TRADITION, 36-37 (1984).

rule, tend to diminish the practical value of Muslim women's theoretical entitlement to certain rights and limit their abilities to realize economic independence and educational and other public achievements.[19] Although women are not prohibited by Shari'a from expressing their opinions in public affairs, and may vote on those competing for public office, the above noted restrictions tended to inhibit their ability to exercise these rights in practice. They are also denied competence to hold general high-ranking public office themselves.[20]

Although Shari'a guarantees members of the family of the deceased specific shares in his or her estate, a woman's guaranteed share in inheritance is generally half the share of a man of the same degree of relationship to the deceased.[21] Restrictions on polygamy generally mean that it is lawful for a man to take up to four wives.[22] In contrast to a woman's right to seek a judicial divorce (before a male judge and for specific grounds) man can divorce his wife at will by unilateral repudiation without having to explain his reasons to anyone.[23] A woman's right to decent treatment is subject to the guardianship which a father, brother, husband, uncle or even a son may have on his women wards.[24]

19. The complex and amorphous subject of the veil and gender segregation with clear cultural variations, does not permit a brief summary. *See, generally*, SEPARATE WORLDS: STUDIES OF PURDAH IN SOUTHEAST ASIA (H. PAPANEK AND G. MINAULT EDS., 1982); WOMEN AND REVOLUTION IN IRAN, *supra* note 13, chapter 7; M.U.H. Kah, Purdah and Pologamy (1983); and F. MERNISSI, BEYOND THE VEIL: MALE-FEMALE DYNAMICS IN MODERN MUSLIM SOCIETY (REV. ED. 1987). It is important to note, however, that the relevant principles and practices do have the very clear and definite sanction of the *Qur'an* as in 33:33 and 53.

20. The disqualification of women to hold high-ranking public office is partly based on what is believed to be Qur'anic requirements of the veil and gender segregation noted above which restrict women's ability to seek and exercise the responsibilities of public office. The more important soures of disqualification, however, are Qur'anic, as in 2:282 and 4:34 and *Sunna* statements which have been given this interpretation by the agreement of all schools of jurisprudence. Cf. Fazlur Rahman *supra* note 13.

21. *Qur'an* 4:11 and 176.

22. *Qur'an* 4:3 authorizes a man to take up to four wives provided that he maintain justice among them. This requirement, when read with verse 129 of the same chapter which rules that justice among co-wives is impossible to achieve, can be used to restrict pologamy. Although this interpretation has been adopted to justify such restrictions in some Muslim countries, the traditional view, which leaves compliance with the requirement of justice to the discretion and subjective responsibility of the husband, continues to prevail among the vast majority of Muslims. For an example of progressive reform of Muslim family law see N. Anderson, *The Tunisian Law of Personal Status*, 7 *International and Comparative Law Quarterly* 262 (1958).

23. *See generally Talak* in SHORTER ENCYCLOPEDIA OF ISLAM, 564-7 (H.A.R. Gibb and J.H. Kramers eds. 1953).

24. *Id.* 633 *et seq.* under *Wilaya*, male guardianship over women. According to *Qur'an* 4:34, the main verse on male guardianship over women, a husband may discipline his wife in a number of ways, to the extent of beating her "lightly" in exercise of his guardianship.

It must be emphasized here that this is Shari'a as accepted by the vast majority of Muslims. Space does not permit statement of slight variations among the various schools of Islamic jurisprudence. In any case, none of these established schools challenges the basic principles of these limitations on women. Moreover, the concern here is not with the justifications of these restrictions on the rights of women because such inquiry will not affect the content of the rules. In a religious legal system such as Shari'a, policy arguments are insufficient bases for challenging the rules and replacing them with an alternative set of rules unless one can also rely on scriptural authority. Although a few Muslims are prepared to challenge Shari'a on the rights of women today,[25] they are a tiny minority while the vast majority of Muslims continue to subscribe to the validity of Shari'a restrictions on the rights of women.

It is true, in my view, that the provisions of the *Qur'an* and *Sunna* on women's rights can be interpreted differently. In fact, I am suggesting that we should now rely on this alternative interpretation of the *Qur'an* and *Sunna* in the reformation of Shari'a on the rights of women. The possibility of an alternative interpretation, however, should not be confused with the current authoritative view of Shari'a as accepted by the vast majority of Muslims. We must state Shari'a for what it is, and deal with it in relation to the rights of women, until we are able to replace it with the proposed alternative interpretation.

In general, Shari'a was concerned with guaranteeing certain minimum rights for women and not with achieving complete legal equality between men and women. It is obviously true that complete legal equality was never achieved anywhere in the world until very recently. Some would contend that it is yet to be achieved by even the most advanced and enlightened human societies. I do not believe, however, that complete legal equality between men and women is achievable and must be our objective in the Muslim world today. Although much needs to be done under even the most progressive legal and social systems, the ideal of substantive equality between men and women has found sufficient expression and concrete realization elsewhere to have had a profound impact on many Muslim women, and on some Muslim men.

---

25. Such as *Ustadh* Mahmous Mohamed Taha. See note 4 *supra*.

THE IMPACT OF SECULARIZATION

Since the nineteenth century, the Muslim peoples have experienced the massive influence of external forces of increasing secularization and westernization.[26] The main centers of Muslim civilization (in Turkey, Egypt, Persia and India) have experienced western cultural influences far greater and more profound than the experiences of military defeat and political subjugation. In due course, especially after the end of the First World War, nationalism and secular constitutions replaced pan-Islamism and the ideal of Shari'a as the sole legitimate system.[27]

During what may be called the liberal age, Muslims borrowed extensively from western ideas of equality and emancipation of women. Even in those Muslim countries which professed an Islamic ideology, many practices and policies incompatible with Shari'a were allowed, or maybe forced themselves into the consciousness and lifestyle of many Muslims. To a varying degree, Muslim women became increasingly successful in claiming equality in education, employment and access to public life.[28] This process, I submit, cannot be expected to completely transform the rights of Muslim women for two reasons.

First, secular movements towards equality and emancipation tend to be largely confined to the urban centers. The rights and actual living conditions of rural and nomadic women, who are the vast majority of Muslim women, are likely to remain substantially unaffected by western ideas and institutions.[29] For the most part, the status and

26. HERBERT J. LIEBESNY, THE LAW OF THE NEAR & MIDDLE EAST, READINGS, CASES & MATERIAL, CHAPTER 3 (1975).

27. *Id.* Chapter 4; and Aharon Layish, *The Contribution of the Modernists to the Secularization of Islamic Law*, 14 *Middle East Studies* 263 (1978).

28. *See*, for example, N. AL-RAZAZ, MUSHARAKAT AL-MAR'A FI AL-HAYAH AL-'AMA FI SURIYA (Participation of Women in Public Life in Syria, in Arabic, 1975); D. INGRAMS, THE AWAKENED: WOMEN IN IRAQ (1983); WOMEN IN IRAN: THE CONFLICT WITH FUNDAMENTALISM IN IRAN, 179 F. AZARI, ED. 1983); and E. SULLIVAN, WOMEN IN EGYPTIAN PUBLIC LIFE (1986).

29. J. Bauer, "Poor Women and Social Consciousness in Revolutionary Iran," in WOMEN AND REVOLUTION IN IRAN, *supra* note 13; and A. MAHDI, WOMEN, RELIGION AND THE STATE: LEGAL DEVELOPMENTS IN TWENTIETH CENTURY IRAN 7 (Michigan State University Working Paper #38, 1983). It is not suggested here that secularization and western cultural influences had no impact whatsoever on rural and nomadic women. Under some trickle-down theory, one can see some benefits reaching rural and nomadic women from the social and legal reforms manifested primarily at the urban centers. What is suggested is that these benefits are so little and are so much successfully resisted and neutralized through traditional adjustment mechanisms in favor of maintaining the *status quo* for these "reforms" that they cannot have a significant and lasting effect on the rights of women in the countryside. This assertion is subject, however, to variations in the degree of penetration of reforms as affected by the clarity and

rights of the vast majority of Muslim women continue to be almost exclusively defined by traditional norms, including Shari'a. Shari'a principles, moreover, are easily used to resist the demands even of urban Muslim women. In particular, the strict application of Shari'a law of personal status in marriage, divorce, custody and inheritance mean that women's rights in these crucial areas are not affected by the secularization and westernization of the legal system as a whole.[30] As a result, a fundamental tension exists between women's civil and political rights under the constitution and the general legal system on the one hand, and their private rights as determined by the Shari'a law of personal status on the other hand.

The second related limitation is the resurgence of the so-called Islamic fundamentalism which challenges the basic premise of secularization of public life. The declared aim of these re-Islamization movements, known by various names in the different regions of the Muslim world, is to re-establish Shari'a as the sole source of all aspects of the law, both public and private.[31] To some extent, these movements can be seen as a reaction to western secularization, which is blamed by many Muslims for the political frustration, economic deprivation and social disorganization of Muslim communities.[32] A more fundamental cause of Islamic resurgence, in my view, is the inherent power of Islam as intellectual and spiritual forces. The forces of Islamization were merely suppressed and never neutralized or assimilated in the secularization processes of the liberal age. The forces are now coming to power in Iran, Pakistan and the Sudan, seeking to reverse changes introduced through secularization. In almost all other Muslim countries, the forces of re-Islamization are undermining recent reforms and

---

determination of governmental policies targeting rural and nomadic populations and the socio-economic factors facilitating or obstructing such penetration.

For an example of the interplay of reform and tradition in a Muslim context, see P. J. Higgins, *Women in the Islamic Republic of Iran: Legal, Social and Ideological Changes*, 20 *Signs: Journal of Women in Culture and Society* 477 (1985).

30. MAHDI *id.* at 5. Even in the most secularized Muslim countries, family law and inheritance continue to be governed by Shari'a. J. SCHACHT, INTRODUCTION TO ISLAMIC LAW 76 (1964).

31. *See generally*, VOICES OF RESURGENT ISLAM (J. L. ESPOSITO ED., 1983), and ISLAMIC RESURGENCE IN THE ARAB WORLD (A.E.H. DESSOUKI, ED. 1982).

32. For an analysis of the causes underlying re-Islamization, or Islamic resurgence, *see* K. Ahmad, "The Nature of the Islamic Resurgence" in VOICES OF RESURGENT ISLAM, *id.* at 218.

resisting further changes that may be introduced through the secularization of constitutions and legal systems and progress in the realization of the rights of women, even in terms of civil and political action of the forces of re-Islamization.[33]

Such reversal and regression, however,[34] are unlikely to be complete because the liberal age has already succeeded in changing the awareness of both women and men. Woman's movements, and liberal political forces in general, have taken root and are expected to struggle to maintain their achievements and resist regression under re-Islamization.[35] The best way for doing this, I suggest, is through what may be described as alternative Islamization through the reformation of Shari'a.[36] Islam is too powerful a political and cultural force to abandon to the fundamentalists. As already demonstrated by their challenge to changes achieved through secularization, Islamic movements can easily mobilize mass support for their agenda by appealing

---

33. In relation to Iran, for example, the Khomeini regime has repealed legislation and reversed policies of the previous regime granting women rights in family and public life. *See* Higgins, *Women in the Islamic Republic of Iran: Legal, Social and Ideological Changes, supra* note 29 at 483; MAHDI, *supra* note 29 at 11; WOMEN IN IRAN, *supra* note 28 at 217-21.

According to sections 5 and 46 of the Retribution Act of 1981, *diyah*, compensation for unlawful homicide, for killing a women is fixed as half that for killing a man. Section 33A of the same Act provides that the testimony of women in homicide cases is completely unacceptable. *See* SUROOSH IRFANI, IRAN'S ISLAMIC REVOLUTION: POPULAR LIBERATION OR RELIGIOUS DICTATORSHIP, 211 (1983).

As reported by Omar Asghar Kan, *Political and Economic Aspects of Islamization* is ISLAM, POLITICS AND STATE: THE PAKISTAN EXPERIENCE 147 (M. A. KHAN, ED. 1985), when Pakistani women protested in February 1983 against legislation aimed at making the evidence of two women equal to that of one man, they were brutally beaten. The author also reported that a section of the 'ulama,' religious scholars, demanded the death penalty for these women whom they regarded as guilty of apostasy (heresy) for demonstrating against Qur'anic injunctions.

It should be noted that the *Qur'an* 2:282 specifically requires two male witnesses or one male and two female witnesses for commercial transactions. To apply Shari'a is therefore to disqualify women as witnesses in homicide cases and hold a woman to be half a witness in commercial matters.

34. A recent good example of organized women's action in support of their rights is the International Conference on the Challenges Facing Arab Women in the Coming Decades — held on September 1-3, 1986 at the Arab League Building, Cairo, Egypt, by the Organization of Arab Women Solidarity. For other evidence of action by women in support of their rights *see* sources cited in *supra* note 28; and IN THE SHADOW OF ISLAM: THE WOMEN'S MOVEMENT IN IRAN (A. TABARI AND N. YEGANEH, EDS. 1982).

35. Added to balance with second 34 in text.

36. The call for reform has so far been confined to efforts to seek favorable formulations of the rules of Shari'a applicable to women from within traditional jurisprudence. This process of selection from the various schools of jurisprudence and the opinions of individual jurists will not, I submit, achieve the necessary degree of reform. Fundamental reform of the basic principles of Shari'a in relation to the rights of women is unavoidable if Muslim women are to achieve complete legal equality with men.

to the religious sentiments and allegiance of the vast majority of Muslims. As evidenced by the vocal presence of educated, intelligent and well-organized fundamentalist women, Islam can motivate women themselves to challenge the achievements of the rights of women when conceived as alien western notions.[37] The best way to challenge this, it would seem, is to show that the rights of women are Islamic and not alien western notions, albeit they may find expression in other cultural and religious traditions, both western and nonwestern.

By alternative Islamization I therefore mean the assumption of an Islamic platform in advocating fundamental reform of Shari'a on the rights of women and the provision of Islamic foundations for these rights. This must be done internally through the adoption of imaginative reform techniques for the evolution and reformulation of Shari'a rules relative to women's rights. The two essential characteristics of an appropriate reform technique are, in my view, the ability to provide Islamic legitimacy and effectiveness in achieving the necessary degree of reform. Without legitimacy, on the one hand, the technique may be defeated as secularist and alien. On the other hand, the rights of women would not be served by an approach which does not change substantially the status and rights of women under Shari'a. The choice of an appropriate reform technique is an internal debate for the Muslim advocates of the rights of women to conduct with other Muslims in light of the suggested dual criteria of legitimacy and efficacy. It can neither be settled, nor should it be addressed, by the present paper.[38] What is relevant and must be addressed here is the role of international law in the advocacy of women's rights in the Muslim world.

37. "Moslem Feminists in Discord," N.Y. Times, July 25, 1985, 15-16. It should not be assumed, however, that women speaking from an Islamic platform express uniform views or accept all the restrictions imposed by the prevailing interpretation of Shari'a. For samples of differences in opinion among Muslim spokeswomen *see* IN THE SHADOW OF ISLAM, *supra* note 34 at 171-200.

38. The position of *Ustadh* Mahmoud Mohamed Taha, *supra* note 4, is an example of a modern Islamic approach to achieving respect for the rights of women from within Islam. As indicated earlier, however, this is a minority position. It is up to the Muslim women themselves, with the support of some sympathetic Muslim men, to advance their cause within their own religious and cultural traditions through the work of the late *Ustadh* Mahmoud or a similar approach.

International Law and the Rights of Women

As in the case of other aspects of human rights, customary international law has very little to say on the rights of women. Since individuals were traditionally regarded as objects rather than direct subjects of international law, custom did not address their rights as such.[39] Therefore, the most significant developments in the rights of women have been achieved through treaties and conventions. This was accomplished by both the general human rights instruments and those specialized in the rights of women. Before offering a brief survey of the provisions of these binding treaties, it may be appropriate to refer to the relevance and force of the Universal Declaration of Human Rights (UDHR) as a non-treaty document of special significance.[40]

The provisions of the UDHR include the fundamental principles of equality and freedom from discrimination on grounds such as sex, in relation to any of the rights set forth in the Declaration.[41] Are any of the provisions of the UDHR, and especially the equality and non-discrimination principles, binding on States as a matter of international law? The UDHR was the first major and most widely supported United Nations document giving an authoritative interpretation to the human rights provisions of the United Nations

39. The abolition of slavery in the nineteenth century may be taken as an example of customary international law protection of a human right. It is hard to think of another example of a human right based on custom. Section 702 of the *Restatement (Revised) of the Foreign Relations Law of the United States* does not include gender discrimination, even as a matter of state policy, in its list of customary international law human rights. Nevertheless, International Law, Cases and Materials (L. Henkin, R. C. Pugh, O. Schachter and H. Smit, editors, 2nd ed. 1987) (hereinafter cited as Henkin *et al.*) at 998 assert that "[w]hile gender-based discrimination is still practiced in many states in varying degrees, freedom from gender discrimination as state policy, in many matters, may already have become a principle of customary international law."

40. G. A. Res. 217A (III), U.N. Doc. A/810, at 71 (1948). This document and all the instruments discussed or cited below may be found in International Human Rights Instruments (R. Lillich, ed. 1985) [hereinafter cited as Lillich 1985]. For the Universal Declaration of Human Rights see *id.* 440.1.

41. Articles 1 and 2 of UDHR. These rights include the right to life, liberty and security of the person (Art. 3); freedom from slavery and servitude (Art. 4); guarantee against torture and cruel, inhuman or degrading treatment or punishment (Art. 5); equality before the law (Art. 7); freedom of movement and residence (Art. 13). Obviously, any of these and the other rights set forth in the UDHR are, however, of special significance to women in the sense explained below, namely that women have traditionally been, and continue to be, the most frequent victims of gross and consistent violations of these rights. These especially significant rights under the UDHR include the right to marry and found a family upon free and full consent and with equality at all stages of marriage (Art. 16), the right to participate in government and have equal access to public service (Art. 21), and rights in relation to work (Art. 23).

Charter which is a binding treaty.[42] As such, the UDHR may have more persuasive authority than other resolutions of the General Assembly. Some would even argue that, when taken together with the United Nations Charter and other developments, the UDHR has achieved the status of binding custom.[43] Whether any of its principles, and if so which ones, have become international custom remains to be seen. In any case, the provisions of the UDHR enjoy special moral and political weight and can be used anywhere in the world to support claims to at least the underlying principles of its main provisions.[44]

In the following brief survey of human rights instruments, the focus will be on rights and principles which are of special significance to women. This should not be taken as implying that women are not concerned with the full ranges of human rights. It simply means that besides being equally affected by and concerned with all the social, economic, cultural, civil and political human rights, women have traditionally been victims of certain types of oppression and discrimination which make certain rights specifically applicable to them. In view of space limitations and the subject of this essay, the following brief survey will focus on this second category of rights.

The general human rights instruments, namely the International Covenant on Social, Economic and Cultural Rights (ICSECR) and the International Covenant on Civil and Political Rights (ICCPR), generally give more precise treaty formulation for the principles of the

42. Article 55 of the United Nations Charter provides that the U.N. shall promote, *inter alia*, "c. universal respect for, and observance of, human rights and fundamental freedoms for all without distinction as to race, sex, language, or religion." The Preamble to the U.N. Charter and Articles 1(3), 13(1)(b), 62(2), 68 and 76(c) also refer to human rights in a variety of contexts. Nevertheless, the Charter neither defines nor enumerates human rights.

Another difficulty with using the U.N. Charter as a treaty source of the rights of women is due to the fact that the Charter is unlikely to be treated as a self-executing treaty directly creating enforceable rights. *See* Henkin *et al.* at 984-85.

43. As early as 1968, the Montreal Statement for the Assembly for Human Rights described the UDHR as "an authoritative interpretation of the [United Nations] Charter of the highest order, and has over the years become a part of customary international law." *See* 9 *Journal of the International Commission of Jurists*, 94 at 95 (June 1968). In M. McDougal, H. Lasswell & L. Chen, Human Rights and World Public Order, 274 (1980), the UDHR is also described as "now hailed as an authoritative interpretation of the human rights provision of the United Nations Charter and as established customary law, having the attributes of *jus cogens* and constituting the heart of a global bill of rights." *See* also Lauterpacht, International Law and Human Rights, 145-60 (1950, 1973), and Schwelb, The International Court of Justice and the Human Rights Clause of the Charter, 66 A.J.I.L. 337 (1972).

44. J. G. Starke, *Human Rights and International Law* in Human Rights, 113 at 122 (E. Kamenka & A.E.S. Tay, eds. 1978).

UDHR, thereby making them legally binding on the States Parties.[45] Both Covenants embody the fundamental principle of non-discrimination on grounds such as sex, in relation to any of the rights enunciated, or recognized, in each Covenant.[46] Moreover, Article 3 of both Covenants specifically provides for the obligation undertaken by the States Parties to ensure the equal right of men and women to the enjoyment of all economic, social and cultural rights, or civil and political rights, set forth in the respective Covenant.

The rights enunciated in the ICSECR which appear to be of special significance to women include the right to freely choose or accept work under just and favorable conditions, especially in relation to equal renumeration for work of equal value and equal opportunity to be promoted on no consideration other than seniority and competence.[47] Also especially significant to women is the recognition of the widest possible protection and assistance to the family. Marriage must be entered into with the free consent of the intending spouses.[48] Moreover, the Covenant provides for special protection to mothers during a reasonable period before and after childbirth when working mothers should be accorded paid leave or leave with adequate social security benefits.[49]

Because of the special problems of implementing the full range of social, economic and cultural rights within the limited resources of many countries, Article 2(1) of ICSECR generally requires of each State Party steps with a view *to achieving progressively the full realization* of the rights recognized in this Covenant.[50] Compliance by the State Parties with their undertakings under the Covenant, in light of this consideration, is supposed to be monitored through State reports

45. International Covenant on Economic, Social and Cultural Rights, G.A. Res. 2200 (XXI), 21 U.N. GAOR, Supp. (No. 16) 49, U.N. Doc. A/6136 at 490 (1966); entered into force on January 3, 1976. International Covenant on Civil and Political Rights, R. A. Res. 2200 (XXI) 21 U.N. GAOR, Supp. (No. 16) 52, U.N. Doc. A/6316 at 52 (1966); entered into force on March 23, 1976. For the texts of both Covenants see Lillich 1985 at 170 and 160, respectively.

46. Articles 2(2) of the IOCSECR and 2(1) of ICCPR. The use of the terms "enunciated" in the ICSECR and "recognized" in the ICCPR may be due to the nature of the rights covered by the particular covenant. This has no bearing, however, on the principle of nondiscrimination on the grounds of sex being emphasized in the present context.

47. Articles 6 and 7 of the ICSECR. The obligation under Article 7(c) to ensure equal opportunity to employment promotion "subject to no considerations other than those of seniority and competence" may create difficulties for adopting policies of affirmative action in favor of women, for example, to compensate for previous discrimination. This, however, is a premature concern for Muslim women who are struggling to establish basic legal equality.

48. *Id.* Article 10(1).

49. *Id.* Article 10(2).

50. Emphasis supplied.

to the Secretary-General of the United Nations, with copies for the consideration of the Economic and Social Council.[51] The Secretary-General must also transmit copies of the reports to the specialized agencies in so far as these reports relate to any matter which falls within the responsibilities of the particular agency.[52] The Covenant also provides for arrangements between the Economic and Social Council and the specialized agencies with respect to progress made in achieving observance of the provisions of the Covenant as well as the study of States' reports and general recommendations by the Commission on Human Rights with opportunities for States and specialized agencies to comment on the general recommendations of the Commission on Human Rights.[53] The Economic and Social Council may also submit occasional reports to the General Assembly reports with general recommendations on information received from the States Parties and specialized agencies on the measures taken and progress made in achieving general observance of the rights recognized in the Covenant.[54] On the whole, it is clear that compliance with the obligations under the ICSECR is dependent on the voluntary cooperation of the States, prompted by any political pressure and persuasion through the Social and Economic Council, specialized agencies and the General Assembly of the United Nations.

The ICCPR recognizes as legally binding treaty obligations several rights which may be especially significant to women, such as guarantees against torture, cruel, inhuman or degrading treatment or punishment,[55] freedom from slavery and servitude,[56] and equality before the law.[57] Of particular significance to Muslim women, however, are the provisions relating to marriage and participation in public affairs. Not only is there a right to marry freely and with full consent, but also a requirement on the States Parties to take appropriate steps to ensure equality of rights and responsibilities of spouses as to marriage, during marriage and at its dissolution.[58] Every citizen (of a State Party), has the right and the opportunity, without any distinctions on grounds such as sex, to take part in the conduct of public affairs; this includes the right to vote and to be elected and to have

51. *Id.* Article 16(2)(a).
52. *Id.* Article 16(2)(b).
53. *Id.* Articles 18 to 20.
54. *Id.* Article 21.
55. ICCPR Article 7.
56. *Id.* Article 8.
57. *Id.* Articles 14 and 26.
58. *Id.* Article 23.

access, on general terms of equality, to public service in his [or her] country.[59]

It seems that general agreement among the States Parties on the feasibility of immediate implementation of the full range of the civil and political rights covered by the ICCPR, unlike those of the ICSECR, permits relatively stronger enforcement mechanisms. Thus, the ICCPR provides for the establishment of a Human Rights Committee which considers reports from the States Parties on the measures they have adopted which give effect to the rights recognized in the Covenant and on the progress made in the enjoyment of these rights.[60] Furthermore, Article 41 of ICCPR provides for an optional feature whereby a State Party may lodge complaints that another State Party is not fulfilling its obligations under this Covenant, provided that the two States have both made declarations accepting this complaint procedure. The Article sets out a three-stage process of direct settlement between the two states, mediation by the Human Rights Committee (with a view towards a friendly solution) or through an ad hoc Conciliation Commission with the prior consent of the States Parties concerned.

It is obvious from the great emphasis placed in this State complaint procedure on the consent of the States Parties, and the need for a friendly or amicable solution, that States are unwilling to surrender their national sovereignty over questions of human rights to independent international adjudication. Nevertheless, this optional procedure is a positive move towards greater international jurisidiction over human rights.

A more positive move, however, is to be found in the Optional Protocol to the ICCPR which provides for a procedure whereby an individual may petition the Human Rights Committee when a violation of the rights set forth in ICCPR occurs by a state to whose jurisdiction the individual is subject.[61] Such individual petition can be received only against States which recognize the competence of the

59. *Id.* Article 25.

60. Articles 28 to 39 of the ICCPR are devoted to the composition and regulation of the Human Rights Committee. Article 40 provides for the obligation of States Parties to submit reports, and the process of consideration of these reports and communications with other organizations and specialized agencies of the U.N.

61. Optional Protocol to the International Covenant on Civil and Political Rights. G.A. Res. 2200 (XXI), 21 U.N. GAOR, Supp. (No. 26), U.N. Doc. A/6316 at 59 (1966); entered into force on March 23, 1976.

It should be noted, however, that as of January 1, 1986, this Optional Protocol was ratified by only 34 states while the ICCPR was ratified by 82 states. Henkin *et al.* 990.

Committee in this regard,[62] and subject to several procedural requirements.[63] The Optional Protocol provides for a timetable for communications, comments and consideration by the Committee in closed meetings, leading up to the formulation by the Committee of its views, which must then be forwarded to the State Party concerned and the individual.[64] Further, the Committee must include a summary of its activities under the Optional Protocol in its annual report.[65] Although ultimately dependent on the voluntary acceptance of its procedure by the States, and on the moral weight of the Committee and possibilities of political pressure on the States Parties to avoid negative publicity, the Protocol is significant in its provision of a treaty framework for individual petition.[66]

Most of the rights of women covered by these general instruments are also provided for in specialized instruments of the International Labor Organization (ILO) and other international conventions. Besides the ILO, there are the 1951 Convention Concerning Equal Renumeration for Men and Women Workers for Work of Equal Value,[67] and the 1958 Convention Concerning Discrimination in Respect of Employment and Occupation.[68] Other specialized international conventions include the 1953 Convention on the Political Rights of Women,[69] the 1958 Convention on the Nationality of Married Women,[70] the 1960 UNESCO Convention Against Discrimination in Education,[71] and the 1962 Convention on the Consent to

62. Article 1 of the Optional Protocol.

63. Such as the requirement of exhaustion of local remedies under *id.* Article 2. Article 3 prescribes that communications or petitions which are anonymous or which the Human Rights Committee consider to be an abuse of the right of submission of such communication or to be incompatible with the provision of the Covenant are all inadmissible.

While space does not permit a discussion of the merits of these procedural requirements, it may be noted that they are likely to inhibit or discourage individual communications, at least from certain countries.

64. *Id.* Article 5.

65. *Id.* Article 6.

66. For a brief discussion of procedure for the consideration of private (individual) communications on human rights violations in the U.N. system, *see* HUMAN RIGHTS IN INTERNATIONAL LAW: LEGAL AND POLICY ISSUES, 384-92 (T. Meron, ed. 1984).

Individual communications are the general rule in the Inter-American system for the protection of human rights while they are only optional under the European Convention for the Protection of Human Rights and Fundamental Freedoms. *See id.* chapters 12 and 13, respectively.

67. ILO No. 100. 165 U.N.T.S. 32. For the text of this Convention *see* Lillich 1985 at 270.

68. ILO No. 111. 362 U.N.T.S. 32. For the text *see* Lillich 1985 at 320.

69. 193 U.N.T.S. 135. For the text *see* Lillich 1985 at 60.

70. 309 U.N.T.S. 65. For the text *see* Lillich 1985 at 310.

71. 429 U.N.T.S. 93. For the text *see* Lillich 1985 at 330.

Marriage, Minimum Age for Marriage and Registration of Marriage.[72]

The most comprehensive and important specialized instrument is the 1979 Convention on the Elimination of All Forms of Discrimination Against Women.[73] This Convention defines discrimination against women as "any distinction, exclusion or restriction made on the basis of sex which has the effect or purpose of impairing or nullifying the recognition, enjoyment or exercise by women, irrespective of their marital status, on a basis of equality of men and women, of human rights and fundamental freedoms in the political, economic, social, cultural, civil or any other field."[74] Other provisions of the Convention impose very specific obligations to eliminate all forms and types of discrimination against women. Besides general condemnation of inequality and requirement of specified types of action to achieve equality and to eliminate discrimination; whether official or private, collective or individual,[75] the Convention follows up with more specific and precise provisions in the fields of political and public life, education, employment, health care, and other areas.[76]

Moreover, this Convention makes a serious attempt at monitoring progress made in the implementation of its provisions through the work of the Committee on the Elimination of Discrimination Against Women.[77] The Committee is required to receive reports from States Parties on the legislative, judicial, administrative or other measures

72. 521 U.N.T.S. 231. For the text see Lillich 1985 at 150.

73. G.A. Res. 34/180, U.N. Doc. A/Res/34/180 (1980); 19 I.L.M. 33 (1980); entered into force on September 3, 1981. For the text of this Convention *see* Lillich 1985 at 220.

74. *Id.* Article 1.

75. *Id.* Article 2. The requirements of this Article include the embodiment of the principle of equality of men and women in national constitutional and other appropriate legislation, ensuring through the law and other appropriate means the practical realization of this principle, and adopting legislative and other measures to prohibit all discrimination against women. Most significantly, this Article also requires States to take appropriate measures to eliminate discrimination against women by any person, organization or enterprise.

76. *Id.* Articles 3 to 16. It is interesting to note that Article 5 requires States Parties to take all appropriate measures to modify the social and cultural patterns of conduct of men and women, with a view to achieving the elimination of prejudices, customs and all other practices which are based on the idea of the inferiority or the superiority of either of the sexes, or on stereotyped roles for men and women. This goes to the heart of the matter because no legal or other official and formal measures can possibly achieve the objectives of equality and human dignity for women without the necessary education and elimination of attitudes and social norms and practices which are antithetical to the rights of women.

77. *Id.* Article 17.

which they have adopted to give effect to the provisions of the Convention, and on the progress made in this respect.[78] The report may indicate factors and difficulties affecting the degree of fulfillment of obligations under the present Convention.[79] The Committee must also report annually to the General Assembly of the United Nations through the Economic and Social Council, with copies transmitted to the Commission on the Status of Women for its information.[80]

In conclusion of this brief survey it may be observed that the relevant international instruments create an impressive body of international standards on the rights of women. Unfortunately, like other aspects of human rights, international law on the rights of women suffers from the inadequacy of enforcement or compliance mechanisms even in relation to the States Parties to the conventions. The reason for this deficiency is presumably the unwillingness of States to submit to international jurisdiction regarding their human rights practices. Since States are likely to continue to be the primary subjects of international law for the foreseeable future, the enforcement of international human rights standards will have to be pursued from within each State. Governments cannot be expected to submit voluntarily to independent international scrutiny without substantial and continuous pressure from their own population. It is with a view to assessing the existence and efficacy of a human rights constituency in the Muslim world, especially in relation to the rights of women, that consideration be given to the record of ratification of the relevant instruments by Muslim countries. It is also extremely important to reflect on possible inconsistencies between Shari'a and the international standards of the rights of women. This is true not only because of the current legal force of certain relevant aspects of Shari'a,[81] but also because of its

78. *Id.* Article 18(1).

79. *Id.* Article 18(2). According to Article 22 of this Convention, specialized agencies are not only entitled to be represented at the consideration of the implementation of such provisions of the Convention as fall within the scope of their activities, but also to be invited by the Committee to submit reports on the implementation of the Convention in areas falling within the scope of their activities.

80. *Id.* Article 21. This annual report may include the Committee's suggestions and general recommendations based on the examination of the State reports and other information received from the States Parties.

81. As noted earlier, note 30, and accompanying text, Shari'a constitutes family law and inheritance for Muslims throughout the Muslim world. The rights of women in these areas, therefore, directly submit to the limitations of Shari'a. Moreover, efforts to implement Shari'a in other spheres have already achieved some success in Iran, Pakistan and the Sudan. In these and other "traditional" muslim countries such as Saudia Arabia and the Gulf States, Shari'a's impact on the rights of women affect a wide range of social, civil and political rights such as access to public office and participation in public life.

continuing strong influence on Muslim public opinion, even where it is not binding as law at the present time.

Muslim Reaction to International Standards on the Rights of Women

Ratification of international instruments by any government, whether of a Muslim or a non-Muslim country, is obviously not conclusive evidence of the actual practice of that country in terms of a given set of rights. What motivates governments to ratify, or fail to ratify, can be a complex phenomenon and may not be necessarily related to the real policies and concrete conditions of life in their countries.

For one thing, a government may have failed to ratify these instruments simply because the issue was not raised at the appropriate levels of decision-making. Alternatively, the issue may have been raised at a politically inopportune moment or the case for ratification may have been made poorly and impersuasively. The mere fact of failure to ratify cannot, therefore, be taken as conclusive evidence of a conscious and deliberate policy rejecting a commitment to the content of the particular international instrument.

Ratification, on the other hand, may have been decided by an individual ruler or official, without sufficient political support from the country as a whole. The official or regime which effected the ratification, may change or be overthrown, with possible significant consequences to the country's commitment to the policy underlying ratification.[82] Alternatively, the decision to ratify may be taken for ulterior motives other than a genuine commitment to the contents of the particular international instruments. On the one hand, ratification may have been effected, for example, to satisfy certain temporary political ends at home or abroad. On the other hand, the decision to ratify or not, may be motivated by some ideological or political considerations unrelated to the specific issue. It therefore may not be valid to

82. In Iran, for example, secular reforms and ratification of international human rights documents by the Shah were effectively reversed after the Islamic revolution of 1979. *See* S. H. Amin, Middle East Legal Systems, chapter 3 (1985). It is not assumed here that the Shah's motives in ratifying human rights conventions were genuine. The point being made here is that his policies, whatever their motives and effects may have been, were reversed after his overthrow.

assume, for example, that a Muslim country refused to ratify a convention on the rights of women specifically because of Shari'a considerations. Finally, ratification may be subject to reservations that substantially diminish its political value.[83]

Thus, neither ratification nor failure to ratify can be taken as conclusive evidence of deliberate and effectively pursued policies. Nevertheless, the ratification or its absence may provide some evidence of policy. So long as one is aware of the complexity of motivation and the possible impact of the nature of the political process in the particular country at a given point in time, the ratification or nonratification of an international instrument may be taken as a relevant consideration. It is in this light that the record of ratification by Muslim countries of the three main instruments relevant to the rights of women will be considered.[84]

The ICSECR, has been ratified by twelve Muslim countries and the ICCPR, by eleven.[85] Special care must be taken with regard to the significance of the ratification of these general human rights documents. Objection to ratification, to the extent that it was a conscious and deliberate decision, may be due to apprehension over some provisions or general implications of rights, other than those especially significant to women. In such cases, women would be affected with the policies which are negative to those other human rights, but there may

83. The example of Egypt's reservation on the Convention on the Elimination of All Forms of Discrimination Against Women is discussed below.

84. The criteria for identifying Muslim countries can be problematic and may depend on the purpose of such identification. For the purposes of this article, all countries where the Muslims constitute over 70% of the total population are taken to be Muslim countries. According to the statistics quoted in WEEKS, MUSLIM PEOPLES at 882-911, the following 32 countries may be regarded as Muslim countries: Afghanistan 99%, Algeria 90%, Bahrain 99.3%, Bangladesh 82.9%, Comoros 99.5%, Djibouti 90%, Egypt 91.1%, The Gambia 87%, Indonesia 80%, Iran 98%, Iraq 96%, Jordan 93%, Kuwait 96%, Libya 98%, Maldive Islands 100%, Mali 80%, Mauritania 99%, Morocco 99%, Niger 87.4%, Oman 99%, Pakistan 97%, Qatar 95%, Saudia Arabia 99%, Senegal 91%, Somalia 99%, Sudan 72%, Syria 87%, Tunisia 99.4%, Turkey 99.2%, United Arab Emirates 90%, Arab Republic of Yemen 99%, Peoples Republic of Yemen 99%.

The vast majority of these countries are not constituted as Islamic states in accordance with Shari'a. Nevertheless, in all of them family law and inheritance for Muslims are governed by Shari'a. Moreover, the fact that Muslims constitute over 70% of the total population indicates, to the present author, that Shari'a considerations are likely to affect the rights of women in these countries.

Since the rights of women provided for in the earlier specialized conventions are now covered by the three main instruments noted below, there is no need to consider Muslim ratification of the earlier specialized conventions.

85. As of June 30, 1986, according to BASIC DOCUMENTS SUPPLEMENT TO INTERNATIONAL LAW: CASES AND MATERIALS, 403 and 388, respectively (L. Henkin, R.C. Pugh, O. Schachter, H. Smit, eds., 2nd ed. 1987).

still be some support in the country for the special rights of women in other areas. The Convention on the Elimination of All Forms of Discrimination Against Women has so far received only five ratifications by Muslim countries.[86]

What are the implications of the fact that the obligations undertaken by Muslim countries under these three main conventions cannot be reconciled with Shari'a rules on the rights of women? As noted above, Shari'a sought to guarantee certain minimum rights for women rather than strive for the complete equality with men. This may have been justified as the only realistic objective in the past, and I believe that it can be so justified, but the result remains that current efforts to achieve complete equality and remove all discrimination are bound to be viewed as contrary to Shari'a.

Nevertheless, several Muslim countries have in fact ratified all the three main instruments. Egypt, Senegal and Turkey, for example, have ratified the extensive and advanced Convention on the Elimination of All Forms of Discrimination Against Women. Since these countries have undertaken international obligations inconsistent with the established Shari'a, as accepted by all Muslims, their position can only be explained in one of three ways: either they do not feel bound by Shari'a; they do not take their international obligations seriously; or they have taken a view of the relevant principles of Shari'a which is consistent with these international obligations. The last mentioned explanation is the one favored by the present author, for reasons explained in the last section of this article.[87] The facts, unfortunately, do not seem to support this as the true explanation of the position of, for example, Egypt.

Egypt has entered reservations with regard to only three Articles of the Convention on Discrimination Against Woman, namely Articles 9, 16 and 29.[88] The reservation with regard to Article 9, granting women equal rights to those of men, with regard to the nationality of their children, may raise serious objection as a matter of principle. The reasons for Egypt's position on this issue may well be due to national policy independent of Shari'a. Again, the reservation on Article 29, regarding submission to arbitration, does not seem to be based on

86. As of June 30, 1986 according to *id.* at 425. Part of the reason for the low ratification of this Convention may be due to its recent adoption, since it was adopted in 1979 and came into force in 1981.

87. *See* text accompanying note 92 *infra.*

88. For the full texts of these reservations *see* Lillich 1985 at 11.

Shari'a. It is Egypt's reservation on Article 16, concerning the equality of men and women in all matters relating to marriage and family relations during the marriage and upon its dissolution, which is clearly based on established Shari'a, as accepted by Muslims in general. In the text of this reservation, Egypt justifies its position by saying that its obligations "must be without prejudice to the Islamic Shari'a provisions . . . . This is out of respect for the sanctity deriving from firm religious beliefs which govern marital relations in Egypt and which may not be called in question . . . ."[89] The reservation cites principles of Shari'a whereby the husband is required to pay bridal money to the wife, maintain her fully out of his own funds and also to make a payment to her upon divorce. The wife retains full rights over her property and is not obliged to spend anything on her keep. The reservations concludes by saying: "The Shari'a therefore restricts the wife's rights to divorce by making it contingent on a judge's ruling, whereas no such restriction is laid down in the case of the husband."[90]

In light of the clear language of the reservation, it can neither be said that Egypt does not feel bound by Shari'a nor that it has developed an alternative view of Shari'a. Paradoxically, Egypt has undertaken other international obligations under the same Convention which are clearly inconsistent with Shari'a.[91] Does this mean that Egypt does not take its international obligations seriously? I think not. Egypt would not have bothered to enter a reservation on Article 16 if it had no intention of attempting to comply. The explanation for this apparent inconsistency in Egypt's position seems to be due to the fact that while Shari'a is the law of personal status for Muslims in Egypt, which would make the country's obligation under Article 16 inconsistent with an unalterable aspect of its current law, other aspects of Egyptian law are not currently based on Shari'a. Therefore, the question is how would the adoption of Shari'a as the sole, or even the main, source of legislation affect the rights of women in Egypt or elsewhere in the Muslim world? If Shari'a is to be strictly applied, no law, policy or practice will be allowed to stand if it is perceived to be in violation of Shari'a.[92] Such is the probable impact of Shari'a on the

89. *Id.*

90. *Id.*

91. The Convention's general prohibition of all discrimination against women, as defined in Article 1, and the specific obligations to eliminate discrimination against women in the field of employment, as defined in Article 11, are impossible to reconcile, for example, with Shari'a rules disqualifying women from holding general judicial office.

92. This is not an unlikely possibility, even in a country like Egypt. Article 2 of the Egyptian Constitution of 1971 used to provide that "Islamic jurisprudence is a principle source of

international standards as applied to the Muslim world, unless a fundamental reformulation of the relevant rules of Shari'a is undertaken.

An Approach to the Rights of Women in Islam

When viewed in the Muslim context, the rights of women are the function of the interplay of two powerful forces. On the one hand, Muslims have a strong and enduring commitment to Shari'a, with its negative implications for the rights of women. On the other hand, secularization and external cultural influence have already transformed the consciousness of Muslim women and men and created an expectation of complete equality and full respect for the rights of women. More recently, emerging international standards on the rights of women have also provided strong support for equality and non-discrimination for all women, including the Muslim women. The question now is how to sustain the emerging Muslim awareness of, and commitment to, the rights of women in the face of likely and powerful opposition by the proponents of Shari'a?

In view of the dominant role of Islam in this part of the world, I believe that the advocacy of the rights of women must come from within the Islamic tradition itself. As indicated at the end of the introduction of this article,[93] to maintain Islamic religious law does not necessarily mean the application of Shari'a in its historical formulations. Reference has also been made to the possibility of an alternative interpretation of Islamic sources. It is true that what has been described in this article as alternative Islamization, is an internal struggle for the adoption of imaginative reform techniques for the evolution and reformulation of Shari'a. The dual essential characteristics of this alternative Islamization are Islamic legitimacy and efficacy in achieving the necessary degree of reform to realize the full rights of equality and freedom from any shade or form of discrimination against women. This article can neither discuss in detail nor hope to win this internal struggle for the Muslim women. However, it may be helpful to reflect on the possible contribution of international advocates of the rights of women. In what ways can they be constructive

legislation." An amendment to the Constitution in 1980 changed that last part of the clause to make Shari'a "the" principle source of legislation. 1985 Facts on File, Inc., August 2, 1985, at 578E1. See volume IV of Constitutions of the Countries of the World - Egypt (A.P. Blaustein ed. 1986). Even if the whole legal system was not transformed over time through this constitutional mandate, it is not unlikely that the rights of women may suffer some regression to bring Egyptian law and practice into greater conformity with Shari'a, international obligations notwithstanding.

93. *See* note 4 *supra* and accompanying text.

or destructive in their efforts to promote the rights of Muslim women? How can international standards be most relevant and helpful to Muslim women?

International standards are meaningless to Muslim women unless they are reflected in the concrete realities of the Muslim environment. Like members of other cultural traditions, Muslims tend to be suspicious and unreceptive towards what they perceive to be an attempt to impose alien standards. To obtain their cooperation in implementing international standards on the rights of women, we need to show the Muslims in general that these standards are not alien at all. They are, in fact, quite compatible with the fundamental values of Islam. In other words, we need to provide Islamic legitimacy for the international standards on the rights of women.

The balance of universality and cultural relativity of human rights, especially the rights of women, is extremely difficult to achieve and maintain in practice.[94] It requires giving each cultural tradition an opportunity to contribute in the standard formulation process without allowing any tradition to dictate to the others. The balance also requires recognition of the ethical standards and substantive norms of the cultural tradition while rejecting or disallowing archaic and oppressive norms. To avoid even the appearance of dictation by outsiders, which is likely only to be counterproductive, the classification of certain cultural (legal or religious) norms, as archaic and oppressive, must be done by the members of the cultural or religious group themselves. Yet, they cannot be left to themselves completely to do whatever they, or their elites, deem fit and appropriate.

There must be room for external influence which is considerate and sensitive to cultural concerns, while committed to enlightened ideals which can be shown to be the common wisdom of mankind. Sensitive and reflective regard to the totality of the human experience, not only to the dominate cultures or that of the rich and developed societies, can provide us with a core of fundamental rights which are either accepted or can be acceptable to all the cultural traditions of the world. We can then act immediately on these core fundamental rights while working progressively towards developing consensus on, and agreed formulations of, more rights.

94. For an explanation of the present author's thesis as applied to the human rights of religious minorities, *see* An-Na'im, *Religious Minorities Under Islamic Law and the Limits of Cultural Relativism*, 9 *Human Rights Quarterly* 1 (1987). Cf. Teson, *International Human Rights and Cultural Relativism*, 25 *Virginia Journal of International Law* 869 (1985).

Both principle and pragmatism, I believe, would recommend this approach to the rights of women. Our commitment should not be to the rights of women in the abstract, or as contained in high-sounding international instruments signed by official delegations. It should be a commitment to the rights of women in practice; the rights of rural and nomadic African and Asian women to live in very "traditional" or tribal communities and practice Islam, or other religious beliefs, out of genuine conviction. These women cannot and should not be invited to subscribe to a supposedly "international" feminist vision without enabling them, at the same time, to live in harmony with their immediate environment. It is irresponsible and inhumane to encourage these women to move too fast, too soon and to repudiate many of the established norms of their culture or religious law, without due regard to the full implications of such action. It must be remembered that it is these women who will have to remain there to endure the full consequences of their actions.

In conclusion, the wholeness of women as human beings must be emphasized. Efforts to promote the full range of human rights, social, economic and cultural, as well as civil and political, are as conducive to maintaining respect for the rights of women, as efforts to promote rights especially significant to women. What does equality with men and freedom from discrimination mean if both men and women are equally poor and hungry? Can women enjoy any rights when their children are starving, their countries ravaged by civil war or external aggression, or their communities denied their collective right to self-determination? In the final analysis, the rights of women are an integral part of the individual and collective human rights of their men and children.

[14]

The Contingent Universality of Human Rights: The Case of Freedom of Expression in African and Islamic Contexts*

I. INTRODUCTION

Mohammed al-Massari, a national of Saudi Arabia who was engaged in vigorous but peaceful criticism of the monarchy in his home country, was asked to leave the United Kingdom in January 1996. The request came after the Saudi government threatened economic retaliation should Britain grant al-Massari's request for political asylum.[1] A television program about female circumcision in Egypt was broadcast by Cable News Network (CNN), an American corporation based in Atlanta, and widely seen throughout the world; the broadcast provoked strong official and public reactions and activities about this traditional practice in Egypt.[2] Taslima Nasreen, a writer

* An earlier preliminary version of the paper was published in THE EMORY LAWYER, Annual Report 11-18 (1994-95).

[1] Anne Widdecombe, an official of the United Kingdom Home Office, said on BBC radio on January 5, 1996, that Mr. al-Massari's activities "have been complicating our relations with the Saudis" and that there have been "various representations from people in British business and the Saudis about the situation," but denied that there have been "the sort of direct, almost blackmailing pressure" to remove him that some reports suggested. John Darnten, *British Government Criticized For Ordering Saudi to Leave*, N.Y. TIMES, Jan. 5, 1996, at A5. The decision to "remove" al-Massari to Dominica (in eastern Caribbean) provoked strong protests inside and outside the United Kingdom. Mr. al-Massari was eventually allowed to stay following judicial review by the High Court of the Home Office decision. *See, e.g.*, HERALD (Glasgow), Jan. 1, 1996, at 1; WASH. POST, Jan. 22, 1996, at A15. I find both the decision to deport him and its reversal significant for my purposes here.

[2] This program was seen in Egypt on CNN's *The World Today* on September 7, 1994, during the convening of the International Conference on Population and Development in Cairo. For information on official and public responses, including law suits, see Robert Fisk, *U.N. Population Conference: Operation on TV Enrages Egypt*, INDEP. (LONDON), Sept. 13, 1994, at 10; *available in* 1994 WL 8841693; Sarah

from Bangladesh, was forced to seek political asylum in Sweden to escape prosecution for blasphemy in her home country. She allegedly attacked the *Qur'an* in comments made to an Indian newspaper, saying that the holy book should be "thoroughly revised."[3] A novel by Salman Rushdie, a British citizen of Indian Muslim origin, was condemned and banned in almost all Islamic countries and the author sentenced to death by the late Ayatollah Khomeini of Iran in 1989.[4] In my view, these and many similar recent examples of the emerging realities of globalization emphasize both the urgent need for, and increasing difficulty of, generating and sustaining global consensus on international human rights norms and stronger commitment to their effective implementation.

The main premise of this paper is that freedom of expression (and other human rights) posesess a contingent universality. The element of contingency lies in the dependence of such human rights norms upon two different sets of facets and processes. These are, first, the dynamic of internal domestic affairs, and, second, the dynamic of external or international affairs. Moreover, these two dynamics carry on a perpetual interaction in which each influences and is influenced by the other. National standards and practice are the bases of international standards and the necessary context of their implementation. Yet national standards and practices are in turn affected by international responses to the poor articulation or persistent violation of human rights at the local level. International recognition of the universality of freedom of expression equally influences, and is affected by, the local national dynamics of articulation, legitimation, and mediation of this and other human rights.

Gauch, *Modern Egypt Says Ancient Rite is Wrong*, CHI. TRIB., Sept. 10, 1995 at 1, *available in* 1995 WL 6244514; Judy Mann, *When Journalist Witness Atrocities*, WASH. POST, Sept. 23, 1994, at E3, *available in* 1994 WL 2441076.

[3] *See* Taslima Nasreen, "*Welcome in France*": AGENCE FRANCE-PRESSE, Oct 16, 1994, *available in* 1994 WL 9625924; Eric Weiner, *Muslim Radicals and Police Hunt Feminist Bangladeshi Writer: A Controversy Surrounds Taslima Nasreen, Whose Works Sparked a Religious Edict Calling For Her Death*, CHRISTIAN SCI. MONITOR, July 26, 1994, at 6, *available in* 1994 WL 8790278. It is interesting to note that Ms. Nasreen had to cancel an initial visit to France because the authorities there granted her a visa for one day only, citing a "security reason," but she was able to visit France subsequently. *Nasreen Receives French Human Rights Award*, AGENCE FRANCE PRESSE, Dec. 1, 1994, *available in* 1994 WL 9641744.

[4] This incident of 1989 continues to generate extensive and vigorous debate and commentary in many parts of the world. *See, e.g.*, Youssef Ibrahim, *Muslim Edicts Take on New Force*, N.Y. TIMES MAG., Feb. 12, 1995, at 14; Alan Riding, *Muslim Thinkers Rally for Rushdie*, N.Y. TIMES, Nov. 4, 1993, at C17; Edward Said, *The Phony Islamic Threat*, N.Y. TIMES, Nov. 21, 1993, at 62.

For a review of the debate and an analysis that is particularly relevant to my approach in this paper, see M.M. Slaughter, *The Salman Rushdie Affair: Apostasy, Honor, and Freedom of Speech*, 79 VA. L. REV. 153 (1993).

Rapidly growing realities of global interdependence makes it increasingly difficult even for the most developed countries to remain insulated from the consequences of human rights crisis abroad.

This interplay of the domestic and the international is evident in the above mentioned situations. We see, for example, from al-Massari's case that even a major former colonial power like the United Kingdom can be confronted with a choice between the economic well-being of its citizens, on the one hand, and its commitment to freedom of expression and protection of refugees, on the other. Egyptian officials and nongovernmental actors alike must now realize from the CNN case that they have to participate in a global effort to protect and regulate freedom of expression because external actors and factors can no longer be excluded or controlled in this age of satellite communications. Unavoidable interaction between domestic political issues and ideological debates, on the one hand, and regional and international law and relations, on the other, is clearly illustrated by the Salman Rushdie affair, a citizen of one country sentenced to death without trial by the head of state of another country for literary expression. In the case of Taslima Nasreen, the nature and scope of freedom of expression, and possibilities of exercising it in practice, can hardly be understood in isolation from the political/ideological struggles over the role of Islam in Bangladesh and South Asia in general.[5] The politics of Islamization in Bangladesh should also be seen in light of India's struggle to maintain its national unity and integrity as a secular state in the face of increasingly violent confrontation between Hindu and Muslim extremists and the demands of segment of its Muslims population in Kashmir to join Pakistan.[6]

This paper explores the nature and dynamics of internal and external variables in relation to the normative and empirical standing of freedom of expression at both the domestic and international levels. A clear understanding of these dynamics, it seems to me, is necessary for the development of appropriate strategies for promoting the universality of freedom of expression. Such strategies must take serious account of the realities of globalization in trying

[5] Note that the prosecution of Ms. Nasreen for blasphemy was based on a remarks attributed to her in an Indian newspaper. Weiner, *supra* note 3. It should be recalled that India lost what is now Bangladesh (then known as East Pakistan) in the partritian of 1947, and subsequently assisted the same territory and population to achieve secession from Pakistan in 1971. *See generally* HASAN ZAHEER, THE SEPARATION OF EAST PAKISTAN: THE RISE AND REALIZATION OF BENGALI MUSLIM NATIONALISM (1994).

[6] *See generally* ROBERT WIRSING, INDIA, PAKISTAN, AND THE KASHMIR DISPUTE ON REGIONAL CONFLICT AND ITS RESOLUTION (1994).

to promote consensus on the concept, content, and implementation of this right. These realities include both traditional power differentials between the developed North and developing South, as well as geopolitical factors that tend to diminish the impact of traditional power relations. But the key to redressing the imbalance in power relations with respect to the "proclaimed" universality of human rights is to engage in the process and adapt it to the respective priorities and concerns of each society, rather than pretend to be unconcerned with its moral and political implications. African and Islamic societies, for example, should seek to promote universality of human rights as a necessary response to the realities of hegemonic neo-colonial designs of the developed world. As I will argue in this paper, the needs of Islamic and African societies to attain and sustain national unity, political stability, and economic development, even as they safeguard their cultural and religious integrity, are all better served by a greater protection and promotion of freedom of expression than by its violation.

As commonly understood today, freedom of expression is one of the "civil liberties" which emerged through a long process of Western philosophical, political, and constitutional developments, especially over the last two centuries, and came to be proclaimed as a universal human right by the United Nations under the 1948 Universal Declaration of Human Rights, and subsequent human rights treaties.[7] To acknowledge this Western origin of the present formulation of this freedom is not to suggest that the concept itself is alien to non-Western cultures. Obviously, the basic concept of freedom of expression has been known to human cultures, past and present. Moreover, the task today is to embed this freedom as a universal human right within the context of the centralized, pervasive power of the nation-state, which is now the norm throughout the world. It is certainly true that possibilities of regression will always remain, even where the right is traditionally respected. The behavior of the British government in al-Massari's case illustrates as much. But as is also shown by that case, this risk only underscores the importance

[7] *See* Universal Declaration of Human Rights, G.A. Res. 217, U.N. GAOR, 3d Sess., at 71. U.N. DOC. A/810 (1948); International Covenant on Civil and Political Rights, Dec. 16, 1966, art. 19, G.A. Res. 2200, U.N. GAOR, 21st Sess., Supp. No. 16, U.N. DOC. A/6316 (1967). Similar formulations can be found in Article 10 of the European Convention for the Protection of Human Rights and Fundamental Freedoms, Nov. 4, 1950, 213 U.N.T.S. 221; Articles 13 and 14 of the American Convention on Human Rights, Nov. 22, 1969, 1144 U.N.T.S. 123; and Article 9 of the African Charter on Human and Peoples' Rights, June 27, 1981 21 I.L.M. 58. However, in addition to significant differences between these and other international formulations, freedom of expression is always made subject to some general or specific limitations and exceptions.

of organized and vocal resistance to such regression.

The universality of a human rights, such as freedom of expression, can refer to either universal validity or universal application. In the first sense, the claim is that freedom of expression is held to be valid by all (or virtually all) human societies, or within all major cultural, philosophical, and religious traditions. Alternatively, universality can refer to the applicability of a given norm to human beings everywhere. Since the two meanings are in fact mutually inclusive and supportive, as discussed below, freedom of expression should in fact mean universality of both validity and application. It should be emphasized, however, that neither sense of universality assumes or implies that freedom of expression is absolute. Rather, it is a claim of universal validity and/or universal application, whatever the accepted scope of the freedom or warranted limitations may be.

It is true that universal acceptance of freedom of expression as a generally applicable norm is only a first step. There is still a considerable range of views on the specific nature and scope of this freedom, and there has not yet arisen a sufficient degree of agreement on effective mechanisms for its universal application. However, this was equally true of the concept when it gradually emerged as a civil liberty under Western constitutional regimes. Moreover, differences over the meaning and scope of this right remain, and will probably continue in the future, within those normative systems. The implementation of freedom of expression as a domestic constitutional norm requires a certain degree of national consensus. Yet, varying degrees of disagreements and significant shifts in the meaning and implications of the concept persist in countries where it is believed to be most securely established.[8] This continuing need for mediation between freedom of expression and other priorities and concerns of each society does not negate its wide acceptance and application as a constitutional norm in most countries of the world today. Similarly, such need for mediation should not negate the universality of free-

---

[8] *See, e.g.*, R. v. Keegstra, 61 S.C.R. 3rd 1 (Can. 1990), in which the Canadian Supreme Court had to decide whether and to what extent "hate speech" (anti-Semitic views in this case) should be protected under section 2 (b) of the Canadian Charter of Rights and Freedoms. There are significant differences not only between Canada, the U.S., and Europe, but also among West European countries. *See generally* OWEN FISS, THE IRONY OF FREE SPEECH (Harvard Univ. Press 1996); CASE AGAINST RACIST SPEECH, HATE, AND PORNOGRAPHY (Laura J. Lederer & Richard Delgado eds., Hill and Wang 1995). For a brief discussion of the jurisprudence of the European Court of Human Rights in this regard, see Gregory P. Propes, *Wherefore Art Thou Deference? The European Court of Human Rights, Military Discipline, and Freedom of Expression*, 19 HOUS. J. INT'L L. 281 (1996).

dom of expression as a human right. But one should not expect the same considerations and processes of mediation to apply at the international level.

To clarify and illustrate the contingent universality of freedom of expression as a human right, I propose to approach the issues from an African and an Islamic perspective because of actual or presumed similarities in the contexts and responses of relevant African and Asian societies to the universality project. It is true that much of the debate and ambivalence about freedom of expression in any part of the world is specific to local context and circumstances, or a particular set of national objectives and concerns. But the similarities of colonial and post-colonial experiences of African and Islamic countries appear to have somehow generated and sustained a shared suspicion of the universality project in general as a neo-colonial tool of cultural imperialism designed to defeat their right to self-determination and to perpetuate their economic and political dependency on the West. In fact, as emphasized earlier, Western as well as African and Asian societies must now formulate and pursue their national objectives in this regard within the context of growing globalization and interdependence, which affects all parts of the world.

To say that universality of freedom of expression has been established by the Universal Declaration of Human Rights and subsequent instrument does not indicate a particular causal relationship between freedom of expression and international human rights law. Is freedom of expression universal because international law says so, or does international law merely declare the already established universality of this right? The "contingency" approach would clearly suggest that the universality of freedom of expression is a product of a combination of the two approaches. The universal validity and application of freedom of expression at the local domestic level is both the cause and effect of its international standing, while such international standing in turn influences and is influenced by universality at the local level. In other words, I suggest a dialectical relationship between the empirical and normative, local and global, standing of freedom of expression. However, that does not mean this dynamic has always been in favor of universal validity and application, or is likely to be so in the foreseeable future. On the contrary, my purpose is to identify and discuss both types of interaction in order to suggest effective strategies for the promotion of universality on realistic foundations.

Accordingly, an analysis of the universality of freedom of expression as a human right can begin from either side of this dialectic—the local/domestic or global/international—as long as it takes into account both the negative and positive aspects of the process. Since the language of universality was first introduced at the international level, it is logical to begin with an examination of the assumptions and implications of that universalist normative claim. Then I will explore theoretically the dynamics of the protection and violation of freedom of expression in the present context of African and Islamic societies to introduce the empirical local/domestic side of the process. That section is followed by a discussion of the possibilities of mobilizing the actual interdependence of relevant actors and factors in promoting the local/domestic validity and application of freedom of expression. The recent experiences of Kenya and Sudan will be considered to illustrate and clarify the preceding theoretical analysis. In conclusion, I summarize my argument and attempt to formulate some strategies for further reflection and action.

II. From Assumed to Constructed Universality of Freedom of Expression

As indicated earlier, the universality of freedom of expression can mean either universal validity, universal application, or a combination of the two; however, they can be supportive. It seems clear that there is a significant relationship between the two senses of universality in that, whereas universal validity is conducive to universal application, the latter is difficult to achieve without the former. Acceptance of freedom of expression as a universal human right by a given society would probably lead to more voluntary compliance than could be expected if the concept itself were not acceptable. Should active enforcement by the states become necessary, the political will to do so is more likely to be generated and sustained if the concept is acceptable to the general population of the country in question. Conversely, universal application in the face of wide scale popular resistance or strong governmental rejection can only be achieved, if at all, through some form of external coercion and imposition.

Some degree of internal enforcement of human rights will always be necessary because it is unrealistic to expect voluntary compliance with the law of the land by the whole population. However, massive coerced enforcement by a government, against its own population, is neither consistent with the nature and justification of human rights in general, nor likely to succeed in practice. Similarly, a degree of external pressure on governments that fail to live up to their international obligations will also be necessary and useful. But to make external pressure the primary instrument of local implementation will not only be seen as an infringement on national sovereignty and a violation of the people's human rights to self-determination, but would also be expensive and difficult to maintain. In any case, experience shows that other governments are rarely able and willing to sustain the economic, political, security, and other costs of pressuring offending governments into greater respect and protection for human rights.[9] In short, the use of coercion as the primary means of enforcement at either the national or international level is neither desirable as a matter of principle nor likely to materialize and be sustained in practice.

In this light, speaking of freedom of expression as a universal human right is both important and useful, but in the sense of a project to be constructed through global dialogue and collaboration, and not as a predetermined concept or accomplished fact. In terms of the thesis of this paper, I emphasize that African and Islamic societies can and should have a distinctive and positive role to play in the construction of such universality from their respective economic, political, and cultural perspectives. These societies should see themselves, and be seen by others, as contributing to a global effort to define, protect, and promote freedom of expression, rather than be expected to adopt a concept developed by other societies out of their own circumstances and traditions. Such inclusion and participation should be in relation to the underlying concepts and assumptions of human rights discourse as well as the actual standards, mechanisms, and strategies for their implementation. The construction of universality of freedom of expression should also incorporate the contributions of nongovernmental organizations in addition to those of intergovernmental and governmental entities.

Because challenges to its universal validity and application are often directed against particular conceptions of this right, developing a definition of freedom of expression is obviously important. However, it would be inconsistent with the premise of this paper to offer a specific definition since my contention is that such a definition should emerge from the interaction of internal and external forces in the context of each society. Nevertheless, I suggest that local definitions should be consistent with the nature of the process I am proposing which require the "popularization" of freedom of expression in order to generate political support for its universal validity and appli-

[9] See INTERNATIONAL HUMAN RIGHTS IN CONTEXT 811-83 (Henry J. Steiner & Philip Alston eds., Clarendon Press 1996) for a wide variety of views and information on American and European approaches to human rights and foreign policy.

cation. For example, in terms of the geographical and cultural focus of this paper, I would call on African and Islamic advocates of freedom of expression to question and seek to supplement the narrow and elitist conceptions of this right which assume or imply that all that is required is the removal of direct official constraints on otherwise articulate, creative, and communicative individuals who have the material resources and ability to exercise their rights. In my view, this liberal "negative" sense of freedom as the absence of direct official constraints (as opposed to indirect limitations such as the lack of resources, self-censorship, or personal inhibitions) is a necessary but insufficient condition for a broader and more inclusive sense of the ability and opportunity for self-expression.[10] Protection of freedom of expression should be conceived not only in terms of removing official constraints from articulate elites to debate issues of public concern, but also by enhancing material resources and practical opportunities for the exercise of this right by more people. That is, the justification and facilitation of freedom of expression need to be supported by deliberate strategies to progressively broaden the base of participation among the general public.

Another aspect of the liberal notion of justiciable civil liberties, "internationalized" as human rights under the Universal Declaration and human rights treaties, is the view that those rights can only be attributed to individual persons who would be able to adjudicate and vindicate their rights against the community as represented in the state. Again, while holding this aspect of the liberal notion of rights to be important, I suggest that freedom of expression as a universal human right should incorporate other conceptions of rights in relation to a variety of implementation mechanisms and strategies. For example, positive conceptions of freedom of expression should be articulated and deployed as a moral norm in the socialization and education of children, and be defined as a clear objective of national politics and in the daily functioning of administrative organs of national and local government. The possibilities and risks of collective exercise of freedom of expression should also be explored in relation to, for example, freedom of conscience and belief in the context of traditional African religions.[11]

---

[10] *See id.* at 166-92 (exploring the question of competing conceptions of rights in human rights theory). The editors briefly discuss "negative" versus "positive" notions of rights. *Id.* at 189-91.

[11] On the collective nature of traditional African religions, see, for example, EMEFIE KENGA METUH, COMPARATIVE STUDIES OF AFRICAN TRADITIONAL RELIGIONS (IMCO Publications 1987). Can freedom of expression play a role in mediating possible tensions between the collective and individual dimensions of freedom of religion in the African context? *See* EMERGING HUMAN RIGHTS: THE AFRICAN POLITICAL ECONOMY CONTEXT (George W. Shepard & Mark O.C. Anikpo eds., Greenwood Press 1990); *see also* RHODA E.

To summarize and emphasize, I suggest that freedom of expression should be understood not only in the "negative" sense of absence of official restraints, so as to *permit* individual persons to express themselves in political, artistic, literary, scholarly, and other ways, but also to include positive action to *enable* inarticulate individual and collective social and cultural forms of self-expression. A modified conception of justiciability and judicial enforcement can be useful in enforcing this broader conception of rights. For example, traditional definitions of standing to sue and judicial remedies for violations of individual rights may need to be revised to allow for the possibility of collective claims. To the extent that judicial protection is not possible or adequate for the purpose, alternative strategies of implementation should be developed to encourage people individually and collectively to express themselves. However, those alternative strategies should not jeopardize the ability of those who are already inclined to express themselves freely and effectively. In other words, the objective in this regard is to *supplement*, rather than replace, liberal notions of rights and their enforcement mechanisms as the basis of freedom of expression as a universal human right.

However, these and other possible mechanisms for the popularization of freedom of expression will, of course, require allocation of financial resources for governmental and nongovernmental action. At one level of analysis, if freedom of expression is accorded the high degree of priority it deserves, such expenditure will easily be viewed as fully justified. Accordingly, the question is whether the criteria and processes of setting national priorities are giving freedom of expression its appropriate weight, relative to other national concerns. There is little practical value, however, to according this right even the highest order of priority if material resources for its promotion are not available. From this perspective, the protection of the "individual" civil and political right to freedom of expression is *contingent* on the availability of material resources that may be lacking in developing countries because of the harsh realities of global economic relations. For advocates of freedom of expression to have credibility in resisting a low standing for this right in the appropriation of national resources, they must also address global conditions of trade and distribution of wealth that diminish the share of developing countries. This confronts traditional supporters of freedom of expression in the capitalist, liberal West with a challenge to redress this dimension of the

HOWARD, HUMAN RIGHTS IN COMMONWEALTH AFRICA 107-12 (1986) (discussing the relationship between religious tolerance and state security).

contingency of this human right.

The need to clarify and broaden the concept of freedom of expression in these ways, it seems, is an indication of a broader concern with what I would call the "culturally-specific" origins and development of universal human rights in general. In a formal legalistic sense, the modern concept of universal human rights first emerged in the aftermath of the Second World War and found international recognition in the 1945 Charter of the United Nations of 1945 and subsequent international and regional treaties.[12] As a matter of intellectual, as well as legal and political, history however, the modern concept of human rights clearly emerged from European and North American experience, particularly in constitutional regimes for the protection of civil liberties and fundamental rights of the last two centuries.[13]

Moreover, little opportunity for contributions by peoples of Africa and Asia at the beginning of the process in the late 1940s existed because the vast majority of these peoples were still suffering from repressive colonial rule by the same European powers who were proclaiming the Universal Declaration of Human Rights at the United Nations. The fact that many African and Islamic countries subsequently endorsed the Universal Declaration and participated in the adoption of subsequent covenants and conventions after they achieved independence from colonial rule in the late 1950s and early 1960s is significant. By that stage, however, those emerging African and Asian states were not only late comers to an already established concept and framework, but also lacked the human and material resources to make a significant original contribution.[14] After all, treaty formulations of human rights and their implementation are premised on the preexisting power-oriented systems of international law and relations that did not accord much weight to emerging poor and underdeveloped countries.

Pointing out these facts and considerations does not mean that human rights as such are not universal, or that the present set of international human rights standards should not be accepted as a valid expression of that universality. Rather, my purpose in recalling those origins and that history is to

---

[12] *See supra* note 9, at 118-31.

[13] *See* Virginia A. Leary, *The Effect of Western Perspectives on International Human Rights*, *in* HUMAN RIGHTS IN AFRICA: CROSS-CULTURAL PERSPECTIVES 15-30 (Abdullahi A. An-Na'im & Francis M. Deng eds., 1990); Jack Donnelly, *Human Rights and Western Liberalism* at 31-55.

[14] Abdullahi A. An-Na'im, *Problems of Universal Cultural Legitimacy for Human Rights*, *in* HUMAN RIGHTS IN AFRICA, *supra* note 13, at 331, 346-52.

reaffirm the universality of human rights based on a clear and realistic understanding of its foundations and limitations as well as a positive appreciation of its liberating force. If these facts are not acknowledged and taken into account by the advocates of universality of human rights, cultural relativists can gain advantage with their constituencies by recalling the origins and development of the present standards in order to conclude that these formulations are necessarily inconsistent with non-Western cultural and religious traditions.

In response to such relativist claims, I would argue that the fact that the present formulations of human rights emerged from Western conceptions of civil liberties does not by itself prove that they are not universal. For one thing, those Western origins, in turn, drew from, and interacted with earlier and wider philosophical and political experiences of the totality of humanity. Another, and perhaps more important fact to note in this regard is that those Western conceptions of civil liberties emerged through a long struggle against the risks of abuse and manipulation of the centralized and all-pervasive powers of the state. With the recent, even greater expansion in the powers of the state, and its ability to affect a wider range of economic, political, educational, cultural, and other vital interests and concerns of individuals as well as communities, those risks are more serious and far reaching today in all parts of the world than they ever were. Whether as a result of colonial imposition or post-colonial adoption and endorsement, all non-Western societies now live under the Western model of the nation-state. Unless and until those societies develop either an alternative model of the state or better safeguards against the abuse and manipulation of its extensive powers, they are better advised to also adopt Western concepts and mechanisms that have already succeeded in providing effective limitations on those powers in Western experience.

In light of these considerations, I suggest, the assumption of the validity of the present human rights standards is supported by the fact that they reflect the normative framework of common human experience in the face of expanding powers of the state, and the realities of globalization, in every part of the world today. Even the rhetoric of cultural relativism cannot afford to do without the present set of internationally recognized human rights as such, because those who are challenging universality rely on, and benefit from, these same rights and freedoms in launching their challenge. That does not mean that the assumption of the universality of the present human rights standards precludes every type and form of challenge or reformulation of specific conceptions or formulations of one right or another. In fact, I am attempting to do precisely that regarding freedom of expression in this paper. What I find conceptually unacceptable and practically dangerous is a counter-assumption of the inherent and irrevocable lack of universality for present internationally-recognized human rights or for the concept itself.

Although well-founded and warranted in my view, the assumption of universality should be substantiated through internal discourse within cultures, and cross-cultural dialogue between cultures (including religious traditions, ideologies, and legal systems) to broaden and deepen genuine consensus on the global validity and application of human rights standards.[15] As clearly demonstrated in the limited discourse and dialogue that we have had since the adoption of the Universal Declaration, there is a growing overlapping consensus in support of the universality of human rights. Daily experience clearly shows that there is agreement among peoples of the world on the universal validity of human rights, and mounting demand for their application to all human beings throughout the world, despite differences as to the internal cultural, religious, or ideological justification of that agreement.

Varying degrees of tension no doubt remain between some formulations of human rights, on the one hand, and certain interpretations of cultural and religious traditions, or ideological and philosophical perspectives, on the other.[16] There are also differences over the precise content and manner of implementation of various rights, as can be seen in relation to freedom of expression not only between American and European societies, but also among European societies.[17] While these sorts of problems are to be expected in relation to such a global and highly complex project, and should be taken seriously, they are not sufficient reason to abandon efforts to broaden and deepen universal consensus on every aspect of content and justification for these rights. The universality project may prove to be untenable in the future, but it is too important to be abandoned without a serious attempt at

[15] *Id.*; *see also* Abdullahi A. An-Na'im, *Toward a Cross-Cultural Approach to Defining International Standards of Human Rights: The Meaning of Cruel, Inhuman and Degrading Treatment or Punishment*, *in* HUMAN RIGHTS IN CROSS-CULTURAL PERSPECTIVES: QUEST FOR CONSENSUS 19-43 (Abdullahi A. An-Na'im ed., University of Pennsylvania Press 1992).

[16] *See supra* note 9, at 226-55.

[17] On the relationship between the European Convention for the Prevention of Human Rights and the domestic legal systems of twenty-six member countries, see MACDONALD ET AL., THE EUROPEAN SYSTEM FOR THE PROTECTION OF HUMAN RIGHTS 26-30 (1993). For further discussion of some cases brought before the Court, see BEDDARD, B., HUMAN RIGHTS AND EUROPE 8-18 (1993).

realizing it as an inclusive and flexible principle.

In conclusion of this section, I suggest that the concept of human rights in general, and freedom of expression in this instance, must remain open and responsive to the changing priorities and concerns of the various peoples of the world. Far from being seen as accomplished or exhausted, the process of articulating and validating universal human rights should allow for refinement and clarification of existing rights, as suggested earlier for freedom of expression, as well as for the conception and articulation of new rights, such as collective human rights to development and protection of the environment, which may not necessarily conform to traditional liberal notions of individual rights.[18] When viewed in this light—as the continuing and inclusive product of an overlapping consensus among peoples of diverse cultural orientation, religious affiliation, and ideological allegiance, rather than as a Western notion to be imposed on others—freedom of expression as a universal human right becomes a useful, indeed indispensable, instrument of liberation.

III. FREEDOM OF EXPRESSION IN AFRICAN AND ISLAMIC CONTEXTS

Colonial repression and exploitation, superpower rivalry during the Cold War, the realities and risks of ethnic and religious conflict or civil war, political instability, economic underdevelopment and marginalization, and technological and intellectual dependency are all matters of great concern to African and Islamic societies. Drawing on that background, ruling elites in these regions claim that violations of freedom of expression should be "tolerated" in the interest of achieving the higher priorities of national unity, political stability and economic development. In addition, these elites seek to rationalize human rights violations in the name of protecting culture and religion. In my view, the exact opposite is achieved in that unity, stability, and development can never be realized or sustained through the violation of freedom of expression. In fact, culture and religion are actually sustained and promoted by the protection of freedom of expression, not by its violation. In this section, I will attempt to develop a theoretical argument in support of the proposition that protection of freedom of expression is conducive to the realization of the same national interests and societal values it is alleged to undermine.

---

[18] For some new perspectives and emerging concerns in this regard see, HUMAN RIGHTS IN THE TWENTY-FIRST CENTURY: A GLOBAL CHALLENGE §§ IV-V (Kathleen E. Mahoney & Paul Mahoney eds., Martinus Nijhoff Publishers 1993).

From the outset, I concede the difficulty of establishing a causal relationship between a certain policy regarding freedom of expression and a specific state of affairs, especially within a relatively short period of time, let alone generalizing about such a causal relationship from one situation to another. That is, it is difficult to show that a certain state of affairs is the direct result or consequence of the existence or denial of freedom of expression. But this is equally true for both sides of the issue; neither the opponents nor the proponents of freedom of expression can easily adduce evidence of a casual relationship in support of their position. One may, however, be able to develop some sense of the conceptual viability and empirical probability of the suppression or protection of freedom of expression by following a hypothetical scenario to its logical conclusion. For example, if freedom of speech is suppressed in the interest of preserving national unity or political stability or pursuing economic development, then ruling elites will have to suppress all opposition to the policies they seek to implement in these fields. With consequent loss of general political legitimacy, ruling elites will have to increasingly rely on a progressively narrowing base of information and support. In time, political leaders and government officials will have no way of verifying whether the information they are receiving and acting upon in formulating and implementing their policies is true or not, let alone being able to accurately evaluate the consequences of those policies. That is, the difficulty of "demonstrating" how protection of freedom of expression would ensure that good policies are in fact adopted does not preclude one from showing that violating this right will likely lead to negative consequences.

The argument for suppressing freedom of expression in the interest of economic development is sometimes said to be supported by the example of countries such as Singapore.[19] In response, I reiterate the difficulty of establishing causal relationships in defined time frames. That is, one cannot assume that the economic success of Singapore is due to suppression of freedom of speech, or that this causal relationship, if it exists, can be sustained over time. Moreover, I seriously question the relative value of the alleged benefit in relation to the price such societies pay. The society is not only denied the opportunity to discover itself and its true potential for social and moral growth, it cannot determine whether it is achieving all the economic success of which it is capable. That is, the costs of subordinating freedom of

---

[19] *See* Bilhari Kausikan, *Asia's Different Standard*, 92 FOREIGN POL'Y 24-42 (1993). *Cf.* Aryeh Neier, *Asia's Unacceptable Standard*, FOREIGN POL'Y 42-51 (1993).

expression to economic development, for example, include uncertainty about the narrow objective itself in addition to sacrificing some broader societal aims to address long-term concerns. Moreover, without freedom of expression, a society has no way of debating the issues regarding the alleged rationale itself.

To induce it to take such a blind leap of faith and surrender its fate to the dictator of the day, a society is told that the surrender is a "temporary measure," and is assured that freedom of expression will be fully restored as soon as unity, stability, development, or some other alleged national goal is achieved. Yet, such a society is not allowed to determine whether those goals are truly desirable, or that such a "trade-off" is in fact necessary or appropriate in relation to the desired goals. Neither is it able to determine the extent or duration of the "postponement" or to decide when the alleged goals have been sufficiently realized for the "temporary" curtailment of freedom of expression to be terminated. In reality, therefore, a people are being asked to forever surrender the ability to reclaim freedom of expression in the future in pursuit of an alleged national goal that they are not even allowed to discuss.

But if such claims are so obviously false, why do elites make them, and how can they get away with this conduct? A brief answer might simply be "because they are in control of the state, and can compel acceptance of their absurd claims." But that is too simplistic and deterministic because it neither explains the nature and source of that power, nor permits ways of challenging it. A more satisfactory answer, in my view, must include an understanding of the nature of the claim and the manner in which it is sustained. Perhaps ruling elites make these types of claims because they believe that they can play on the strong appeal of the type of public good that they are promising. Furthermore, these elites stress the notion that the interests of the many should take precedence over those of the few. The mechanics of achieving this "confidence" trick is to control any possibility of challenge to such claims at both the normative and empirical levels. When no one is able to question the validity of such claims in a general or abstract sense, or to challenge their application to the facts of the situation (and perhaps not even to determine what the facts are), who is to know of the double fallacy, and what can they do about it? That is precisely why freedom of expression is usually one of the first human rights to be violated, since its exercise is the only way the fallacy of the rationale of its own violation (and that of all other rights) can be exposed.

Since the explanation of the loss of freedom of expression is in that very fact—that ruling elites are able to get away with its violation by violating it—it follows that the protection of freedom of expression is in its exercise. The logic of this proposition is not as circular as it first appears. As will be discussed in the next section, in violating human rights, ruling elites in fact rely on the support of the same people whose human rights they are violating. In the case of freedom of expression, instead of violating the right all at once, ruling elites begin by a gradual erosion coupled with reinforcement of the assumptions underlying their claims. The less resistance they encounter on either front, the bolder they get in violating this right and justifying its progressive violation. In other words, freedom of expression is lost by its beneficiaries more than "taken away" by its violators. At the theoretical level discussed in this section, the relevance of this analysis to a strategy of resistance can be explained as follows.

First, it is important to understand the dynamic relationship between the underlying assumptions and the progressive violation of freedom of expression in the context of one society or another, and to incorporate such understanding in the strategies of resistance. While it is useful to draw on the experiences of other societies, there is no real substitute for intimate knowledge of the nature and methods of the ruling elites of the country in question, and the urgent public concerns they are manipulating. Otherwise, no effective strategy of resistance can be devised or implemented in a particular setting.

Second, there is the need for formulating adequate responses to the underlying assumptions about, for example, the relative size of the beneficiaries of this freedom, or the presumed contradiction between its exercise and the achievement of alleged national objectives. On the first count, advocates of freedom of expression must expand their constituency and build effective channels of communication with the public at large. This action must be undertaken as a matter of principle as well as a strategy for frustrating the forthcoming attack by the ruling elites. Otherwise, claims by the elites that freedom expression is a privilege of a few articulate intellectuals, rather than of the public at large, might sound more plausible, thereby setting the scene for an alleged conflict between public good and private luxury.

Third, having established and maintained their credibility and ability to communicate with the widest possible constituency, advocates of freedom of expression should immediately challenge any alleged conflict between the popular exercise of this freedom and the achievement of the public good of national unity, stability, or economic development. Proponents of freedom of expression should strive to show its importance to all citizens and society at large, and not just to a few educated elites. They should also demonstrate that freedom of expression is essential for achieving national goals. For example, it is important to demonstrate that freedom of expression is essential for ensuring that national unity is based on solid foundations of justice and equality of ethnic, cultural, or religious groups. Moreover, it is needed for defining the objectives of sustainable economic development and for monitoring its effective realization. Freedom of expression is also essential for ensuring that political stability is achieved through the widest possible participation of the population, and genuine legitimacy of the state and its institutions and processes, instead of by silencing dissent and repressing opposition. As demonstrated by the experiences of countries like Algeria, Iraq, Liberia, Mauritania, Rwanda, Somalia, and Sudan, denial of freedom of expression is more frequently associated with severe political strife and civil war than with unity, peace, and stability. The post-independence experiences of almost all African and Islamic countries also clearly show that decades of bad planning and poor implementation of economic policies, corruption and incompetence were sustained in part through systematic denial of freedom of expression.[20]

The efforts of ruling elites to rationalize violations of freedom of expression through the need to protect the integrity of culture and religion are explicitly or implicitly premised on arguments and assumptions about the relationship between African and Islamic countries and the colonial and neo-colonial West. Freedom of expression is represented as a Western ploy designed to confuse and weaken African and Islamic societies, and to alienate them from their own traditional cultures and religions. Ruling elites also often misrepresent formulations of freedom of expression as an absolute and unqualified right, or emphasize exaggerated forms of its practice in some Western societies, in order to "demonstrate" its incompatibility with prevailing perceptions of cultural and religious norms and institutions. For example, according to such misrepresentations and exaggerations, the sole purpose of freedom of expression is to promote "hard" pornography and decadent literature.

This sort of rationalization presents the advocates of freedom of expression with the following challenges: (1) how to acknowledge the realities of past and present Western hegemony without encouraging siege mentality and defensive hostility to any universalist project among African and Islamic

---

[20] The underdevelopment of Africa is attributed to the post-colonial repression of civil liberties and human rights. GEORGE W. SHEPARD & MARK O.C. ANIKPO, EMERGING HUMAN RIGHTS 57-65 (1990).

societies; (2) how to define the limitations of freedom of expression without providing ruling elites with justification for its progressive curtailment; and (3) how to defend freedom of expression as compatible with cultural and religious traditions without accepting the supremacy of all prevailing conceptions of those traditions, some of which are inconsistent with, for example, the human rights of women or ethnic and religious minorities. The complex and protracted issues raised by these dilemmas can best be addressed over time and in the specific context of particular societies. However, the following general remarks may provide some guidance in responding to such challenges.

On the first dilemma, it would be futile to deny the obvious fact of Western hegemony, or to pretend that protection of freedom of expression will immediately and completely redress the underlying differential in power relations between Western and African or Islamic societies. Instead, the issue should be that the protection of these human rights would better prepare African and Islamic societies for resisting all hegemonies, whether Western, Eastern, or from within. It should be noted that Western societies which practice a high degree of freedom of expression are in fact stronger and more developed than the African and Islamic societies which have failed to protect this right. Although the relative historical evolution of societies should not be simplified, its association with freedom of expression should still be considered.

Regarding the second dilemma, the definition of freedom of expression, as indicated earlier, is a matter for negotiation by each society, within the framework of internal and international interdependence. The most fundamental requirement for the validity of this process of definition and specification is that it must be open to all segments and points of view within society, including subsequent generations. No group or segment of society should monopolize the power to define freedom of expression for all present and future generations. Such opportunities for constant debate and reevaluation of the definition exist when freedom of expression is protected, not where it is suppressed.

As to the third dilemma, I argue that perceptions of conflict or tension between freedom of expression, on the one hand, and cultural and religious norms, on the other, are the product of particular interpretations of culture and religion which can and should be both challenged and changed. In fact, the integrity and proper functioning of cultural and religious traditions themselves need to be reaffirmed and verified through open and free discussion, including the possibility of reformulation and reinterpretation, if the values and institutions of culture and religion are to maintain the confidence and allegiance of their constituencies, and continue to inform and guide their behavior.[21]

In a sense, the contest between the proponents and opponents of freedom of expression can be seen as one version of the age-old struggle over power in which the modern idea of human rights is used as a political tool by rivals competing for dominance and privilege. The significant difference can be, however, that where traditional struggles over power were about the replacement of one group of ruling elites by another to the exclusion of the public at large, the essence of freedom of expression is to ensure the diffusion and sharing of power among the whole population. For this shift in perceptions of struggles over power and their objectives to materialize, however, freedom of expression must be seen as a vital concern and immediate relevance and of use to the totality of the population, and not only of one small group of elites. It is for this reason that I have emphasized a more proactive and inclusive definition of freedom of expression.

IV. MOBILIZING THE DYNAMICS OF INTERDEPENDENCE

The precise definition and implications of freedom of expression are to be negotiated by each society over time within the framework of internal and international interdependence. But it is clear that in any society, the freedom to express oneself is neither absolutely secured nor fundamentally repudiated or repressed.[22] The very existence of another person to whom (or group to which) the self is being expressed implies limitation on freedom of expression since the response of that other person (or entity) to the form, manner, content, or consequences of expression would need to be taken into account. By the same token, since other individuals and society at large would not seek to restrict or regulate expression they do not find objectionable, there

---

[21] Further development of this argument from an Islamic perspective can be found in Abdullahi A. An-Na'im, *Toward an Islamic Hermeneutics for Human Rights*, *in* HUMAN RIGHTS AND RELIGIOUS VALUES (Abdullahi A. An-Na'im et al., eds, William B. Eerdmans Pub. 1995); Abdullahi A. An-Na'im, *Islamic Foundations for Religious Human Rights*, *in* RELIGIOUS HUMAN RIGHTS IN GLOBAL PERSPECTIVES: RELIGIOUS PERSPECTIVES 337-60 (John Witte & Johan van der Vyver eds., Martinus Nijhoff 1996).

[22] For an example of the concept and role of freedom of expression in a traditional African context, see Bonnie L. Wright, *The Power of Articulation*, *in* CREATIVITY OF POWER: COSMOLOGY AND ACTION IN AFRICAN SOCIETIES 39-57 (W. Arens & Ivan Karp eds., 1989).

will always be some scope for freedom of expression, even in the most repressive and authoritarian settings. There are always limitations on the concept and practical exercise of expression, even in the most liberal societies. There is always some scope in principle and space in practice for expression in the most authoritarian or traditional societies. From this general point of view, the question is never whether there is any freedom of expression, but rather what limits and possibilities exist for it or ought to be provided.[23]

From a human rights perspective, however, freedom of expression is not simply about expressing one's self to others in general everyday interactions. Rather it is about one's right and ability to *contest the limits of permissibility* with a view to expanding political, social, and moral "space" for freedom of expression and challenging arbitrary or unwarranted restrictions.[24] To have the right to contest the limits does not necessarily mean, of course, that the desired expansion of the scope of the right, or improvement in the circumstances of its exercise, will be realized in practice. What is important is the right and ability to contest, and to seek to improve one's case and win more support for it. For example, it is universally agreed that one's exercise of his freedom of expression should not be allowed to cause "harm" to other persons or to the community at large. What is at issue in this context is the right to debate and contest the meaning and degree of "harm" — what level or type of harm should justify what degree or form of restriction on freedom of expression. The right to contest the limits also include possibilities of challenging the manner in which legitimate restrictions might be specified and applied in practice, again with a view to expanding the scope and improving the quality of freedom of expression.

Another general point to note is that many, perhaps most, situations of potential or actual conflict over freedom of expression are successfully resolved through some form of negotiation and mediation short of adjudication. Structural, economic, sociological, cultural, and other factors may "persuade"

---

[23] For example, the International Covenant on Civil and Political Rights of 1966 guarantees the right to freedom of expression, and then proceeds to recognize that certain restrictions on freedom of expression are permissible, but "only as provided for by law and are necessary, (1) for respect of the rights or reputations of others, (2) for the protection of national security or of public order (*ordre public*), or of public health or morals." Arts. 19.2, 19.3. A discussion of the appropriateness of this or other specific definitions of freedom of expression is beyond the scope of this paper.

[24] Some who contest the limits of freedom of expression with a view to reducing the scope of permissibility, see their effort as necessary for protecting the human dignity and rights of women, or some other legitimate human rights concern. *See generally* CATHARINE A. MACKINNON, ONLY WORDS (1993).

one person to abandon a possible claim of freedom of expression in a given situation, or "induce" another to accept or tolerate what they would have challenged or contested under different circumstances. What might appear to be consensus over the toleration or rejection of certain types of expression could in fact be a reflection of realities of power relations or lack of means and opportunity to assert the freedom, or to challenge its purported exercise in a given case. A case that might be characterized as self-censorship by an individual or an instance of tolerance by others could in fact be the realization that there is no point in trying to assert freedom of expression, or in resisting such a claim. Yet whatever may be the possible motives and reasons for an apparently successful resolution or mediation, one can easily find numerous and routine examples of conflict over the scope, manner, and content of freedom of expression in every society.

Therefore, it is reasonable to assume that there is some level of freedom of expression in all societies, for whatever reasons or motivations, and that most potential disputes are resolved through some sort of compromise and informal mediation. Nevertheless, there still remains the need for definition and adjudication in hard cases when there is conflict between those who seek expression and those who oppose it. Granted that there are things one would not want to express for whatever reasons he or she may have, and there are expressions of things which would not bother or concern other persons, or the community or state at large. The contested field of freedom of expression is that middle ground between the two ends: what one side wishes to express and what other persons or entities find objectionable. An arbiter is therefore needed to adjudicate in case of conflict when there is an assertion of freedom of expression in the face of opposition or resistance by others in a given situation.

In the modern context, the state is supposed to act as arbiter. The state is the politically constituted authority with a monopoly of the legitimate use of force and the ability to mobilize social and material resources. But the state itself is not, and cannot be, neutral in this conflict. The state is controlled by specific individual and group actors who will always have their own perspective and interests to promote or protect in any dispute over the scope and manner of expression. In other words, those in control of the apparatus of the state are usually parties to disputes over freedom of expression, either in favor or against the assertion of the right in a given situation. Consequently, on the one hand, each side to a dispute over expression will need the support of other persons and the community against the possibility of bias by state actors. State actors, on the other hand, will need the support of one side to the conflict, and of the public at large, in trying to adjudicate a dispute between the parties, to protect their own interests, or promote their perspectives on the issues. When the state is openly or clearly party to a dispute over a freedom of expression issue in its own cause, it will still need broader political support from significant individuals and the public at large in seeking to impose its will in any particular case.

Thus, an important aspect of the struggle over freedom of expression is about the dynamics of this tripartite relationship of mutual conflict and interdependence between those seeking self-expression and others who oppose it, as well as between such parties and the state, who is supposed to be the arbiter. An individual or group seeking protection of freedom of expression in a specific case or situation will need to rely on the support of other individuals and groups, and of the community at large, in checking or countering the bias or self-interest of state actors. For that support to be forthcoming, however, other individuals, groups and the community must appreciate the value of protecting freedom of expression in general, and be persuaded that the particular case is worthy of their support. Others who object to an assertion of freedom of expression in broader terms or with regard to the case in question will also no doubt try to influence state actors, other individuals, and the community at large in favor of their position, including responding to the terms and purported justification of the original claim. Such challenges and their strategies and rationale should, in turn, be anticipated and responded to by the claimant or advocates of freedom of expression.

A recent example from Egypt clearly illustrates some of the complexities and subtleties of these dynamics of interdependence. Nasr Hamid Abu Zeid, an Associate Professor of Arabic at Cairo University at the time, applied for promotion to the rank of full professor in 1993. In accordance with normal academic procedures, he submitted his publications for review by departmental and university committees. All of his senior colleagues on those committees were impressed by the applicant's scholarship and recommended promotion, except one professor who objected strongly on the ground that some of the ideas expressed by Abu Zeid in his writings about the *Qur'an* amounted to apostasy (a repudiation of his faith in Islam). Soon after, this internal academic matter exploded into a major controversy in the Egyptian media, among political parties, trade union organizations, mosques, and other religious and intellectual fora throughout civil society, and even within official government circles.[25]

In this case, almost every segment or group of participants, including the government, is pursuing the issues (the controversy continues at the time of writing) from its own political, religious, organizational, and professional perspective. While some are genuinely concerned with the civil liberties and human rights implications and consequences of the case, others are using it primarily as a proxy for other political or intellectual objectives. The controversy is further complicated by the fact that someone instituted a personal law suit to have Professor Abu Zeid's wife divorced from him by judicial decree because, as an apostate from Islam, his marriage to a Muslim women is null and void.[26] That suit brought additional concerns about Islamic *Shari'a* law as personal law for Muslims in Egypt, issues of independence of the judiciary, and so forth. While some resent the power of the courts to annul a marriage against the wishes of both spouses, others insist that the couple would be "living in sin" should the marriage be allowed to stand. To a third group, the question could simply provide an opportunity to insist on expanding or restricting the application of *Shari'a*, regardless of the merits of the case at hand. Alliances among various protagonists were built and dissolved according to their political or other objectives, irrespective of the consequences for Abu Zeid personally, or for freedom of expression as an abstract principle.

There are also regional and international dimensions to this dynamic of interdependence between claimants whose petitions are determined by con-

---

[25] For an overview of this controversy, see CHRISTIAN SCI. MONITOR, Jun. 23, 1995, at 1; CHI. TRIB., Jul. 4, 1995, at 1; 42 WORLD PRESS REV., Oct. 1995, at 18; Deborah Pugh, *Court Case Casts Doubt on Secularism in Egypt Accused of Apostacy*, CHRISTIAN SCI. MONITOR, June 24, 1993, at 1; Stover H. Rawley, *Egyptian Intellectuals Feel Trapped, Strict Islamic Law Ensnarls Professor*, CHI. TRIB. July, 4, 1995, at 1; Amira Howeidy Mara Nahhas Mara Anis, *The Persecution of Abu Zeid*, WORLD PRESS REV., Oct. 1995, at 18.

[26] The divorce case has come to an alarming conclusion because the Supreme Court of Egypt upheld the rulings of lower courts to dissolve the marriage for apostasy. Another cycle begins, a court of first instance has refused to enforce that judgment on the grounds that the applicant lacks standing (has no personal interest) in the matter. That decision is being appealed by the applicant at the time of writing (January 1997). Observers believe that both the judiciary and the government of Egypt hope for a protracted appellate process that will ease political and legal tensions in this case. That is no consolation, however, to Professor Abu Zeid, who stands guilty of apostasy, nor his wife, who was legally divorced from her husband against her will and his. Another appeal by Abu Zeid's lawyers against the apostasy ruling has also been lodged, but Abu Zeid and his wife are currently forced to live abroad for fear that Islamic extremists will decide to "execute" the death penalty for apostasy on the couple. For recent developments in this case, see Judith Miller, *New Tuck for Egypt's Islamic Militants: Imposing Divorce*, N.Y. TIMES, Dec. 28, 1996, at 19.

cerns not necessarily related to freedom of expression. For example, it is obvious that the cases of Salman Rushdie and Taslima Nasreen, mentioned earlier, raise fundamental issues of freedom of expression in Islamic societies. But it would be extremely naive and misleading to present these issues without also considering the long and complex history of the relationship between the Islamic countries and Western and regional powers. To all sides of the issue, the controversy over the CNN report on female circumcision in Egypt was more about issues of self-determination, national sovereignty and pride, the role of Islamic political activism in the country, the human rights of women, and Western cultural imperialism than freedom of expression. In all three cases, international actors were equally as involved and as capable of influencing the course and outcome of events as internal actors. This broader and more realistic understanding of the complexities of these situations is necessary both for determining the scope, objectives, and beneficiaries of freedom of expression and for developing strategies for overcoming the obstacles facing the realization of this right in specific Islamic societies and beyond.

These internal and external processes of interdependence are simplified here for the sake of argument. In reality, issues will rarely be presented in such clear-cut terms of support or opposition to freedom of expression as such, or even to the particular claim. In all probability, a claim to freedom of expression will not be presented, supported, or opposed in its own specific terms, but rather as part of broader issues or concerns. Both supporters and opponents would usually consist of coalitions of actors who may be pursuing political or other objectives that have little to do with freedom of expression in an abstract sense. The whole process, moreover, will be greatly influenced, if not determined for all practical purposes, by such factors as the general dynamics of political, economic, social, and cultural power relations in the given situation, the timing of the claim in relation to other issues and concerns, and the psychology and inter-personal or inter-group relations of relevant actors. The same freedom of expression issue may evoke different responses, depending on whether it is presented in a form perceived to threaten fundamental interests of dominant individuals or groups, at a time of general crisis, or in a manner that is offensive to potential allies or conciliatory to possible opponents.

The point I wish to emphasize is that freedom of expression, like all other human rights, should not be conceived, articulated, or asserted in abstract terms. Rather, its nature should be informed by its internal and external political, economic, social, and cultural context. Whether locally, regionally, or globally, freedom of expression can only be practiced within a specific framework of human relations and material circumstances. I would hasten to add, however, that to acknowledge this obvious fact is not to take a deterministic or apologetic view of the concept, scope, and practice of freedom of expression in any given society or situation. Rather, my purpose here is to take a visionary and forward-looking, yet realistic and practicable, view of the concept and its implementation. As I have argued earlier, situations restrictive of freedom of expression can and must be changed, and violations of this human right should never be rationalized on cultural or contextual grounds. But any successful strategy for changing restrictive circumstances or challenging cultural and contextual justifications of violation must clearly identify and address a variety of underlying issues, even though some of them may not appear to be directly relevant to freedom of expression as such.

V. Freedom of Expression in Kenya and Sudan

In this section, I propose to apply the preceding analysis to the prospects of freedom of expression in Kenya and Sudan. In view of the difficulty noted earlier of establishing a causal relationship between either suppression or protection of freedom of expression, on the one hand, and a certain state of affairs, on the other, my argument is as follows. First, I argue that although freedom of expression had little chance to be secured and institutionalized under post-colonial conditions, the actual record shows that its suppression did not prove to be conducive to the achievement of the objectives of national unity, stability, or development. Here, I simply associate suppression of free expression with failure to achieve those national objectives which are commonly cited as justifications for such suppression. However, the implication is that protecting freedom of expression will yield better results. To support this proposition, I will briefly propose a strategy for integrating protection of freedom of expression in the political and legal systems of African countries as a more viable means of achieving legitimate national and communal objectives, as well as safeguarding individual dignity and human rights. Given the realities of weak articulation and lack of institutionalized protection of this freedom in the two countries, however, I will draw on preceding sections of this paper to try to imagine how universality of validity and application of freedom of expression might work in the harsh realities of Kenya and Sudan.

To place this discussion in context, one should begin with a brief overview of the postcolonial history of the two countries. With such a perspective, one may understand the realistic prospects for freedom of expression at the time of independence and its subsequent fate at the hands of the African elites who took over. Reflecting on recent history, however, one is immediately struck by a paradox. These countries were supposed to have inherited constitutional order and democratic government from their colonial rulers, with freedom of expression playing a central role. However, colonialism and its aftermath burdened these nations with structural obstacles that impeded the progress of constitutionalism and democracy. As the total negation of sovereign constitutional and democratic self-governance, colonialism could not have possibly prepared the peoples of these countries for what they were supposed to be. This is not a justification for oppression and violation of rights by native ruling elites since independence, but an attempt to understand how and why these tragic consequences came about, in order to better redress them.

After a long history of encouraging and institutionalizing European settlement of Kenya and the total subjugation of its native African population, Britain was finally forced to return the country to its own people with little preparation for democratic self-governance.[27] For example, the so-called "Council of Ministers" appointed by the British government in 1954 to run the daily administration of Kenya consisted of three Europeans, two Asians, and one African. As late as 1959, the British government, had decided that Kenya was to achieve full independence in 1975. Within a year, however, the British government was obliged by a combination of Kenyan agitation and international pressure for decolonization to convene a "constitutional conference" in London to renegotiate the political future of the country. Full independence came by December of 1963, after two national elections (1961 and 1963) and another constitutional conference in between the elections that resulted in massive transfers of land from European settlers to African hands, paid for by funds from the World Bank. Instead of being "prepared" for independence, which was supposed to materialize some sixteen years after the unilateral colonial decision of 1959, Kenya was pushed into full sovereign statehood within three years.

Upon achieving full independence in December of 1963, Kenya adopted a

---

[27] DECOLONIZATION AND INDEPENDENCE IN KENYA 1948-93 (B.A. Ogot & W.R. Ochieng eds., Ohio University Press 1995); NORMAN N. MILLER, KENYA: THE QUEST FOR PROSPERITY (1984).

constitution establishing a parliamentary system of government and providing for fundamental rights including freedom of expression.[28] The Constitution, written in London and enacted by the British Parliament, purported to establish Kenya as an independent state within the British Commonwealth, with the Queen of the United Kingdom as its head of state. The first amendment of the Constitution in 1964 severed the colonial link to make Kenya a republic, but subsequent amendments in 1979, 1983, 1988, 1991, and 1992 were enacted for internal political purposes. The struggle for independence and immediate postcolonial politics were dominated by two political parties: Kenya African National Union (KANU) and the Kenya African Democratic Union (KADU). Although the country became a de facto single party state with the merger of these two parties in 1964, the Constitution was amended in 1982 to formalize the political reality of a single party state, only to be amended again in 1991 to relegalize multiparty politics. While KANU continues to rule, ten opposition parties are now recognized and operational, but only with great difficulty and no real prospects of challenging KANU's monopoly of power.[29]

Consider the implications of Kenya's rapid transition from total colonial rule to complete independence without the requisite political and legal institutions or economic infra-structure, but with the dangers of ethic hostility, regional instability, global economic adversity, and cold war rivalries. For example, Kenya has been plagued by intense ethnic politics since the struggle for independence, when smaller ethnic groups supported the KADU to guard against a KANU comprised of the Kikuyu and Luo.[30] Recently, political and economic competition between Kenya's ethnic groups has resulted in more than 1,500 deaths and the displacement of over 300,000 in the Rift Valley region.[31] Those events and their local security consequences are often cited by the government to justify emergency measures, including severe restrictions on freedom of expression. Regional developments over the last three

---

[28] For a discussion of the creation of the Independence Constitution and subsequent changes, see INFORMATION, FREEDOM AND CENSORSHIP: THE ARTICLE 19 WORLD REPORT 31 (1988).

[29] For a discussion on the relationship between the political parties, the state and civil society, see JENNIFER A. WINDER, THE RISE OF A PARTY-STATE IN KENYA 162-97 (1992).

[30] Current estimates of ethnic divisions are as follows: Kikuyu 22%, Luhya 14%, Luo 13%, Kalenjin 12%, Kamba 11%, Kisii 6%, Asian, European and Arab 1%, other 15%. CHRISTOPHER J.S. VANCE, CIA WORLD FACTBOOK <http://www.adfa.oz.au:80/CS/flags/ke/95.txt>.

[31] *See* U.S. DEP'T OF STATE, *Country Reports on Human Rights Practices for 1995: Kenya* 127 (1996); *Migrants and Refugees in Africa* (discussed in EMERGING HUMAN RIGHTS 145-62 (1990); *see also* JENNIFER A. WIDNER, THE RISE OF A PARTY-STATE IN KENYA 81 (1992).

decades, from extreme political instability and civil war in four of its five neighbors (Ethiopia, Somalia, Sudan, and Uganda), to the collapse of the East African Community in 1977, have also had immediate and drastic economic and security consequences for Kenya.[32] The country's economy is extremely vulnerable to the unmitigated impact of global economic factors, from dramatic fluctuations in the prices of coffee and tea, its main exports, to massive rises in the cost of its fuel imports in 1973, 1974, and 1979.[33]

A similar analysis applies to the situation of Sudan, which achieved independence in 1956 from Anglo-Egyptian colonial rule in the same hurried and disorganized manner that was subsequently experienced by Kenya and many other African countries.[34] Sudan is also vulnerable to global economic forces and is severely affected by regional instability and civil war, such as the thirty years of Eritrean struggle for independence from Ethiopia and the cycles of civil war in Chad and Uganda. But Sudan's difficulties are most clearly reflected in its own combination of civil war and the role of Islam in national politics.[35] The first civil war broke out in southern Sudan in 1955 and continued through cycles of civilian and military rule until it was temporarily settled in 1972, only to be resumed from 1983 to the present. Neither political stability nor economic and social development have been possible because of this protracted and highly destructive civil war. Adding to the complex and deep rooted causes of the north-south conflict, political Islam has surfaced and rendered peaceful resolution with unity extremely difficult.

Sudan was united for the first time, within more or less its present boundaries, by the Ottoman Egyptian invasion of 1820, though the process of unification and "pacification" took many decades. That phase of colonial rule ended in 1884 when the nationalist religious leader Muhammed Ahmed (Al-Mahdi) culminated his military success by capturing Khartoum and establish-

---

[32] *See* Miller, *supra* note 27, at 137-38 (discussing the failure of the East African Community); *see also* Katete Orwa, *Foreign Policy, 1963-86, in* A MODERN HISTORY OF KENYA 1895-1980, 234-41 (William R. Ochieng ed., 1989) (discussing the return to equilibrium following the end of the EAC).

[33] *See* WIDNER, *supra* note 31, at 183-87 (material regarding the effect the policies of President Moi and the KANU on the effectiveness of the coffee and tea export industry); Miller, *supra* note 27, at 111-16 (discussing oil import prices and coffee and tea).

[34] On Sudan's transition to independence and subsequent politcal and economic developments see MUDDATHI ABD AL-RAHIM, IMPERIALISM AND NATIONALISM IN THE SUDAN (1969); TIM NIBLOCK, CLASS AND POWER IN SUDAN: THE DYNAMICS OF SUDANESE POLITICS 1898-1985 (1987).

[35] For various perspectives on the civil war, see CIVIL WAR IN THE SUDAN (M.W. Daly & Ahmad Alawad Sikainga eds., British Academic Press 1993); FRANCIS M. DENG, WAR OF VISIONS: CONFLICT OF IDENTITIES IN THE SUDAN (1995).

ing the first "Islamic" state in the history of the region. However, the Mahdist state was destroyed thirteen years later with the Anglo-Egyptian conquest of 1898 and the establishment of a joint colonial administration in which Britain acted as the senior partner, occupying Egypt itself at the time to "protect" British and other European interests in the region. But the rivalry between the two colonial powers ultimately facilitated the independence of the country in 1956, the first in sub-Saharan Africa.

Colonial administrations are by definition exploitative and oppressive, but the more serious legacy of these two phases of colonialism in Sudan is their role in fermenting the ethnic and political divisiveness that continues to haunt the country to the present day. For example, while both colonial administrations maintained the geographical unity of the entire country by force for their own exploitative reasons, they did nothing to promote ethnic harmony or political and social cohesion. On the contrary, the Ottoman-Egyptian colonial rule of the last century continued the slave trade for most of its reign, with the southern part of the country as the source of slaves and some northern Sudanese acting as intermediaries.[36] The native Mahdist state practiced institutionalized chattel slavery for the duration of its rule. The British rulers of the country during the Anglo-Egyptian phase prohibited slavery, but kept the southern region strictly closed to northern Sudanese until the mid 1940s, less than ten years before independence.[37] Both phases of colonial rule (Ottoman-Egyptian and Anglo-Egyptian) totally excluded the local population from the government of their own land, relying on the expediency of traditional rulers to collect taxes and minimize the costs of administration. Yet, Sudan was supposed to emerge as a sovereign democratic country, enjoying the benefits of constitutional government and the rule of law, with the politics of "divide and conquer" as its only legacy from colonial rule.

Profound ambivalence among ruling northern Sudanese elites about the role of Islam in politics was always a destabilizing factor and an obstacle to constitutionalism since independence.[38] But the negative consequences have mounted since the National Islamic Front (NIF), a small Islamic fundamen-

---

[36] On slavery in Sudan and the region in general see ALLAN G.B. FISHER, SLAVERY AND MUSLIM SOCIETY IN AFRICA: THE INSTITUTION IN SAHARAN AND SUDANIC AFRICA AND THE TRANS-SAHAHRAN TRADE (1971).

[37] For British Closed Districts policy and general colonial practices, see M.O. BESHIR, THE SUDAN: BACKGROUND TO CONFLICT (1968).

[38] Abdullahi Ahmed An-Na'im, *The Elusive Islamic Constitution: The Sudanese Experience*, *in* ORIENT 329-40 (1985).

talist party, seized power through a military coup in June 1989. The insistence of the NIF regime to maintain and expand the application of *Shari'a* (historical formulations of Islamic law) means reducing all women and non-Muslim Sudanese to the status of second class citizens in their own country.[39] The totalitarian project of the NIF regime also devastated the already weakened institutions of state and civil society, as the government purged thousands of qualified Sudanese from the judiciary, civil, and diplomatic services, as well as the armed and security forces, to replace them with unqualified and highly politicized NIF cadres.[40] This regime also destroyed the educational system in an attempt to remold it in its own ideological image. Furthermore, the regime undermined the economy and security of the country by antagonizing most of Sudan's neighbors and much of the international community at large.

Both the governments of Kenya and Sudan have persistently responded to the difficulties of their respective countries with massive and systematic human rights violations.[41] In particular, freedom of expression was suppressed in Kenya for most of the thirty-five years of KANU.[42] This freedom was also suppressed by the three military regimes which ruled Sudan for thirty of its forty years of independent statehood.[43] Yet three to four decades after independence, the two countries continue to suffer from the same severe and protracted problems. As indicated earlier, it is important to my argument that the suppression of freedom of expression in Kenya and Sudan has not yielded better results for national unity, political stability, or economic development.

---

[39] Abdullah Ahmed An-Na'im, *Constitutional Discourse and the Civil War in the Sudan*, *in* CIVIL WAR IN THE SUDAN, *supra* note 35, at 97-116.

[40] ANN E. MAYER, ISLAM AND HUMAN RIGHTS: TRADITION AND POLITICS 25-29, 112-13, 157-59 (1995).

[41] *See, e.g.*, KENYA: SHADOW JUSTICE (London: African Rights, 1996) HUMAN RIGHTS WORLD REPORT 1993, 1994, 1995, Kenya (New York: Human Rights Watch, 1995); and U.S. DEP'T OF STATE, KENYA HUMAN RIGHTS PRACTICES, 1994 (1995).

On Sudan see, for example, BEHIND THE RED LINE: POLITICAL REPRESSION IN SUDAN (New York: Human Rights Watch, 1996), and reports of Casper Biro, the Special Rapporteur of the United Nations (1992-93).

[42] U.S. DEPARTMENT OF STATE, COUNTRY REPORTS ON HUMAN RIGHTS PRACTICES FOR 1995: KENYA 128-31 (1996).

[43] Two years after independence in 1956, Sudan had its first military regime which ruled until 1964. The second phase of civilian parliamentary government lasted only five years until the military took over again in May 1969, and ruled until 1985, when a combined military and civilian transitional government ruled for a year before handing the state over to civilian rule by April 1986. This third phase of civilian rule ended three years later with the NIF military coup of June 1989, which continues to rule until the time of writing (January 1997).

Thus, consider the following situations with a view towards reflecting on whether protecting freedom of expression would have been more conducive to addressing such matters of legitimate and fundamental national concern.

As can be expected, many local and national political and economic factors contribute to the continuing Rift Valley crisis in Kenya that resulted in massive killings and displacement of populations. One aspect of the crisis is ethnic competition over land and access to political power.[44] But upon closer examination, the evidence indicates that the government has manipulated existing tensions for its own political ends.

> On September 17 [1992], the Parliament's Select Committee on Ethnic Clashes released a report concluding that the violence was politically motivated and often incited by provincial officials. It called for criminal investigations of all politicians who had made inflammatory statements during the violence, and alleged that Nicholas Biwott and Ezekiel Barng'etuny, close associates of President Moi, were involved in organizing and financing the fighting.[45]

Whereas these politicians and local officials have been able to speak on the issues from their own perspective, others were denied the right to present their point of view.

Conflict in the Rift Valley or any other part of Kenya will continue, as it has done in all human societies throughout history, because people disagree over the distribution of wealth and power, and have different priorities and competing visions about matters of general concern. The role of government is to regulate the political and legal mediation and resolution of such conflicts, instead of attempting to suppress it or arbitrarily take one side against another. But those in control of the apparatus of the state are also human beings, with their own interests and biases. Ruling elites are also politically dependent upon the population at large in attempting to arbitrate between competing claims or seeking to promote their own. This is what I referred to earlier as interdependence of actors and factors within the country. Given this reality, it would seem obvious that protecting the freedom of expression of all concerned is the best means of mediating conflict. In view of the fact that those in control of the state are fallible human beings, the real possibilities of error, let alone bias or corrupt motives, cannot be exposed and scrutinized

---

[44] *See* WIDNER, *supra* note 31, at 77-84.

[45] HUMAN RIGHTS WATCH WORLD REPORT 1993, 17 (New York: Human Rights Watch, 1992).

without freedom of expression.

Similar analysis applies with regard to the role of Islam in the national politics of Sudan, which is also relevant to the civil war. The NIF is a small political party that advocates the establishment of an Islamic state and application of *Shari'a* throughout Sudan. It was part of the democratic process, represented in Parliament and briefly a partner in a coalition government in 1988, until it seized power through a military coup in 1989. Once in power through this fundamentally illegal manner, the NIF regime suspended the Constitution, banned all political parties and organizations, canceled all existing licences for publication or broadcast of any kind, and declared any political opposition by any means a capital offense punishable by death if done in collaboration with another.[46] Thus, the NIF installed itself as the sole legal political party in total control of the entire country, and then made it a serious crime for any person to even point out those obvious facts. Moreover, in addition to the usual psychological difficulty of Muslims to oppose the application of *Shari'a*, expressing such views can be deemed to constitute apostasy (for a Muslim to repudiate his or her faith in Islam) which is punishable by death under Section 126 of the Penal Code of 1991.[47] These are not merely theoretical possibilities because, as the record shows since the NIF came to power in 1989, severe restrictions on freedom of expression, among many other human rights violations, are indeed endemic in Sudan today.[48]

This state of affairs is totally unacceptable by its own alleged logic that the Muslims of Sudan are exercising their right to self-determination to establish an Islamic state governed by *Shari'a*. If that is the case, then why not allow the Muslims of Sudan to express that view and elect their constitutional government accordingly? What about the rights of Muslims, like myself, who disagree with the very concept of an Islamic state advocated by the NIF and oppose the application of *Shari'a* from an Islamic point of view?[49] More importantly, what about the rights of millions of non-Muslim Sudanese who are not accepted by *Shari'a* as equal citizens of an Islamic state? It is, therefore, not surprising that the role of Islam in national politics is a contributing factor to the continuation of the civil war. Moreover, while the NIF regime has

---

[46] Constitutional Decree Number 2 (1989) (published in Arabic *in* 1 LAWS OF SUDAN 3-5 (1992)).

[47] *Id.* at 84.

[48] *See, e.g.*, BEHIND THE RED LINE—POLITICAL REPRESSION IN SUDAN 142-63 (New York: Human Rights Watch, 1996).

[49] *See generally* ABDULLAHI AHMED AN-NA'IM, TOWARD AN ISLAMIC REFORMATION: CIVIL LIBERTIES, HUMAN RIGHTS, AND INTERNATIONAL LAW (1990).

characterized its war effort as *jihad* to defend Islam and the Islamic state, it also claims that the southern region of the country is exempt from the application of *Shari'a*. However, such exemption is neither permitted by *Shari'a* itself nor supported in practice. Yet, Sudanese of all religious and ethnic backgrounds are not allowed to verify the facts for themselves, or debate any of these matters of fundamental national importance and their far-reaching consequences.

The strategy I propose for integrating protection of freedom of expression in the political and legal systems of African countries is premised on the preceding discussion of the contingent universality of this human right. This notion of contingency means that a certain configuration of factors and forces may lead to the persistent, perhaps even structural or institutionalized violation of freedom of expression, while another configuration may lead to its systematic and institutionalized protection. But to identify one configuration would not by itself result in a significant change in the dynamics of such contingency that produces a different and sustainable outcome. It is important to devise and implement specific strategies to address adverse factors in order to make the situation as a whole more conducive to the protection of freedom of expression. Although such strategies will of course have to be tailored to the particular circumstances of each situation, the following broad framework might be useful in devising and implementing them in practice.

1) However obvious or self-evident one may believe the universal validity and utility of freedom of expression to be, that does not mean it will materialize by a simple proclamation or affirmation of this fact. Nevertheless, the widest possible appreciation of such universal validity and utility is crucial for generating positive political and legal support for this right, as well as in anticipation of rationalizations of its violation or "postponement" in the name of achieving some alleged public good or another.

2. Because of the obvious universal validity and utility of freedom of expression, it is unlikely to be challenged openly and as a matter of principle. Instead, some argument would be advanced to justify or rationalize violation or postponement. Moreover, such arguments or rationalizations will probably have some apparent plausibility to the constituency for which they are intended. Otherwise, there will be no expectation of benefit or advantage to those who make such claims. Therefore, to dismiss such arguments or rationalizations without careful consideration and response, addressed to the same constituency, plays into the hands of those who make them, who will then have the political support of the constituency in question.

3. One should also consider the possibility of some underlying legitimate concern or public interest that appears to be better served by denying or restricting freedom of expression in general, or in a given limited sense. To the extent that such concerns or interests exist, one should address them in a deliberate strategy of response. For example, the government of Kenya claims that it is necessary to suppress expressions of ethnic hatred or incitement to violence in the Rift Valley. Simply denying that such a risk exists can be counter-productive, not only because the public at large appreciates the risk and may have personal experience of it, but also fails to account for such considerations in the definition and practice of freedom of expression. It is, therefore, better to acknowledge the risk and show how freedom of expression can help reduce, rather than increase ethnic tensions.

4. It is neither practical in realistic political terms, nor desirable as a matter of principle, to pursue the promotion of freedom of expression by drawing on the support of a narrow constituency or in disregard to public opinion at large. Advocates of this right must continue to strive to expand political support for their objectives among all segments of the population, and build alliances with advocates of other causes. Both aspects of this process should be pursued through long and short term plans as stages in a process, and with a serious expectation of set-backs or loss on one aspect or another.

5. It should also be emphasized that the struggle for securing the protection of this right never ends, even in societies in which the right appears to enjoy wide acceptance and implementation. For one thing, if one takes a proactive and affirmative view of the right as enabling all people to express themselves, and not merely preventing governmental restraints, much needs to be done to realize that vision in all societies. Moreover, there are always risks of regression or gradual erosion of freedom of expression. Consequently, strategies should include a constant push to expand the scope of the right, and defensive measures to sustain it in daily life.

6. Both of these dimensions require institutional and educational measures to secure achieved gains and promote further development of the right. Since legal mechanisms do not work in a cultural and political vacuum, strategies should include early socialization and continuous education of the entire population on the vital importance and practical utility of freedom of expression in everyday life, as well as with regard to major national and societal issues and concerns. In particular, freedom of expression must be shown as conducive to the achievement of all desirable objectives, and never as an obstacle to their realization. This will require clearer definitions and more careful

implementation of the right.

7. Due regard must also be given to the role of external factors and actors, both in favor and against the protection and promotion of freedom of expression. While idealism is important for sustaining the endless effort that needs to be made, naivety is counter-productive. Not all proclaimed advocates of human rights are genuine, and most have mixed motives for their agenda. Even the most enlightened and humane of foreign governments have to cope with competing claims on their resources at home and abroad.

These are some general principles and guidelines that I believe to be useful in constructing local, national, and global strategies for the promotion and protection of freedom of expression. As emphasized earlier, each situation must be taken on its own terms, and in relation to its particular combination of factors and forces, both for and against the universal validity and application of human rights. In relation to Kenya and Sudan, for example, one would have to begin with the stark realities of institutionalized and structural suppression of freedom of expression, and political and economic oppression in general. Moreover, as indicated earlier, not all sources of such suppression and oppression are internal to these and other African countries. But I believe that there is an appropriate and effective response to each and every set of obstacles and difficulties, whether it is local, national, or global. The only unsurmountable obstacle is the limitations we place on our own imagination and will to act accordingly.

VI. Conclusions

In this paper, I attempt to make a case for a more nuanced understanding of the universal validity and application of freedom of expression as a *contingent project* that needs to draw on a wide range of internal and external actors and factors for its realization. Given this dynamic of local, regional, and global determinants, universal validity and application should be promoted from both sides of the process: from the specific practice to global consensus and vice versa. My analysis has only touched on some of the issues in order to explain and substantiate the proposed framework of contingent universality. Realizing the difficulty of establishing causal connections between the status of freedom of expression in a specific context and a certain state of affairs, I have tried to present a general framework for strategies for promoting the universality of this fundamental human right. Similar analysis can be made, and strategies drawn, in relation to other human rights. But I also realize that much of my tentative analysis and conclusions can benefit from further reflection and elaboration.

I also wish to conclude this essay by calling on human rights advocates throughout the world to contribute to the promotion of the universality of this and other human rights with a carefully considered and realistic understanding of the true nature, possibilities, and limitations of any universalist project. Such understanding should also include problems associated with the circumstances of realizing human rights in national struggles and within the framework of power-oriented international law and relations. Given the need to substantiate assumptions of universality, and opportunity to contribute to its construction through overlapping consensus among the peoples of the world, all advocates of freedom of expression must debate, articulate, and struggle for their own conceptions of, and priorities in pursuing, the protection of this and other human rights. This needs to be done, moreover, through the mobilization of political support and other resources within a framework of interdependence at home and abroad, and in the context of the terms and objectives of power struggles at the national and global levels.

While human rights advocates within each society can expect assistance from external allies who support freedom of expression as a universal human right, they must rely primarily on their own "home" constituencies because that is where the cause is won or lost in the most concrete and specific terms. Far from voluntarily surrendering their power and privilege, ruling elites will employ every tool at their disposal to maintain control, including the manipulation of public opinion against the protection of human rights. Other groups competing for power in their own narrowly-defined self-interest will attempt to do the same, thereby confusing the issues for the public at large even further. Abuses of freedom of expression by transnational actors constitute another source of confusion. Nevertheless, human rights advocates must compete with all these forces, and overcome all possibilities of confusion and manipulation, in seeking to secure sufficient political support for their cause, at both the national and international levels. To be effective in doing so, however, they need the empathetic understanding and active support of fellow advocates from other parts of the world.

Though detailed strategies for protecting and promoting freedom of expression are bound to differ from one situation to another, as well as over time, I suggest the popularization of this human right be a permanent feature. Whatever else may succeed in enlisting political support and generate legal protection for freedom of expression, a strong sense of its relevance and utility to the public at large is indispensable. To this end, this freedom must neither be perceived to be the exclusive domain of the literate, articulate, and creative few, nor be allowed to be seen as threatening other national or societal objectives that are more easily appreciated by the public at large. On the contrary, it must be appreciated for its effective service of all legitimate public (national, social) objectives, as well as gratifying private and personal aims of intellectual and emotional growth and fulfillment.

In light of this analysis, I conclude that since the status of freedom of expression at any given point in time and place is a product of the abovementioned internal and external interdependence of forces, both in favor of and against this right, and that the balance of these forces can change in either direction, freedom of expression is neither totally secured nor completely lost at the local, regional, or global levels. Advocates of freedom of expression have to work within their actual societies and cultures, and perhaps seek support and forge alliances with some of the same political configurations which may initially be hostile or indifferent to freedom of expression. They also need to work within the regional and global situation and circumstances of their societies, and seek support and forge alliances at that external level as well. In the process of transforming their societies and cultures towards greater respect for, and protection of, freedom of expression in local as well as broader regional and international contexts, advocates of freedom of expression have to work within those societies, and their contexts, as they exist and not as they wish them to be. To devise and implement effective strategies for the protection of freedom of expression, they need to understand their societies and characterize their political configurations with regard to this universal human right, as well as the nature and impact of external actors and factors. They need to know, and learn to draw upon, all internal and external resources available to them in this struggle.

[15]

Why should Muslims abandon *Jihad*? Human Rights and the Future of International Law

ABSTRACT *This article examines the basis and reality of international legality and the universality of human rights from an Islamic perspective. The author calls for principled commitment and systematic respect for the institutional framework of international legality and the rule of law to encourage Muslims to abandon traditional notions of* jihad. *Similarly, since the institutional framework of legality and the rule of law in international relations is necessary for the protection of human rights as well, the absence of this framework would undermine the credibility and viability of human rights norms.*

The question in this title is intended in both real and rhetorical senses, questioning the basis of prohibition of *jihad* and upholding the universality of human rights in ways that can reaffirm the commitment of Muslims to international legality. While it is clear that the term '*jihad*' has many meanings, and there are various requirements for its proper application or deployment,[1] I am using it here to refer to the unilateral use of force by Muslims in pursuit of political objectives and outside the institutional framework of international legality and the rule of law in general. Since the framework of legality and the rule of law is lacking in 'the real world', there would be no basis for expecting Muslims to abandon *jihad*, as defined here. Moreover, since this institutional framework of legality of the rule of law in international relations is necessary for the protection of human rights as well, the absence of this framework undermines the credibility and viability of human rights norms.

My own position is that human beings everywhere are responsible for protecting each other against the risks of our shared vulnerability to arbitrary violence, poverty and injustice generally. As clearly shown by the terrorist attacks in New York, Madrid and London, the most technologically advanced countries are as vulnerable to arbitrary violence as the least developed ones, anywhere in the world.[2] The question for me is how can we all fulfil this mutual responsibility, instead of seeing the issues in terms of an 'Islamic threat' to human rights or to the security of some Western countries?

But this objective would neither be coherent nor politically viable in the absence of consistent observance of these norms and mechanisms of the rule of law in international relations. If that is the case, then Muslims should still abandon *jihad* in favour of upholding international law and human rights around the world, but should also realise that such calls will not be heeded in practice if those principles are not also honoured by other societies. Moreover, these principles cannot be true to their underlying rationale if they are not inclusive of all of humanity, including Muslims.

Muslims constitute about one-fifth of the total world population, living in every continent and region, though predominantly in Africa and Asia, and constituting the clear majority of the population in 44 states.[3] Such demographic facts confirm the reality of linkages between Islam and international law, but do not define the terms of this relationship one way or the other. As briefly explained below, the relationship between religion, human rights and international law should be examined regarding all religious traditions, and not only those of Islam. In all cases, however, the issue can be meaningful only when it is about believers and not the religion in the abstract, that is, it is about Muslims not Islam, Jews not Judaism, and so forth, thereby raising the same question for all religious traditions. Once framed in this way the issue becomes about people in their social, economic and political context, in relation to their understanding or practice of their religion. For all believers the question is how do human beings negotiate the relationships between their religious beliefs and practice, on the one hand, and mundane concerns with security and well-being, on the other? This perspective also emphasises that such questions are asked about specific Muslims or Hindus, for instance, and not about all Muslims as a monolithic undifferentiated global community.

Regarding the subject of this article, the manner in which different Islamic societies are likely to interact with international law or human rights will probably be influenced by the same sort of factors and conditions that affect other human societies. The so-called 'Islamic factor' is only one among others in this process, and outcomes also tend to be affected by other factors and context. For example, as briefly explained below, the controversy about the publication of cartoons of the Prophet in Denmark is more about the socioeconomic situation of Muslims in Europe, political conditions in Islamic majority countries and their neo-colonial relations with Western powers than it is about Islam and Muslims as such. Islam and Islamic identity are indeed relevant, but they are neither definitive causes of how Muslims behave nor isolated factors to the extent they are relevant.

How international and lawful is international law?

My purpose here is to affirm and promote the legitimacy and efficacy of international law as the indispensable means for realising universal ideals of peace, development and the protection of human rights, everywhere. From this perspective the issue cannot be about the so-called 'West' being the primary author of international law and fully conforming to its principles and underlying values, while the rest of the world is struggling to subscribe to and comply with them. For international law to play its role in realising shared ideals of justice and equality under the rule of law for all human beings it must be both truly international and legitimately lawful. It has to be equally accepted and implemented by all human societies, not something that some may choose to ignore while others are required to observe it.

Although there have been several parallel systems for regulating inter-state relations throughout human history until the mid-20th century, there can now be only one system of international law in the present globally integrated, and interdependent, world. But international law cannot be limited to the European system of inter-state relations that has evolved since the 18th century, and which was simply a regional system, like the Chinese, Hindu, Roman and Islamic systems that preceded it. The fact that the European powers managed to extend the domain of their regional system further and more completely than any of the earlier imperial powers does not make it truly international. After all, that parochial European system, often called 'traditional international law', had justified the military conquest and colonisation of much of Asia, almost all of Africa and elsewhere on the basis of European conceptions of sovereignty and legality. The vast majority of the peoples of Africa and Asia had no possibility of being true subjects of international law until the decolonisation process after the Second World War. Native populations of the Americas and Australia are unlikely ever to be considered subjects of traditional international law because they are not allowed to have 'sovereignty' in European terms.

From this perspective I am using the term 'international law' here to refer to the legal system that has evolved since the end of the Second World War, especially through the United Nations and the decolonisation process of the second half of the 20th century. It is only during this phase of decolonisation that international law has become the legitimate legal framework for recognition of national sovereignty and territorial jurisdiction throughout the world, including in all Islamic countries. It is also the legal framework for international relations in matters ranging from issues of international peace and security to countless routine yet essential daily transactions in such fields as health, postal services, trade, travel and the environment.

Accordingly, I take the Charter of the United Nations of 1945 to be the most authoritative normative framework of international law we have so far, although it is certainly not sufficient for addressing some of the fundamental challenges facing the prospects of international legality today. The UN Charter is foundational not only as the most widely binding treaty that establishes a viable institutional framework for realising the fundamental purposes and rationale of international law, but also because of its commitment to the self-determination and equal sovereignty of all the peoples of the world. It clearly follows from this premise that the use of military force is not allowed except in accordance with the Charter of the United Nations, namely, in strict self-defence under Article 51 of the Charter, or when sanctioned by the Security Council under Chapter VII. There cannot be any possibility of lawful use of force beyond these two grounds, whether claimed as 'pre-emptive self-defence', 'just war' or Islamic *jihad*.

The point I am making here is stronger than simply saying that it is illegal as a matter of international law to use military force beyond the strict limits of the UN Charter. My point is that it is *theoretically incoherent and practically impossible* to maintain such limitations unless it is done regarding every actor, whether acting under the auspices of a state or not. It is incoherent and futile to prohibit aggressive Islamic *jihad* without doing the same for any use of force outside the ambit of the UN Charter in the name of national self-interest. From this perspective, there is no moral, political or practical difference between international terrorism in the name of Islamic *jihad*, on the one hand, and so-called pre-emptive self-defence or humanitarian intervention claimed by the USA in Iraq, on the other. Both are instances of 'self-regulated' use of force outside the institutional framework of the UN, and are so inherently arbitrary and unaccountable that they undermine the very possibility of international law. One of the primary constraints of the Charter's framework, however, is that it is limited to states, although the UN has managed to include civil society organisations, especially in the human rights field. But it is not possible to redress this situation unless international law is consistently observed by states as its primary subjects. It is futile for state actors to demand observance of international law principles by non-state actors when they are unwilling to abide by those principles themselves.

The necessary qualities of being *both* 'international' *and* 'law' that I am concerned with in raising these issues relate to the normative underpinnings or guiding principles as well as to the objectives and methods of the system as a whole. They also pertain to the relationship between international law and its subjects, that is, how its subjects are identified and how they contribute to the making and implementation of the law. International law cannot command the allegiance and co-operation of international actors, who are no longer limited to states, unless it is able to include them in its principles and institutions. In other words, the exclusion of other appropriate subjects in addition to states denies those other social agents the possibility of contributing to the making of the law and enhancing its legitimacy through broader democratic participation and accountability.

There is therefore an urgent need for an *imaginative* approach to include other types of international actors as subjects of international law, and to international law reform more generally. This inclusive and imaginative approach is particularly urgent in the present context of intensified globalisation, which is diminishing state sovereignty, and of the mounting role of various non-state actors in international relations. Globalisation has accelerated and intensified the complexities of social identities and social interactions, in addition to creating new kinds of frameworks of internationality which are different from the international law model of territorial states.[4] In my view the emerging international law principle of universal jurisdiction and establishment of the International Criminal Court illustrate this more inclusive approach by extending their reach to more subjects, such as perpetrators of crimes against humanity and their victims.

The impressive record of daily success of international law in a wide range of fields, including international peace and security and facilitating trade and co-operation in the fields of health, postal services, trade, travel and the environment, is often overlooked because of understandable concerns about a few highly visible apparent failures in securing international peace and security. This concern with peace and security cannot be addressed except through strict compliance with international law by all states, without exception. In fact, compliance by the most powerful states is a stronger indication of the legal authority of international law, as the practice of weak states is likely to be dismissed as more motivated by fear of retaliation or opportunistic calculations than by a sense of legal obligation. As explained later, this point is underscored by both the terrorist attacks of 9/11/2001 in the USA and by the global crusade by the USA and its allies, especially the military invasion and colonisation of Iraq in March 2003.

It is equally clear that the ability of international law to achieve its objectives is contingent on the willingness and ability of a wide range of actors voluntarily to comply with its dictates. The total and continuous coercive enforcement of any legal system is both impossible in practice and also assumes high levels of political commitment and institutional capacity that may not necessarily be available or forthcoming. Since no enforcement regime can cope with massive and persistent violations, any legal system must assume a high level of voluntary compliance in order to have the will and ability to enforce its rules in the exceptional cases when that is necessary. This is not to suggest that coercive enforcement is immaterial, but only to emphasise that its role is both limited and contingent. Direct use of force or the threat of it may ensure compliance with rules in the short term, but it is not sustainable over time. That is, the limited though important role of coercive enforcement should be understood in a broader context of the other factors that make a legal system work. In particular, it is necessary to understand the factors that motivate or encourage the subjects of a legal system to comply voluntarily with its dictates to a sufficient degree that makes coercive enforcement possible, when necessary.

As a general rule states do in fact comply with the vast majority of international law norms, for the same sorts of reasons people have for obeying any legal system, such as self-interest and fear of retaliation by others. In particular, the clear limitations of the military or economic power of all states, including the USA as the so-called sole superpower, mean that all of them have to rely on international legality for their own survival. Events like the terrorist attacks of 9/11 clearly show that even the most powerful states are vulnerable to the arbitrary action of individual international terrorists, for whose crimes no state can be held accountable under traditional notions of state responsibility. I would therefore conclude that it is both dangerously unrealistic and unnecessarily limiting to focus exclusively on 'state practice' as the primary source of international law. For example, it is dangerous to emphasise traditional notions of exclusive territorial jurisdiction when national boundaries are being violated by many unaccountable, sometimes undetectable, actors.[5]

In conclusion of this section I would emphasise the paramount importance of reaffirming our principled and systematic commitment to a globally inclusive international law. Since it is impossible to reverse the process of decolonisation and self-determination, selective assertions of principles of international law or territorial sovereignty will simply provoke retaliatory responses by others. Before offering further reflections in relation to Islamic societies in particular, let me introduce the second theme of this article.

Universality of human rights

Regarding the other side of the title of this article, human rights by definition are rights which are due to every human being by virtue of his or her humanity, without any requirement of membership of any group or other qualification. It is wrong, in my view, to attribute this idea to such documents as the English Bill of Rights, the American Declaration of Independence and the Constitution or the French Declaration of the Rights of Man and the Citizen. This is because those documents were explicitly about the rights of citizens of specific territorial states, not of human beings everywhere. The point is clearly illustrated by the brutal colonial expansion of England and France in Africa and Asia under the auspices of their respective 'foundational' documents. Similarly, it took an intensive civil war and constitutional amendment to end slavery in the USA almost a century after independence, while the genocide of those native inhabitants known as American Indians continued into the 20th century.

In fact, the idea of the universal rights of all human beings as such was inconceivable before the Charter of the United Nations of 1945, establishment of the United Nations and the consequent process of decolonisation during the subsequent decades. The vast majority of Africans and Asians could not have had any possibility of human rights under European colonialism. Yet those earlier English, French and American documents did in fact shape the 'content' of human rights texts once the idea was established through the UN Charter and the Universal Declaration of Human Rights of 1948.[6]

Given the large numbers of Muslims around the world, as noted earlier, it is clear that one cannot speak of universal human rights without taking into consideration the perspectives and experiences of Islamic societies. But in what sense are the Islamic beliefs of Muslims anywhere relevant to their acceptance or implementation of human rights standards in theory or practice? Since Islam, or any other religion for that matter, cannot be the sole source or cause of the behaviour of believers, Muslims may accept or reject human rights norms regardless of what is believed to be the prevalent Islamic view on the subject. The level of compliance with human rights norms is more likely to be associated with such conditions as the degree of political stability and economic and social development in post-colonial Islamic societies than with Islam as such. To the extent that Islam is a relevant factor, its impact or influence cannot be understood in isolation from those broader conditions, as well as from the specific interpretation of Islamic precepts that are prevalent in the particular country or region. It is not possible therefore to predict or explain the degree or quality of human rights compliance as the necessary or unavoidable consequence of the relationship between Islam and human rights in an abstract theoretical sense.

In practice, moreover, the vast majority of Islamic states (in the sense of Muslims being the majority of the population) have ratified most international human rights treaties, and their record of compliance is similar or comparable to that of other countries in their regions. That is, the human rights record of Islamic countries in East or West Africa, South or Southeast Asia is similar to that of other countries in those regions, presumably because of shared factors, such as level of political stability, economic development, legal systems and institutional capacity. Many Muslims, whether in a majority or minority situation, have also expressed their acceptance of human rights by struggling for the protection of those rights locally, and in collaboration and solidarity with other persons and civil society organisations throughout the world.[7]

To my knowledge, there are no studies showing that having a Muslim majority or significant minority of the population is correlated with a lower human rights performance by states or that Muslims have less of a commitment to human rights than non-Muslims in comparable situations. On the contrary, some studies show that Muslims share commitments to these values.[8] The Islamic tradition at large is basically consistent with most human rights norms, except for some specific, albeit very serious, aspects of the rights of women and freedom of religion and belief. In other words, there are no factual or normative bases for the negative perception about Islam and Muslims in relation to human rights, although certain aspects of *Shari'a* are problematic in this regard. It is not possible to discuss these problematic aspects of the rights of women and freedom of religion here, and I have proposed elsewhere ways of overcoming them from an Islamic perspective.[9] The premise of the approach I support is that it is better to seek to transform the understanding of Muslims of those aspects of *Shari'a*, than to confront them with a stark choice between Islam and human rights. Such a choice is not only an offensive violation of freedom of religion or belief, but will also certainly result in the rejection of the human rights paradigm itself by most Muslims.

I find that framing the issue in terms of transforming attitudes and values is more constructive than simplistic assertions of the compatibility or incompatibility of Islam and human rights which take both sides of this relationship in static essentialist terms. This approach is necessary for mediating the paradox of the idea of universal human rights in a world of profound and permanent cultural and contextual difference. Because all human beings are entitled to these rights by virtue of their humanity, without any distinction on grounds of race, sex, religion, language or national origin, no person should be required to give up any of these essential aspects of his or her identity in order to qualify for these rights.

My framing of the issue also includes a clear appreciation of the permanent social, cultural and political diversity among Muslims, particularly in relation to their understanding and practice of Islam. That diversity testifies to the impact of contextual and historical factors in the theological or legal development of the Islamic traditions. Being Muslim (or other believer) has not in fact had the same meaning in different places or over time. From an Islamic perspective the reality and permanence of difference among all human beings, Muslims and non-Muslims alike, is expressly affirmed in, for example, the Qur'an 10:93; 11:118-119; 32:25; and 45:17 (cited by number of chapter followed by number of verse). This permanent reality is one reason why the protection of such human rights as freedom of belief, opinion and expression, is imperative from an Islamic point of view in order to protect the rights of Muslims to be believers in their own way, without risk to life and livelihood. After all, without the existence of the right to disbelieve, there is no possibility of any genuine belief.

It may also be helpful to consider the implications of this reality of Islamic diversity for the nature or basis of religious beliefs. The fact that specific verses in the Qur'an are taken to authorise or require certain actions does not explain why some Muslims choose to act on one understanding of such verses, while others act on a different understanding, or have a different relationship to the text altogether. Such choices are the product of the human agency of believers, not the inherent or eternal meaning of Islam as such, independent of all material conditions under which Muslims live and interact with others. If beliefs regarding the rights of women are the direct meaning of Islamic texts, there would not be so much disagreement among Muslims on these issues.[10] This is not to suggest that any of established schools of Islamic jurisprudence (*madhahib*) already accept equality for women from an Islamic point of view, because that is simply not true. Rather, my purpose here is to emphasise the possibility of changing the attitudes and practice of Muslims in these matters in favour of the equal human rights of women, or some other issue. Since any interpretation of *Shari'a* is the product of human agency, in a specific time and place, it can change through the same process, over time.

From this framing of the question it is clear that the manner in which Muslims are likely to interact with human rights will be conditioned by such factors as what other societies are doing about the same issues, and the orientation, motivation or objectives of various actors on all sides. For instance, Muslims' responses are likely to be affected by whether they perceive that they are required to 'prove' their allegiance to the human rights paradigm while others are not expected or required to do so. Muslims are more likely to resist commitment to these rights when they are presented as being alone in struggling with the principle, while the commitment of other cultural or religious traditions is taken for granted. This dimension also includes broader issues of the nature and operation of international law and institutions as the underlying legal framework of human rights, as outlined earlier. Concerns about historical exclusion and present hegemony are sometimes reflected in patterns of reciprocal treatment and mutual hostility or suspicion, as well as deeply entrenched bias or distortion in how and by whom the information about the attitudes and practice of various societies regarding human rights is collected and assessed. This web of interactive and dialectal factors and relationships provides a useful framework for understanding the recent controversy over the publication of cartoons of the Prophet.

WHY SHOULD MUSLIMS ABANDON *JIHAD*?

Cartoons depicting the Prophet of Islam, Muhammad, in demeaning images, including some representing him as a terrorist, were published by a Danish newspaper in September 2005. These cartoons were republished in newspapers throughout the world in January and February 2006, including in Denmark, France, Germany, Spain, Switzerland and Hungary, with affirmations of freedom of speech. In contrast, many Muslim leaders perceived the republication of these offensive cartoons as deliberate provocation to 'spite the Muslims'.[11] Muslims around the world protested in large demonstrations and made threats of sanctions against Denmark. Some of these demonstrations have turned violent, especially in Afghanistan and Nigeria, sometimes resulting in the death of local civilians. The Danish and Norwegian embassies in Syria and Lebanon were burnt.[12] There were also some large-scale protests by Muslims in other countries with a sizeable number of Muslims, from New Zealand to the USA. The response also included diplomatic sanctions by countries with predominant Muslim populations against Denmark and its products (the Danish–Swedish dairy giant Arla Foods says its sales in the Middle East have plummeted to zero).[13] The governments of Western Europe and North America tended to affirm freedom of expression, but some also played the issue to their own political advantage. In the weeks after the republication of the cartoons, the Bush administration has shifted its strategy from one of condemnation of the actual republication of the cartoons to condemnation of the violent response by the Muslim community.[14] Perhaps as a self-serving manoeuvre, the shift in policy by the Bush administration targeted particular countries, especially Iran and Syria, with the charge of exploiting the controversy to incite unrest and protests in the Middle East.

While expecting conflicting interpretations to continue to evolve around this and related issues in the future, I would emphasise the need to place such episodes in appropriate perspective and context. In terms of the framing and analysis presented above this sequence of events should not be understood simply as religious reaction by Muslims because they are Muslims, nor should it be thought that the manner and scope of the actions is dictated or determined by an 'Islamic quality' of the subject or actors. In brief, Islam and Islamic identity just happened to be the medium in which a range of issues were being mediated, negotiated and contested in this situation. At one level this episode was about the grievances of Muslim immigrants and refugees in Denmark, which should be understood and assessed against the backdrop of the recent history of racial and inter-religious relations in Western Europe generally. At another level the whole situation can be seen as a process of negotiating and mediating competing human rights, rather than their categorical rejection by either side. Muslim protestors did not simply reject the human rights of freedom of speech or expression, but rather asserted that the publication of the cartoons constituted an abuse or excess of this right. Those who objected to or even resented the protests by Muslims also accept the need to respect the dignity and religious identity of persons and religious or ethnic communities. People holding various positions along a spectrum of views accept that there are fundamental human rights, including those implicated in this situation, but also appreciate that none of those rights is absolute. In other words, the issue to all sides was about where to draw the line between the proper and improper application of one human right or another, and not about disputing any of those competing rights.

Beyond Denmark and Western Europe the controversy was also about various issues for different constituencies, sometimes used by some actors as a proxy for other concerns or to achieve various political objectives that may have had little to do with the cartoons as such. To Islamic political groups and activists in particular, the controversy was an opportunity to demonstrate their ability to organise mass protests, a way of sending their own message to the governments of their countries, and to other political competitors. Governments and some other political actors in the country or region in general did not want to concede the political gains the Islamists were making, or appear to be indifferent to the honour of the Prophet and dignity of Muslims at large. But, whether genuinely or opportunistically, those competing actors were not denying the human right of freedom of speech and expression in principle, but only questioning its proper limits. In fact, demonstrations and other protests were themselves instances of exercising fundamental human rights of freedom of speech and demands for greater political participation. In the final analysis, I suggest, the whole episode should be seen as part of the process of defining and exercising human rights, not a negation or repudiation of those rights or their foundation on international legality.

Mutual responsibilities for shared vulnerabilities

As noted earlier, the premise of this article is that we must all honour our mutual responsibilities for our shared human vulnerabilities. In the present context these vulnerabilities include the human suffering perpetrated by the terrorists as well as by those who engage in arbitrary and indiscriminate retaliation which in fact reinforces and legitimises the distorted logic of terrorism in the name of combating it. I have emphasised this point from the start by equally strongly condemning both the terrorist attacks and the unilateral military retaliation by the USA and its allies. But it is also important to note that all of us share in the responsibilities of combating both terrorism and arbitrary retaliation, because we all benefit when these responsibilities are discharged properly, and suffer when they are not.

For our purposes here we can begin with either side of the present failure to honour our mutual responsibilities, as the history and dynamics of both aspects are intertwined and dialectical. Terrorist atrocities like 9/11 were not the beginning and retaliatory actions will not be the end, as both aspects draw on perceptions of history and play out into future consequences. It is also clear that the consequences of these events in the future can either perpetuate the cycle of violence and counter-violence or evolve towards accountability and peaceful mediation of conflict. In this light I will consider both sides of the equation, interchangeably, shifting back and forth among different aspects of the aftermath of 9/11, without implying that either side justifies or legitimises the other. My purpose is to highlight some aspects of the risks of our shared vulnerabilities and benefits of our mutual responsibilities on all sides of the issue with a view to addressing such failures and safeguarding against future risks, rather than simply blaming one side or the other.

I find that the grossly disproportionate and aggressive foreign policy of the USA after 9/11, especially the attempted colonisation of Iraq since March 2003, is particularly damaging for the human rights paradigm. The Iraq occupation has been a colonial venture because colonialism, by definition, is the seizure of the sovereignty of a people by military conquest without legal justification, whether as self-defence or authorised by the Security Council of the United Nations. The invasion of Iraq is so fundamentally illegal and counter-productive that it undermines the foundations of the rule of law in international relations. After all, there is no international law when powerful states simply appropriate to themselves the right to invade and occupy other countries for whatever reasons they deem fit, without even a national debate on the legality of such action. Since the universality of human rights is legally premised on the binding force of international law obligations, such repudiation of international legality is a negation of the possibility of international human rights.

It is also important to note, however, that there were many positive developments, like the massive protests by citizens of the USA, UK, Spain and Italy against the invasion of Iraq even before it started, and the subsequent official national inquiries that proved the fallacy of the reasons given for the war.[15] There is hope even in this distressing regression to 19th century colonialism at the dawn of the 21st century because it is the first colonial venture that has been so vigorously protested at by the citizens of the colonial powers and across the world. It is also significant that the USA and UK had to resort to the same United Nations they had bypassed in the rush to war in order to negotiate how to vacate the dubious position of being 'occupying powers' and return sovereignty to a native Iraqi government by the end of June 2004.[16] The question remains how to develop the necessary institutions and global culture of the rule of law in international relations and the protection of human rights throughout the world. But that challenge will hopefully now be confronted with a renewed determination to restore the vision of the Charter of the United Nations to prohibit wars of aggression like the invasion of Iraq, to punish terrorist acts as crimes against humanity, and to uphold legality in international relations.

On the Islamic side of the issue, the persistent failure of Muslims to respond effectively enough to the responsibilities of sovereignty at home and peaceful international relations abroad is as damaging for the prospects of international legality and universality of human rights as the unilateral invasion of Iraq by the USA. Since colonialism was initially a consequence of the internal weakness of colonised societies, the effective and sustainable termination of colonialism requires enhancing the genuine sovereignty and independence of formerly colonised societies. Muslim failures in this regard can be seen in the conduct of countries like Afghanistan under the Taliban, of the Kingdom of Saudi Arabia, as well as of Iraq under the Baa'th regime of

Saddam Hussain, among others. After all, freedom is always earned, never granted, and is sustained through constant vigilance to safeguard it.

A critical part of that process in the present global context is to confront terrorism within our own societies, as it is ultimately a challenge to our human decency and to responsibility for what we do, or is done in our name, whether with our approval or acquiescence. Terrorism could not exist or thrive as it does at present if we have not somehow supported or encouraged it, at least by our indifference to the broader phenomenon of political violence and its underlying causes. The degree of our individual and collective responsibility and failure varies according to our locations and what we can do in combating the culture of violence and lawless retaliation in our own societies, but each of us should look for his or her share, and for what we can do about it. Too much of our effort is squandered in a futile apologia for Islam as a religion, or in viewing our societies as oppressed and marginalised, instead of accepting responsibility for our lives. The ability of perpetrators to use terrorist acts, and the willingness of the wider population to tolerate such behaviour, indicate an underlying disregard for the safety and well-being of others. Confronting terrorism would therefore include combating this underlying culture of political violence, as well as the immediate causes and consequences of the use of arbitrary and indiscriminate violence in the furtherance of political ends, whoever the perpetrators and however we may feel about their alleged justification.

Notes

1 Abdullahi Ahmed An-Na'im, 'Islamic ambivalence to political violence: Islamic law and international terrorism', *German Yearbook of International Law*, 31, 1988, pp 307–336.

2 'A strike at Europe's heart', *Time Europe*, 22 March 2004; 'Four from Britain carried out terror blasts, police say', *New York Times*, 13 July 2005; and 'London hit again', *Daily Telegraph*, 22 July 2005.

3 CIA, *The World Fact Book*, at http://www.cia.gov/cia/publications/factbook/geos/xx.html, select 'World', last updated 18 December 2003. Reference to a country as Islamic can only mean that the majority of its population are Muslims, and not that the state itself is Islamic, which is an incoherent claim. See Abdullahi Ahmed An-Na'im, '*Shari'a* and positive legislation: is an Islamic state possible or viable?', in Eugene Cotran & Chibli Mallat (eds), *Yearbook of Islamic and Middle Eastern Law*, 5, 1998–99, pp 29–42.

4 Arjun Appadurai, 'Disjuncture and difference in the global cultural economy', in Dimon During (ed), *The Cultural Studies Reader*, London: Routledge, 1993, pp 220–230.

5 Jonathan I Charney, 'Universal international law', *American Journal of International Law*, 87, 1993, p 529.

6 Eva Brems, *Human Rights: Universality and Diversity*, The Hague: Kluwer Law International, 2001, pp 17–25.

7 *Ibid*, pp 194–206. For debates around these issues among Muslim scholars, see, for example, Mashood A Baderin, *International Human Rights and Islamic Law*, Oxford: Oxford University Press, 2003; Yvonne Yazbeck Haddad & Barbara Freyer Stowasser (eds), *Islamic Law and Challenges of Modernity*, Walnut Creek, CA: AltaMira Press, 2004; and Ausaf Ali, *Modern Muslim Thought*, Vols 1–2, Karachi: Royal Book Company.

8 See, for example, Roland Inglehart & Pippa Norris, 'The true clash of civilizations', *Foreign Policy*, March/April 2003, pp 62–70.

9 See, for example, Abdullahi Ahmed An-Na'im, *Toward an Islamic Reformation: Civil Liberties, Human Rights and International Law*, Syracuse, NY: Syracuse University Press, 1990; and An-Na'im, 'Islamic foundations of religious human rights', in John Witte, Jr & Johan D van der Vyver (eds), *Religious Human Rights in Global Perspectives: Religious Prospectives*, The Hague: Martinus Nijhoff, 1996, pp 337–359.

WHY SHOULD MUSLIMS ABANDON *JIHAD*?

10 For competing interpretations of the role of women, see Ausaf Ali, *Modern Muslim Thought*, Karachi: Royal Book Company, Vol 1, pp 226–227, 256–263 and Fatima Mernissi, *Women in Islam: An Historical and Theological Enquiry*, trans Mary Jo Lackland, Oxford: Basil Blackwell, 1991, pp 49–81.

11 'Muhammad cartoon row intensifies', *BBC News*, 1 February 2006, at http://news.bbc.co.uk/1/hi/world/europe/4670370.stm.

12 'Protesters burn consulate over cartoons', *CNN*, 5 February 2006, at http://www.cnn.com/2006/WORLD/asiapcf/02/05/cartoon.protests.

13 *Ibid.*

14 'Bush condemns violence in protests over cartoons', *Boston Globe*, 9 February 2006, at http://www.boston.com/news/nation/washington/articles/2006/02/09/bush_condemns_violence_in_protests_over_cartoons.

15 'Thousands of protestors march to mark Iraq war', *USA Today*, 20 March 2004, at http://www.usatoday.com/news/world/iraq/2004-03-20-world-war-protests_x.htm; 'Italy protests greet Bush visit', *BBC News*, 5 June 2004, at http://news.bbc.co.uk/go/pr/fr/-/1/hi/world/europe/3777281.stm; 'Million march against Iraq', *BBC News*, 16 February 2003, at http://news.bbc.co.uk/1/hi/uk/2765041.stm; and 'Bush orders intelligence review', *BBC News*, 2 February 2004, at http://news.bbc.co.uk/go/pr/fr/-/1/hi/world/americas/3450151.stm.

16 See, for example, 'Remarks by the President on Iraq and the war on terror', United States Army War College, 24 May 2004, at http://www.whitehouse.gov/new/releases/2004/05/20040524-10.html; and Phyllis Bennis, 'Talking points: the US begs for UN backing in Iraq', 29 June 2004, at http://www.unitedforpeace.org/article.php?id=2261.

Part Four

Conclusion: A Theory of Interdependence

[16]
The Interdependence of Religion, Secularism, and Human Rights: Prospects for Islamic Societies

Religion, secularism, and human rights are interdependent, and the apparent tensions between any or among all of them can be overcome by their conceptual synergy. Given the obviously problematic features of their relationships, however, the interdependence of the three should be deliberately reinforced and stressed now; indeed each of the three should undergo an internal transformation to strengthen the already existing synergy. I am using the term *synergy* to indicate that the internal transformation of each paradigm or discourse (religion, secularism, human rights) is not only necessary for promoting relationships among the three but is also facilitated by it: each of the three tends toward transformation in favor of the other two. Each needs the other two to fulfill its own rationale and to sustain its relevance and validity for its own constituency.

I hasten to add that I am not suggesting the collapse of all related ideas, institutions, and policies into the framework I am describing. My purpose here is to highlight the dynamics of one complex process that might contribute to individual freedom and social justice. Moreover, while I believe that what I am proposing is potentially applicable to various religious and political contexts, my primary concern as a Muslim is the prospect for this approach in Islamic societies. That is, I would like to encourage the determined promotion—the strengthening—of this synergy in the interest of legitimizing human rights, regulating the role of religion in public life, and affirming the positive place of secularism in Islamic societies. Being from Sudan myself, I am acutely aware that hundreds of thousands have died, and millions continue to endure untold suffering, because of widespread confusion over just these issues. Some politicians manipulate that confusion for their own purposes and thus we require a framework that minimizes it.[1] While attempting to outline a theoretical framework that could be of use in Islamic societies, I hope that others may seek to use it in their own religious and political contexts.

This task might be approached from a variety of perspectives, but I prefer to begin by considering the moral and philosophical foundation of human rights since it most clearly highlights both the reality of tension and the possibilities of mediation among the three paradigms. Article 1 of the Universal Declaration of Human Rights (UDHR), issued by the United Nations in 1948, asserts that "all human beings are born free and equal in dignity and rights. They are endowed with reason and conscience and should act towards one another in a spirit of brotherhood." No specific foundation for the equality of human beings in dignity and rights, whether religious or secular, is stated, and the omission was apparently designed in the interest of achieving consensus. But more than fifty years later, the question—what is the moral or philosophical foundation of universal human rights?—remains difficult to answer, and answering it remains crucial for the practical implementation of those rights.

The difficulty in achieving agreement—agreement among all communities—on a single foundation for human rights indicates that we should promote instead an overlapping consensus among multiple foundations. Each community could then subscribe to a global agreement on the validity and application of universal rights without concluding that the agreement was an alien imposition. I hope to show that an overlapping consensus is best achieved by encouraging and even exploiting the interdependence of religion, secularism, and human rights.

Working Definitions

The term *human rights* is often used, in a rough and intuitive way, to signify the objectives or the implications of historic struggles for freedom and justice. But the term can also refer, more particularly, to the conception of individual free-

1. One such politician is Dr. Hassan Al-Turabi who led the National Islamic Front (NIF) in Sudan from 1964 until 1999, when he lost an internal struggle for power. The NIF took control of the state in the military coup of June 1989. See, e.g., John L. Esposito and John O. Voll, *Makers of Contemporary Islam* (Oxford: Oxford University Press, 2001), 118.

dom and social justice articulated in the UDHR and further specified in subsequent treaties that enable its implementation. In this latter sense of the term—the sense in which I use it here—human rights are due to all human beings by virtue of their humanity, without distinction on grounds such as race, sex, religion, language, or national origin. The key feature of human rights, by this definition, is universality.[2] When the definition was first made in the wake of World War II, it was viewed by some and opposed as a pretext for imposing the values of one culture on others, and the definition continues to be opposed from this and related perspectives.[3] The idea of overlapping consensus that I will explore takes into account the conceptual and practical difficulties associated with universality and seeks to resolve them.

The working definition of religion that I use here must focus, obviously, on those aspects of religion that have special relevance to human rights and secularism. For this limited purpose, religion can be defined as a system of beliefs, practices, institutions, and relationships within a community that distinguishes itself from other communities. The key feature of religion in this sense is the exclusivity of any community of believers, but that is not to say that understanding some religious traditions in more inclusive terms is impossible. In fact, I am counting on just that possibility to enable an overlapping consensus about universal human rights. But initiatives like the one I am proposing should be founded on a realization that some form or degree of exclusion (at least moral—and often material—exclusion) seems necessary for vindicating the faith of one religious community and distinguishing it from that of all others. "The denial of other views," as William Paden has written, "is typically a consequence of the need to protect or affirm one's own. We reject other views when the truth of our own does not appear to be acknowledged in them."[4] In contrast, human rights, by the UDHR definition, are by nature inclusive of all human beings, irrespective of membership in any social group.

For the limited purposes of this discussion, secularism may be defined as a principle of public policy, applied variously in distinct contexts, for organizing the relationship between religion and state. Historical experience shows that religious exclusivity tends to undermine solidarity and even peaceful coexistence among differing communities of belief, and secularism apparently evolved as a means of encouraging pluralism in the state. In any case, my concern with secu-

2. Abdullahi Ahmed An-Na'im, "What Do We Mean by Universal?" *Index on Censorship* 4/5 (September–October 1994): 120.

3. See American Anthropological Association, "Statement on Human Rights," *American Anthropologist* 49.4 (1947): 539.

4. William E. Paden, *Interpreting the Sacred: Ways of Viewing Religion* (Boston: Beacon Press, 1992), 126.

larism here is its ability to safeguard political pluralism, though I will argue that the principle can be applied differently under various regimes of government.

The Universality of Human Rights

The modern concept of human rights has emerged from European and American experiences since the eighteenth century. Those rights were premised, as is commonly acknowledged, on principles of the Enlightenment rather than on Christian or Jewish theologies, though the latter have tended to reconcile themselves with the former over time.[5] In view of the "universalization" of the European model of the nation-state through colonialism, the basic purpose of the UDHR appears to have been to put protections of individual freedoms in place and thus safeguard against abuse by the expansive powers of new states. While initially limited by Western experience, the rights that have emerged since 1948 are broader in scope than those guaranteed under the constitutional system of any Western country. The Western origins and immediate antecedents of human rights have been overtaken by developments reflecting the experiences and expectations of other peoples of the world.

Given that they are intended to protect individuals and groups against the contingencies of national politics, human rights are supposed to be the product of international agreement. But the claim of the international community to act as arbiter in safeguarding minimum standards is not plausible without the corresponding commitment of each member state to encourage and support each other in the process. That encouragement and support is crucial in view of significant differences in degrees of political will and in institutional capacity and material resources for the application of these rights in different parts of the world. It thus follows that one cannot rely on a horizontal enforcement mechanism for human rights among states without a broader cooperative framework of implementation among a variety of actors. The universal recognition of a single set of rights is not likely to be useful in practice without international cooperation in implementing it.

Moreover, it is important to recognize that, since the vast majority of African and Asian peoples still suffered under European colonialism in 1946–48, the process by which the UDHR was drafted and adopted was not globally inclusive and so the universality of the rights it proclaimed was contingent on subsequent developments.[6] It can be argued that genuine universality was to some extent attained through the affirmation of the UDHR by African and Asian states upon

5. Hilary Charlesworth, "The Challenges of Human Rights Law for Religious Traditions," in *Religion and International Law*, ed. Mark W. Janis and Carolyn Evans (The Hague: Martinus Nijhoff, 1999), 401–15.

6. See Henry J. Steiner and Philip Alston, *International Human Rights in Context: Law, Politics, and Morals*, 2d ed. (Oxford: Oxford University Press, 2000), 136–46.

achieving political independence and through their participation in the drafting and adoption of subsequent treaties on human rights. But it is also clear that the challenge of relevance and efficacy remains and will continue: serious cultural and ideological differences—differences that have significant practical consequences—are obscured by the consensus that presently obtains. While problems in non-Western cultures with respect, for example, to the rights of women are well known, there is little awareness of Western cultural or ideological problems with economic, social, and cultural rights (such as the right to housing and education) that many societies take to be as fundamental as the civil and political rights (such as freedom of belief and expression) so valued in the West. Widely ratified treaties provide for both sets of rights. Still, Western governments and public opinion alike find it difficult to accept that economic, social, and cultural rights are human rights in the current sense of the term. Western and non-Western societies face the same challenge—that of accepting the universal validity of one or more rights established as pertaining to every culture.

The problem of self-exemption from certain rights is doubtless related to the process by which the relevant treaties were negotiated. Agreement on international standards of human rights was only possible on the understanding that they be implemented through the agency of sovereign states. Given prevalent understandings of national sovereignty and international relations at the time, it was imperative for the United Nations Charter (1945) and the UDHR (1948) to strike a balance between international protection for human rights and respect for the domestic jurisdiction of nation-states.[7] That individual states regulate their own performance with regard to universal criteria is paradoxical, and to make the system work demands understanding of the local, national, and international actors and processes that influence the conduct of states, including the roles of the various religious communities and their views of secularism. The limitations of the system by which human rights are enforced are unlikely to be overcome without solidarity among religious communities. Since that degree of cooperation is not readily available within current understandings of religion (understandings that are exclusive and excluding), the enforcement of human rights and the introduction or strengthening of secularism are needed to help along an internal transformation of religious doctrine.

The Exclusivity of Religion

It may be useful to distinguish between the universalizing normative claims of some religions and the universality of human rights. The universal normative

7. David J. Bederman, *International Law Frameworks* (New York: Foundation, 2001), 96.

claims of Christianity and Islam, for instance, call for all human beings to accept the one true faith. In contrast, the universality of human rights represents, or is meant to represent, a convergence of differing traditions on a set of universal commitments to all human beings without regard to particularities of (for example) religion. The former is premised on the superiority of one religion; the latter, on the equality in principle of differing religious (and cultural) traditions. In other words, the rationale of religious solidarity is an exclusive one, while that of human rights is inclusive—though the potential for universality of the latter remains to be fully realized. The premise of equality requires that no religious or cultural tradition claim to be the sole foundation for the universality of human rights. Accordingly, when the foundations for human rights differ across cultures, we should view them as interdependent and mutually supportive, not antagonistic and mutually exclusive. The existence of varying foundations for human rights is intrinsic to the enterprise.

The question is whether, and if so how, religious traditions—which are of necessity exclusive—can participate in an overlapping consensus on a set of universal human rights. Since religions divide rather than unite human beings, so the argument goes, it is better to avoid religion altogether when seeking common ground. But to concede this argument is problematic because the more religious perspectives are excluded from the conversation, the less likely are religious adherents to accept the universality of human rights. Still, religions are unlikely to play a positive role until each undergoes an internal transformation. Fortunately, that transformation is possible as well as necessary because of what might be termed the secular dimension of religions. Since the transcendental dimension of religions is supposed to address the experience of their communities in the phenomenal world, interpretations of religious doctrine (along with the behavioral implications of each) are bound to be in competition and to reflect extant power relations. For the fair and sustainable mediation of these competing claims, secularism and the enforcement of human rights are critical both within each community of believers and between communities at odds. It is the very place of particularist religions in the world that makes secularism and human rights essential: the opposition of particularist religions to secular "encroachments" and to human rights (as defined internationally) is more apparent than real.

The Specificity of Secularism

Widespread confusion and suspicion are attendant on the term *secularism*, especially in Islamic societies, which regard it as a European, Christian concept imposed by colonial and neocolonial forces. It is thus necessary to clarify and substantiate a definition that is deeply contextual and dynamic. Etymologically, the word *secular* derives from the Latin *saeculum*, meaning "great span of time" or perhaps "spirit of the age." Later, *secular* came to mean "of this world" (a conception presuming more than one world), and eventually the distinction between secular and religious came to overlap with that between the temporal and the spiritual.[8] In the European context, secularization initially meant privatization or nationalization or confiscation of church lands, but eventually the gerund was applied to politics and then to art and economics.[9] This evolution is reflected in the common definition of secularism as "indifference to or rejection or exclusion of religion or religious considerations."[10] Equally common is the definition of secularism as "the doctrine that morality should be based solely on regard to the well-being of mankind in the present life, to the exclusion of all considerations drawn from belief in God or in a future state."[11]

Larry Shiner has identified, and distinguished among, five definitions of secularism as (1) the decline of religion, (2) conformity to the norms of the present world, (3) disengagement and differentiation of society from religion, (4) transposition of religious beliefs and institutions (the shift in focus, for example, from divine to human power and creativity), and (5) the desacralization of the world and the sacralization of rationality.[12] Yet all these views are at best reflections of how the concept has evolved in various European and North American settings. Secularism is multidimensional and reflects elements of the historical, political, social, and economic landscape of individual nations.[13] In the United States today, secularism requires a wall between church and state (a permeable wall, albeit: sessions of the Supreme Court open with the proclamation, "God bless this honorable Court"). Mexican secularism requires a separation of religion and politics so strict that Catholic priests are not allowed to vote, and secularism in France is if anything even more jealously guarded (Islamic and Jewish headcoverings are, as of this writing, to be proscribed in public schools). But in the secular Republic of Ireland, the Catholic Church wields so much power politically that abortion remains illegal on the grounds that it violates church doctrine. Essentially, as Asghar Ali Engineer has argued, "each country has its own specificity as far as the concept of secularism is concerned. This specificity depends on its historical evolution as well as on contemporary social conditions."[14]

Secularism in Islamic societies will not succeed if based on preconceived

8. Uday Mehta, "Secularism, Secularization, and Modernity: A Sociological Perspective of the Western Model," in *State Secularism and Religion: Western and Indian Experience*, ed. Asghar Ali Engineer and Mehta (Delhi: Ajanta, 1998), 24–25.

9. Hugh McLeod, *Secularisation in Western Europe, 1848–1914* (New York: St. Martin's, 2000), 1.

10. *Merriam-Webster's Collegiate Dictionary*, 10th ed., s.v. "secularism."

11. *Oxford Short Dictionary*, as cited in Engineer and Mehta, *State Secularism*, 2.

12. Larry Shiner, "The Concept of Secularization in Empirical Research," *Journal for the Scientific Study of Religion* 6.2 (fall 1967): 207–20.

13. Mehta, "Secularism, Secularization, and Modernity," 25.

14. Engineer, "Secularism in India—Theory and Practice," in Engineer and Mehta, *State Secularism*, 202.

Western notions of the concept and thus understood locally as an imposition. In particular, I believe (and as I have written before) that "it is grossly misleading to speak of complete separation or total union of any religion and the state. Any state, as well as its constituent organs and institutions, are conceived and operated by people whose religious or philosophical beliefs will necessarily be reflected in their thinking and behavior."[15] Entire separation of religion and state is not possible, nor in my view desirable, because religion is not separable from politics. How can citizens be prevented from acting politically according to their most basic beliefs? Even were such a requirement established, how could it be enforced in a way consistent with the integrity and legitimacy of the political process?

There is, theoretically, a continuum of "secularisms" from the extreme of fusion to that of absolute separation between religion and state. The question is therefore which forms are more consistent with the rationale of secularism adopted here. Drawing on the premise that secularism is dynamic and deeply contextual, a recent study of the relationship between religion and state in Britain, Germany, the Netherlands, the United States, and Australia has concluded that the minimum requirement for a positive relationship is neutrality: "that people are neither advantaged or [*sic*] disadvantaged by their adherence to their secular or faith-based tradition."[16] The state should neither favor nor disfavor one particular religious tradition over another.[17] The problem with this minimum requirement, however clearly it is necessary, is that no public policy is ever completely neutral: citizens are always believers (in something). The question, then, is how people can exercise free democratic choice in accordance with their own beliefs (religious or otherwise) while the neutrality of the state is maintained. Again, my conclusions are that (a) the possibility exists only if belief systems are internally transformed and that (b) belief systems will be transformed only where the interdependence of religion, secularism, and human rights is well established.

But belief systems—religions—are not the only paradigm that requires transformation in this dynamic. Secularism suffers from a basic limitation or, rather, a need for limitation: it must confine its normative content to a minimum if it is to achieve its purpose—safeguarding political pluralism in heterogeneous societies. In other words, secularism is able to unite diverse communities of belief and practice into one political community precisely and only because the moral claims it makes are miminal. All secularisms, it is true, prescribe a civic ethos on the basis of some specific understanding of the individual's relation to the com-

15. An-Na'im, "*Sharia* and Positive Legislation: Is an Islamic State Possible or Viable?" in *Yearbook of Islamic and Middle Eastern Law 1998/1999*, vol. 5, ed. Eugene Cotran (The Hague: Kluwer, 2000), 40. See also Harold J. Berman, *Faith and Order: The Reconciliation of Law and Religion* (Atlanta, GA: Scholars, 1993), 1–20, 35–52.

16. Stephen V. Monsma and J. Christopher Soper, *The Challenge of Pluralism: Church and State in Five Democracies* (Lanham, MD: Rowman and Littlefield, 1997), 209.

17. Monsma and Soper, *Challenge of Pluralism*, 209.

munity. But my point here is that the content of most varieties of secularism is so narrow that it cannot serve as an interreligious and cross-cultural foundation for human rights as a universal norm. From a pragmatic or political viewpoint, this limitation is serious because religious believers will fail to be inspired by the doctrine of human rights if founded solely on secular grounds. It may be necessary, indeed, to seek a religious justification for the principle of secularism itself. I am not saying that a serious engagement of religion is essential for either human rights or secularism to be legitimized (everywhere and always) but rather that that engagement is necessary to obtain the consent of most religious believers. And religious adherents constitute the clear majority of all human beings.

A related concern is that secularism is unable to address the objections or reservations that religious believers may have about particular standards of human rights or specific principles of secular governance. For instance, since discrimination against women is often justified on religious grounds (in many societies throughout the world), these systematic and gross violations of human rights cannot be eliminated without addressing their allegedly religious rationale. To do so, however, risks violating freedom of religion, a fundamental human right as well. A purely secular discourse can be respectful of religion in general, but its rebuttal of one religion's justifications for discrimination against women is unlikely to convince that religion's adherents. In other words, the minimal normative content that makes secularism conducive to interreligious coexistence diminishes its capacity to support human rights as a universal principle without reference to some other moral source. Likewise secularism by definition fails to address the need of religious believers to express the moral implications of their faith in the public domain. Secularism alone, then, is a necessary but insufficient condition for realizing the political stability that forms part of its own rationale. But secularism can be enhanced by insisting on a contextual understanding of the rationale and functioning of secular government in each location.

The Role of Human Agency

When I say that every society can insist on change—on the sorts of change that I suggest—I am referring to the individual members of those societies. I do not discount the impact of cultural, structural, and environmental factors in the processes of social change. Neither do I disregard religious, ideological, and other motivations that people have in acting or in refraining from action. Nor do I suggest that people are all equally able and willing to play an active role in demanding and effecting change. But each paradigm under discussion—religion, secularism, human rights—is both enabling of human agency and susceptible to influence by it. The question is how to secure the best conditions for human agency to achieve the transformations required: the decisions that individuals must reach will not follow as a matter of course. The agency of some actors will tend to diminish the social and political "space" for the agency of others, and moreover the outcome of every act is likely to be objectionable from some other actor's point of view. Each negative result of human agency will need to be ameliorated by further acts on the part of individuals.

Most people will consider taking such steps only when conditions enable them to believe in the possibility of deliberate change. When religious doctrines (and, for that matter, the doctrines of secularism) are open to free interpretation and thus renewal, those conditions flourish best. Human agency is always integral to the interpretation and implementation of every doctrine. Yet the guardians of orthodoxy everywhere claim eternal validity for their own interpretation and practice. While such claims can only be challenged from within the given tradition of belief and practice, and while there are always believers able to play that role, the process requires a level of security and stability for dissidents to make their case and for the body of believers to hear and make up their own minds without fear of retaliation. Those conditions are more likely to be guaranteed from outside than from inside any given tradition—guaranteed, that is, by the principles of human rights. Again, each element in the tripartite relationship I have been describing can be called upon to support the other two. They paradoxically, but reliably, depend upon one another.

Prospects for Interdependence

The first step in promoting the interdependence of human rights, religion, and secularism is to understand how each paradigm depends upon the other two for achieving its own objectives—to understand that this interdependence is already operative but also how it might be improved and promoted deliberately. The second step is to appreciate fully the role of human agency (as well as the obstacles to its exercise) in promoting the transformations necessary within each paradigm to support an increasing interdependence and synergy among the three.

The relationships among human rights, religion, and secularism should be methodically summarized before I elaborate on each of them further:

1. Human rights need religion to validate their moral foundation and to mobilize religious adherents (the vast majority, globally) in support of universal rights.
2. Religion needs human rights to protect the dignity and rights of religious adherents within any political system, but human rights also ensure freedom of belief and practice within each religion itself and thus ensure the evolution and continuing relevance of each religion to its own membership.

3. Human rights need secularism to provide the political stability and peace among communities of believers and nonbelievers that are necessary for the protection of those rights.
4. Secular governments need human rights for normative guidance in the daily protection of people against the abuse of state power.
5. Secularism needs religion to provide a widely accepted source of moral guidance for the political community, as well as to help satisfy and discipline the nonpolitical needs of believers within that community.
6. Religion needs secularism to mediate relations between different communities (whether religious or antireligious or nonreligious) that share the same political space.

However reasonable and clear these and other possible dimensions of interdependence may seem, one should not expect them to be appreciated or acted upon readily. Once again: human agency is crucial. It is individuals who must address the challenge that faces each of the three paradigms—the challenge to remain true to its own purposes. The overall advantage of each paradigm's remaining true is that those purposes make beneficial change inevitable for all three. Examples follow.

Human Rights Depend on Both Secularism and Religion

Human rights as defined in the UDHR are the current expression of ancient struggles for social justice and human dignity. The validity and sustainability of human rights in the former (the current and specific) sense depend on their vindication in the latter (the more general and historic) sense. The specifics embodied in the UDHR are appropriate for our time: they respond to the extensive powers of the state over every aspect of life and provide safeguards and mechanisms to protect rights and promote justice. But the adoption of the UDHR does not mean that its paradigm for human rights has achieved legitimacy in all states, for all peoples; and the paradigm must respond continually to difficult challenges.

The essence of the paradigm is that the entitlements spelled out in the UDHR be provided as of right, not as an incidental outcome of social policy: rights are not subject to the contingencies of political process. The political and civil rights defined in the declaration are not, in this respect, different from—they are not prior and superior to—the social and economic rights listed there. Rather, these two sorts of human rights depend on and are reinforced by one another. I said that people are more likely to accept the specific terms of the UDHR definition of rights to the extent that it corresponds to their understanding of human rights in the more general sense of social justice and human dignity. What I meant is that the political and civil rights enshrined in the declaration will be attractive to the extent that they are understood as means for realizing higher claims upon the state. For example, freedom of expression has traditionally been understood as a negative freedom: the state should refrain from action that infringes on the right of people to express their opinions. But taken as an affirmative obligation, this right would do more than allow for the passive consumption of others' free expression. The state would implement this right by providing educational and other public facilities enabling all segments of the population to pursue knowledge, exchange information, and formulate independent views. But the people for whom that education, that expansion of the right to free expression, would be most meaningful tend to be those who lack shelter and food or are ravaged by disease. It is therefore sensible and imperative to abandon efforts to classify human rights or to establish some categories as superior to others. Moreover, this evolution in the meaning and implications of each right would make the UDHR relevant and useful for the majority of the peoples of the world, not only for privileged elites, and would thus make human rights at last universally human.

It is also accepted by now that the so-called individual human rights can be achieved only in the context of family and community. This consensus is clearly reflected in the text of more recent UN treaties like the Convention on the Elimination of All Forms of Discrimination against Women (1979) and the Convention on the Rights of the Child (1989), as well as in regional documents like the African Charter on Human and Peoples' Rights (1981) and its subsequent development in other instruments. Even for so-called traditional human rights, it is clear that respect for freedom of expression is dependent on a contextually appropriate education that draws on the cultural traditions of a community. Language is obviously fundamental to freedom of expression as well as to education, but language is anything but individual and private. Thus it would be useful to transcend the conventional distinction between so-called civil and political rights, on the one hand, and economic, social, and cultural rights, on the other hand. It would be equally wise and useful to accept at least the possibility of collective or group rights as integral to the protection of individual rights. If human rights are about protecting human dignity, and human dignity is defined for some in their relation to others, then human rights may also be about protecting collective dignity.[18] I am not suggesting that every claim to a collective right should be accepted, but rather that such claims should be given serious consideration rather than dismissed as simply inconsistent with the individual focus of human rights doctrine.

I have already indicated that the main challenge for human rights law is to

18. See Rhoda Howard, "Dignity, Community, and Human Rights," in *Human Rights in Cross-Cultural Perspectives: A Quest for Consensus*, ed. An-Na'im (Philadelphia: University of Pennsylvania Press, 1992), 81.

reconcile the international respect for state sovereignty with the international commitment to protect human dignity. Even a state that refuses to commit to a positive obligation, as embodied in a treaty, may still in international law be bound to uphold that obligation if it is held to be *jus cogens*, an overriding general principle. These principles include proscriptions of slavery, genocide, torture, and apartheid. State sovereignty is subordinated to *jus cogens* in these instances; but with respect to most human rights, sovereignty takes precedence in international law. It is principally this problem that mandates transformation of the UDHR paradigm for human rights: if state sovereignty is regarded in international law as above most concerns for rights, then human agency must operate resourcefully to ensure enforcement of the UDHR within recalcitrant states. I do not believe that sovereignty should be minimized and human rights enforced by the international community. While intellectuals and governments alike are beginning to regard human rights enforcement as the humane side of globalization, there is also evidence that powerful states will further their own foreign-policy objectives by claiming to enforce human rights in developing countries. Still, the dynamics associated with globalization—economic and security interdependence—can be used to redress these drastically negative consequences. The global nature of political coercion and economic deprivation calls for correspondingly global strategies of response, and these are facilitated by the same mechanisms and technologies that make the negative consequences possible.

I do not mean to suggest that human rights provide the answer to all problems of differential power relations, whether locally or beyond. Rather, my point is that human rights need to be "owned" by different peoples differently, otherwise they will be perceived as simply another mode of Western coercion. In other words, legitimating human rights in local cultures and religious traditions is a matter of vital importance for the survival and future development of the human rights paradigm itself. Religions must also be encouraged, from within, to provide moral underpinnings for fresh development of the paradigm in order to address emerging issues in differing contexts. The contribution of secularism to these critical developments must be to provide the political stability and communal security essential for negotiating a unique and dynamic relationship between human rights and religion in every setting internationally.

Religion Depends on Both Secularism and Human Rights

Shifting to the role of religion, I want immediately to stress that the internal transformation of religions is critical not just for the flourishing of human rights and secular government but also for the survival of religious traditions and the legitimacy of religious experience. Every orthodox precept that believers take for granted today began as a heresy from the perspective of some other orthodox doctrine and may well continue to be considered heretical by some believers in a major branch of the same religion. Without such human rights as freedom of belief and expression, there is no possibility of development (which is to say, life) within the doctrine of any religion, and no possibility of peace within or between religious communities. This same need is served by secularism: as a principle of public policy, it ensures that an exclusivist and authoritarian religious group, while it could dominate the government of the day by majority will, would be unable (at least in theory) to threaten the essential interests of any segment of the population.

I hope it is clear that I am not urging the development of liberal or liberation theologies within the framework of each major world religion. What I am saying is that problems of authority and representation often frustrate the circulation of such views among believers. If a community defines itself to the exclusion of others, it is unlikely to listen to outsiders defining or contesting its religious doctrine or its behavioral precepts. The dilemma is how to encourage credible agents of internal religious change when the critique that they would undertake is believed to serve the interests of alien religions, cultures, powers. The more a religious community feels threatened by internal instability or external domination, the less likely will it be tolerant of religious dissent. Questions are raised about any dissenter's piety and authority in order to discredit his or her views. Moreover, when dissidents are defended from outside the religious community, upholders of the status quo often take that defense as proof that dissidents are intent on undermining the community of believers from within. This tendency of orthodox communities limits the utility of both human rights and secularism in protecting the rights of religious dissidents. But the tendency is less problematic where religious justifications have been found for human rights and secular government.

The scope of human agency has always been contested: this generalization has resonance for secular ideologies, as illustrated by recent experience with Marxism and nationalism, but is probably most valid in religious contexts because of the transcendental (superhuman) nature of most religious doctrine and the consequent reluctance to permit change. Given these tendencies, a prerequisite to the internal transformation of a religion is to emphasize the social and political implications of religious doctrine for the everyday lives of individuals and communities. Since an exclusively religious frame of reference for assessing those implications is likely to do no more than reinforce orthodox views, human rights and secularism can provide some commonly agreed criteria for the purpose. Dissidents, in other words, can point to international consensus on the universality of human rights and describe the experience of other societies with secularism in support of their own critique of religious hegemony. But these are issues of structure and not of content: where dissidents rely on what is thought an external justification for an inauthentic innovation in religious doctrine or practice, their views are naturally rejected by their communities. Arguing effectively for human rights and secularism, on the other hand, ensures that minority voices can compete on their own merits, rather than be suppressed because they disagree with prevailing views. Arguing on intercultural terms for the toleration of dissent is not the same as arguing on intercultural terms for the reform of local theology and religious practice, but the former can help protect the latter from persecution. This protection is especially important where there is a need for fundamental change (short of founding a new religion). What is required is a contextual critique of the basic assumptions (including assumptions about methodology) of currently orthodox doctrines without reference to those of other religious traditions—a critique unlikely to occur without the extracontextual safeguards that are enhanced by secularism and human rights.

Secularism Depends on Both Religion and Human Rights

On the other hand, the capacity of secularism to offer dissidents the protection to operate more freely in religious discourse is dependent on secularist doctrine maintaining a minimal normative content. On the positive side, secularism precludes any specific understanding of religious doctrine from being enforced consciously as state policy. This feature conduces to internal religious transformation because believers are less threatened by views that, while unorthodox, are not forced on them through organs of the state. Moreover, novel ideas have a better chance of consideration on their own merit when there is no chance of their being declared official state policies. What is known as "separation of church and state" is necessary for the health of individual religions (though that is not all that their health requires).

To play this constructive role in national politics, secularism depends on the normative guidance supplied by human rights doctrine and on the moral justification provided by religion. The importance of human rights standards is obvious because secularism on its own may not be enough for safeguarding individual freedoms and social justice—as illustrated by recent experience with secular totalitarianism in Russia, Germany, and elsewhere. What is not sufficiently appreciated is the importance of a religious rationale for secularism. While the material conditions of coexistence may force a level of religious tolerance and diversity, this situation is likely to be seen as merely expedient and temporary by religious adherents unless they are also able to find tolerance and diversity consistent with (or preferably, implied or stipulated by) their religious doctrine. This requirement is not as difficult to achieve as it may superficially appear: the dichotomy demanding a choice between religion and secularism has already failed because, as Talal Asad writes, the "concept of the secular cannot do without the idea of religion."[19] Politics and religion do not operate in distinct realms; the one continually informs and is informed by the other. The concept of the secular lacks motivating power and lives off that of the religions it checks and balances. As Harold Berman puts it: "people will not give their allegiance to a political and economic system, and even less to a philosophy, unless it represents for them a higher, sacred truth. People will desert institutions that do not seem to them to correspond to some transcendent reality in which they believe—believe in with their whole beings, and not just believe about with their minds."[20] Secularism cannot motivate individuals to uphold its own basic principles; it paradoxically requires religious motives to energize it.

Interdependence in Islamic Contexts

My test case for the generalizations I have offered thus far is that of theology and politics in Islamic contexts. Religious transformation in Islam requires a theological argument for change and a political and social context within which that change may be realized in practice. On the theological side, it is necessary to first recognize the role of human agency in Islam through understanding of the Qur'an and Sunna (traditions of the Prophet) in historical context. Wide recognition of the centrality of human agency in Islam is critical for appreciating that secularism is in fact integral to the religion, rather than opposed to it, and for accepting human rights as a framework for the transformation of Islamic doctrine and practice. But for either of the two to play its role, secularism and human rights themselves must be open to their own internal transformations in response to the various challenges that Islam presents.

I must preface this discussion with two sets of general remarks about the place of religion in Islamic communities today. First, while many Muslims may claim that Islam is definitive in their private and communal lives, it is not the sole determinant of their behavior or the sole basis of social and political organization, even in purportedly Islamic states like Iran, Saudi Arabia, and Sudan.[21] In fact, some Islamic communities (in India, for instance) may have more in common

19. Talal Asad, "Religion, Nation-State, Secularism," in *Nation and Religion*, ed. Peter van der Veer and Hartmut Lehmann (Princeton, NJ: Princeton University Press, 1999), 192.

20. Harold Berman, *The Interaction of Law and Religion* (Nashville, TN: Abingdon, 1974), 73.

21. A Saudi newspaper editor, for example, recently described a "split" between what he called "virtual Saudi Arabia" and the "real Saudi Arabia." "The virtual Saudi Arabia actually exists in its rules and in the minds of the people. . . . For instance, in virtual Saudi Arabia there is no satellite television. In principle, and by law, you are not allowed to own a satellite dish. But in reality we are the biggest consumers of satellite television in the Middle East. Not only that, Saudi businessmen are also the biggest investors in satellites. In principle, and by law, Saudi Arabia is not supposed to have interest-based banking, but in fact 90 percent of our banking system is interest-based. And it goes on and on. The solution for Saudi problems is to bring the virtual world and the real world together." Lawrence Wright, "The Kingdom of Silence," *New Yorker*, January 5, 2004, 54.

with neighboring non-Islamic communities that share their ethnic and cultural affiliations, historical experiences, economic resources, and political and security concerns than they have in common with other Islamic communities (say, in sub-Saharan Africa). In other words, Muslims' understanding and practice of Islam are conditioned more by what may be regarded as "extra-religious" factors than they are by any abstract, settled, and in whatever way divinely sanctioned conception of the religion.

Second, there has always been a significant diversity of theological and jurisprudential views—and of political opinion and practice—within and between Islamic communities. Profound political and theological differences have divided Muslims from the beginning in the Arabia of the seventh century, leading to civil wars over issues of political power within three decades of the Prophet's death in 632. Serious disagreements over the interpretation and implementation of Islamic doctrine have long since resulted in the distinctive religious factions and schools of jurisprudence called *madhahib* (singular *madhhab*), as well as in wide differences of opinion within each school. Muslim scholars and communities at large routinely cite this diversity of opinions and beliefs as a positive feature of their faith. This diversity is likely to become more intense and widespread under modern conditions of education and communication. There are now greater opportunities for disagreement (as well as consensus) as more Muslims, women included, are educated enough to assess the Qur'an, Sunna, and Islamic history for themselves and to communicate with others around the world about theological and political issues of common concern. Disagreement is logically integral to religious experience because human beings do not truly *believe* where disbelief is not an option. This proposition may sound modern and liberal but is made in 114 verses of the Qur'an (and is rooted in Islamic theological and philosophical discourse since the eighth century). Verse 18 of chapter 29, for example, reads: "Tell them that Truth is revealed from God, and let those who wish to believe, do so, and those who wish to disbelieve, do so." But as I have argued elsewhere, the real issue is the "framework of interpretation" and not simply the presence of texts that can be variously understood.[22] In other words, it is human agency that determines which texts are relevant to the issue at hand and how they should be interpreted.

Islamic life today is not guided solely by Muslim principles, and religious views within the Islamic world are and always have been very diverse: it is in light of these two recognitions that Islamic communities need to consider the relationship between Islam (under its various interpretations) and the global doctrines of secular government and human rights. First, it must be recognized that any

22. An-Na'im, "Toward an Islamic Hermeneutics for Human Rights," in *Human Rights and Religious Values*, ed. An-Na'im, Jerald D. Gort, Henry Jansen, and Hendrik M. Vroom (Amsterdam: Rodopi; Grand Rapids, MI: William B. Eerdmans, 1995), 229–42.

sharp distinction between the sacred and the secular in the Islamic world itself is misleading. Muslims believe that the Qur'an is the literal and final word of God and that Sunna is the second divinely inspired source of Islam. But the Qur'an was revealed in Arabic, a human language that evolved historically, and many normative parts of the Qur'an address situations in Mecca and Medina specific to the time that the Prophet conveyed them. Sunna, moreover, responded to immediate concerns that emerged in specifiable contexts, whatever the broader implications that Sunna may have for later times and different places. Human agency, in other words, was integral to the revelation, interpretation, and practice of Islam from its beginning in the seventh century. In any case, the Qur'an and Sunna cannot be understood except as applied by human beings temporally and in particular contexts. Religious precepts necessarily respond to the temporal, secular concerns of human beings and have practical relevance only because those responses are believed to be practically useful in the daily lives of the people they address. Some Muslims think that these propositions undermine belief in the divine source of Islam. They fail to appreciate, however, that the Qur'an and Sunna are not manifestations of divinity in the abstract; they are directed at human beings living human lives.

The presumed incompatibility of Islam and secularism derives from terminological as well as substantive confusions, and clarifying matters of definition should help frame the substantive issues in more precise terms. The main problem, from this perspective, is the tendency to limit understanding of secularism to the Western experience with Christianity since the eighteenth century. Whether viewed as "separation of church and state" or "disestablishment of religion," such definitions are specific to given settings and do not address the continuing social and political role of religion in public life even in those settings. For instance, efforts to sever institutional links between religion and the state cannot apply to the role of religion in politics: there is no way of knowing, much less disallowing, the motives of an individual's political action. It is also problematic to equate secularism with disregard for religion, or with a diminishing role for religion in public life, as some scholars have done.[23] To say that religion has no influence in societies with secular governments is obviously false, so the question becomes what sort of influence and, if the influence is diminishing, in what ways? It is time that we rethink secularism as a kind of relationship between religion and state that varies, religion by religion and state by state. The form that this relationship takes in a given setting is the product of organic development over time and needs, if it is to succeed, to be accepted as legitimate by the population at large; it cannot be expected to drastically change a political and religious situation instantaneously via constitutional enactment or political rhetoric.

23. See notes 10–12 and related text, above.

As a matter of terminology, secularism in its West European and North American sense came to Africa and Asia in the suspect company of other items of colonial vocabulary. Secularism is commonly associated, especially in Islamic societies, with the militantly antireligious attitudes of the French Revolution; and generally, non-Christians think of the concept as related to Christianity in particular. Nevertheless, the term is applicable to the experience of African and Asian societies, provided it is understood and applied in the specific context of each society, rather than as a feature of a supposedly global and context-free liberalism. The most compelling argument for developing a specifically Muslim rationale for secularism is the necessity of secular guarantees for the freedom of religion in pluralistic nation-states. The states of the Islamic world are simply not, as many in the West presume they are, religiously uniform. Whether it is the Shi'a of eastern Saudi Arabia, Sunni of Iran, or Shi'a of Pakistan, Muslims can suffer serious violations of the right to live by their belief in what they understand Islam to command and claim. It is worth observing that many Muslim intellectuals and political dissidents—including leaders of Islamist movements like Rashid Qanushi of Tunisia (as I write, he is living in the United Kingdom)—have taken or are seeking refuge in Western countries because they enjoy more freedom of belief when living in "Christendom," which by now is mostly secular, than in states with large Muslim majorities.

But a Muslim rationale for secularism is not far to seek. It is commonly claimed that Islam mandates the establishment of an "Islamic state" to enforce Shari'a (the normative system of Islam) as the law of the land. But the notion of an Islamic state is a contradiction in terms. Principles of Shari'a enacted by the state as positive law cease, once enacted and enforced by the state, to be part of the normative system of Islam. Since there is so much diversity of opinion among Islamic schools of thought and among Islamic scholars, any enactment of Shari'a principles as law must accept some opinions over others, with the result that believers would be denied freedom of choice among the equally legitimate competing opinions on any legal question. Moreover, as even advocates of an Islamic state must concede, the only such state in Muslim history has been that of the Prophet in Medina, and it was in many ways too exceptional an entity to be useful now as a model. The implementation of Shari'a as state law is, as I have argued at some length elsewhere, untenable for any nation-state in the present economic and political context globally.[24]

My basic points have been, in summary, (1) that Muslims need human rights to protect them from government abuse and (2) that every Muslim needs secularism to secure his or her freedom to be the kind of Muslim that he or she wishes to

24. For further elaboration on and substantiation of these views, see An-Na'im, "*Shari'a* and Positive Legislation," 29–42.

be, but (3) that these two needs cannot be satisfied without transformation of the standard ways of understanding Islam. These three points make my theoretical case for the synergy and interdependence of Islam, secularism, and the modern doctrine of human rights. But the synergy I propose is already developing in a variety of Islamic societies, and what is needed are ways of facilitating these processes and overcoming the limitations and difficulties that such developments are bound to face. What follows, accordingly, are three very brief case studies to highlight this perspective.

Women's Rights in Egypt

The women's movement in Egypt is multifaceted or perhaps fractured, a characteristic often explained as a rift between Islamist conservatives and secular liberals.[25] According to one good survey, however, the "secular" branch of the women's movement is united not by an antireligious or anti-Islamic position, but rather by the view that Shari'a should not be the main or sole source of legislation in Egypt (1–4). The majority of women in the "secular" women's movement describe themselves as very religious (142).[26] Many of these women do not see religion as antithetical to feminism, and they perceive religious affiliation as integral to their struggle for human rights. It is simply, according to this survey, that "most secular women activists [recognize] that religion does not constitute the only source of values and axis of orientation in people's lives" (142). There are, however, some women activists who view Islamic tradition as inherently tainted by the patriarchal system in which it was created more than a thousand years ago, and they therefore reject the religious tradition (141). The best way, then, to conceive of religious and secular attitudes in Egypt is not as a dichotomy but as a continuum. Dichotomous conceptions sustain the Islamist notion of secularism as meaning "against religion" (147).

The case of the Egyptian women's movement supports the idea that religion needs both secularism and human rights. Muslim women, for one thing, believe in their own ability to promote understanding and practice of the three paradigms in tandem: in Egypt, they are reinterpreting and renewing their reli-

25. See Nadje Al-Ali, *Secularism, Gender, and the State in the Middle East: The Egyptian Women's Movement* (Cambridge: Cambridge University Press, 2000), 3.

26. Al-Ali's study reveals that trying to categorize these women, as some other scholars have done, engenders artificial distinctions. The author argues that categorizing Egyptian feminists as Islamist, Muslim, or secular is misleading. Specifically, Al-Ali challenges the definition of secular feminists by Azza Karam in *Women, Islamisms, and the State: Contemporary Feminism in Egypt* (Basingstoke, U.K.: Macmillan; New York: St. Martin's, 1998): Karam argues that secular feminists center their discourse in the language of international human rights rather than that of religion. To Al-Ali, "views and opinions about secularism and religion are extremely complex and variable even among members of the same group. Moreover, international conventions of human rights constitute only one reference point among many." *Secularism, Gender, and the State*, 140–41.

gious traditions in order to do so. And the Western origin of human rights doctrine does not prevent these women from claiming UDHR rights for themselves or from seeking to reevaluate and adapt those norms to suit their own cultural, religious, and political situations (142–48). Freedom of religion, a norm of human rights doctrine, gives these women the power to choose, among Islamic traditions, those most compatible with their own belief in other UDHR rights. Invoking global norms of human rights enables Muslims like these Egyptian women to challenge dated and regressive understandings and practices. Thus, human rights and secularism help such Muslims avoid the difficult choice of either rejecting their religion entirely or abandoning their own human dignity.

At the same time, the invocation of human rights, and also secularism, enables those who feel more completely alienated to leave the Muslim religion altogether, as some members of the secular women's movement in Egypt have indeed chosen to do. It is critical for the moral integrity of the religion itself that people be free to stay or leave the community at will—that they not be forced or intimidated into the pretense of belief and hypocritical practice. The relative neutrality of the Egyptian state in religious matters is important in maintaining peace and stability in a country that has a significant Christian minority as well as the usual diversity of beliefs among its Muslims.[27] Unfortunately, in attempting to respond to the threat of militant Islamic fundamentalism, the present Egyptian government tends to limit freedom of religion and other human rights for all segments of its population.[28] For example, in 1992 private mosques in Egypt were "nationalized" so that sermons promoting violent extremism could be censored. Ironically, while this state control of Islamic discourse tends to inhibit the exercise of human rights among the majority of Muslims, it is not always successful in suppressing Islamic militancy. The fact that the mosque has become a contested political arena undermines the secular nature of the state and its role as guardian of human rights. A better appreciation of the interdependence of religion, secular government, and human rights would enable the state and civil society to cooperate in upholding the integrity of all three paradigms as the foundation of political pluralism.

Negotiating Islamic Identity and Politics: The Case of Sunni Sudan

In view of the intense and long-standing religious diversity in all countries with Muslim majorities, secularism is, as I have argued, crucial for the good of both

27. Egypt is approximately 90 percent Muslim, mostly Sunni, with a tiny Shi'i minority, and 7 to 10 percent Coptic Christian. Denis J. Sullivan and Sana Abed-Kotob, *Islam in Contemporary Egypt: Civil Society vs. the State* (Boulder, CO: Lynne Rienner, 1999), 19.

28. Sullivan and Abed-Kotob, *Islam in Contemporary Egypt*, 122.

human rights and religion throughout the Islamic world. Recent developments in Sudan illustrate how ambiguities about the relationship between Islam and the state have figured in the political instability and retarded socioeconomic development of the country since it gained independence from colonial rule in 1956. These ambiguities are also among the causes of the civil war waged in the southern part of the country, first from 1955 to 1972, then again from 1983 to the present.[29] The main political parties in the northern part of the country, which is predominantly Muslim, are unable to dispute claims made by the National Islamic Front that the country must be governed by an Islamic state and Shari'a enforced as the law of the land.[30] This situation has given the National Islamic Front a grossly exaggerated influence in the country and has promoted a general belief that the "removal of Islam from public life in Sudan is not an option."[31] On the other hand, the notion of an Islamic state is obviously untenable in view of the profound religious and cultural diversity of the country as a whole.[32] The imposition of a particular understanding of Islamic law violates the human rights of Muslim as well as non-Muslim citizens of the country.[33] To the extent that Shari'a is taken to be of divine origin, any political opposition to the government of the day becomes tantamount to apostasy—a capital crime punishable by death under section 126 of the Sudan Penal Code of 1991.[34] And minority religious traditions will suffer serious violations of their most fundamental rights.[35]

The benefits of secularism, and the protection of human rights, are in such a context obvious, but neither is achievable in a sustainable manner until the role of Islam in national politics is clarified. That is, given widespread belief in the necessity of a role for Islam in public life, human rights cannot be secured, and secularism cannot be established as a guarantor of human rights, until both obtain credible justifications in Islamic terms. Yet the process by which those justifications could be developed depends itself on the protection offered by the

29. For a comprehensive history and analysis, see, for example, Francis M. Deng, *War of Visions: Conflict of Identities in the Sudan* (Washington, DC: Brookings Institution, 1995).

30. According to the National Islamic Front in Sudan, an Islamic state "is an ideological movement that seeks comprehensive reform of Muslim society for the establishment of a just social order centered on faith." This formulation means that the tenets of Islam would dictate all religious, social, political, economic, and legal aspects of life. See Lawyers Committee for Human Rights, *Beset by Contradictions: Islamization, Legal Reform and Human Rights in Sudan* (New York: Lawyers Committee for Human Rights, 1996), 84.

31. A. H. Abdel Salam, "Constitutional Challenges of Transition," in *The Phoenix State: Civil Society and the Future of Sudan*, by Abdel Salam and Alex de Waal (Trenton, NJ: Red Sea, 2001), 21.

32. As of 2001, 70 percent of Sudanese adhere to Islam, while 20 percent are Christians. Abdel Salam and de Waal, *Phoenix State*, 53.

33. Abdel Salam and de Waal, *Phoenix State*, 22–23.

34. Donna E. Artz, "The Treatment of Religious Dissidents under Classical and Contemporary Islamic Law," in *Religious Human Rights in Global Perspective: Religious Perspectives*, ed. John Witte and Johan D. van der Vyver (The Hague: Martinus Nijhoff, 1996), 405–6.

35. Abdel Salam and de Waal, *Phoenix State*, 22–23.

right to freedom of belief and dissent.[36] Sudan is thus a clear case of the need for us—for the individuals involved—to nurture the existing synergy of Islam, religiously neutral governance, and UDHR rights.

Negotiating Islamic Identity and Politics: The Case of Shi'a Iran

The condition of Iran under the Islamic Republic proclaimed in April 1979 supports the same conclusion. The Iranian state since that time has been fused with one particular interpretation of Islam—an interpretation exceptional even within the distinctive Shi'a tradition of Iran itself—under "guardianship by the clergy" (*vilayat-i faqih*).[37] The Iranian constitution is a complex of paradoxes and contradictions.[38] For example, article 2 states that "the Islamic Republic is a system based on belief in . . . One God . . . His exclusive sovereignty and right to legislate, and the necessity of submission to His commands." Article 4 states that "all civil, penal, economic, administrative, cultural, military, political, and other laws and regulations must be based on Islamic criteria." But contradicting these assertions, article 6 states that "the affairs of the country must be administered on the basis of public opinion, expressed by means of elections." While establishing Islam as the "eternally immutable" religion of Iran, the constitution bestows recognition on Zoroastrianism, Judaism, and Christianity (though only those three) as religious minorities, allowing their adherents freedom of religion "within the limits of the law." An "absolute religious Leader and the Leadership of the Ummah" have ultimate authority in the executive branch of government, but the Islamic Assembly contains guaranteed seats for non-Muslims: "the Zoroastrians and Jews will elect one representative; Assyrian and Chaldean Christians will jointly elect one representative; and Armenian Christians in the north and in the south of the country will each elect one representative." Further, the constitution ensures equal rights for women but only "in conformity with Islamic criteria."

Mixing notions of divine authority (exercised fallibly by the "absolute religious Leader") with modern ideas of popular sovereignty and democratic elections has resulted in suffering for all segments of the population, including the Shi'a majority itself. Political struggles among competing religious and civic authorities have locked the state in unworkable policies and forced the country into a devastating international isolation. Reports of the United Nations' Special

36. See An-Na'im, "Islamic Foundations of Religious Human Rights," in Witte and van der Vyver, *Religious Human Rights*, 341.

37. Michael M. J. Fisher, "Legal Postulates in Flux: Justice, Wit, and Hierarchy," in *Iran in Law and Islam in the Middle East*, ed. Daisy Hilse Dwyer (New York: Bergin and Garvey, 1990), 115. This notion of a Shi'a state was based on Khomeini's ideas (see, for example, Ayatollah Ruhollah Khomeini, *Islamic Government*, trans. Joint Publications Research Service [New York: Manor, 1979], which represented a break from the traditional view of the "Twelvers Shi'a" school that prevails in Iran today).

38. Steiner and Alston, *International Human Rights*, 459–62, quoting *Constitution of Iran*, 1979 (as amended).

Representative on Iran in 1991 and 1998 documented horrendous violations of human rights throughout the country.[39] Yet the fact that the second UN report also documented some improvement indicates a possibility of recovery from the disaster of the 1980s and early 1990s. What is clear from the sad, yet hopeful, experience of Iran with the project of creating an Islamic state is that a secular space between religion and state is indispensable for the political stability, social and economic development, and general well-being of Islamic societies. From an internal point of view, the well-documented, daily violations of human rights by a purportedly Islamic state undermine not only the notion of Islamic government but, for some, even the validity of Islam. When government is identified with religion, both are blamed for the social and political problems of the country.

Some Implications for Policy

Religion, secularism, and human rights are not autonomous concepts or paradigms; they exist in constant interaction with each other and with political, economic, constitutional, and governmental processes and institutions, both locally and globally. Given this reality of interdependence, neither the ratification of international treaties nor the adoption of national legislation can guarantee progress of the kind that I am hoping may ensue. Neither secular government in Sudan nor the rights of women in Egypt and Iran will be made real simply by proclaiming them or even by amending national constitutions. In each case, the success or failure of any initiative will depend on the development and wide comprehension of clear principles, on consistent practice in accordance with them, and on a well-informed and active civil society intent on holding its government officials accountable for their acts. The model that I have drawn and advocated here, if found plausible and useful, must be further developed, adapted, and applied on a case by case basis in order to clarify the relationships among religion, secularism, and human rights in any given society. This much, however, may be said, across the board, with confidence: a constitution that reflects particular religious beliefs will be static (a grounding in divine authority can sanction little change) and therefore doomed in a changing world. States that adopt religious law as national law and allot political positions according to religious affiliation discover eventually that religious adherents do not necessarily act politically in terms of their religious beliefs and that religions suffer by their association with the exigencies of politics. Religion and politics are not well mixed—and Muslim history offers ample evidence of that generalization.

39. UN Doc. E/CN.4/1991/35, and UN Doc. E/CN.4/1999/32. See Steiner and Alston, *International Human Rights*, 624–29.

I have tried to underscore that peoples and individuals need make no choice among religion, secularism, and human rights. The three can work in synergy. But there is a related choice that does need to be made: whether or not to attempt mediating tensions among the three paradigms. I would myself urge both scholars and policymakers to take responsibility for that mediation rather than permit further damage to be done by belief in the incompatibility of religion with secular government and human rights. Whether we should adopt, develop, and implement any given approach to this mediation (the one that I have outlined here or any other approach) is not a foregone conclusion, imposed by impersonal forces. It is a human choice and will be made by individuals.

Name Index

Abu Hanifa 21
Abu Zeid, Nasr Hamid xxxv, 313–14
Ali 72, 120
Anderson, J.N.D. 123
An-Na'im, Abdullahi Ahmed xiii–xxxix *passim*, 3–11, 13–31, 33–45, 47–56, 57–63, 67–106, 107–33, 135–66, 167–202, 203–15, 219–46, 247–64, 265–90, 291–328, 329–41, 345–69
Asad, Talal 359
Ataturk, Mustafa Kemal 9

Badawi, Zaki xxvi, 178
Barng'etuny, Ezekiel 322
Berman, Harold 360
Bhutto, Benazir 81, 98
Bhutto, Zulfikar Ali 80–81
Biwott, Nicholas 322
Bourguiba, Habib 9

Carter, Jimmy 209
Chirac, Jacques 179
Coulson, N.J. 123

Dzhabbarov, Sandzhar 191

El Koussy, Rachad 11
Elizabeth II, Queen of England 318
Engineer, Asghar Ali 351

Fatima 72
Featherstone, Mike 174
Fierman, William 189

Gorbachev, Mikhail 192
Gross, Jo-Ann 190

Hassan II, King of Morocco 87
Henkin, Louis 63
Herskovits, Melville J. 251
Hussein, Saddam xix, 47, 340

Ibn Abd al-Wahab, Muhammad 83–4
Ibn Abdillah, Mohammed *see* Muhammad the Prophet
Ibn Abi Talib, Ali 18

Karimov, Islam 177, 187–9
Khomeini, Ayatollah xvi, 38–9, 87, 258, 292
Koven, Ronald 179–80

al-Madhi, Muhammad Ahmad 220, 319
Maritain, Jacques 8
al-Massari, Mohammed 291, 293–4
Mayer, Ann 114
Moi, Daniel Arap 322
Muhammad (Mohammed) the Prophet 6, 8, 14, 16–17, 22, 30, 39–40, 50, 60, 71–3, 83, 87, 100, 118–20, 125–6, 191, 214–15, 226, 233–5, 237, 261–3, 330, 336–8, 360–62, 363

Nasreen, Taslima 291, 293, 315
Numeri, Ja'far xxxi, 219–20, 222–4, 227–8, 232–3

Osman 261

Paden, William 347
Piscatori, J. 83
Polatov, Abdoumannob 189
Polatov, Abdurahim 189
Pulatov, Abdurakhim 187

Qanushi, Rashid 50, 363

Rahman, Fazlur xxvi, 178
Razig, Ali Abdel 30
Rushdie, Salman xvi, 5, 10, 38–9, 292–3, 315

Sadat, Anwar El 145
Salih, Mohammed 188
al-Shafi'i, Imam 73
Shiner, Larry 351
Smith, W. 85
Suharto, General 80–81

Taha, Mahmoud Mohamed (Muhammad) xviii, xix, xxiii, xxxi, xxxviii, 30–31, 37, 42, 100, 219–20, 225–33, 237–9, 263–4

Timur Link 177, 184
at-Turabi, Hassan 223

Umar 120
Uthman 120

Wafi, Ali A. 76

Zia ul-Haq, Muhammad 80–81, 90, 98–9

For Product Safety Concerns and Information please contact our EU
representative GPSR@taylorandfrancis.com
Taylor & Francis Verlag GmbH, Kaufingerstraße 24, 80331 München, Germany

www.ingramcontent.com/pod-product-compliance
Ingram Content Group UK Ltd.
Pitfield, Milton Keynes, MK11 3LW, UK
UKHW022111190926
475702UK00013B/1386
* 9 7 8 1 0 3 2 0 9 9 4 4 6 *